RANDOM
HOUSE

LARGE
PRINT

RANDOM
HOUSE
LARGE
PRINT

PRINCE HARRY

SPARE

R A N D O M H O U S E
L A R G E P R I N T

Published in the United States of America by Random House Large Print in association with Random House, an imprint and division of Penguin Random House LLC, New York.

Published in the United Kingdom by Transworld Publishers Ltd, a division of Penguin Random House UK and in Canada by Random House Canada.

Part Two opening photograph © MoD/Newspix International

Cover design: Christopher Brand
Front-cover photograph: Ramona Rosales

Prince Harry wishes to support British charities with donations from his proceeds from **SPARE**. The Duke of Sussex has donated $1,500,000 to Sentebale, an organization he founded with Prince Seeiso in their mothers' legacies, which supports vulnerable children and young people in Lesotho and Botswana affected by HIV/AIDS. Prince Harry will also donate to the nonprofit organization WellChild in the amount of £300,000. WellChild, which he has been Royal patron of for fifteen years, makes it possible for children and young people with complex health needs to be cared for at home instead of hospital, wherever possible.

The Library of Congress has established a Cataloging-in-Publication record for this title.

ISBN: 978-0-593-67786-5

www.penguinrandomhouse.com/large-print-format-books

FIRST LARGE PRINT EDITION

Printed in the United States of America

10 9 8 7 6 5 4 3 2 1

This Large Print edition published in accord with the standards of the N.A.V.H.

FOR MEG AND ARCHIE AND LILI . . .
AND, OF COURSE, MY MOTHER

The past is never dead. It's not even past.

—WILLIAM FAULKNER

WE AGREED TO MEET a few hours after the funeral. In the Frogmore gardens, by the old Gothic ruin. I got there first.

I looked around, saw no one.

I checked my phone. No texts, no voicemails.

They must be running late, I thought, leaning against the stone wall.

I put away my phone and told myself: Stay calm.

The weather was quintessentially April. Not quite winter, not yet spring. The trees were bare, but the air was soft. The sky was gray, but the tulips were popping. The light was pale, but the indigo lake, threading through the gardens, glowed.

How beautiful it all is, I thought. And also how sad.

Once upon a time, this was going to be my forever home. Instead it had proved to be just another brief stop.

When my wife and I fled this place, in fear for our sanity and physical safety, I wasn't sure when I'd ever come back. That was January 2020. Now, fifteen months later, here I was, days after waking to thirty-two missed calls and then one short, heart-racing talk with Granny: **Harry . . . Grandpa's gone.**

The wind picked up, turned colder. I hunched my

shoulders, rubbed my arms, regretted the thinness of my white shirt. I wished I'd not changed out of my funeral suit. I wished I'd thought to bring a coat. I turned my back to the wind and saw, looming behind me, the Gothic ruin, which in reality was no more Gothic than the Millennium Wheel. Some clever architect, some bit of stagecraft. Like so much around here, I thought.

I moved from the stone wall to a small wooden bench. Sitting, I checked my phone again, peered up and down the garden path.

Where are they?

Another gust of wind. Funny, it reminded me of Grandpa. His wintry demeanor, maybe. Or his icy sense of humor. I recalled one particular shooting weekend years ago. A mate, just trying to make conversation, asked Grandpa what he thought of my new beard, which had been causing concern in the family and controversy in the press. **Should the Queen Force Prince Harry to Shave?** Grandpa looked at my mate, looked at my chin, broke into a devilish grin. **THAT'S no beard!**

Everyone laughed. To beard or not to beard, that was the question, but leave it to Grandpa to demand **more** beard. **Let grow the luxurious bristles of a bloody Viking!**

I thought of Grandpa's strong opinions, his many passions—carriage driving, barbecuing, shooting, food, beer. The way he embraced **life**. He had that in common with my mother. Maybe that was why he'd been such a fan. Long before she was Princess

Diana, back when she was simply Diana Spencer, kin-
dergarten teacher, secret girlfriend of Prince Charles,
my grandfather was her loudest advocate. Some said
he actually brokered my parents' marriage. If so, an
argument could be made that Grandpa was the Prime
Cause in my world. But for him, I wouldn't be here.

Neither would my older brother.

Then again, maybe our mother **would** be here. If
she hadn't married Pa . . .

I recalled one recent chat, just me and Grandpa, not
long after he'd turned ninety-seven. He was thinking
about the end. He was no longer capable of pursu-
ing his passions, he said. And yet the thing he missed
most was work. Without work, he said, everything
crumbles. He didn't seem sad, just ready. **You have to
know when it's time to go, Harry.**

I glanced now into the distance, towards the
mini skyline of crypts and monuments alongside
Frogmore. The Royal Burial Ground. Final resting
place for so many of us, including Queen Victoria.
Also, the notorious Wallis Simpson. Also, her doubly
notorious husband Edward, the former King and my
great-great-uncle. After Edward gave up his throne
for Wallis, after they fled Britain, both of them fretted about their ultimate return—both obsessed about
being buried right here. The Queen, my grandmother,
granted their plea. But she placed them at a distance
from everyone else, beneath a stooped plane tree.
One last finger wag, perhaps. One final exile, maybe.
I wondered how Wallis and Edward felt now about
all their fretting. Did any of it matter in the end? I

wondered if they wondered at all. Were they floating in some airy realm, still mulling their choices, or were they Nowhere, thinking Nothing? Could there really be Nothing after this? Does consciousness, like time, have a stop? Or maybe, I thought, just maybe, they're here right now, next to the fake Gothic ruin, or next to me, eavesdropping on my thoughts. And if so . . . **maybe my mother is too?**

The thought of her, as always, gave me a jolt of hope, and a burst of energy.

And a stab of sorrow.

I missed my mother every day, but that day, on the verge of that nerve-racking rendezvous at Frogmore, I found myself longing for her, and I couldn't say just why. Like so much about her, it was hard to put into words.

Although my mother was a princess, named after a goddess, both those terms always felt weak, inadequate. People routinely compared her to icons and saints, from Nelson Mandela to Mother Teresa to Joan of Arc, but every such comparison, while lofty and loving, also felt wide of the mark. The most recognizable woman on the planet, one of the most beloved, my mother was simply indescribable, that was the plain truth. And yet . . . how could someone so far beyond everyday language remain so real, so palpably present, so exquisitely vivid in my mind? How was it possible that I could see her, clear as the swan skimming towards me on that indigo lake? How could I hear her laughter, loud as the songbirds in the bare trees—still? There was so much I didn't remember, because I was so young when she died, but the greater miracle was all that I did. Her devastating smile, her vulnerable eyes, her childlike love of movies and music and clothes and sweets—and us. Oh how she loved my brother and me. **Obsessively**, she once confessed to an interviewer.

Well, Mummy . . . vice versa.

Maybe she was omnipresent for the very same reason that she was indescribable—because she was light, pure and radiant light, and how can you really describe light? Even Einstein struggled with that one. Recently, astronomers rearranged their biggest telescopes, aimed them at one tiny crevice in the cosmos, and managed to catch a glimpse of one breathtaking sphere, which they named Earendel, the Old English word for Morning Star. Billions of miles off, and probably long vanished, Earendel is closer to the Big Bang, the moment of Creation, than our own Milky Way, and yet it's somehow still visible to mortal eyes because it's just so awesomely bright and dazzling.

That was my mother.

That was why I could see her, sense her, always, but especially that April afternoon at Frogmore.

That—and the fact that I was carrying her flag. I'd come to those gardens because I wanted peace. I wanted it more than anything. I wanted it for my family's sake, and for my own—but also for hers.

People forget how much my mother strove for peace. She circled the globe many times over, traipsed through minefields, cuddled AIDS patients, consoled war orphans, always working to bring peace to someone somewhere, and I knew how desperately she would want—no, **did** want—peace between her boys, and between us two and Pa. And among the whole family.

For months the Windsors had been at war. There had been strife in our ranks, off and on, going back centuries, but this was different. This was a full-scale public rupture, and it threatened to become irreparable. So, though I'd flown home specifically and solely for Grandpa's funeral, while there I'd asked for this secret meeting with my older brother, Willy, and my father to talk about the state of things.

To find a way out.

But now I looked once more at my phone and once more up and down the garden path and I thought: Maybe they've changed their minds. Maybe they're not going to come.

For half a second I considered giving up, going for a walk through the gardens by myself or heading back to the house where all my cousins were drinking and sharing stories of Grandpa.

Then, at last, I saw them. Shoulder to shoulder, striding towards me, they looked grim, almost menacing. More, they looked tightly aligned. My stomach dropped. Normally they'd be squabbling about one thing or another, but now they appeared to be in lockstep—in league.

The thought occurred: Hang on, are we meeting for a walk . . . or a duel?

I rose from the wooden bench, made a tentative step towards them, gave a weak smile. They didn't smile back. Now my heart really started thrashing in my chest. Deep breaths, I told myself.

Apart from fear, I was feeling a kind of hyper-awareness, and a hugely intense vulnerability, which I'd experienced at other key moments of my life.

Walking behind my mother's coffin.

Going into battle for the first time.

Giving a speech in the middle of a panic attack.

There was that same sense of embarking on a quest, and not knowing if I was up to it, while also fully knowing that there was no turning back. That Fate was in the saddle.

OK, Mummy, I thought, picking up the pace, here goes. Wish me luck.

We met in the middle of the path. **Willy? Pa? Hello.**

Harold.

Painfully tepid.

We wheeled, formed a line, set off along the gravel path over the little ivy-covered stone bridge.

The way we simply fell into this synchronous alignment, the way we wordlessly assumed the same measured paces and bowed heads, plus the nearness of those graves—how could anyone not be reminded of Mummy's funeral? I told myself not to think about that, to think instead about the pleasing crunch of our footsteps, and the way our words flew away like wisps of smoke on the wind.

Being British, being Windsors, we began chatting casually about the weather. We compared notes about Grandpa's funeral. He'd planned it all himself, down

to the tiniest detail, we reminded each other with rueful smiles.

Small talk. The smallest. We touched on all sec-
ondary subjects and I kept waiting for us to get to the
primary one, wondering why it was taking so long
and also how on earth my father and brother could
appear so calm.

I looked around. We'd covered a fair bit of terrain,
and were now smack in the middle of the Royal Burial
Ground, more up to our ankles in bodies than Prince
Hamlet. Come to think of it . . . didn't I myself once
ask to be buried here? Hours before I'd gone off to
war my private secretary said I needed to choose the
spot where my remains should be interred. **Should
the worst happen, Your Royal Highness . . . war
being an uncertain thing . . .**

There were several options. St. George's Chapel?
The Royal Vault at Windsor, where Grandpa was
being settled at this moment?

No, I'd chosen this one, because the gardens were
lovely, and because it seemed peaceful.

Our feet almost on top of Wallis Simpson's face,
Pa launched into a micro-lecture about this personage over here, that royal cousin over there, all the
once-eminent dukes and duchesses, lords and ladies,
currently residing beneath the lawn. A lifelong student of history, he had loads of information to share,
and part of me thought we might be there for hours,
and that there might be a test at the end. Mercifully,
he stopped, and we carried on along the grass around

the edge of the lake, arriving at a beautiful little patch of daffodils.

It was there, at last, that we got down to business.

I tried to explain my side of things. I wasn't at my best. For starters, I was still nervous, fighting to keep my emotions in check, while also striving to be succinct and precise. More, I'd vowed not to let this encounter devolve into another argument. But I quickly discovered that it wasn't up to me. Pa and Willy had their parts to play, and they'd come ready for a fight. Every time I ventured a new explanation, started a new line of thought, one or both of them would cut me off. Willy in particular didn't want to hear anything. After he'd shut me down several times, he and I began sniping, saying some of the same things we'd said for months—years. It got so heated that Pa raised his hands. **Enough!**

He stood between us, looking up at our flushed faces: **Please, boys—don't make my final years a misery.**

His voice sounded raspy, fragile. It sounded, if I'm being honest, old.

I thought about Grandpa.

All at once something shifted inside of me. I looked at Willy, really looked at him, maybe for the first time since we were boys. I took it all in: his familiar scowl, which had always been his default in dealings with me; his alarming baldness, more advanced than my own; his famous resemblance to Mummy, which was fading with time. With age. In some ways he was my mirror, in some ways he was my opposite. My beloved brother, my arch nemesis, how had that happened?

I felt massively tired. I wanted to go home, and I realized what a complicated concept home had become. Or maybe always was. I gestured at the gardens, the city beyond, the nation, and said: **Willy, this was supposed to be our home. We were going to live here the rest of our lives.**

You left, Harold.

Yeah—and you know why.

I don't.

You . . . don't?

I honestly don't.

I leaned back. I couldn't believe what I was hearing. It was one thing to disagree about who was at fault or how things might have been different, but for him to claim total ignorance of the reasons I'd fled the land of my birth—the land for which I'd fought and been ready to die—my Mother Country? That fraught phrase. To claim no knowledge of why my wife and I took the drastic step of picking up our child and just running like hell, leaving behind everything—house, friends, furniture? Really?

I looked up at the trees: **You don't know!**

Harold . . . I honestly don't.

I turned to Pa. He was gazing at me with an expression that said: **Neither do I.**

Wow, I thought. Maybe they really don't.

Staggering. But maybe it was true.

And if they didn't know why I'd left, maybe they just didn't know me. At all.

And maybe they never really did.

And to be fair, maybe I didn't either.

The thought made me feel colder, and terribly alone.

But it also fired me up. I thought: **I have to tell them.**

How can I tell them?

I can't. It would take too long.

Besides, they're clearly not in the right frame of mind to listen.

Not now, anyway. Not today.

And so:

Pa? Willy?

World?

Here you go.

part 1 out of the night that covers me

1.

THERE WERE ALWAYS STORIES.

People would whisper now and then about folks who hadn't fared well at Balmoral. The long-ago Queen, for instance. Mad with grief, she'd locked herself inside Balmoral Castle and vowed never to come out. And the very proper former prime minister: he'd called the place "surreal" and "utterly freaky."

Still, I don't think I heard those stories until much later. Or maybe I heard them and they didn't register. To me Balmoral was always simply Paradise. A cross between Disney World and some sacred Druid grove. I was always too busy fishing, shooting, running up and down "the hill" to notice anything off about the feng shui of the old castle.

What I'm trying to say is, I was happy there.

In fact, it's possible that I was never happier than that one golden summer day at Balmoral: August 30, 1997.

We'd been at the castle for one week. The plan was to stay for another. Same as the previous year, same as the year before that. Balmoral was its own micro-season, a two-week interlude in the Scottish

Highlands to mark the turn from high summer to early autumn.

Granny was there too. Naturally. She spent most of every summer at Balmoral. And Grandpa. And Willy. And Pa. The whole family, with the exception of Mummy, because Mummy was no longer part of the family. She'd either bolted or been thrown out, depending on whom you asked, though I never asked anyone. Either way, she was having her own holiday elsewhere. Greece, someone said. No, Sardinia, someone said. No, no, someone chimed in, your mother's in Paris! Maybe it was Mummy herself who said that. When she phoned earlier that day for a chat? Alas, the memory lies, with a million others, on the other side of a high mental wall. Such a horrid, tantalizing feeling, to know they're over there, just on the other side, mere inches away—but the wall is always too high, too thick. Unscalable.

Not unlike the turrets of Balmoral.

Wherever Mummy was, I understood that she was with her new **friend**. That was the word everyone used. Not boyfriend, not lover. Friend. Nice enough bloke, I thought. Willy and I had just met him. Actually, we'd been with Mummy weeks earlier when **she** first met him, in St. Tropez. We were having a grand time, just the three of us, staying at some old gent's villa. There was much laughter, horseplay, the norm whenever Mummy and Willy and I were together, though even more so on that holiday. Everything about that trip to St. Tropez was heaven. The weather was sublime, the food was tasty, Mummy was smiling.

Best of all, there were jet skis.

Whose were they? Don't know. But I vividly remember Willy and me riding them out to the deepest part of the channel, circling while waiting for the big ferries to come. We used their massive wakes as ramps to get airborne. I'm not sure how we weren't killed.

Was it after we got back from that jet-ski misadventure that Mummy's friend first appeared? No, more likely it was just before. **Hello there, you must be Harry.** Raven hair, leathery tan, bone-white smile. **How are you today? My name is blah blah.** He chatted us up, chatted Mummy up. Specifically Mummy. Pointedly Mummy. His eyes plumping into red hearts.

He was cheeky, no doubt. But, again, nice enough. He gave Mummy a present. Diamond bracelet. She seemed to like it. She wore it a lot. Then he faded from my consciousness.

As long as Mummy's happy, I told Willy, who said he felt the same.

2.

A SHOCK TO THE SYSTEM, going from sun-drenched St. Tropez to cloud-shadowed Balmoral. I vaguely remember that shock, though I can't remember much else about our first week at the castle. Still, I can almost guarantee it was spent mostly outdoors. My family lived to be outdoors, especially Granny, who got cross if she didn't breathe at least an hour of fresh air each day. What we did outdoors, however, what we said, wore, ate, I can't conjure. There's some reporting that we journeyed by the royal yacht from the Isle of Wight to the castle, the yacht's final voyage. Sounds lovely.

What I do retain, in crisp detail, is the physical setting. The dense woods. The deer-nibbled hill. The River Dee snaking down through the Highlands. Lochnagar soaring overhead, eternally snow-spattered. Landscape, geography, architecture, that's how my memory rolls. Dates? Sorry, I'll need to look them up. Dialogue? I'll try my best, but make no verbatim claims, especially when it comes to the nineties. But ask me about any space I've occupied—castle, cockpit, classroom, stateroom, bedroom, palace, garden, pub—and I'll re-create it down to the carpet tacks.

Why should my memory organize experience like this? Is it genetics? Trauma? Some Frankenstein-esque combination of the two? Is it my inner soldier, assessing every space as potential battlefield? Is it my innate homebody nature, rebelling against a forced nomadic existence? Is it some base apprehension that the world is essentially a maze, and you should never be caught in a maze without a map?

Whatever the cause, my memory is my memory, it does what it does, gathers and curates as it sees fit, and there's just as much truth in what I remember and how I remember it as there is in so-called objective facts. Things like chronology and cause-and-effect are often just fables we tell ourselves about the past. **The past is never dead. It's not even past.** When I discovered that quotation not long ago on BrainyQuote.com, I was thunderstruck. I thought, Who the **fook** is Faulkner? And how's he related to us Windsors?

And so: Balmoral. Closing my eyes, I can see the main entrance, the paneled front windows, the wide portico and three gray-black speckled granite steps leading up to the massive front door of whisky-colored oak, often propped open by a heavy curling stone and often manned by one red-coated footman, and inside the spacious hall and its white stone floor, with gray star-shaped tiles, and the huge fireplace with its beautiful mantel of ornately carved dark wood, and to one side a kind of utility room, and to the left, by the tall windows, hooks for fishing rods and walking sticks and rubber waders and heavy waterproofs—so many waterproofs, because summer could be wet and cold all over Scotland, but it was biting in this Siberian nook—and then the light brown wooden door leading to the corridor with the crimson carpet and the walls papered in cream, a pattern of gold flock, raised like braille, and then the many rooms along the corridor, each with a specific purpose, like sitting or reading, TV or tea, and one special room for the pages, many of whom I loved like dotty uncles, and finally the castle's main chamber, built in the nineteenth century, nearly on top of the site of another castle dating to the fourteenth century, within a few generations of another Prince Harry, who got himself exiled, then came back and annihilated everything and everyone in sight. My distant kin. My kindred spirit, some would claim. If nothing else, my namesake. Born

September 15, 1984, I was christened Henry Charles Albert David of Wales.

But from Day One everyone called me Harry.

In the heart of this main chamber was the grand staircase. Sweeping, dramatic, seldom used. Whenever Granny headed up to her bedroom on the second floor, corgis at her heels, she preferred the lift.

The corgis preferred it too.

Near Granny's lift, through a pair of crimson saloon doors and along a green tartan floor, was a smallish staircase with a heavy iron banister; it led up to the second floor, where stood a statue of Queen Victoria. I always bowed to her as I passed. **Your Majesty!** Willy did too. We'd been told to, but I'd have done it anyway. I found the "Grandmama of Europe" hugely compelling, and not just because Granny loved her, nor because Pa once wanted to name me after her husband. (Mummy blocked him.) Victoria knew great love, soaring happiness—but her life was essentially tragic. Her father, Prince Edward, Duke of Kent and Strathearn, was said to be a sadist, sexually aroused by the sight of soldiers being horsewhipped, and her dear husband, Albert, died before her eyes. Also, during her long, lonely reign, she was shot at eight times, on eight separate occasions, by seven different subjects.

Not one bullet hit the mark. Nothing could bring Victoria down.

Beyond Victoria's statue things got tricky. Doors became identical, rooms interlocked. Easy to get lost. Open the wrong door and you might burst in on Pa while his valet was helping him dress. Worse, you might blunder in as he was doing his headstands. Prescribed by his physio, these exercises were the only effective remedy for the constant pain in Pa's neck and back. Old polo injuries, mostly. He performed them daily, in just a pair of boxers, propped against a door or hanging from a bar like a skilled acrobat. If you set one little finger on the knob you'd hear him begging from the other side: **No! No! Don't open! Please God don't open!**

Balmoral had fifty bedrooms, one of which had been divided for me and Willy. Adults called it the nursery. Willy had the larger half, with a double bed, a good-sized basin, a cupboard with mirrored doors, a beautiful window looking down on the courtyard, the fountain, the bronze statue of a roe deer buck. My half of the room was far smaller, less luxurious. I never asked why. I didn't care. But I also didn't need to ask. Two years older than me, Willy was the Heir, whereas I was the Spare.

This wasn't merely how the press referred to us—though it was definitely that. This was shorthand often used by Pa and Mummy and Grandpa. And even Granny. The Heir and the Spare—there was no judgment about it, but also no ambiguity. I was the shadow, the support, the Plan B. I was brought into the world in case something happened to Willy. I was summoned to provide backup, distraction, diversion and, if necessary, a spare part. Kidney, perhaps. Blood transfusion. Speck of bone marrow. This was all made explicitly clear to me from the start of life's journey and regularly reinforced thereafter. I was twenty the first time I heard the story of what Pa allegedly said to Mummy the day of my birth: **Wonderful! Now you've given me an Heir and a Spare—my work is done.** A joke. Presumably. On the other hand, minutes after delivering this bit of high comedy, Pa was said to have gone off to meet with his girlfriend. So. Many a true word spoken in jest.

I took no offense. I felt nothing about it, any of it. Succession was like the weather, or the positions of the planets, or the turn of the seasons. Who had the time to worry about things so unchangeable? Who could bother with being bothered by a fate etched in stone? Being a Windsor meant working out which truths were timeless, and then banishing them from your mind. It meant **absorbing** the basic parameters of one's identity, knowing by instinct who you were, which was forever a byproduct of who you weren't.

I wasn't Granny.

I wasn't Pa.

I wasn't Willy.

I was third in line behind them.

Every boy and girl, at least once, imagines themselves as a prince or princess. Therefore, Spare or no Spare, it wasn't half bad to actually **be** one. More, standing resolutely behind the people you loved, wasn't that the definition of honor?

Of love?

Like bowing to Victoria as you passed?

3.

NEXT TO MY BEDROOM was a sort of round sitting room. Round table, wall mirror, writing desk, fireplace with cushioned hearth surround. In the far corner stood a great big wooden door that led to a bathroom. The two marble basins looked like prototypes for the first basins ever manufactured. Everything at Balmoral was either old or made to look so. The castle was a playground, a hunting lodge, but also a stage.

The bathroom was dominated by a claw-footed tub, and even the water spurting from its taps seemed old. Not in a bad way. Old like the lake where Merlin helped Arthur find his magic sword. Brownish, suggestive of weak tea, the water often alarmed weekend guests. **Sorry, but there seems to be something wrong with the water in my loo?** Pa would always smile and assure them that nothing was wrong with the water; on the contrary it was filtered and sweetened by the Scottish peat. **That water came straight off the hill, and what you're about to experience is one of life's finest pleasures—a Highland bath.**

Depending on your preference, your Highland bath could be Arctic cold or kettle hot; taps throughout the castle were fine-tuned. For me, few pleasures compared with a scalding soak, but especially while gazing out of the castle's slit windows, where archers, I imagined, once stood guard. I'd look up at the starry sky, or down at the walled gardens, picture myself floating over the great lawn, smooth and green as a snooker table, thanks to a battalion of gardeners. The lawn was so perfect, every blade of grass so precisely mown, Willy and I felt guilty about walking across it, let alone riding our bikes. But we did it anyway, all the time. Once, we chased our cousin across the lawn. We were on quads, the cousin was on a go-kart. It was all fun and games until she crashed head-on into a green lamppost. Crazy fluke—the only lamppost within a thousand miles. We shrieked with laughter, though the lamppost, which had recently been a tree in one of the nearby forests, snapped cleanly in two and fell on top of her. She was lucky not to be seriously hurt.

On August 30, 1997, I didn't spend a lot of time looking at the lawn. Both Willy and I hurried through our evening baths, jumped into our pajamas, settled eagerly in front of the TV. Footmen arrived, carrying trays covered with plates, each topped with a silver dome. The footmen set the trays upon wooden stands, then joked with us, as they always did, before wishing us bon appétit.

Footmen, bone china—it sounds posh, and I suppose it was, but under those fancy domes was just kiddie stuff. Fish fingers, cottage pies, roast chicken, green peas.

Mabel, our nanny, who'd once been Pa's nanny, joined us. As we all stuffed our faces we heard Pa padding past in his slippers, coming from his bath. He was carrying his "wireless," which is what he called his portable CD player, on which he liked to listen to his "storybooks" while soaking. Pa was like clock-work, so when we heard him in the hall we knew it was close to eight.

Half an hour later we picked up the first sounds of the adults beginning their evening migration down-stairs, then the first bleaty notes of the accompanying bagpipes. For the next two hours the adults would be held captive in the Dinner Dungeon, forced to sit around that long table, forced to squint at each other in the dim gloom of a candelabra designed by Prince Albert, forced to remain ramrod straight before china plates and crystal goblets placed with math-ematical precision by staff (who used tape measures), forced to peck at quails' eggs and turbot, forced to make idle chitchat while stuffed into their fanciest kit. Black tie, hard black shoes, trews. Maybe even kilts.

I thought: What hell, being an adult!

Pa stopped by on his way to dinner. He was running late, but he made a show of lifting a silver dome—**Yum, wish I was having that!**—and taking a long sniff. He was always sniffing things. Food, roses, our hair. He must've been a bloodhound in another life. Maybe he took all those long sniffs because it was hard to smell anything over his personal scent. **Eau Sauvage.** He'd slather the stuff on his cheeks, his neck, his shirt. Flowery, with a hint of something harsh, like pepper or gunpowder, it was made in Paris. Said so on the bottle. Which made me think of Mummy.

Yes, Harry, Mummy's in Paris.

Their divorce had become final exactly one year before. Almost to the day.

Be good, boys.

We will, Pa.

Don't stay up too late.

He left. His scent remained.

Willy and I finished dinner, watched some more TV, then got up to our typical pre-bedtime hijinks. We perched on the top step of a side staircase and eavesdropped on the adults, hoping to hear a naughty word or story. We ran up and down the long corridors, under the watchful eyes of dozens of dead stag heads. At some point we bumped into Granny's piper. Rumpled, pear-shaped, with wild eyebrows and a tweed kilt, he went wherever Granny went, because she loved the sound of pipes, as had Victoria, though Albert supposedly called them a "beastly instrument." While summering at Balmoral, Granny asked that the piper play her awake and play her to dinner.

His instrument looked like a drunken octopus, except that its floppy arms were etched silver and dark mahogany. We'd seen the thing before, many times, but that night he offered to let us hold it. Try it.

Really?

Go on.

We couldn't get anything out of the pipes but a few piddly squeaks. We just didn't have the puff. The piper, however, had a chest the size of a whisky barrel. He made it moan and scream.

We thanked him for the lesson and bade him good night, then took ourselves back to the nursery, where Mabel monitored the brushing of teeth and the washing of faces. Then, to bed.

My bed was tall. I had to jump to get in, after which I rolled down into its sunken center. It felt like climbing onto a bookcase, then tumbling into a slit trench. The bedding was clean, crisp, various shades of white. Alabaster sheets. Cream blankets. Eggshell quilts. (Much of it stamped with ER, **Elizabeth Regina**.) Everything was pulled tight as a snare drum, so expertly smoothed that you could easily spot the century's worth of patched holes and tears.

I pulled the sheets and covers to my chin, because I didn't like the dark. No, not true, I loathed the dark. Mummy did too, she told me so. I'd inherited this from her, I thought, along with her nose, her blue eyes, her love of people, her hatred of smugness and fakery and all things posh. I can see myself under those covers, staring into the dark, listening to the clicky insects and hooty owls. Did I imagine shapes sliding along the walls? Did I stare at the bar of light along the floor, which was always there, because I always insisted on the door being left open a crack? How much time elapsed before I dropped off? In other words, how much of my childhood remained, and how much did I cherish it, savor it, before groggily becoming aware of—

Pa?

He was standing at the edge of the bed, looking down. His white dressing-gown made him seem like a ghost in a play.

Yes, darling boy.

He gave a half-smile, averted his gaze.

The room wasn't dark anymore. Wasn't light either.

Strange in-between shade, almost brownish, almost like the water in the ancient tub.

He looked at me in a funny way, a way he'd never looked at me before. With . . . fear?

What is it, Pa?

He sat down on the edge of the bed. He put a hand on my knee. **Darling boy, Mummy's been in a car crash.**

I remember thinking: Crash . . . OK. But she's all right? Yes?

I vividly remember that thought flashing through my mind. And I remember waiting patiently for Pa to confirm that indeed Mummy was all right. And I remember him not doing that.

There was then a shift internally. I began silently pleading with Pa, or God, or both: **No, no, no.**

Pa looked down into the folds of the old quilts and blankets and sheets. **There were complications. Mummy was quite badly injured and taken to hospital, darling boy.**

He always called me "darling boy," but he was saying it quite a lot now. His voice was soft. He was in shock, it seemed.

Oh. Hospital?

Yes. With a head injury.

Did he mention paparazzi? Did he say she'd been chased? I don't think so. I can't swear to it, but probably not. The paps were such a problem for Mummy, for everyone, it didn't need to be said.

I thought again: Injured . . . but she's OK. She's

been taken to hospital, they'll fix her head, and we'll go and see her. Today. Tonight at the latest.

They tried, darling boy. I'm afraid she didn't make it.

These phrases remain in my mind like darts in a board. He did say it that way, I know that much for sure. **She didn't make it.** And then everything seemed to come to a stop.

That's not right. Not **seemed**. Nothing at all **seemed**. Everything distinctly, certainly, irrevocably, came to a stop.

None of what I said to him then remains in my memory. It's possible that I didn't say anything. What I do remember with startling clarity is that I didn't cry. Not one tear.

Pa didn't hug me. He wasn't great at showing emotions under normal circumstances, how could he be expected to show them in such a crisis? But his hand did fall once more on my knee and he said: **It's going to be OK.**

That was quite a lot for him. Fatherly, hopeful, kind. And so very untrue.

He stood and left. I don't recall how I knew that he'd already been in the other room, that he'd already told Willy, but I knew.

I lay there, or sat there. I didn't get up. I didn't bathe, didn't pee. Didn't get dressed. Didn't call out to Willy or Mabel. After decades of working to reconstruct that morning I've come to one inescapable conclusion: I must've remained in that room, saying nothing, seeing no one, until nine A.M. sharp, when the piper began to play outside.

I wish I could remember what he played. But maybe it doesn't matter. With bagpipes it's not the tune, it's the tone. Thousands of years old, bagpipes are built to amplify what's already in the heart. If you're feeling silly, bagpipes make you sillier. If you're angry, bagpipes bring your blood to a higher boil. And if you're in grief, even if you're twelve years old and don't know you're in grief, maybe **especially** if you don't know, bagpipes can drive you mad.

4.

IT WAS SUNDAY. So, as always, we went to church. Crathie Kirk. Walls of granite, large roof of Scottish pine, stained-glass windows donated decades earlier by Victoria, perhaps to atone for the upset she caused in worshipping there. Something about the head of the Church of England worshipping in the Church of Scotland—it caused a stir, which I never understood.

I've seen photographs of us going into the church that day, but they bring back no memories. Did the minister say anything? Did he make it worse? Did I listen to him or stare at the back of the pew and think about Mummy?

On the way back to Balmoral, a two-minute drive, it was suggested that we stop. People had been gathering all morning outside the front gates, some had begun leaving things. Stuffed animals, flowers, cards. Acknowledgment should be made.

We pulled over, stepped out. I could see nothing but a matrix of colored dots. Flowers. And more flowers. I could hear nothing but a rhythmic clicking from across the road. The press. I reached for my father's hand, for comfort, then cursed myself, because that gesture set off an explosion of clicks.

I'd given them exactly what they wanted. Emotion. Drama. Pain.

They fired and fired and fired.

5.

HOURS LATER PA LEFT FOR PARIS. Accompanied by Mummy's sisters, Aunt Sarah and Aunt Jane. They needed to learn more about the crash, someone said. And they needed to arrange for the return of Mummy's body.

Body. People kept using that word. It was a punch in the throat, and a bloody lie, because Mummy wasn't dead.

That was my sudden insight. With nothing to do but roam the castle and talk to myself, a suspicion took hold, which then became a firm belief. This was all a trick. And for once the trick wasn't being played by the people around me, or the press, but by Mummy. **Her life's been miserable, she's been hounded, harassed, lied about, lied to. So she's staged an accident as a diversion and run away.**

The realization took my breath away, made me gasp with relief.

Of course! It's all a ruse, so she can make a clean start! At this very moment she's undoubtedly renting an apartment in Paris, or arranging fresh flowers in her secretly purchased log cabin somewhere way up high in the Swiss Alps. Soon, soon, she'll send for me and Willy. It's all so obvious! Why didn't I see it before? Mummy isn't dead! She's hiding!

I felt so much better.

Then doubt crept in.

Hang on! Mummy would never do this to us. This unspeakable pain, she'd never allow that, let alone cause it.

Then back to relief: **She had no choice. It was her only hope of freedom.**

Then doubt again: **Mummy wouldn't hide, she's too much of a fighter.**

Then relief: **This is her way of fighting. She'll be back. She has to be. It's my birthday in two weeks.**

But Pa and my aunts came back first. Their return was reported by every TV channel. The world watched as they stepped onto the tarmac at RAF Northolt. One channel even added music to the arrival: someone mournfully singing a psalm. Willy and I were kept from the TV, but I think we heard that.

The next few days passed in a vacuum, no one saying anything. We all remained ensconced inside the castle. It was like being inside a crypt, except a crypt where everyone's wearing trews and keeping to normal routines and schedules. If anyone talked about anything, I didn't hear them. The only voice I heard was the one droning in my head, arguing with itself.

She's gone.

No, she's hiding.

She's dead.

No, she's playing **dead.**

Then, one morning, it was time. Back to London. I remember nothing about the trip. Did we drive? Did we fly on the Royal Flight? I can see the reunion with Pa, and the aunts, and the pivotal encounter with Aunt Sarah, though it's wreathed in fog and might be slightly out of sequence. At times my memory places it right there, in those horrid first days of September. But at other times memory casts it forward, to many years later.

Whenever it happened, it happened like this:

William? Harry? Aunt Sarah has something for you, boys.

She stepped forward, holding two tiny blue boxes.

What's this?

Open it.

I lifted off the top of my blue box. Inside was . . . a moth?

No.

A mustache?

No.

What's . . . ?

Her hair, Harry.

Aunt Sarah explained that, while in Paris, she'd clipped two locks from Mummy's head.

So there it was. Proof. **She's really gone.**

But then immediately came the reassuring doubt, the lifesaving uncertainty: **No, this could be anybody's hair.** Mummy, her beautiful blond hair intact, was out there somewhere.

I'd know if she weren't. My body would know. My heart would know. And neither knows any such thing.

Both were just as full of love for her as ever.

6.

WILLY AND I WALKED UP and down the crowds outside Kensington Palace, smiling, shaking hands. As if we were running for office. Hundreds and hundreds of hands were thrust continually into our faces, the fingers often wet.

From what? I wondered.

Tears, I realized.

I disliked how those hands felt. More, I hated how they made me feel. Guilty. Why were all these people crying when I wasn't—and hadn't?

I wanted to cry, and I'd tried to, because Mummy's life had been so sad that she'd felt the need to disappear, to invent this massive charade. But I couldn't squeeze out one drop. Maybe I'd learned too well, absorbed too deeply, the ethos of the family, that crying wasn't an option—ever.

I remember the mounds of flowers all around us. I remember feeling unspeakable sorrow and yet being unfailingly polite. I remember old ladies saying: **Oh,**

my, how polite, the poor boy! I remember muttering thanks, over and over, thank you for coming, thank you for saying that, thank you for camping out here for several days. I remember consoling several folks who were prostrate, overcome, as if they knew Mummy, but also thinking: You didn't, though. You act as if you did . . . **but you didn't know her.**

That is . . . you **don't** know her. Present tense.

After offering ourselves up to the crowds, we went inside Kensington Palace. We entered through two big black doors, into Mummy's apartment, went down a long corridor and into a room off the left. There stood a large coffin. Dark brown, English oak. Am I remembering or imagining that it was draped in . . . **a Union Jack?**

That flag mesmerized me. Maybe because of my boyish war games. Maybe because of my precocious patriotism. Or maybe because I'd been hearing rumblings for days about the flag, the flag, the flag. That was all anyone could talk about. People were up in arms because the flag hadn't been lowered to half-mast over Buckingham Palace. They didn't care that the Royal Standard never flew at half-mast, no matter what, that it flew when Granny was in residence, and didn't fly when she was away, full stop. They cared only about seeing some official show of mourning, and they were enraged by its absence. That is, they were whipped into rage by the British papers, which were trying to deflect attention from their role in Mummy's disappearance. I recall one headline, addressed pointedly at Granny: **Show Us You Care.**

How **rich**, coming from the same fiends who "cared" so much about Mummy that they chased her into a tunnel from which she never emerged.

By now I'd overheard this "official" version of events: Paps chased Mummy through the streets of Paris, then into a tunnel, where her Mercedes crashed into a wall or cement pillar, killing her, her friend, and the driver.

Standing before the flag-draped coffin, I asked myself: Is Mummy a patriot? What does Mummy really think of Britain? Has anyone bothered to ask her?

When will I be able to ask her myself?

I can't recollect anything the family said in that moment, to each other or to the coffin. I don't recall a word that passed between me and Willy, though I do remember people around us saying "the boys" look "shell-shocked." Nobody bothered to whisper, as if we were so shell-shocked that we'd gone deaf.

There was some discussion about the next day's funeral. Per the latest plan, the coffin would be pulled through the streets on a horse-drawn carriage by the King's Troop while Willy and I followed on foot. It seemed a lot to ask of two young boys. Several adults were aghast. Mummy's brother, Uncle Charles, raised hell. **You can't make these boys walk behind their mother's coffin! It's barbaric.**

An alternative plan was put forward. Willy would walk alone. He was fifteen, after all. **Leave the younger one out of it.** Spare the Spare. This alternative plan was sent up the chain.

Back came the answer.

It must be both princes. To garner sympathy, presumably.

Uncle Charles was furious. But I wasn't. I didn't want Willy to undergo an ordeal like that without me. Had the roles been reversed, he'd never have wanted me—indeed, allowed me—to go it alone.

So, come morning, bright and early, off we went, all together. Uncle Charles on my right, Willy to his right, followed by Grandpa. And on my left was Pa. I noted at the start how serene Grandpa looked, as if this was merely another royal engagement. I could see his eyes, clearly, because he was gazing straight ahead. They all were. But I kept mine down on the road. So did Willy.

I remember feeling numb. I remember clenching my fists. I remember keeping a fraction of Willy always in the corner of my vision and drawing loads of strength from that. Most of all I remember the sounds, the clinking bridles and clopping hooves of the six sweaty brown horses, the squeaking wheels of the gun carriage they were hauling. (A relic from the First World War, someone said, which seemed right, since Mummy, much as she loved peace, often seemed a soldier, whether she was warring against the paps or Pa.) I believe I'll remember those few sounds for the rest of my life, because they were such a sharp contrast to the otherwise all-encompassing silence. There wasn't one engine, one lorry, one bird. There wasn't one human voice, which was impossible, because two million people lined the roads. The only hint that we were marching through a canyon of humanity was the occasional wail.

After twenty minutes we reached Westminster Abbey. We filed into a long pew. The funeral began with a series of readings and eulogies, and culminated with Elton John. He rose slowly, stiffly, as if he was one of the great kings buried for centuries beneath the abbey, suddenly roused back to life. He walked to the front, seated himself at a grand piano. Is there anyone who doesn't know that he sang "Candle in the Wind," a version he'd reworked for Mummy? I can't be sure the notes in my head are from that moment or from clips I've seen since. Possibly they're vestiges of recurring nightmares. But I do have one pure, indisputable memory of the song climaxing and my eyes starting to sting and tears nearly falling.

Nearly.

Towards the end of the service came Uncle Charles, who used his allotted time to blast everyone—family, nation, press—for stalking Mummy to her death. You could feel the abbey, the nation outside, recoil from the blow. Truth hurts. Then eight Welsh Guards moved forward, hoisted the enormous lead-lined coffin, which was now draped in the Royal Standard, an extraordinary break with protocol. (They'd also yielded to pressure and lowered the flag to half-mast; not the Royal Standard, of course, but the Union Jack—still, an unprecedented compromise.) The Royal Standard was always reserved for members of the Royal Family, which, I'd been told, Mummy wasn't anymore. Did this mean she was forgiven? By Granny? Apparently.

But these were questions I couldn't quite formulate, let alone ask an adult, as the coffin was slowly carried outside and loaded into the back of a black hearse. After a long wait the hearse drove off, rolled steadily through London, which surged on all sides with the largest crowd that ageless city had ever seen—twice as large as the crowds that celebrated the end of the Second World War. It went past Buckingham Palace, up Park Lane, towards the outskirts, over to the Finchley Road, then Hendon Way, then the Brent Cross flyover, then the North Circular, then the M1 to Junction 15a and northwards to Harlestone, before passing through the iron front gate of Uncle Charles's estate.

Althorp.

Willy and I watched most of that car ride on TV. We were already at Althorp. We'd been speeded ahead, though it turned out there was no need to hurry. Not only did the hearse go the long way round, it was delayed several times by all the people heaping flowers onto it, blocking the vents and causing the engine to overheat. The driver had to keep pulling over so the bodyguard could get out and clear the flowers off the windscreen. The bodyguard was Graham. Willy and I liked him a lot. We always called him Crackers, as in Graham Crackers. We thought that was hysterical.

When the hearse finally got to Althorp the coffin was removed again and carried across the pond, over a green iron bridge hastily positioned by military engineers, to a little island, and there it was placed upon a platform. Willy and I walked across the same bridge to the island. It was reported that Mummy's hands were folded across her chest and between them was placed a photo of me and Willy, possibly the only two men who ever truly loved her. Certainly the two who loved her most. For all eternity we'd be smiling at her in the darkness, and maybe it was this image, as the flag came off and the coffin descended to the bottom of the hole, that finally broke me. My body convulsed and my chin fell and I began to sob uncontrollably into my hands.

I felt ashamed of violating the family ethos, but I couldn't hold it in any longer.

It's OK, I reassured myself, it's OK. There aren't any cameras around.

Besides, I wasn't crying because I believed my mother was in that hole. Or in that coffin. I promised myself I'd never believe that, no matter what anyone said.

No, I was crying at the mere idea.

It would just be so unbearably tragic, I thought, if it was actually true.

7.

THEN EVERYONE MOVED ON.
The family went back to work, and I went back to school, same as I did after every summer holiday.

Back to normal, everyone said cheerily.

From the passenger seat of Pa's open-topped Aston Martin everything certainly looked the same. Ludgrove School, nestled in the emerald Berkshire countryside, looked as ever like a country church. (Come to think of it, the school motto was from Ecclesiastes: **Whatsoever thy hand findeth to do, do it with thy might.**) Then again, not many country churches could boast two hundred acres of woodland and meadows, sports fields and tennis courts, science labs and chapels. Plus a well-stocked library.

If you wanted to find me in September 1997, the library would've been the last place to look. Better to check the woods. Or the sports fields. I was always trying to keep moving, keep busy.

I was also, most often, alone. I liked people, I was gregarious by nature, but just then I didn't want anyone too close. I needed space.

That was a tall order, however, at Ludgrove, where more than one hundred boys lived in proximity. We ate together, bathed together, slept together, sometimes ten to a room. Everyone knew everyone's business, down to who was circumcised and who wasn't. (We called it Roundheads versus Cavaliers.)

And yet I don't believe one boy so much as mentioned my mother when that new term began. Out of respect?

More likely fear.

I certainly said nothing to anyone.

Days after my return I had a birthday. September 15, 1997. I turned thirteen. By long-standing Ludgrove tradition there would be a cake, sorbet, and I was allowed to choose two flavors. I chose black currant.

And mango.

Mummy's favorite.

Birthdays were always a huge deal at Ludgrove, because every boy, and most teachers, had a ravenous sweet tooth. There was often a violent struggle for the seat next to the birthday boy: that's where you'd be assured of the first and biggest slice. I don't remember who managed to win the seat beside me.

Make a wish, Harry!

You want a wish? All right, I wish my mother was—

Then, out of nowhere—

Aunt Sarah?

Holding a box. **Open it, Harry.**

I tore at the wrapping paper, the ribbon. I peered inside.

What . . . ?

Mummy bought it for you. Shortly before . . .

You mean in Paris?

Yes. Paris.

It was an Xbox. I was pleased. I loved video games.

That's the story, anyway. It's appeared in many accounts of my life, as gospel, and I have no idea if it's true. Pa said Mummy hurt her head, but perhaps I was the one with brain damage? As a defense mechanism, most likely, my memory was no longer recording things quite as it once did.

8.

DESPITE ITS TWO MALE HEADMASTERS—Mr. Gerald and Mr. Marston, both legends—

Ludgrove was largely run by women. We called them the matrons. Whatever tenderness we got, day to day, came from them. The matrons hugged us, kissed us, bandaged our injuries, wiped our tears. (All except mine, that is. After that one graveside outburst I'd not cried again.) They fancied themselves our surrogates. Mums-Away-From-Mums, they'd always chirp, which had always been odd, but now was especially confusing, because of Mummy's disappearance, and also because the matrons were suddenly . . . hot.

I had a crush on Miss Roberts. I felt certain I'd marry her one day. I also recall two Miss Lynns. Miss Lynn Major and Miss Lynn Minor. They were sisters. I was deeply smitten with the latter. I reckoned I'd marry her too.

Three times a week, after dinner, the matrons would assist the youngest boys with the nightly wash. I can still see the long row of white baths, each with a boy reclining like a little pharaoh, awaiting his personalized hair-washing. (For older boys who'd reached puberty there were two tubs in a separate room, behind a yellow door.) The matrons came down the row of tubs with stiff brushes, bars of floral soap. Every boy had his own towel, embossed with his school number. Mine was 116.

After shampooing a boy the matrons would ease back his head, give him a slow and luxurious rinse.

Confusing as hell.

Matrons would also help with the crucial extraction of lice. Outbreaks were common. Nearly every week another boy would come down with a fierce case. We'd all point and laugh. **Nyah, nyah, you've got nits!** Before long a matron would be kneeling over the patient, rubbing some solution into his scalp, then scraping out the dead beasts with a special comb.

As a thirteen-year-old I graduated from matronly bathing assistance. But I still depended on their nightly tuck-ins, still treasured their morning greetings. They were the first faces we saw each day. They swept into our rooms, threw open our curtains. **Morning, boys!** Bleary, I'd gaze up into a beautiful visage framed by a halo of sun . . .

Is that . . . could that be . . . ?

It never was.

The matron I dealt with the most was Pat. Unlike the other matrons, Pat wasn't hot. Pat was cold. Pat was small, mousy, frazzled, and her hair fell greasily into her always tired eyes. Pat didn't seem to get much joy out of life, though she did find two things reliably satisfying—catching a boy somewhere he wasn't supposed to be, and shutting down any bouts of roughhousing. Before every pillow fight we'd put a sentry on the door. If Pat (or the headmasters) approached, the sentry was instructed to cry: **KV! KV!** Latin, I think? Someone said it meant: The head's coming! Someone else said it meant: Beware!

Whichever, when you heard it you knew to get out of there. Or pretend to be asleep.

Only the newest and stupidest boys would go to Pat with a problem. Or, worse, a cut. She wouldn't bandage it: she'd poke it with a finger or squirt something into it that hurt twice as much. She wasn't a sadist, she just seemed "empathy-challenged." Odd, because she knew about suffering. Pat had many crosses to bear.

The biggest seemed her knees and spine. The latter was crooked, the former chronically stiff. Walking was hard, stairs were torture. She'd descend backwards, glacially. Often we'd stand on the landing below her, doing antic dances, making faces.

Do I need to say which boy did this with the most enthusiasm?

We never worried about Pat catching us. She was a tortoise and we were tree frogs. Still, now and then the tortoise would luck out. She'd lunge, grab a fistful of boy. Aha! That lad would then be well and truly fucked.

Didn't stop us. We went on mocking her as she came down the stairs. The reward was worth the risk. For me, the reward wasn't tormenting poor Pat, but making my mates laugh. It felt so good to make others laugh, especially when I hadn't laughed for months.

Maybe Pat knew this. Now and then she'd turn, see me being a perfect ass, and she'd laugh too. That was the best. I loved cracking up my mates, but nothing quite did it for me like making the otherwise miserable Pat bust a gut.

9.

WE CALLED THEM GRUB DAYS.
They were Tuesday, Thursday, and Saturday, I think. Immediately after lunch we'd queue in the

corridor, along the wall, craning to see, just ahead, the grub table, piled high with sweets. Munchies, Skittles, Mars Bars and, best of all, Opal Fruits. (I took great offense when Opal Fruits changed their name to Starburst. Pure heresy. Like Britain changing its name.)

Just the sight of that grub table made us swoon. Mouths watering, we'd talk about the impending sugar rush as farmers in a drought talk about a forecast of rain. Meanwhile, I devised a way of super-sizing my sugar rush. I'd take all my Opal Fruits and squeeze them together into one massive gobstopper, then jam it into the side of my mouth. As the wad melted my bloodstream would become a frothy cataract of dextrose. **Whatsoever thy hand findeth to do, do it with thy might.**

The opposite of grub day was letter-writing day. Every boy was required to sit down and compose a missive to his parents. At the best of times this was drudgery. I could barely remember when Pa and Mummy weren't divorced, so writing to them without touching on their mutual grievances, their messy breakup, required the finesse of a career diplomat.

Dear Pa, How's Mummy?

Hm. No.

Dear Mummy, Pa says you haven't . . .

No.

But after Mummy disappeared, letter-writing day became impossible.

I've been told the matrons asked me to write a "final" letter to Mummy. I have a vague memory of wanting to protest that she was still alive, and yet not doing so, for fear they'd think I was mad. Also, what was the point? Mummy would read the letter when she came out of hiding, so it wouldn't be a total waste of effort.

I probably dashed off something pro forma, saying I missed her, school was fine, so on and so forth. I probably folded it once and handed it to the matron. I remember, immediately thereafter, regretting that I hadn't taken the writing more seriously. I wished I'd dug deep, told my mother all the things weighing on my heart, especially my regret over the last time we'd spoken on the phone. She'd called early in the evening, the night of the crash, but I was running around with Willy and my cousins and didn't want to stop playing. So I'd been short with her. Impatient to get back to my games, I'd rushed Mummy off the phone. I wished I'd apologized for it. I wished I'd searched for the words to describe how much I loved her.

I didn't know that search would take decades.

10.

A MONTH LATER it was half-term. I was going home at last.

Wait—no, I wasn't.

Pa, apparently, didn't want me to spend the break wandering aimlessly around St. James's Palace, where he'd been mostly living since his breakup with Mummy, and where Willy and I had lived whenever it was our allotted time with Pa. He feared what I might get up to in that big palace all by myself. He feared I might glimpse a newspaper, overhear a radio. More, he feared I might be photographed through an open window, or while playing with my toy soldiers in the gardens. He could imagine reporters trying to speak to me, shouting questions. **Hi, Harry, do you miss your mum?** The nation was in a state of hysterical grief, but the press's hysteria had veered into psychosis.

Worst of all, Willy wouldn't be at home to watch over me. He was at Eton.

So Pa announced that he'd be taking me with him on a planned work trip. To South Africa.

South Africa, Pa? Really?

Yes, darling boy. Johannesburg.

He had a meeting with Nelson Mandela . . . and the Spice Girls?

I was thrilled. And baffled. The Spice Girls, Pa? He explained that the Spice Girls were giving a concert in Johannesburg, so they were calling on President Mandela to pay their respects. Great, I thought, that explains why **the Spice Girls** are going to be there . . . what about us? I didn't get it. I'm not sure Pa wanted me to get it.

The truth was, Pa's staff hoped a photo of him standing alongside the world's most revered political leader and the world's most popular female musical act would earn him some positive headlines, which he sorely needed. Since Mummy's disappearance he'd been savaged. People blamed him for the divorce and thus for all that followed. His approval rating around the world was single digits. In Fiji, to pick just one example, a national holiday in his honor had been rescinded.

Whatever the official reason for the trip, I didn't care. I was just glad to be going along. It was a chance to get away from Britain. Better yet, it was proper time with Pa, who seemed sort of checked out.

Not that Pa hadn't always been a bit checked out. He'd always given an air of being not quite ready for parenthood—the responsibilities, the patience, the time. Even he, though a proud man, would've admitted as much. But single parenthood? Pa was never made for that.

To be fair, he tried. Evenings, I'd shout downstairs: **Going to bed, Pa!** He'd always shout back cheerfully: **I'll be there shortly, darling boy!** True to his word, minutes later he'd be sitting on the edge of my bed. He never forgot that I didn't like the dark, so he'd gently tickle my face until I fell asleep. I have the fondest memories of his hands on my cheeks, my forehead, then waking to find him gone, magically, the door always considerately left open a crack.

Other than those fleeting moments, however, Pa and I mostly coexisted. He had trouble communicating, trouble listening, trouble being intimate face-to-face. On occasion, after a long multi-course dinner, I'd walk upstairs and find a letter on my pillow. The letter would say how proud he was of me for something I'd done or accomplished. I'd smile, place it under my pillow, but also wonder why he hadn't said this moments ago, while seated directly across from me.

Thus the prospect of days and days of unrestricted Pa time was exhilarating.

Then came the reality. This was a work trip for Pa. And for me. The Spice Girls concert represented my first public appearance since the funeral, and I knew, through intuition, through bits of overheard conversations, that the public's curiosity about my welfare was running high. I didn't want to let them down, but I also wanted them all to go away. I remember stepping onto the red carpet, screwing a smile onto my face, suddenly wishing I was in my bed at St. James's Palace.

Beside me was Baby Spice, wearing white plastic shoes with chunky twelve-inch platform heels. I fixated on those heels while she fixated on my cheeks. She kept pinching them. So chubby! So cute! Then Posh Spice surged forward and clutched my hand. Farther down the line I spied Ginger Spice, the only Spice with whom I felt any connection—a fellow ginger. Also, she was world-famous for recently wearing a minidress made of the Union Jack. **Why's there a Union Jack on the coffin?** She and the other Spices were cooing at me, saying things I didn't understand, while bantering with the journalists, who were shouting at me. **Harry, over here, Harry, Harry, how are you doing, Harry?** Questions that weren't questions. Questions that were traps. Questions that were flung at my head like cleavers. The journalists didn't give a toss how I was doing, they were trying to get me to say something messy, newsy.

I gazed into their flashes, bared my teeth, said nothing.

If I was intimidated by the flashes, the Spice Girls were intoxicated. Yes, yes, a thousand times yes, that was their attitude every time another flash went off. Fine by me. The more out-front they were, the more I could fade into the woodwork. I remember they talked to the press about their music and their mission. I didn't know they had a mission, but one Spice compared the group's crusade against sexism to Mandela's struggle against apartheid.

At last someone said it was time for the concert to begin. **Off you go. Follow your father.**

Concert? Pa?

Impossible to believe. Even more impossible while it was actually happening. But I saw it with my own eyes, Pa gamely nodding to the beat and tapping his foot:

If you want my future, forget my past
If you wanna get with me, better make it fast

After, on the way out, there were more flashes. This time the Spice Girls weren't there to deflect attention. It was just Pa and me.

I reached for him, grabbed his hand—hung on.

I recall, bright as the flashes: Loving him.

Needing him.

11.

THE NEXT MORNING PA and I went to a beautiful lodge on a snaky river. KwaZulu-Natal. I knew about this place, where Redcoats and Zulu warriors clashed in the summer of 1879. I'd heard all the stories, legends, and I'd seen the movie **Zulu** countless times. But now I was going to become a bona fide expert, Pa said. He'd arranged for us to sit on camp chairs before a log fire and listen to a world-famous historian, David Rattray, re-create the battle.

It might've been the first lecture to which I ever really paid attention.

The men who fought on this ground, Mr. Rattray said, were heroes. On both sides—heroes. The Zulus were ferocious, utter wizards with a short spear known as the **iklwa**, which was named for the sucking sound it made when pulled from a victim's chest. And yet a mere 150 British soldiers on hand managed to hold off four thousand Zulus, and that improbable stand, called Rorke's Drift, instantly became part of British mythology. Eleven soldiers were awarded the Victoria Cross, the greatest number ever won in one battle by a single regiment. Another two soldiers, who held off the Zulus one day before Rorke's Drift, became the first to win the Victoria Cross posthumously.

Posthumously, Pa?

Er, yes.

What does it mean?

After they, you know.

What?

Died, darling boy.

Though a source of pride for many Britons, Rorke's Drift was the outgrowth of imperialism, colonialism, nationalism—in short, theft. Great Britain was trespassing, invading a sovereign nation and trying to steal it, meaning the precious blood of Britain's finest lads had been wasted that day, in the eyes of some, among them Mr. Rattray. He didn't glide over such difficult facts. When necessary, he condemned the British roundly. (Locals called him the White Zulu.) But I was too young: I heard him and also didn't hear. Maybe I'd seen the movie **Zulu** too many times, maybe I'd waged too many pretend battles with my toy Redcoats. I had a view of battle, of Britain, which didn't permit new facts. So I zoomed in on the bits about manly courage, and British power, and when I should've been horrified, I was inspired.

On the way home I told myself the whole trip had been a smash. Not only a terrific adventure, but a bonding experience with Pa. Surely life would now be altogether different.

12.

MOST OF MY TEACHERS WERE kind souls who just let me be, who understood all that I was dealing with and didn't want to give me more. Mr. Dawson, who played the organ in the chapel, was extremely gentle. Mr. Little, the drum teacher, was exceedingly patient. Confined to a wheelchair, he'd turn up for drum lessons in his van, and it would take us forever to get him out of the van and into the classroom, and then we'd have to leave enough time to get him back into the van after the lesson, so we'd never have more than twenty minutes of actual teaching. I didn't mind, and in return Mr. Little didn't ever complain that my drumming wasn't really improving.

Some teachers, however, gave me no quarter. Like my history teacher, Mr. Hughes-Games.

Day and night, from Mr. Hughes-Games's bungalow beside the sports fields, came the shrill yelps of his pointers, Tosca and Beade. They were beautiful, spotted, gray-eyed, and Mr. Hughes-Games cherished them as children. He kept silver-framed photos of them on his desk, which was one reason many boys thought Mr. Hughes-Games a tad eccentric. So it came as a roaring shock when I realized that Mr. Hughes-Games believed me to be the odd one. What could be odder, he said to me one day, than a British prince not knowing British history?

I cannot fathom it, Wales. We're talking about your blood relatives—does that mean nothing to you?

Less than nothing, sir.

It wasn't just that I didn't know anything about my family's history: I didn't want to know anything.

I liked British history **in theory**. I found certain bits intriguing. I knew a few things about the signing of the Magna Carta, for instance—June 1215, at

Runnymede—but that was because I'd once glimpsed the place where it happened through the window of Pa's car. Right by the river. Looked beautiful. Perfect spot to establish peace, I thought. But micro details about the Norman Conquest? Or the ins and outs of the beef between Henry VIII and the Pope? Or the differences between the First and Second Crusades?

Please.

It all came to a head one day when Mr. Hughes-Games was talking about Charles Edward Stuart, or Charles III, as he thought of himself. Pretender to the Throne. Mr. Hughes-Games had strong opinions about the fellow. While he shared them with us, in a hot rage, I stared at my pencil and tried not to fall asleep.

Suddenly Mr. Hughes-Games stopped and posited a question about Charles's life. The answer was a cinch if you'd done the reading. No one had.

Wales—you must know this.

Why must I?

Because it's your family!

Laughter.

I dropped my head. The other boys knew I was royal, of course. If they forgot for half a second, my omnipresent bodyguard (armed) and uniformed police scattered across the grounds would be more than happy to remind them. But did Mr. Hughes-Games need to shout it from the rooftops? Did he need to use that loaded word—family? My family had declared me a nullity. The Spare. I didn't complain about it, but I didn't need to dwell on it either. Far better, in my mind, not to think about certain facts, such as the cardinal rule for royal travel: Pa and William could never be on the same flight together, because there must be no chance of the first and second in line to the throne being wiped out. But no one gave a damn whom I traveled with; the Spare could always be spared. I knew this, knew my place, so why go out of my way to study it? Why memorize the names of past spares? What was the sense in that?

More, why trace my family tree when all tracery led to the same severed branch—Mummy?

After class I went up to Mr. Hughes-Games's desk and asked him to please stop.

Stop what, Wales?

Embarrassing me, sir.

His eyebrows flew up to his hairline, like startled birds.

I argued that it would be cruel to single out any other boy the way he did me, to ask any other student at Ludgrove such pointed questions about his great-great-grand-whatever.

Mr. Hughes-Games harrumphed and snuffled. He'd overstepped, he knew it. But he was stubborn.

It's good for you, Wales. The more I call on you, the more you'll learn.

Days later, however, at the start of class, Mr. Hughes-Games made a proffer of peace, Magna Carta style. He presented me with one of those wooden rulers, engraved along both sides with the names of every British monarch since Harold in 1066. (Rulers, get it?)

The royal line, inch by inch, right up to Granny. He said I could keep it at my desk, refer to it as needed.

Gosh, I said. Thanks.

13.

LATE AT NIGHT, AFTER lights-out, some of us would sneak out, go roaming up and down the corridors. A strict violation of the rules, but I was lonely and homesick, probably anxious and depressed, and I couldn't abide being locked into my dormitory.

There was one particular teacher who, whenever he caught me, would give me a tremendous clout, always with a copy of the **New English Bible**. The hardback version. It is indeed, I always thought, a very hard back. Getting hit with it made me feel bad about myself, bad about the teacher, and bad about the Bible. Nevertheless, the next night I'd go right back to flouting the rules.

If I wasn't roaming the corridors, I was roaming the school grounds, usually with my best mate, Henners. Like me, Henners was officially a Henry, but I always called him Henners, and he called me Haz.

Skinny, with no muscles, and hair that stood up in permanent surrender, Henners was all heart. Whenever he smiled, people melted. (He was the only boy who mentioned Mummy to me after she disappeared.) But that winning smile, that tender nature, made you forget that Henners could be **quite** naughty.

A huge "pick your own" farm lay beyond the school grounds, on the other side of a low fence, and one day Henners and I hopped over, landing face-first in carrot furrows. Row after row. Nearby were some fat, juicy strawberries. We went along, stuffing our mouths, popping up now and then like meerkats to make sure the coast was clear. Whenever I bite into a strawberry I'm there again, in those furrows, with lovely Henners.

Days later we went back. This time, after we'd eaten our fill and hopped over the fence, we heard our names.

We were heading along a cart track in the direction of the tennis courts and slowly we turned. Coming straight for us was one of the teachers.

You there! Stop!

Hello, sir.

What are you two doing?

Nothing, sir.

You've been to the farm.

No!

Open your hands.

We did. Busted. Crimson palms. He reacted as if it were blood.

I can't remember what punishment we received. Another clout with the **New English Bible?** Detention? (Often called det.) A trip to Mr. Gerald's office? Whatever it was, I know I didn't mind. There was no torture Ludgrove could dish out that surpassed what was going on inside me.

14.

Mr. Marston, while patrolling the dining room, often carried a little bell. It reminded me of the bell on the front desk of a hotel. **Ding, have you a room?** He'd ring the bell whenever he wanted to get a group of boys' attention. The sound was constant. And utterly pointless.

Abandoned children don't care about a bell.

Frequently Mr. Marston would feel the need to make an announcement during meals. He'd begin speaking and no one would listen, or even lower their voice, so he'd ring his bell.

Ding.

A hundred boys would keep on talking, laughing.

He'd ring it harder.

Ding! Ding! Ding!

Each time the bell failed to bring silence, Mr. Marston's face would grow a shade redder. **Fellas! Will you LISTEN?**

No, was the simple answer. We would not. It wasn't disrespect, however; it was simple acoustics. We couldn't hear him. The hall was too cavernous, and we were too absorbed in our conversations.

He didn't accept this. He seemed suspicious, as if our disregard of his bell was part of some greater coordinated plot. I don't know about the others, but I was part of no plot. Also, I wasn't disregarding him. Quite the contrary: I couldn't take my eyes off the man. I often asked myself what an outsider might say if they could witness this spectacle, a hundred boys chatting away while a grown man stood before them frantically and uselessly abusing a tiny brass bell.

Adding to this general sense of bedlam was the psychiatric hospital down the road. Broadmoor. Some time before I came to Ludgrove, a Broadmoor patient had escaped and killed a child in one of the nearby villages. In response Broadmoor installed a warning siren, and now and then they'd test it, to make sure it was in working order. A sound like Doomsday. Mr. Marston's bell on steroids.

I mentioned this to Pa one day. He nodded sagely. He'd recently visited a similar place as part of his charitable work. The patients were mostly gentle, he assured me, though one stood out. A little chap who claimed to be the Prince of Wales.

Pa said he'd wagged a finger at this impostor and severely reprimanded him. **Now look here. You cannot be the Prince of Wales! I'm the Prince of Wales.**

The patient merely wagged his finger back. **Impossible! I'm the Prince of Wales!**

Pa liked telling stories, and this was one of the best in his repertoire. He'd always end with a burst of philosophizing: If this mental patient could be so thoroughly convinced of his identity, no less than Pa, it raised some very Big Questions indeed. Who could say which of us was sane? Who could be sure **they** weren't the mental patient, hopelessly deluded, humored by friends and family? **Who knows if**

I'm really the Prince of Wales? Who knows if I'm even your real father? Maybe your real father is in Broadmoor, darling boy!

He'd laugh and laugh, though it was a remarkably unfunny joke, given the rumor circulating just then that my actual father was one of Mummy's former lovers: Major James Hewitt. One cause of this rumor was Major Hewitt's flaming ginger hair, but another cause was sadism. Tabloid readers were delighted by the idea that the younger child of Prince Charles wasn't the child of Prince Charles. They couldn't get enough of this "joke," for some reason. Maybe it made them feel better about their lives that a young prince's life was laughable.

Never mind that my mother didn't meet Major Hewitt until long after I was born, the story was simply too good to drop. The press rehashed it, embroidered it, and there was even talk that some reporters were seeking my DNA to prove it—my first intimation that, after torturing my mother and sending her into hiding, they would soon be coming for me.

To this day nearly every biography of me, every longish profile in a paper or magazine, touches on Major Hewitt, treats the prospect of his paternity with some seriousness, including a description of the moment Pa finally sat me down for a proper heart-to-heart, reassuring me that Major Hewitt wasn't my real father. Vivid scene, poignant, moving, and wholly made up. If Pa had any thoughts about Major Hewitt, he kept them to himself.

15.

MY MOTHER LEGENDARILY SAID there were three people in her marriage. But her maths was off.

She left Willy and me out of the equation.

We didn't understand what was going on with her and Pa, certainly, but we intuited enough, we sensed the presence of the Other Woman, because we suffered the downstream effects. Willy long harbored suspicions about the Other Woman, which confused him, tormented him, and when those suspicions were confirmed he felt tremendous guilt for having done nothing, said nothing, sooner.

I was too young, I think, to have suspicions. But I couldn't help but feel the lack of stability, the lack of warmth and love, in our home.

Now, with Mummy missing, the maths swung hard in Pa's favor. He was free to see the Other Woman, openly, as often as he liked. But seeing wasn't sufficient. Pa wanted to be public about it. He wanted to be aboveboard. And the first step towards that aim was to bring "the boys" into the fold.

Willy went first. He'd bumped into the Other Woman, once, at the palace, but now he was formally summoned from Eton for a high-stakes private meeting. At Highgrove, I think. Over tea, I believe. It went well, I gathered from Willy later, though he didn't go into details. He merely gave me the impression that the Other Woman, Camilla, had made an effort, which he appreciated, and that was all he cared to say.

My turn came next. I told myself: No big deal. Just like getting an injection. Close your eyes, over before you know it.

I have a dim recollection of Camilla being just as calm (or bored) as me. Neither of us much fretted about the other's opinion. She wasn't my mother, and I wasn't her biggest hurdle. In other words, I wasn't the Heir. This bit with me was mere formality.

I wonder what we found to talk about. Horses, probably. Camilla loved them, and I knew how to ride. Hard to think of any other subject we might've scrounged up.

I recall wondering, right before the tea, if she'd be mean to me. If she'd be like all the wicked stepmothers in storybooks. But she wasn't. Like Willy, I did feel real gratitude for that.

At last, with these strained Camilla summits behind us, there was a final conference with Pa.

So, what do you boys think?

We thought he should be happy. Yes, Camilla had played a pivotal role in the unraveling of our parents' marriage, and yes, that meant she'd played a role in our mother's disappearance, but we understood that she'd been trapped like everyone else in the riptide of events. We didn't blame her, and in fact we'd gladly forgive her if she could make Pa happy. We could see that, like us, he wasn't. We recognized the vacant looks, the empty sighs, the frustration always visible on his face. We couldn't be absolutely sure, because Pa didn't talk about his feelings, but we'd pieced together, through the years, a fairly accurate portrait of him, based on little things he'd let slip.

For instance, Pa confessed around this time that he'd been "persecuted" as a boy. Granny and Grandpa, to toughen him up, had shipped him off to Gordonstoun, a boarding school, where he was horrendously bullied. The most likely victims of Gordonstoun bullies, he said, were creative types, sensitive types, bookish types—in other words, Pa. His finest qualities were bait for the toughs. I remember him murmuring ominously: **I nearly didn't survive.** How had he? Head down, clutching his teddy bear, which he still owned years later. Teddy went everywhere with Pa. It was a pitiful object, with broken arms and dangly threads, holes patched up here and there. It looked, I imagined, like Pa might have after the bullies had finished with him. Teddy expressed eloquently, better than Pa ever could, the essential loneliness of his childhood.

Willy and I agreed that Pa deserved better. Apologies to Teddy, Pa deserved a proper companion. That was why, when asked, Willy and I promised Pa that we'd welcome Camilla into the family.

The only thing we asked in return was that he not marry her. You don't need to remarry, we pleaded. A wedding would cause controversy. It would incite the press. It would make the whole country, the whole world, talk about Mummy, compare Mummy and Camilla, and nobody wanted that. Least of all Camilla.

We support you, we said. We endorse Camilla, we said. **Just please don't marry her. Just be together, Pa.**

He didn't answer.

But she answered. Straightaway. Shortly after our private summits with her, she began to play the long game, a campaign aimed at marriage and eventually the Crown. (With Pa's blessing, we presumed.) Stories began to appear everywhere, in all the papers, about her private conversation with Willy, stories that contained pinpoint accurate details, none of which had come from Willy, of course.

They could only have been leaked by the one other person present.

And the leaking had obviously been abetted by the new spin doctor Camilla had talked Pa into hiring.

16.

IN THE EARLY AUTUMN of 1998, having completed my education at Ludgrove the previous spring, I entered Eton.

A profound shock.

The finest school in the world for boys, Eton was **meant** to be a shock, I think. Shock must've been part of its original charter, even perhaps a part of the instructions given to its first architects by the school's founder, my ancestor Henry VI. He deemed Eton some sort of holy shrine, a sacred temple, and to that end he wanted it to overwhelm the senses, so visitors would feel like meek, abased pilgrims.

In my case, mission accomplished.

(Henry even vested the school with priceless religious artifacts, including part of Jesus's Crown of Thorns. One great poet called the place "Henry's holy shade.")

Over the centuries Eton's mission had become somewhat less pious, but the curriculum had become more shockingly rigorous. There was a reason Eton now referred to itself not as a school but simply as . . . School. For those in the know, there simply was no other choice. Eighteen prime ministers had been molded in Eton's classrooms, plus thirty-seven winners of the Victoria Cross. Heaven for brilliant boys, it could thus only be purgatory for one very unbrilliant boy.

The situation became undeniably obvious during my very first French lesson. I was astounded to hear the teacher conducting the entire class in rapid, non-stop French. He assumed, for some reason, that we were all fluent.

Maybe everyone else was. But me? Fluent? Because I did passably well on the entrance exam? **Au contraire, mon ami!**

Afterwards I went up to him, explained that there'd been a dreadful mistake and I was in the wrong class. He told me to relax, assured me I'd be up to speed in no time. He didn't get it; he had faith in me. So I went to my housemaster, begged him to put me with the slower talkers, the more glacial learners, boys **exactement comme moi**.

He did as I asked. But it was a mere stopgap.

Once or twice I'd confess to a teacher or fellow student that I wasn't merely in the wrong class but in the wrong location. I was in way, way over my head. They'd always say the same thing: Don't worry, you'll be all right. **And don't forget you always have your brother here!**

But I wasn't the one forgetting. Willy told me to pretend I didn't know him.

What?

You don't know me, Harold. And I don't know you.

For the last two years, he explained, Eton had been his sanctuary. No kid brother tagging along, pestering him with questions, pushing up on his social circle. He was forging his own life, and he wasn't willing to give that up.

None of which was all that new. Willy always hated it when anyone made the mistake of thinking us a package deal. He loathed it when Mummy dressed us in the same outfits. (It didn't help that her taste in children's clothes ran to the extreme; we often looked like the twins from **Alice in Wonderland**.) I barely took notice. I didn't care about clothes, mine or anyone else's. So long as we weren't wearing kilts, with that worrisome knife in your sock and that breeze up your arse, I was good. But for Willy it was pure agony to wear the same blazer, the same tight shorts, as me. And now, to attend the same school, was pure murder.

I told him not to worry. **I'll forget I ever knew you.**

But Eton wasn't going to make that easy. Thinking to be helpful, they put us under the same bloody roof. Manor House.

At least I was on the ground floor.

Willy was way upstairs, with the older boys.

17.

MANY OF THE SIXTY BOYS in Manor House were as welcoming as Willy. Their indifference, however, didn't unsettle me as much as their **ease**. Even the ones my age acted as if they'd been born on the school grounds. Ludgrove had its problems, but at least I knew my way around, knew how to fox Pat, knew when sweets got handed out, how to survive letter-writing days. Over time I'd scratched and clawed my way to the top of the Ludgrove pyramid. Now, at Eton, I was at the bottom again.

Starting over.

Worse, without my best friend, Henners. He was attending a different school.

I didn't even know how to get dressed in the morning. Every Etonian was required to wear a black tailcoat, white collarless shirt, white stiff collar pinned to the shirt with a stud—plus pinstripe trousers, heavy black shoes, and a tie that wasn't a tie, more like a cloth strip folded into the white detachable collar. Formal kit, they called it, but it wasn't formal, it was funereal. And there was a reason. We were supposed to be in perpetual mourning for old Henry VI. (Or else for King George, an early supporter of the school, who used to have the boys over to the castle for tea—or something like that.) Though Henry was my great-great-great-great-great-great-grandfather, and though I was sorry for his passing, and for whatever pain it had caused those who loved him, I wasn't keen on mourning the man around the clock. Any boy might balk at taking part in a never-ending funeral, but for a boy who'd just lost his mum it was a daily kick in the balls.

First morning: It took forever to fasten my trousers, button my waistcoat, fold my stiff collar, before finally getting out the door. I was frantic, desperate not to be late, which would mean being forced to write my name in a large ledger, the Tardy Book, one of many new traditions I'd need to learn, along with a long list of new words and phrases. Classes were no longer classes: they were divs. Teachers were no longer teachers: they were beaks. Cigarettes were tabbage. (Seemingly everyone had a raging tabbage habit.) Chambers was the mid-morning meeting of the beaks, when they discussed the students, especially the problem students. I often felt my ears burning during Chambers.

Sport, I decided, would be my thing at Eton. Sporty boys were separated into two groups: dry bobs and wet bobs. Dry bobs played cricket, football, rugby, or polo. Wet bobs rowed, sailed, or swam. I was a dry who occasionally got wet. I played every dry sport, though rugby captured my heart. Beautiful game, plus a good excuse to run into stuff very hard. Rugby let me indulge my rage, which some had now taken to calling a "red mist." Plus, I simply didn't feel pain the way other boys did, which made me scary on a pitch. No one had an answer for a boy actually **seeking** external pain to match his internal.

I made some mates. It wasn't easy. I had special requirements. I needed someone who wouldn't tease me about being royal, someone who wouldn't so much as mention my being the Spare. I needed someone who'd treat me normal, which meant ignoring the armed bodyguard sleeping down the hall, whose job was to keep me from being kidnapped or assassinated. (To say nothing of the electronic tracker and panic alarm I carried with me at all times.) My mates all met these criteria.

Sometimes my new mates and I would escape, head for Windsor Bridge, which connected Eton to Windsor over the River Thames. Specifically we'd head to the underside of the bridge, where we could smoke tabbage in privacy. My mates seemed to enjoy the naughtiness of it, whereas I just did it because I was on autopilot. Sure, I fancied a cig after a McDonald's, who didn't? But if we were going to bunk off, I'd much prefer heading over to Windsor Castle golf course, knocking a ball around, while drinking a wee beer.

Still, like a robot, I took every cig offered me, and in the same automatic, unthinking way, I soon graduated to weed.

18.

THE GAME REQUIRED A BAT, a tennis ball, and a total disregard for one's physical safety. There were four players: a bowler, a batsman, and two fielders stationed mid-corridor, each with one foot in the corridor and one in a room. Not always our rooms. We often intruded on other boys trying to work. They'd beg us to go away.

Sorry, we said. **This** is **our** work.

The radiator represented the wicket. There was an endless debate about what constituted a catch. Off the wall? Yes, catch. Off a window? No catch. One hand, one bounce? Half out.

One day the sportiest member of our group hurled himself at a ball, trying to make a tricky catch, and landed face-first on a fire extinguisher hooked to the wall. His tongue split wide open. You'd think after that, after the carpet had been permanently soiled with his blood, we'd have called an end to Corridor Cricket.

We didn't.

When not playing Corridor Cricket we'd loll in our rooms. We got very good at affecting postures of supreme indolence. The point was to look as if you had no purpose, as if you'd bestir yourself only to do something bad or, better yet, stupid. Near the end of my first half we hit on something supremely stupid.

Someone suggested that my hair was a complete disaster. Like grass on the moors.

Well . . . what can be done?

Let me have a go at it.

You?

Yeah. Let me shave it off.

Hm. That didn't sound right.

But I wanted to go along. I wanted to be a top bloke. A funny bloke.

All right.

Someone fetched the clippers. Someone pushed me into a chair. How quickly, how blithely, after a lifetime of healthy growth, it all went cascading off my head. When the cutter was done I looked down, saw a dozen pyramids of ginger on the floor, like red volcanoes seen from a plane, and knew I'd made a legendary mistake.

I ran to the mirror. Suspicion confirmed. I screamed in horror.

My mates screamed too. With laughter.

I ran in circles. I wanted to reverse time. I wanted to scoop up the hair from the floor and glue it back on. I wanted to wake from this nightmare. Not knowing where else to turn, I violated the sacred rule, the one shining commandment never to be broken, and ran upstairs to Willy's room.

Of course, there was nothing Willy could do. I was just hoping he'd tell me it would be OK, don't freak out, keep calm, Harold. Instead, he laughed like the others. I recall him sitting at his desk, bent over a book, chuckling, while I stood before him fingering the nubs on my newly bare scalp.

Harold, what have you done?

What a question. He sounded like Stewie from **Family Guy.** Wasn't it obvious?

You shouldn't have done it, Harold!

So we're just stating the obvious now?

He said a few more things that were immensely unhelpful and I walked out.

Worse ridicule was yet to come. A few days later, on the front page of the **Daily Mirror,** one of the tabloids, there I was with my new haircut.

Headline: **Harry the Skinhead.**

I couldn't imagine how they'd got wind of the story. A schoolmate must have told someone who told someone who told the papers. They had no photo, thank goodness. But they'd improvised. The image on the front page was a "computer-generated" rendering of the Spare, bald as an egg. A lie. More than a lie, really.

I looked bad, but not that bad.

19.

I DIDN'T THINK it could get worse. What a grievous mistake it is for a member of the Royal Family, when considering the media, to imagine that things can't get worse. Weeks later the same newspaper put me on the front page again.

HARRY'S HAD AN ACCIDENT.

I'd broken a bone in my thumb playing rugby, no big deal, but the paper decided to make out that I was on life support. Bad taste, under any circumstances, but a little more than a year after Mummy's alleged accident?

C'mon, fellas.

I'd dealt with the British press all my life, but they'd

never before singled me out. In fact, since Mummy's death an unspoken agreement had governed press treatment of both her sons, and the agreement went like this: **Lay off.**

Let them have their education in peace.

Apparently that agreement had now expired, because there I was, splattered across the front page, made out to seem a delicate flower. Or an ass. Or both.

And knocking on death's door.

I read the article several times. Despite the somber subtext—something's very wrong with Prince Harry—I marveled at its tone: larky. My existence was just fun and games to these people. I wasn't a human being to them. I wasn't a fourteen-year-old boy hanging on by his fingernails. I was a cartoon character, a glove puppet to be manipulated and mocked for fun. So what if their fun made my already difficult days more difficult, made me a laughingstock before my schoolmates, not to mention the wider world? So what if they were torturing a child? All was justified because I was royal, and in their minds royal was synonymous with non-person. Centuries ago royal men and women were considered divine; now they were insects. What fun, to pluck their wings.

Pa's office lodged a formal complaint, publicly demanded an apology, accused the paper of bullying his younger son.

The newspaper told Pa's office to sod off.

Before trying to move on with my life I took one last look at the article. Of all the things that surprised me about it, the truly flabbergasting thing was the absolutely shitty writing. I was a poor student, a dreadful writer, and yet I had enough education to recognize that this right here was a master class in illiteracy.

To take one example: After explaining that I'd been grievously injured, that I was nearly at death's door, the article went on to caution breathlessly that the exact nature of my injury couldn't be revealed because the Royal Family had forbidden the editors to do so. (As if my family had any control over these ghouls.) "To reassure you, we can say that Harry's injuries are NOT serious. But the accident was considered grave enough for him to be taken to hospital. But we believe you are entitled to know if an heir to the throne is involved in any accident, however small, if it results in injury."

The two "buts" in a row, the smug self-regard, the lack of coherence and absence of any real point, the hysterical nothingness of it all. This dog's dinner of a paragraph was said to be edited—or, more likely, written—by a young journalist whose name I scanned and then quickly forgot.

I didn't think I'd ever run across it, or him, again. The way he wrote? I couldn't imagine he'd be a working journalist much longer.

20.

I FORGET WHO USED THE WORD FIRST. Someone in the press, probably. Or one of my teachers.

Whoever—it took hold and circulated. I'd been cast in my role in the Rolling Royal Melodrama. Long before I was old enough to drink a beer (legally) it became dogma.

Harry? Yeah, he's the naughty **one.**

Naughty became the tide I swam against, the headwind I flew against, the daily expectation I could never hope to shake.

I didn't want to be naughty. I wanted to be noble. I wanted to be good, work hard, grow up and do something meaningful with my days. But every sin, every misstep, every setback triggered the same tired label, and the same public condemnations, and thereby reinforced the conventional wisdom that I was innately naughty.

Things might have been different if I'd achieved good grades. But I didn't and everyone knew it. My reports were in the public domain. The whole Commonwealth was aware of my academic struggles, which were largely due to being overmatched at Eton.

But no one ever discussed the **other** probable cause. Mummy.

Study, concentration, requires an alliance with the mind, and in my teen years I was waging all-out war with mine. I was forever fending off its darkest thoughts, its basest fears—its fondest memories. (The fonder the memory, the deeper the ache.) I'd found strategies for doing this, some healthy, some not, but all quite effective, and whenever they were unavailable—for instance, when I was forced to sit quietly with a book—I freaked out. Naturally, I avoided such situations.

At all costs, I avoided sitting quietly with a book.

It struck me at some point that the whole basis of education was memory. A list of names, a column of numbers, a mathematical formula, a beautiful poem—to learn it you had to upload it to the part of the brain that stored stuff, but that was the same part of my brain I was resisting. My memory had been spotty since Mummy disappeared, by design, and I didn't want to fix it, because memory equaled grief.

Not remembering was balm.

It's also possible that I'm misremembering my own struggles with memory from back then, because I do recall being very good at memorizing **some** things, like long passages from **Ace Ventura** and **The Lion King**. I'd recite them often, to mates, to myself. Also, there's a photo of me, sitting in my room, at my pull-out desk, and there amid the cubbyholes and chaotic papers sits a silver-framed photo of Mummy. So. Despite my clear memory of not wanting to remember her, I was also trying gamely not to forget her.

Difficult as it was for me to be the naughty one, and the stupid one, it was anguish for Pa, because it meant I was his opposite.

What troubled him most was how I went out of my way to avoid books. Pa didn't merely enjoy books, he exalted them. Especially Shakespeare. He adored **Henry V**. He compared himself to Prince Hal. There were multiple Falstaffs in his life, like Lord Mountbatten, his beloved great-uncle, and Laurens van der Post, the irascible intellectual acolyte of Carl Jung.

When I was about six or seven, Pa went to Stratford and delivered a fiery public defense of Shakespeare. Standing in the place where Britain's greatest writer was born and died, Pa decried the neglect of Shakespeare's plays in schools, the fading of Shakespeare from British classrooms, and from the nation's collective consciousness. Pa peppered this fiery oration with quotations from **Hamlet, Macbeth, Othello, The Tempest, The Merchant of Venice**—he plucked the lines from thin air, like petals from one of his homegrown roses, and tossed them into the audience. It was showmanship, but not in an empty way. He was making the point: You should all be able to do this. You should all know these lines. They're our shared heritage, we should be cherishing them, safeguarding them, and instead we're letting them die.

I never doubted how much it upset Pa that I was part of the Shakespeare-less hordes. And I tried to change. I opened **Hamlet**. Hmm: Lonely prince, obsessed with dead parent, watches remaining parent fall in love with dead parent's usurper . . . ?

I slammed it shut. No, thank you.

Pa never stopped fighting the good fight. He was spending more time at Highgrove, his 350-acre estate in Gloucestershire, and it was just down the road from Stratford, so he made a point of taking me now and then. We'd turn up unannounced, watch whatever play they were putting on, it didn't matter to Pa. Didn't matter to me either, though for different reasons.

It was all torture.

On many nights I didn't understand most of what was taking place or being said onstage. But when I did understand, worse for me. The words burned. They troubled. Why would I want to hear about a grief-stricken kingdom "contracted in one brow of woe"? That just put me in mind of August 1997. Why would I want to meditate upon the inalterable fact that "all that lives must die, passing through nature to eternity . . ."? I had no time to think about eternity.

The one piece of literature I remember enjoying, even savoring, was a slender American novel. **Of Mice and Men** by John Steinbeck. We were assigned it in our English divs.

Unlike Shakespeare, Steinbeck didn't need a translator. He wrote in plain, simple vernacular. Better yet, he kept it tight. **Of Mice and Men**: a brisk 150 pages.

Best of all, its plot was diverting. Two blokes, George and Lennie, gadding about California, looking for a place to call their own, trying to overcome their limitations. Neither's a genius, but Lennie's trouble seems to be more than low IQ. He keeps a dead mouse in his pocket, strokes it with his thumb— for comfort. He also loves a puppy so much that he kills it.

A story about friendship, about brotherhood, about loyalty, it was filled with themes I found relatable. George and Lennie put me in mind of Willy and me. Two pals, two nomads, going through the same things, watching each other's back. As Steinbeck has one character say: "A guy needs somebody—to be near him. A guy goes nuts if he ain't got nobody."

So true. I wanted to share it with Willy.

Too bad he was still pretending not to know me.

21.

MUST'VE BEEN EARLY spring, 1999. I must've been home from Eton for the weekend.

I woke to find Pa on the edge of my bed, saying I was going back to Africa.

Africa, Pa?

Yes, darling boy.

Why?

It was the same old problem, he explained. I was facing a longish school holiday, over Easter, and something needed to be done with me. So, Africa. Botswana, to be precise. A safari.

Safari! With you, Pa?

No. Alas, he wouldn't be going along this time. But Willy would.

Oh, good.

And someone very special, he added, acting as our African guide.

Who, Pa?

Marko.

Marko? I barely knew the man, though I'd heard good things. He was Willy's minder, and Willy seemed to like him very much. Everyone did, for that matter.

Of all Pa's people there was consensus that Marko was the best. The roughest, the toughest, the most dashing.

Longtime Welsh Guard. Raconteur. Man's man, through and through.

I was so excited about the prospect of this Marko-led safari, I don't know how I got through the following weeks of school. I don't actually **recall** getting through them, in fact. Memory winks out completely, right after Pa delivered the news, then snaps back into focus as I'm boarding a British Airways jet with Marko and Willy and Tiggy—one of our nannies. Our favorite nanny, to be accurate, though Tiggy couldn't stand being called that. She'd bite the head off anyone who tried. **I'm not the nanny, I'm your friend!**

Mummy, sadly, didn't see it that way. Mummy saw Tiggy not as a nanny but as a rival. It's common knowledge that Mummy suspected Tiggy was being groomed as her future replacement. (Did Mummy see Tiggy as her Spare?) Now this same woman whom Mummy feared as her possible replacement was her actual replacement—how dreadful for Mummy. Every hug or head pat from Tiggy, therefore, must've unleashed some twinge of guilt, some throb of disloyalty, and yet I don't remember that. I remember only heart-racing joy to have Tiggy next to me, telling me to buckle my seatbelt.

We flew direct to Johannesburg, then by prop plane to Maun, the largest city in northern Botswana. There we met up with a large group of safari guides, who steered us into a convoy of open-topped Land

Cruisers. We drove off, straight into pure wilderness, towards the vast Okavango Delta, which I soon discovered was possibly the most exquisite place in the world.

The Okavango is often called a river, but that's like calling Windsor Castle a house. A vast inland delta, smack in the middle of the Kalahari Desert, one of the largest deserts on earth, the lower Okavango is bone dry for part of the year. But come late summer it begins to fill with floodwaters from upstream, little droplets that begin as rainfall in the Angola highlands and slowly swell to a trickle, then a flow, which steadily transforms the delta into not one river but dozens. From outer space it looks like the chambers of a heart filling with blood.

With water comes life. A profusion of animals, possibly the most biodiverse collection anywhere, they come to drink, bathe, mate. Imagine if the Ark suddenly appeared, then capsized.

As we neared this enchanted place, I had trouble catching my breath. Lions, zebras, giraffes, hippos—surely this was all a dream. At last we stopped—our campsite for the next week. The spot was bustling with more guides, more trackers, a dozen people at least. Lots of high fives, bear hugs, names flung at us. **Harry, William, say hello to Adi!** (Twenty years old, long hair, sweet smile.) **Harry, William, say hi to Roger and David.**

And at the center of it all stood Marko, like a traffic cop, directing, cajoling, embracing, barking, laughing, always laughing.

In no time he'd pulled our campsite into shape. Big green canvas tents, soft canvas chairs grouped in circles, including one enormous circle around a stone-rimmed campfire. When I think about that trip, my mind goes immediately to that fire—just as my skinny body did then. The fire was where we'd all collect at regular intervals throughout the day. First thing in the morning, again at midday, again at dusk—and, above all, after supper. We'd stare into that fire, then up at the universe. The stars looked like sparks from the logs.

One of the guides called the fire Bush TV.

Yes, I said, every time you throw a new log on, it's like changing the channel.

They all loved that.

The fire, I noticed, hypnotized, or narcotized, every adult in our party. In its orange glow their faces grew softer, their tongues looser. Then, as the hour got later, out came the whisky, and they would all undergo another sea change.

Their laughter would get . . . louder.

I'd think: **More of this, please.** More fire, more talk, more loud laughter. I'd been scared of darkness all my life, and it turned out Africa had a cure.

The campfire.

22.

MARKO, THE LARGEST MEMBER OF THE GROUP, also laughed the loudest. There was some ratio between the size of his body and the radius of his bellows. Also, there was a similar link between the volume of his voice and the bright shade of his hair. I was a ginger, self-conscious about it, but Marko was an **extreme** ginger and owned it.

I gawped at him and thought: **Teach me to be like that.**

Marko, however, wasn't your typical teacher. Perpetually moving, perpetually **doing,** he loved many things—food, travel, nature, guns, us—but he had no interest in giving lectures. He was more about leading by example. And having a good time. He was one great big ginger Mardi Gras, and if you wanted to join the party, wonderful, and if not, that was grand too. I wondered many times, watching him wolf his dinner, gulp his gin, shout another joke, slap another tracker on the back, why more people weren't like this guy.

Why didn't more at least try?

I wanted to ask Willy what it was like to have such a man minding him, guiding him, but apparently the Eton rule carried over to Botswana: Willy didn't want to know me in the bush any more than he did back at school.

The one thing about Marko that gave me pause was his time in the Welsh Guards. I'd sometimes look at him on that trip and see those eight Welsh Guards in their red tunics, hoisting that coffin onto their shoulders and marching down the abbey aisle . . . I tried to remind myself that Marko wasn't there that day. I tried to remind myself that, anyway, the box was empty.

All was well.

When Tiggy "suggested" I go to bed, always before everyone else, I didn't squawk. The days were long, the tent was a welcome cocoon. Its canvas smelt pleasantly of old books, its floor was covered with soft antelope skins, my bed was wrapped in a cozy African rug. For the first time in months, years, I'd drop off straightaway. Of course it helped to have that campfire glowing against the wall, to hear those adults on the other side, and the animals beyond. Screeches, bleats, roars, what a racket they made after dark—their busy time. Their rush hour. The later it got, the louder they got. I found it soothing. I also found it hilarious: no matter how loud the animals, I could still hear Marko laughing.

One night, before I fell asleep, I made myself a promise: I'm going to find a way to make that guy laugh.

23.

Like me, Marko had a sweet tooth. Like me, he particularly loved puddings. (He always called them "puds.") So I got the idea of spiking his pudding with Tabasco sauce.

At first he'd howl. But then he'd realize it was a trick, and laugh. Oh, how he'd laugh! Then he'd realize it was me. And laugh louder!

I couldn't wait.

The next night, as everyone tucked into their

dinner, I tiptoed out of the meal tent. I went down the footpath, fifty meters, into the kitchen tent, and poured a whole teacup of Tabasco into Marko's bowl of pudding. (It was bread and butter, Mummy's favorite.) The kitchen crew saw me, but I put a finger to my lips. They chuckled.

Scurrying back into the meal tent, I gave Tiggy a wink. I'd already taken her into my confidence and she thought the whole caper brilliant. I don't remember if I told Willy what I was up to. Probably not. I knew he wouldn't have approved.

I squirmed, counting the minutes until dessert was served, fighting back giggles.

Suddenly someone cried out: **Whoa!**

Someone else cried: **What the—!**

In unison we all turned. Just outside the open tent was a tawny tail swishing through the air.

Leopard!

Everyone froze. Except me. I took a step towards it.

Marko gripped my shoulder.

The leopard walked away, like a prima ballerina, across the footpath where I'd just been.

I turned back in time to see the adults all look at one another, mouths open. **Holy fuck.** Then their eyes turned towards me. **Holy fuuuuck.**

They were all thinking the same thing, picturing the same banner headline back home.

Prince Harry Mauled by Leopard.

The world would reel. Heads would roll.

I wasn't thinking about any of that. I was thinking

about Mummy. That leopard was **clearly** a sign from her, a messenger she'd sent to say:

All is well. And all will be well.

At the same time I also thought: The horror!

What if Mummy were to come out of hiding at last, only to learn that her younger son had been eaten alive?

24.

AS A ROYAL YOU WERE ALWAYS TAUGHT to maintain a buffer zone between you and the rest of Creation. Even working a crowd you always kept a discreet distance between Yourself and Them. Distance was right, distance was safe, distance was survival. Distance was an essential bit of **being** royal, no less than standing on the balcony, waving to the crowds outside Buckingham Palace, your family all around you.

Of course, family included distance as well. No matter how much you might love someone, you could never cross that chasm between, say, monarch and child. Or Heir and Spare. Physically, but also emotionally. It wasn't just Willy's edict about giving him space; the older generation maintained a nearly zero-tolerance prohibition on all physical contact. No hugs, no kisses, no pats. Now and then, maybe a light touching of cheeks . . . on special occasions.

But in Africa none of this was true. In Africa

distance dissolved. All creatures mingled freely. Only the lion walked with his head in the air, only the elephant had an emperor's strut, and even they weren't totally aloof. They mingled daily among their subjects. They had no choice. Yes, there was predation and prey, life could be nasty and brutish and short, but to my teenage eyes it all looked like distilled democracy. Utopia.

And that wasn't even counting the bear hugs and high fives from all the trackers and guides.

On the other hand, maybe it wasn't the mere closeness of living things that I liked. Maybe it was the mind-boggling number. In a matter of hours I'd gone from a place of aridity, sterility, death, to a wetland of teeming fertility. Maybe that was what I yearned for most of all—life.

Maybe that was the real miracle I found in the Okavango in April 1999.

I don't think I blinked once that whole week. I don't think I stopped grinning, even while asleep. Had I been transported back to the Jurassic period, I couldn't have been more awed—and it wasn't just **T. rex**es that had me captivated. I loved the littlest creatures too. And the birds. Thanks to Adi, clearly the savviest guide in our group, I began to recognize hooded vultures, cattle egrets, southern carmine bee-eaters, African fish eagles, in flight. Even the bugs were compelling. Adi taught me to really **see** them. Look down, he said, note the different species of beetle, admire the beauty of larvae. Also, appreciate the baroque architecture of termite mounds—the tallest structures built by any animal besides humans.

So much to know, Harry. To appreciate.

Right, Adi.

Whenever I went with him on a wander, whenever we'd come upon a fresh carcass crawling with maggots or wild dogs, whenever we'd stumble on a mountain of elephant dung sprouting mushrooms that looked like the Artful Dodger's top hat, Adi never cringed. **Circle of life, Harry.**

Of all the animals in our midst, Adi said, the most majestic was the water. The Okavango was just another living thing. He'd walked its entire length as a boy, with his father, carrying nothing but bedrolls. He knew the Okavango inside and out, and felt for it something like romantic love. Its surface was a poreless cheek, which he often lightly stroked.

But he also felt for the river a kind of sober awe. Respect. Its innards were death, he said. Hungry crocs, ill-tempered hippos, they were all down there, in the dark, waiting for you to slip up. Hippos killed five hundred people a year; Adi drummed it into my head over and over, and all these years later I can still hear him: **Never go into the dark water, Harry.**

One night around the fire, all the guides and trackers discussed the river, shouting stories about riding it, swimming it, boating it, fearing it, everyone talking over each other. I heard it all that night, the mysticism of the river, the sacredness of the river, the weirdness of the river.

Speaking of weirdness . . . The smell of marijuana wafted on the air.

The stories grew louder, sillier.

I asked if I could try.

Everyone guffawed. **Sod off!**

Willy looked at me in horror.

But I wouldn't back off. I pleaded my case. I was **experienced,** I said.

Heads swung round. **Oh really?**

Henners and I had recently pinched two six-packs of Smirnoff Ice and drunk them till we passed out, I boasted. Plus, Tiggy always let me have a nip of her flask on stalking trips. (Sloe gin, she was never without it.) I thought it best to leave out the full breadth of my experience.

The adults exchanged sly glances. One shrugged, rolled a new joint, passed it to me.

I took a puff. Coughed, retched. African weed was much harsher than Eton weed. And the high was less too.

But at least I was a man.

No. I was still a wee baby.

The "joint" was just fresh basil wrapped in a bit of filthy rolling paper.

25.

HUGH AND EMILIE were old friends of Pa's. They lived in Norfolk, and we often went to visit them for a week or two, during school holidays and summers. They had four sons with whom Willy and I were always thrown together, like pups into a bunch of pit bulls.

We played games. One day Hide and Seek, the next Capture the Flag. But whatever the game it was always an excuse for a massive scrap, and whatever the scrap, there were no winners because there were no rules. Hair-pulling, eye-gouging, arm-twisting, sleeper holds, all was fair in love and war and at Hugh and Emilie's country house.

As the youngest and smallest I always took the brunt. But I also did the most escalating, the most asking for it, so I deserved everything I got. Black eye, violet welt, puffed lip, I didn't mind. On the contrary. Maybe I wanted to look tough. Maybe I just wanted to feel **something**. Whatever my motivation, my simple philosophy when it came to scrapping was: More, please.

The six of us cloaked our pretend battles in historic names. Hugh and Emilie's house would often be converted into Waterloo, the Somme, Rorke's Drift. I can see us charging each other, screaming: **Zulu!**

Battle lines were often blood lines, though not always. It wasn't always Windsor versus Others. We'd mix and match. Sometimes I was fighting alongside Willy, sometimes against. No matter the alliances, though, it often happened that one or two of Hugh and Emilie's boys would turn and set upon Willy. I'd hear him crying out for help and down would come the red mist, like a blood vessel bursting behind my eyes. I'd lose all control, all ability to focus on anything but family, country, tribe, and hurl myself at someone, everyone. Kicking, punching, strangling, taking out legs.

Hugh and Emilie's boys couldn't deal with that. There **was** no dealing with it.

Get him off, he's mad!

I don't know how effective or skilled a fighter I was. But I always succeeded in providing enough diversion for Willy to get away. He'd check his injuries, wipe his nose, then jump straight back in. When the scrap finally ended for good, when we hobbled away together, I always felt such love for him, and I sensed love in return, but also some embarrassment. I was half Willy's size, half his weight. I was the younger brother: he was supposed to save me, not the other way around.

Over time the scraps became more pitched. Small-arms fire was introduced. We'd hurl Roman candles at each other, make rocket launchers from golf-ball tubes, stage night battles with two of us defending a stone pillbox in the middle of an open field. I can still smell the smoke and hear the hiss as a projectile rocketed towards a victim, whose only armor would be a puffer jacket, some wool mittens, maybe some ski goggles, though often not.

Our arms race accelerated. As they do. We began to use BB guns. At close range. How was no one maimed? How did no one lose an eye?

One day all six of us were walking in the woods near their house, looking for squirrels and pigeons to cull. There was an old army Land Rover. Willy and the boys smiled.

Harold, jump in, drive away, and we'll shoot you.

With what?

Shotgun.

No, thanks.

We're loading. Either get in and drive or we shoot you right here.

I jumped in, drove away.

Moments later, **bang.** Buckshot rattling off the back.

I cackled and hit the accelerator.

Somewhere on their estate was a construction site. (Hugh and Emilie were building a new house.) This became the setting for possibly our fiercest battle. It was around dusk. One brother was in the shell of the new house, taking heavy fire. When he retreated we bombarded him with rockets.

And then . . . he was gone.

Where's Nick?

We shone a torch. No Nick.

We marched forward, steadily, came upon a giant hole in the ground, almost like a square well, alongside the construction site. We peered over the edge and shone the torch down. Far below, lying on his back, Nick was moaning. Damned lucky to be alive, we all agreed.

What a great opportunity, we said.

We lit some firecrackers, big ones, and dropped them down into the pit.

26.

WHEN THERE WERE NO other boys around, no other common enemies, Willy and I would turn on each other.

It happened most often in the back seat while Pa drove us somewhere. A country house, say. Or a salmon stream. Once, in Scotland, on the way to the River Spey, we started scuffling, and soon were in a full scrap, rolling back and forth, trading blows.

Pa swerved to the side of the road, shouted at Willy to get out.

Me? Why me?

Pa didn't feel the need to explain. **Out.**

Willy turned to me, furious. He felt I got away with everything. He stepped out of the car, stomped to the backup car with all the bodyguards, strapped himself in. (We always wore seatbelts after Mummy's disappearance.) The convoy resumed.

Now and then I peered out the back window.

Behind us, I could just make out the future King of England, plotting his revenge.

27.

THE FIRST TIME I KILLED anything, Tiggy said: **Well done, darling!**

She dipped her long, slender fingers into the rabbit's body, under the flap of smashed fur, scooped out a dollop of blood and smeared it tenderly across my forehead, down my cheeks and nose. **Now**, she said, in her throaty voice, **you are blooded**.

Blooding—a tradition from the ages. A show of respect for the slain, an act of communion by the slayer. Also, a way to mark the crossing from boyhood into . . . not manhood. No, not that. But something close.

And so, notwithstanding my hairless torso and chirpy voice, I considered myself, post-blooding, to be a full-fledged stalker. But around my fifteenth birthday I was informed that I'd be undertaking the true stalker initiation.

Red deer.

It happened at Balmoral. Early morning, fog on the hills, mist in the hollows. My guide, Sandy, was a thousand years old. He looked as if he'd stalked mastodons. Proper old-school, that was how Willy and I described him and other such gents. Sandy talked old-school, smelt old-school, and definitely dressed old-school. Faded camo jacket over ragged green sweaters, Balmoral tweed plus fours, socks covered with burrs, Gore-Tex walking boots. On his head was a classic tweed flat cap, thrice my age, browned by eons of sweat.

I crept beside him through the heather, through the bog, all morning long. My stag appeared ahead. Inching closer, ever closer, we finally stopped and watched the stag munch some dry grass. Sandy made sure we were still downwind.

Now he pointed at me, pointed at my rifle. Time.

He rolled away, giving me space.

He raised his binoculars. I could hear his rattly breath as I took slow aim, squeezed the trigger. One sharp, thunderous crack. Then, silence.

We stood, walked forward. When we reached the stag I was relieved. Its eyes were already cloudy. The worry was always that you'd merely cause a flesh wound and send the poor animal dashing into the woods to suffer alone for hours. As its eyes turned more and more opaque, Sandy knelt before it, took out his gleaming knife, bled it from the neck and slit open the belly. He motioned for me to kneel. I knelt.

I thought we were going to pray.

Sandy snapped at me: **Closer!**

I knelt closer, close enough to smell Sandy's armpits. He placed a hand gently behind my neck, and now I thought he was going to hug me, congratulate me. **Atta boy.** Instead he pushed my head inside the carcass.

I tried to pull away, but Sandy pushed me deeper. I was shocked by his insane strength. And by the infernal smell. My breakfast jumped up from my stomach. **Oh please oh please do not let me vomit inside a stag carcass.** After a minute I couldn't smell anything, because I couldn't breathe. My nose and mouth were full of blood, guts, and a deep, upsetting warmth.

Well, I thought, so this is death. The ultimate blooding.

Not what I'd imagined.

I went limp. Bye, all.

Sandy pulled me out.

I filled my lungs with fresh morning air. I started to

wipe my face, which was dripping, but Sandy grabbed my hand. **Nae, lad, nae.**

What?

Let it dry, lad! Let it dry!

We radioed back to the soldiers in the valley. Horses were sent. While waiting, we got down to work, gave the stag a full gralloching, the Old Scottish word for disemboweling. We removed the stomach, scattered the junky bits on the hillside for hawks and buzzards, carved out the liver and heart, snipped the penis, careful not to pop the cord, which would douse you with urine, a stench that ten Highland baths wouldn't cleanse.

The horses arrived. We slung our gralloched stag across a white drum stallion, sent it off to the larder, then walked shoulder to shoulder back to the castle.

As my face dried, as my stomach settled, I felt swelling pride. I'd been good to that stag, as I'd been taught. One shot, clean through the heart. Besides being painless, the instant kill had preserved the meat. Had I merely wounded him, or let him get a glimpse of us, his heart would've raced, his blood would've filled with adrenaline, his steaks and fillets would've been inedible. This blood on my face contained no adrenaline, a credit to my marksmanship.

I'd also been good to Nature. Managing their numbers meant saving the deer population as a whole, ensuring they'd have enough food for winter.

Finally, I'd been good to the community. A big stag in the larder meant plenty of good meat for those living around Balmoral.

These virtues had been preached to me from an early age, but now I'd lived them, and felt them on my face. I wasn't religious, but this "blood facial" was, to me, baptismal. Pa was deeply religious, he prayed every night, but now, in this moment, I too felt close to God. If you loved Nature, Pa always said, you had to know when to leave it alone, and when to manage it, and managing meant culling, and culling meant killing. It was all a form of worship.

At the larder Sandy and I took off our clothes and checked each other for ticks. Red deer in those woods were rife and once a tick got onto your leg it would burrow deep under the skin, often crawl up into your balls. One poor gamekeeper had recently been felled by Lyme disease.

I panicked. Every freckle looked like doom. **Is that a tick? Is that?**

Nae, lad, nae!

I got dressed.

Turning to Sandy to say goodbye, I thanked him for the experience. I wanted to shake his hand, give him a hug. But a small, still voice inside me said:

Nae, lad. Nae.

28.

WILLY ENJOYED STALKING too, so that was his excuse for not coming to Klosters that year. He preferred to stay behind at Granny's estate in

Norfolk, twenty thousand acres we both adored: Sandringham.

Rather shoot partridges, he told Pa.

A lie. Pa didn't know it was a lie, but I did. The real reason Willy was staying at home was that he couldn't face the Wall.

Before skiing at Klosters we'd always have to walk to a designated spot at the foot of the mountain and stand before seventy or so photographers, arranged in three or four ascending tiers—the Wall. They'd point their lenses and shout our names and shoot us while we squinted and fidgeted and listened to Pa answer their daft questions. The Wall was the price we paid for a hassle-free hour on the slopes. Only if we went before the Wall would they briefly leave us in peace.

Pa disliked the Wall—he was famous for disliking it—but Willy and I **despised** it.

Hence, Willy was at home, taking it out on the partridges. I'd have stayed with him, if I could, but I wasn't old enough to assert myself like that.

In Willy's absence, Pa and I had to face the Wall ourselves, which made it that much more unpleasant. I stuck close to Pa's side while the cameras whirred and clicked. Memories of the Spice Girls. Memories of Mummy, who also despised Klosters.

This is why she's hiding, I thought. This right here. This shit.

Mummy had other reasons besides the Wall for hating Klosters. When I was three, Pa and a friend were involved in a gruesome accident on the slopes there. A massive avalanche overtook them. Pa narrowly escaped, but the friend didn't. Buried under that wall of snow, the friend's final breaths must have been snow-filled gasps. Mummy often spoke of him with tears in her eyes.

After the Wall, I tried to put my mind to having fun. I loved skiing and I was good at it. But once Mummy was in my thoughts, I was buried under my own private avalanche of emotions. And questions. **Is it wrong to enjoy a place that Mummy despises? Am I being mean to her if I have fun today on these slopes? Am I a bad son for feeling excited to get on the chairlift alone with Pa? Will Mummy understand that I miss her and Willy but also enjoy having Pa briefly to myself?**

How would I explain any of this to her when she returned?

Some time after that trip to Klosters I shared my theory with Willy, about Mummy being in hiding. He admitted that he'd once entertained a similar theory. But, ultimately, he'd discarded it.

She's gone, Harold. She's not coming back.

No, no, no, I wouldn't hear such a thing. **Willy, she always said she wanted to just disappear! You heard her!**

Yes, she did. But, Harold, she'd never do this to us!

I'd had the very same thought, I told him. **But she wouldn't die either, Willy! She'd never do that to us either!**

Fair point, Harold.

29.

WE ROLLED DOWN THE LONG DRIVE, past Granny's white stag ponies through the golf course, past the green where the Queen Mother once scored a hole in one, past the policeman in his little hut (crisp salute) and over a couple of speed bumps, then over a small stone bridge and onto a quiet country lane.

Pa, driving, squinted through the windscreen. **Splendid evening, isn't it?**

Balmoral. Summer. 2001.

We went up a steep hill, past the whisky distillery, along a blowy lane and down between sheep fields, which were overrun by rabbits. That is, those lucky enough to escape us. We'd shot a bunch earlier that day. After a few minutes we turned onto a dusty track, drove four hundred meters to a deer fence. I hopped out, opened the padlocked gate. Now, at last, because we were on remote private roads, I was allowed to drive. I jumped behind the wheel, hit the accelerator, put into practice all those driving lessons from Pa through the years, often seated on his lap. I steered us through the purple heather into the deepest folds of that immense Scottish moorland. Ahead, like an old friend, stood Lochnagar, splotchy with snow.

We came to the last wooden bridge, the tires making that soothing lullaby I always associated with Scotland. **Da dong, da dong . . . da dong, da dong.** Just below us, a burn seethed after recent heavy rain up top. The air was thick with midges. Through the trees, in the last moments of daylight, we could faintly make out huge stags peering at us. Now we arrived in a great clearing, an old stone hunting lodge to the right, the cold stream running down to the river through the wood on our left, and there she was. Inchnabobart!

We ran inside the lodge. The warm kitchen! The old fireplace! I fell onto the fender, with its worn red cushion, and inhaled the smell of that huge pyramid of silver birch firewood stacked beside it. If there's a smell more intoxicating or inviting than silver birch, I don't know what it could be. Grandpa, who'd set off half an hour before us, was already tending his grill at the back of the lodge. He stood amid a thick cloud of smoke, tears streaming from his eyes. He wore a flat cap, which he took off now and then to mop his brow or smack a fly. As the fillets of venison sizzled he turned them with a huge pair of tongs, then put on a loop of Cumberland sausages. Normally I'd beg him to make a pot of his specialty, spaghetti Bolognese. This night, for some reason, I didn't.

Granny's specialty was the salad dressing. She'd whisked a large batch. Then she lit the candles down the long table and we all sat on wooden chairs with creaky straw seats. Often we had a guest for these dinners, some famous or eminent personage. Many times I'd discussed the temperature of the meat or the coolness of the evening with a prime minister or bishop. But tonight it was just family.

My great-grandmother arrived. I jumped up, offered

her my hand. I always offered her my hand—Pa had drummed it into me—but that night I could see Gan-Gan really needed the extra help. She'd just celebrated her 101st birthday and was looking frail.

Still natty, however. She wore blue, I recall, all blue. Blue cardigan, blue tartan skirt, blue hat. Blue was her favorite color.

She asked for a martini. Moments later, someone handed her an ice-cold tumbler filled with gin. I watched her take a sip, expertly avoiding the lemon floating along the top, and on an impulse I decided to join her. I'd never had a cocktail in front of my family, so this would be an event. A bit of rebellion.

Empty rebellion, it turned out. No one cared. No one noticed. Except Gan-Gan. She perked up for a moment at the sight of me playing grown-up, gin and tonic in hand.

I sat beside her. Our conversation started out as lively banter, then evolved, gradually settling into something deeper. A connection. Gan-Gan was really speaking to me that night, really listening. I couldn't quite believe it. I wondered why. Was it the gin? Was it the four inches I'd grown since last summer? At six foot I was now one of the tallest members of the family. Combined with Gan-Gan's shrinkage, I towered over her.

I wish I could recall specifically what we talked about. I wish I'd asked more questions, and jotted down her answers. She'd been the War Queen. She'd lived at Buckingham Palace while Hitler's bombs rained from the skies. (Nine direct hits on the Palace.)

She'd dined with Churchill, wartime Churchill. She'd once possessed a Churchillian eloquence of her own. She was famous for saying that, no matter how bad things got, she'd never, ever leave England, and people loved her for it. I loved her for it. I loved my country, and the idea of declaring you'd never leave struck me as wonderful.

She was, of course, **infamous** for saying other things. She came from a different era, enjoyed being Queen in a way that looked unseemly to some. I saw none of that. She was my Gan-Gan. She was born three years before the aeroplane was invented yet still played the bongo drums on her hundredth birthday. Now she took my hand as if I were a knight home from the wars, and spoke to me with love and humor and, that night, that magic night, respect.

I wish I'd asked about her husband, King George VI, who died young. Or her brother-in-law, King Edward VIII, whom she'd apparently loathed. He gave up his crown for love. Gan-Gan believed in love, but nothing transcended the Crown. She also reportedly despised the woman he'd chosen.

I wish I'd asked about her distant ancestors in Glamis, home to Macbeth.

She'd seen so much, knew so much, there was so much to be learned from her, but I just wasn't mature enough, despite the growth spurt, or brave enough, despite the gin.

I did, however, make her laugh. Normally that was Pa's job; he had a knack for finding Gan-Gan's funny bone. He loved her as much as he loved anybody in the world, perhaps more. I recall him glancing over several times and looking pleased that I was getting such good giggles out of his favorite person.

At one point I told Gan-Gan about Ali G, the character played by Sacha Baron Cohen. I taught her to say **Booyakasha**, showing her how to flick her fingers the way Sacha did. She couldn't grasp it, she had no idea what I was talking about, but she had such fun trying to flick and say the word. With every repetition of that word, **Booyakasha**, she'd shriek, which would make everyone else smile. It tickled me, thrilled me. It made me feel . . . a part of things.

This was my family, in which I, for one night at least, had a distinctive role.

And that role, for once, wasn't the Naughty One.

30.

WEEKS LATER, BACK at Eton, I was walking past two blue doors, almost exactly the same blue as one of Gan-Gan's kilts. She'd have liked these doors, I thought.

They were the doors to the TV room, one of my sanctuaries.

Almost every day, straight after lunch, my mates and I would head to the TV room and watch a bit of **Neighbours**, or maybe **Home and Away**, before going off to sports. But this day in September 2001 the room was packed and **Neighbours** wasn't on.

The news was on.

And the news was a nightmare.

Some buildings on fire?

Oh, wow, where's that?

New York.

I tried to see the screen through all the boys massed in the room. I asked the boy to my right what was going on.

He said America was under attack.

Terrorists had flown planes into the Twin Towers in New York City.

People were . . . jumping. From the tops of buildings half a kilometer high.

More and more boys gathered, stood around, biting their lips, their nails, tugging their ears. In stunned silence, in boyish confusion, we watched the only world we'd ever known disappear in clouds of toxic smoke.

World War Three, someone muttered.

Someone propped open the blue doors. Boys kept streaming in.

None made a sound.

So much chaos, so much pain.

What can be done? What can we do?

What will we be called to do?

Days later I turned seventeen.

31.

I'D OFTEN SAY IT TO MYSELF first thing in the morning: **Maybe this is the day.**

I'd say it after breakfast: **Maybe she's going to reappear this morning.**

I'd say it after lunch: **Maybe she's going to reappear this afternoon.**

It had been four years, after all. Surely she'd established herself by now, forged a new life, a new identity. **Maybe, at long last, she's going to emerge today, hold a press conference—shock the world.** After answering the shouted questions from the astonished reporters, she'd lean into the microphone: **William! Harry! If you can hear me, come to me!**

At night I had the most elaborate dreams. They were essentially the same, though the scenarios and costumes were slightly different. Sometimes she'd orchestrate a triumphant return; other times I'd simply bump into her somewhere. A street corner. A shop. She was always wearing a disguise—a big blond wig. Or big black sunglasses. And yet I'd always recognize her.

I'd step forward, whisper: **Mummy? Is it you?**

Before she could answer, before I could find out where she'd been, why she hadn't come back, I'd snap awake.

I'd look around the room, feeling the crushing disappointment.

Only a dream. Again.

But then I'd tell myself: **Maybe that means . . . today's the day?**

I was like those religious fanatics who believe the world will end on such and such a date. And when the date passes uneventfully, their faith remains undaunted.

I must've misread the signs. Or the calendar.

I suppose I knew the truth deep in my heart. The illusion of Mummy hiding, preparing to return, was never so real that it could blot out reality entirely. But it blotted it out enough that I was able to postpone the bulk of my grief. I still hadn't mourned, still hadn't cried, except that one time at her grave, still hadn't processed the bare facts. Part of my brain knew, but part of it was wholly insulated, and the division between those two parts kept the parliament of my consciousness divided, polarized, gridlocked. Just as I wanted it.

Sometimes I'd have a stern talk with myself. **Everyone else seems to believe that Mummy is dead, full stop, so maybe you should get on board.**

But then I'd think: I'll believe it when I have proof.

With solid proof, I thought, I could properly mourn and cry and move on.

32.

I DON'T REMEMBER how we got the stuff. One of my mates, I expect. Or maybe several. Whenever we found ourselves in possession, we'd commandeer a tiny upstairs bathroom, wherein we'd implement a surprisingly thoughtful, orderly assembly line. Smoker straddled the loo beside the window, second boy leaned against the basin, third and fourth boys sat in the empty bath, legs dangling over, waiting their turns. You'd take a hit or two, blow the smoke out of the window, then move on to the next station, in rotation, until the spliff was gone. Then we'd all head to one of our rooms and giggle ourselves sick over an episode or two of a new show. **Family Guy**. I felt an inexplicable bond with Stewie, prophet without honor.

I knew this was bad behavior. I knew it was wrong. My mates knew too. We talked about it often, while stoned, how stupid we were to be wasting an Eton education. Once, we even made a pact. At the start of exam period, called Trials, we vowed to quit cold turkey, until after the final Trial. But the very next night, lying in bed, I heard my mates in the hall, cackling, whispering. Headed to the loo. **Bloody hell, they're already breaking the pact!** I got out of bed, joined them. As the assembly line cranked up, bath to basin to loo, as the weed began to take effect, we shook our heads.

What idiots we were, thinking we could change.

Pass the spliff, mate.

One night, straddling the loo, I took a big hit and gazed up at the moon, then down at the school grounds. I watched several Thames Valley police officers marching back and forth. They were stationed out there because of me. But they didn't make me feel safe. They made me feel caged.

Beyond them, however, that was where safety lay. All was peaceful and still **out there**. I thought: How beautiful. So much peace in the wider world . . . for some. For those free to search for it.

Just then I saw something dart across the quad. It froze under one of the orange streetlights. I froze too, and leaned out of the window.

A fox! **Staring straight at me! Look!**

What, mate?

Nothing.

I whispered to the fox: **Hello, mate. How's it going?**

What are you on about?

Nothing, nothing.

Maybe it was the weed—undoubtedly it was the weed—but I felt a piercing and powerful kinship with that fox. I felt more connected to that fox than I did to the boys in the bathroom, the other boys at Eton—even the Windsors in the distant castle. In fact, this little fox, like the leopard in Botswana, seemed like a messenger, sent to me from some other realm. Or perhaps from the future.

If only I knew who sent it.

And what the message was.

33.

WHENEVER I WAS HOME from school, I hid.

I hid upstairs in the nursery. I hid inside my new video games. I played Halo endlessly against an American who called himself Prophet and knew me only as BillandBaz.

I hid in the basement beneath Highgrove, usually with Willy.

We called it Club H. Many assumed the H stood for Harry, but in fact it stood for Highgrove.

The basement had once been a bomb shelter. To get down to its depths you went through a heavy white ground-level door, then down a steep flight of stone stairs, then groped your way along a damp stone floor, then descended three more stairs, walked down a long damp corridor with a low arched roof, then past several wine cellars, wherein Camilla kept her fanciest bottles, on past a freezer and several storerooms full of paintings, polo gear, and absurd gifts from foreign governments and potentates. (No one wanted them, but they couldn't be regifted or donated, or thrown out, so they'd been carefully logged and sealed away.) Beyond that final storeroom were two green doors with little brass handles, and on the other side of those was Club H. It was windowless, but the brick walls, painted bone white, kept it from feeling claustrophobic. Also, we kitted out the space with nice pieces from various royal residences. Persian rug, red Moroccan sofas, wooden table, electric dartboard. We also put in a huge stereo system. It didn't sound great, but it was loud. In a corner stood a drinks trolley, well stocked, thanks to creative borrowing, so there was always a faint aroma of beer and other booze. But thanks to a big vent in good working order, there was also the smell of flowers. Fresh air from Pa's gardens was pumped in constantly, with hints of lavender and honeysuckle.

Willy and I would start a typical weekend evening

by sneaking into a nearby pub, where we'd have a few drinks, a few pints of Snake Bite, then round up a group of mates and bring them back to Club H. There were never more than fifteen of us, though somehow there were never less than fifteen either.

Names float back to me. Badger. Casper. Nisha. Lizzie. Skippy. Emma. Rose. Olivia. Chimp. Pell. We all got on well, and sometimes a bit more than well. There was plenty of innocent snogging, which went hand in hand with the not-so-innocent drinking. Rum and Coke, or vodka, usually in tumblers, with liberal splashes of Red Bull.

We were often tipsy, and sometimes smashed, and yet there wasn't a single time that anyone used or brought drugs down there. Our bodyguards were always nearby, which kept a lid on things, but it was more than that. We had a sense of boundaries.

Club H was the perfect hideout for a teenager, but especially this teenager. When I wanted peace, Club H provided. When I wanted mischief, Club H was the safest place to act out. When I wanted solitude, what better than a bomb shelter in the middle of the British countryside?

Willy felt the same. I often thought he seemed more at peace down there than anywhere else on earth. And it was a relief, I think, to be somewhere that he didn't feel the need to pretend I was a stranger.

When it was just the two of us down there, we'd play games, listen to music—talk. With Bob Marley, or Fatboy Slim, or DJ Sakin, or Yomanda thumping in the background, Willy sometimes tried to talk about Mummy. Club H felt like the one place secure enough to broach that taboo subject.

Just one problem. I wasn't willing. Whenever he went there . . . I changed the subject.

He'd get frustrated. And I wouldn't acknowledge his frustration. More likely, I couldn't even recognize it.

Being so obtuse, so emotionally unavailable, wasn't a choice I made. I simply wasn't capable. I wasn't close to ready.

One topic that was always safe was how wonderful it felt to be unseen. We talked at length about the glory, the luxury, of privacy, of spending an hour or two away from the press's prying eyes. Our one true haven, we said, where those lot can never ever find us.

And then they found us.

At the tail end of 2001 Marko visited me at Eton. We met for lunch at a café in the heart of town, which I thought quite a treat. Plus an excuse to bunk off, leave school grounds? I was all smiles.

But no. Marko, looking grim, said this was no larky outing.

What's up, Marko?

I've been asked to find out the truth, Harry.

About what?

I suspected he was referring to my recent loss of virginity. Inglorious episode, with an older woman. She liked horses, quite a lot, and treated me not unlike a young stallion. Quick ride, after which she'd smacked my rump and sent me off to graze. Among the many things about it that were wrong: It happened in a grassy field behind a busy pub.

Obviously someone had seen us.

The truth, Marko?

About whether or not you're doing drugs, Harry.

What?

It seemed that the editor of Britain's biggest tabloid had recently phoned my father's office to say she'd uncovered "evidence" of my doing drugs in various locations, including Club H. Also, a bike shed behind a pub. (Not the pub where I'd lost my virginity.) My father's office immediately dispatched Marko to take a clandestine meeting with one of this editor's lieutenants, in some shady hotel room, and the lieutenant laid out the tabloid's case. Now Marko laid it out for me.

He asked again if it was true.

Lies, I said. All lies.

He went item by item through the editor's evidence. I disputed all of it. Wrong, wrong, wrong. The basic facts, the details, it was all wrong.

I then questioned Marko. Who the hell is this editor?

Loathsome toad, I gathered. Everyone who knew her was in full agreement that she was an infected pustule on the arse of humanity, plus a shit excuse for a journalist. But none of that mattered, because she'd managed to wriggle her way into a position of great power and lately she was focusing all that power upon . . . me. She was hunting the Spare, straight out, and making no apologies for it. She wouldn't stop until my balls were nailed to her office wall.

I was lost. **For doing basic teenage stuff, Marko?**

No, boy, no.

In this editor's estimation, Marko said, I was a drug addict.

A what?

And one way or another, Marko said, that was the story she was going to publish.

I offered a suggestion about what this editor could do with her story. I told Marko to go back, tell her she had it all wrong.

He promised he would.

He rang me days later, said he'd done what I asked, but the editor didn't believe him, and she was now vowing not only to get me, but to get Marko.

Surely, I said, Pa will do something. Stop her.

Long silence.

No, Marko said. Pa's office had decided on a . . . different approach. Rather than telling the editor to call off the dogs, the Palace was opting to play ball with her. They were going full Neville Chamberlain.

Did Marko tell me why? Or did I learn only later that the guiding force behind this putrid strategy was the same spin doctor Pa and Camilla had recently hired, the same spin doctor who'd leaked the details of our private summits with Camilla? This spin doctor, Marko said, had decided that the best approach in this case would be to spin me—right under the bus. In one swoop this would appease the editor and also bolster the sagging reputation of Pa. Amid all this unpleasantness, all this extortion and gamesmanship, the spin doctor had discovered one silver lining, one shiny consolation prize for Pa. No more the unfaithful husband, Pa would now be presented to the world as the harried single dad coping with a drug-addled child.

34.

I WENT BACK TO ETON, tried to put all this out of my mind, tried to focus on my schoolwork.

Tried to be calm.

I listened over and over to my go-to soothing CD: **Sounds of the Okavango.** Forty tracks: Crickets. Baboons. Rainstorm. Thunder. Birds. Lions and hyenas scrapping over a kill. At night, shutting off the lights, I'd hit play. My room sounded like a tributary of the Okavango. It was the only way I could sleep.

After a few days the meeting with Marko receded from consciousness. It began to feel like a nightmare.

But then I woke to the actual nightmare.

A blaring front-page headline: **Harry's Drugs Shame.**

January 2002.

Spread over seven pages inside the newspaper were all the lies Marko had presented to me, and many more. The story not only had me down as a habitual drug user, it had me recently going to rehab. **Rehab!** The editor had got her mitts on some photos of Marko and me paying a visit to a suburban rehab center, months earlier, a typical part of my princely charitable work, and she'd repurposed the photos, made them visual aids for her libelous fiction.

I gazed at the photos and read the story in shock. I felt sickened, horrified. I imagined everyone, all my countrymen and countrywomen, reading these things, believing them. I could hear people all across the Commonwealth gossiping about me.

Crikey, the boy's a disgrace.

His poor dad—after all he's been through?

More, I felt heartbroken at the idea that this had been partly the work of my own family, my own father and future stepmother. They'd abetted this nonsense. For what? To make their own lives a bit easier?

I phoned Willy. I couldn't speak. He couldn't either. He was sympathetic, and more. (**Raw deal, Harold.**) At moments he was even angrier about the whole thing than I was, because he was privy to more details about the spin doctor and the backroom dealings that had led to this public sacrifice of the Spare.

And yet, in the same breath, he assured me that there was nothing to be done. This was Pa. This was Camilla. This was royal life.

This was our life.

I phoned Marko. He too offered sympathy.

I asked him to remind me, What was this editor's name? He said it, and I committed it to memory, but in the years since then I've avoided speaking it, and I don't wish to repeat it here. Spare the reader, but also myself. Besides, can it possibly be a coincidence that the name of the woman who pretended I went to **rehab** is a perfect anagram for . . . **Rehabber** Kooks? Is the universe not saying something there?

Who am I not to listen?

Over several weeks, newspapers continued to rehash the Rehabber Kooks libels, along with various new and equally fabricated accounts of goings-on in Club H. Our fairly innocent teenage clubhouse was made to sound like Caligula's bedchamber.

Around this time one of Pa's dearest friends came to Highgrove. She was with her husband. Pa asked me to give them a tour. I walked them around the gardens, but they didn't care about Pa's lavender and honeysuckle.

The woman asked eagerly: **Where's Club H?**

An avid reader of all the papers.

I led her to the door, opened it. I pointed down the dark steps.

She breathed in deeply, smiled. **Oh, it even smells of weed!**

It didn't, though. It smelt of damp earth, stone and moss. It smelt of cut flowers, clean dirt—and maybe a hint of beer. Lovely smell, totally organic, but the power of suggestion had taken hold of this woman. Even when I swore to her that there was no weed, that we'd never once done drugs down there, she gave me a wink.

I thought she was going to ask me to sell her a bag.

35.

OUR FAMILY WAS NO longer getting larger. There were no new spouses on the horizon, no new babies. My aunts and uncles, Sophie and Edward, Fergie and Andrew, had stopped growing their families. Pa, too, of course. An era of stasis had set in.

But now, in 2002, it dawned on me, dawned on all of us, that the family wasn't static after all. We were about to get smaller.

Princess Margaret and Gan-Gan were both unwell.

I didn't know Princess Margaret, whom I called Aunt Margo. She was my great-aunt, yes, we shared 12.5 percent of our DNA, we spent the bigger holidays together, and yet she was almost a total stranger. Like most Britons, I mainly knew **of** her. I was conversant with the general contours of her sad life. Great loves thwarted by the Palace. Exuberant streaks of self-destruction splashed across the tabloids. One hasty marriage, which looked doomed at the outset and ended up being worse than expected. Her husband leaving poisonous notes around the house, scalding lists of things wrong with her. **Twenty-four reasons why I hate you!**

Growing up, I felt nothing for her, except a bit of pity and a lot of jumpiness. She could kill a houseplant with one scowl. Mostly, whenever she was around, I kept my distance. On those rarer-than-rare occasions when our paths crossed, when she deigned to take notice of me, to speak to me, I'd wonder if she had any opinion of me. It seemed that she didn't. Or else, given her tone, her coldness, the opinion wasn't much.

Then one Christmas she cleared up the mystery. The whole family gathered to open gifts on Christmas Eve, as always, a German tradition that survived the anglicizing of the family surname from Saxe-Coburg-Gotha to Windsor. We were at Sandringham in a big room with a long table covered with white cloth and white name cards. By custom, at the start of the night, each of us located our place, stood before our mound of presents. Then suddenly, everyone began opening at the same time. A free-for-all, with scores of family members talking at once and pulling at bows and tearing at wrapping paper.

Standing before my pile, I chose to open the smallest present first. The tag said: **From Aunt Margo.**

I looked over, called out: **Thank you, Aunt Margo!**
I do hope you like it, Harry.

I tore off the paper. It was . . .

A biro?

I said: **Oh. A biro. Wow.**

She said: **Yes. A biro.**

I said: **Thank you so much.**

But it wasn't just any biro, she pointed out. It had a tiny rubber fish wrapped around it.

I said: **Oh. A fish biro! OK.**

I told myself: That is cold-blooded.

Now and then, as I grew older, it struck me that Aunt Margo and I should've been friends. We had so much in common. Two Spares. Her relationship with Granny wasn't an **exact** analog of mine with Willy, but pretty close. The simmering rivalry, the intense competition (driven largely by the older sibling), it all looked familiar. Aunt Margo also wasn't that dissimilar from Mummy. Both rebels, both labeled as sirens. (Pablo Picasso was among the many men obsessed with Margo.) So my first thought when I learned in early 2002 that she'd been taken ill was to wish there'd been more time to get to know her. But we were well past that. She was unable to care for herself. After badly burning her feet in a bath, she was confined to a wheelchair, and said to be swiftly declining.

When she died, February 9, 2002, my first thought was that this would be a heavy blow to Gan-Gan, who was also in decline.

Granny tried to talk Gan-Gan out of attending the funeral. But Gan-Gan dragged herself out of her sickbed, and shortly after that day took a bad fall.

It was Pa who told me she'd been confined to her bed at Royal Lodge, the sprawling country house in which she'd lived part-time for the last fifty years, when she wasn't at her main residence, Clarence House. Royal Lodge was three miles south of Windsor Castle, still in Windsor Great Park, still part of the Crown Estate, but like the castle it had one foot in another world. Dizzyingly high ceilings. Pebbled driveway winding serenely through vivid gardens.

Built not long after the death of Cromwell.

I felt comforted to hear that Gan-Gan was there, a place I knew she loved. She was in her own bed, Pa said, and not suffering.

Granny was often with her.

Days later, at Eton, while studying, I took the call. I wish I could remember whose voice was at the other end; a courtier, I believe. I recall that it was just before Easter, the weather bright and warm, light slanting through my window, filled with vivid colors.

Your Royal Highness, the Queen Mother has died.

Cut to Willy and me, days later. Dark suits, down-cast faces, eyes filled with déjà vu. We walked slowly behind the gun carriage, bagpipes playing, hundreds of them. The sound threw me back in time.

I began shaking.

Once again we made that hideous trek to Westminster Abbey. Then we stepped into a car, joined the cortège—from the center of town, along Whitehall, out to the Mall, on to St. George's Chapel.

Throughout that morning my eye kept going to the top of Gan-Gan's coffin, where they'd set the crown. Its three thousand diamonds and jeweled cross winked in the spring sunlight. At the center of the cross was a diamond the size of a cricket ball. Not just a dia-mond, actually; the Great Diamond of the World, a 105-karat monster called the Koh-i-Noor. Largest diamond ever seen by human eyes. "Acquired" by the British Empire at its zenith. Stolen, some thought. I'd heard it was mesmerizing, and I'd heard it was cursed. Men fought for it, died for it, and thus the curse was said to be masculine.

Only women were permitted to wear it.

36.

STRANGE, AFTER so much mourning, to just . . . **party**. But months later came the Golden Jubilee. Fiftieth anniversary of Granny's reign.

Over four days that summer of 2002, Willy and

I were constantly pulling on another set of smart clothes, jumping into another black car, rushing to yet another venue for another party or parade, reception or gala.

Britain was intoxicated. People did jigs in the streets, sang from balconies and rooftops. Everyone wore some version of the Union Jack. In a nation known for its reticence, this was a startling expression of unbridled joy.

Startling to me anyway. Granny didn't seem startled. I was startled at how unstartled she was. It wasn't that she felt no emotions. On the contrary, I always thought that Granny experienced all the normal human emotions. She just knew better than the rest of us mortals how to control them.

I stood beside or behind her through much of the Golden Jubilee Weekend and I often thought: If this can't shake her then she's truly earned her reputation for imperturbable serenity. In which case, I thought, maybe I'm a foundling? Because I'm a nervous wreck.

There were several reasons for my nerves, but the main one was a brewing scandal. Just before the Jubilee I'd been summoned by one of the courtiers to his little office and without much buildup he'd asked: **Harry—are you doing cocaine?**

Shades of my lunch with Marko.

What? Am I—? How could—? No!

Hm. Well. Could there be a photo out there? Is it possible that someone somewhere might have a photo of you doing cocaine?

God, no! That's ridiculous! Why?

He explained that he'd been approached by a newspaper editor who claimed to have come into possession of a photo showing Prince Harry snorting a line.

He's a liar. It's not true.

I see. Be that as it may, this editor is willing to lock the photo into his safe forever. But in exchange he wants to sit down with you and explain that what you're doing is very damaging. He wants to give you some life advice.

Ah. Creepy. And devious. Diabolical, in fact, because if I agree to this meeting, then I'm admitting guilt.

Right.

I told myself: After Rehabber Kooks, they all want a go at me. She'd scored a direct hit, and now her competitors are lining up to be next.

When will it end?

I reassured myself that the editor had nothing, that he was just fishing. He must've heard a rumor and he was tracking it down. Stay the course, I told myself, and then I told the courtier to call the journalist's bluff, vigorously refute the claim, turn down the deal. Above all, reject the proffered meeting.

I'm not going to submit to blackmail.

The courtier nodded. Done.

Of course . . . I **had** been doing cocaine around this time. At someone's country house, during a shooting weekend, I'd been offered a line, and I'd done a few more since. It wasn't much fun, and it didn't make me particularly happy, as it seemed to make everyone around me, but it did make me feel **different**, and that was the main goal. Feel. Different. I was a deeply unhappy seventeen-year-old boy willing to try almost anything that would alter the status quo.

That was what I told myself anyway. Back then, I could lie to myself as effortlessly as I'd lied to that courtier.

But now I realized coke hadn't been worth the candle. The risk far outweighed the reward. Threatened with exposure, faced with the prospect of fouling up Granny's Golden Jubilee, walking a knife's edge with the mad press—nothing was worth any of that.

On the bright side, I'd played the game well. After I'd called the journalist's bluff, he went silent. As suspected, he had no photo, and when his con game didn't work, he slithered off. (Or not quite. He slithered into Clarence House, and became very good friends with Camilla and Pa.) I was ashamed for lying. But also proud. In a tight spot, a hugely scary crisis, I hadn't felt any serenity, like Granny, but at least I'd managed to project it. I'd channeled **some** of her superpower, her heroic stoicism. I regretted giving the courtier a cock-and-bull story, but the alternative would've been ten times worse.

So . . . job well done?

Maybe I wasn't a foundling after all.

37.

ON TUESDAY, THE CULMINATING day of the Jubilee, millions watched Granny go from Palace to church. A special thanksgiving service. She rode with Grandpa in a carriage of gold—all of it, every square inch, lustrous gold. Gold doors, gold wheels, gold roof, and on top of it all a gold crown, held aloft by three angels cast in glowing gold. The carriage was built thirteen years before the American Revolution, and still ran like a top. As it sped her and Grandpa through the streets, somewhere in the distance a massive choir blasted the coronation anthem. **Rejoice! Rejoice!** We did! We did! For even the grumpiest antimonarchists, it was hard not to feel at least one goosebump.

There was a luncheon that day, I think, and a dinner party, but it all felt a bit anticlimactic. The main event, everyone acknowledged, had taken place the night before, in the gardens outside Buckingham Palace—a performance by some of the greatest musical artists of the century. Paul McCartney sang "Her Majesty." Brian May, on the roof, played "God Save the Queen." How marvelous, many said. And how miraculous that Granny should be so hip, so modern, that she should allow, indeed relish, all this modern rock.

Sitting directly behind her, I couldn't help thinking the same thing. To see her tapping her foot, and swaying in time, I wanted to hug her, though of course I didn't. Out of the question. I never had done and couldn't imagine any circumstance under which such an act might be sanctioned.

There was a famous story about Mummy trying to hug Granny. It was actually more a lunge than a hug, if eyewitnesses can be believed; Granny swerved to avoid contact, and the whole thing ended very awkwardly, with averted eyes and murmured apologies. Every time I tried to picture the scene it reminded me of a thwarted pickpocketing, or a rugby tap-tackle. I wondered, watching Granny rock out to Brian May, if Pa ever tried? Probably not. When he was five or six, Granny left him, went off on a royal tour lasting several months, and when she returned, she offered him a firm handshake. Which may have been more than he ever got from Grandpa. Indeed, Grandpa was so aloof, so busy traveling and working, he barely saw Pa for the first several years of his life.

As the concert went on and on, I began to feel tired. I had a headache from the loud music, and from the stress of the last few weeks. Granny, however, showed no signs of fading. Still going strong. Still tapping and swaying.

Suddenly, I looked closer. I noticed something in her ears. Something—gold?

Gold as the golden carriage.

Gold as the golden angels.

I leaned forward. Maybe not quite gold.

No, maybe it was more yellow.

Yes. Yellow ear plugs.

I looked into my lap and smiled. When I lifted my head again, I watched with glee as Granny kept time to music she couldn't hear, or music she'd found a clever and subtle way of . . . distancing. Controlling.

More than ever before, I wanted to give my Granny a hug.

38.

I SAT DOWN WITH PA that summer, possibly at Balmoral, though it might've been Clarence House, where he was now living more or less full-time. He'd moved in shortly after Gan-Gan's death, and wherever he lived, I lived.

When I wasn't living at Manor House.

My final year at Eton drawing near, Pa wanted to chat about how I envisaged my life post-Eton. Most of my mates would be headed off to university. Willy was already at St. Andrews and thriving. Henners had just finished his A levels at Harrow School and was planning to go to Newcastle.

And you, darling boy? Have you given any thought to . . . the future?

Why, yes. Yes, I had. For several years I'd talked in all seriousness about working at the ski resort in Lech am Arlberg, where Mummy used to take us. Such wonderful memories. Specifically, I wanted to work at the fondue hut in the center of town, which Mummy loved. That fondue could change your life. (I really was that mad.) But now I told Pa I'd given up the fondue fantasy, and he sighed with relief.

Instead I was taken with notions of becoming a ski instructor . . .

Pa tensed again. **Out of the question.**

OK.

Long pause.

How about . . . safari guide?

No, darling boy.

This wasn't going to be easy.

Part of me really did want to do something totally outside the box, something that would make everyone in the family, in the country, sit up and say: **What the—**? Part of me wanted to drop out, disappear— as Mummy did. And other princes. Wasn't there one in India, a long time ago, a bloke who just walked out of the palace and sat under a lovely banyan tree? We'd read about him at school. Or, we were supposed to.

But another part of me felt hugely ambitious. People assumed that the Spare wouldn't or shouldn't have any ambition. People assumed that royals generally had no career desires or anxieties. You're royal, everything's done for you, why worry? But in fact I worried quite a lot about making my own way, finding my purpose in this world. I didn't want to be one of those cocktail-slurping, eyeroll-causing sloths everyone avoided at family gatherings. There had been plenty of those in my family, going back centuries.

Pa, in fact, might've become one. He'd always been discouraged from hard work, he told me. He'd been advised that the Heir shouldn't "do too much," shouldn't try too hard, for fear of outshining the monarch. But he'd rebelled, listened to his inner voice, discovered work that excited him.

He wanted that for me.

That was why he didn't press me to go to university. He knew it wasn't in my DNA. Not that I was anti-university, **per se**. In fact, the University of Bristol looked interesting. I'd pored over its literature, even considered a course in art history. (Lots of pretty girls took that subject.) But I just couldn't picture myself spending years bent over a book. My Eton housemaster couldn't either. He'd told me straight-out: **You're not the university type, Harry.** Now Pa added his assent. It was no secret, he said gently, that I wasn't the "family scholar."

He didn't mean it as a dig. Still, I winced.

He and I went round and round, and in my head I went back and forth, and by a process of elimination we landed on the Army. It made sense. It aligned with my desire to be outside the box, to disappear. The military would take me away from the prying eyes of the public and the press. But it also fitted with my hope of making a difference.

And it accorded with my personality. My prized toys as a boy had always been miniature soldiers. I'd spent thousands of hours planning and waging epic battles with them at Kensington Palace and in Highgrove's Rosemary Verey–designed gardens. I'd also treated every game of paintball as though the future of the Commonwealth depended on the outcome.

Pa smiled. **Yes, darling boy. The Army sounds like just the thing.**

But first, he added . . .

Many people took a gap year as a matter of course. Pa, however, considered a gap year to be one of the most formative periods in a person's life.

See the world, darling boy! Have adventures.

So I sat down with Marko and tried to decide what those adventures might look like. We settled first on Australia. Spend half the year working on a farm.

Excellent.

As for the second half of the year, Africa. I told Marko I'd like to join the fight against AIDS. That this would be an homage to Mummy, an explicit continuation of her work, didn't need to be spelled out.

Marko went away, did some research, came back to me and said: Lesotho.

Never heard of it, I confessed.

He educated me. Landlocked country. Lovely country. Bordering South Africa. Lots of need, loads of work to be done.

I was overjoyed. A plan—at last.

Soon after, I visited Henners. A weekend in Edinburgh. Autumn 2002. We went to a restaurant and I told him all about it. **Good for you, Haz!** He was taking a gap year as well, in East Africa. Uganda, as I recall. Working in a rural school. At the moment, however, he was working a part-time job— at Ludgrove. Working as a stooge. (The Ludgrovian word for "handyman.") It was a very cool job, he said. He got to be with kids, got to fix things all over the grounds.

Plus, I teased him: **All the free strawberries and carrots you can eat!**

But he was quite serious about it. **I like teaching, Haz.**

Oh.

We talked excitedly about Africa, made plans to meet up there. After Uganda, after college, Henners too would probably go into the Army. He was going to be a Green Jacket. It wasn't really a decision; his family had been in uniform for generations. We talked about meeting up there too. Maybe, we said, we'll find ourselves side by side one day, marching into battle or helping people on the other side of the world.

The future. We wondered aloud what it held. I worried about it, but not Henners. He didn't take the future seriously, didn't take anything seriously. Life as it comes, Haz. That was Henners, always and forever. I envied his tranquility.

For now, however, he was heading to one of Edinburgh's casinos. He asked if I wanted to come along. Ah, can't, I said. I couldn't possibly be seen in a casino. It would cause a huge scandal.

Too bad, he said.

Cheers, we both said, promising to talk again soon.

Two months later, a Sunday morning—just before Christmas 2002. The news must have come in the form of a phone call, though I only dimly recall holding the phone, hearing the words. Henners and another boy, leaving a party near Ludgrove, drove into a tree. Though the call's a blur, I vividly remember my reaction. Same as when Pa told me about Mummy. **Right . . . so Henners was in an accident. But he's in hospital, right? He's going to be OK?**

No, he wasn't.

And the other boy, the driver, had been critically injured.

Willy and I went to the funeral. A little parish church down the road from where Henners grew up. I remember hundreds of people squeezing into creaky wooden pews. I remember, after the service, queueing up to hug Henners's parents, Alex and Claire, and his brothers, Thomas and Charlie.

I think, while we waited, I overheard whispered discussions of the crash.

It was foggy, you know . . .

They weren't going far . . .

But where were they going?

And at that time of night?

They were at a party and the sound system was knackered!

So they ran off to get another.

No!

They went to borrow a CD player from a friend. Short distance, you know . . .

So they didn't bother with seatbelts . . .

Just like Mummy.

And yet, unlike Mummy, there was no way to spin this as a disappearance. This was death, no two ways about it.

Also, unlike Mummy, Henners wasn't going that fast.

Because he wasn't being chased.

Twenty miles an hour, tops, everyone said.

And yet the car went straight into an old tree.

Old ones, someone explained, are much harder than young ones.

39.

THEY WOULDN'T LET ME out of Eton until I acted. That was what they said: I needed to take part in one of their formal dramas before they'd punch my ticket and release me into the wild.

It sounded ridiculous, but theater was deadly serious at Eton. The drama department staged several productions each year, and the year-end production was always the most major of them all.

In the late spring of 2003 it was Shakespeare's **Much Ado About Nothing**.

I was cast as Conrade. Minor character. He was, perhaps, a drinker, perhaps a drunkard, which gave the press all sorts of clever openings for calling me a drunkard too.

What's this? Bit of typecasting, is it?

Stories wrote themselves.

Eton's drama teacher said nothing about typecasting when he gave me the role. He just told me I was Conrade—**Have fun with it, Harry**—and I didn't question his motives. I wouldn't have questioned them even if I'd suspected he was taking the piss, because I wanted to get out of Eton, and to get out of Eton you had to act.

Among other things, I learned from studying the play that it was wrongheaded, and reductive, to focus on Conrade's alcohol consumption. He was a fascinating guy, really. Loyal, but also immoral. Full of advice, but essentially a follower. Above all, he was a henchman, a sidekick, whose main function, seemingly, was to give the audience a laugh or two. I found it easy to throw myself into such a role, and discovered during dress rehearsals that I had a hidden talent. Being royal, it turned out, wasn't all that far from being onstage. Acting was acting, no matter the context.

Opening night, my father sat dead center in a packed Farrer Theatre and no one had a better time. Here it was, his dream come true, a son performing Shakespeare, and he was getting his money's worth. He roared, he howled, he applauded. But, inexplicably, at all the wrong moments. His timing was bizarrely off. He sat mute when everyone else was laughing. He laughed when everyone else was silent. More than noticeable, it was bloody distracting. The audience thought Pa was a plant, part of the performance. **Who's that over there, laughing at nothing? Oh—is that the Prince of Wales?**

Later, backstage, Pa was all compliments. **You were wonderful, darling boy.**

But I couldn't help looking cross.

What's the matter, darling boy?

Pa, you laughed at all the wrong times!

He was baffled. I was too. How could he have no idea what I was talking about?

Slowly it became clear. He'd told me once that, when he was my age, acting in his own school performance of Shakespeare, Grandpa turned up and did exactly the same thing. Laughed at all the wrong times. Made a complete spectacle. Was Pa modeling his own father? Because he knew no other way to parent? Or was it more subliminal, some recessive gene expressing itself? Is each generation doomed to unwittingly repeat the sins of the last? I wanted to know, and I might've asked, but that wasn't the sort of thing you could ever raise with Pa. Or Grandpa. So I put it out of my mind and tried to focus on the good.

Pa is here, I told myself, and he's proud, and that's not nothing.

That was more than a lot of kids had.

I thanked him for coming, gave him a kiss on each cheek.

As Conrade says: **Can you make no use of your discontent?**

40.

I COMPLETED MY EDUCATION AT Eton in June 2003, thanks to hours of hard work and some extra tutoring arranged by Pa. No small feat for one so un-scholarly, so limited, so distracted, and while I wasn't proud of myself, exactly, because I didn't know how to be proud of myself, I felt a distinct pause in my non-stop internal self-criticism.

And then I was accused of cheating.

An art teacher came forward with evidence of cheat-ing, which turned out not to be evidence of cheating. It turned out to be nothing at all, and I was later cleared by the exam board. But the damage was done. The accusation stuck.

Brokenhearted, I wanted to release a statement, hold a press conference, tell the world: I did the work! I didn't cheat!

The Palace wouldn't let me. In this, as in most things, the Palace stuck fast to the family motto: **Never complain, never explain.** Especially if the complainer was an eighteen-year-old boy.

Thus I was forced to sit by and say nothing while the papers called me a cheat and a dummy every day. (Because of an art project! I mean, how do you "cheat" on an art project?) This was the official start of that dreaded title: Prince Thicko. Just as I was cast as Conrade without my consultation or consent, I was now cast in this role. The difference was, we did **Much Ado About Nothing** for three nights. This had the look of a role that would last a lifetime.

Prince Harry? Oh, yeah, not too bright.

Can't pass a simple test without cheating, that's what I read!

I talked to Pa about it. I was near despair.

He said what he always said.

Darling boy, just don't read it.

He never read it. He read everything else, from Shakespeare to white papers on climate change, but never the news. (He did watch the BBC, but he'd often end up throwing the controller at the TV.) The problem was, everyone else read it. Everyone in my family claimed not to, just like Pa, but even as they were making this claim to your face, liveried footmen were bustling around them, fanning every

British newspaper across silver platters, as neatly as the scones and marmalades.

41.

THE FARM WAS CALLED Tooloombilla. The people who owned it were the Hills.

Noel and Annie. They'd been friends of Mummy. (Annie had been Mummy's flatmate when she first started dating Pa.) Marko helped me find them, and somehow persuaded them to let me be their unpaid summer jackaroo.

The Hills had three children. Nikki, Eustie, and George. The eldest, George, was exactly my age, though he looked much older, perhaps due to years and years of toil under the boiling Australian sun. Upon arriving I learned that George would be my mentor, my boss—my headmaster, in a way. Though Tooloombilla was nothing like Eton.

In fact it was like no place I'd ever been.

I came from a green place. The Hills' farm was an ode to brown. I came from a place where every move was monitored, catalogued, and subjected to judgment. The Hills' farm was so vast and remote that no one would see me for most of each day but George. And the odd wallaby.

Above all, I came from a place that was temperate, rainy, cool. The Hills' farm was hot.

I wasn't sure I could endure this kind of hot. The Australian Outback had a climate I didn't understand

and which my body couldn't seem to accept. Like Pa, I wilted at the mere **mention** of heat: how was I supposed to put up with an oven inside a blast furnace inside a nuclear reactor set on top of an active volcano?

Bad spot for me, but worse for my bodyguards. Those poor lads—of all the assignments. Plus, their lodging was extra spartan, an outbuilding on the edge of the farm. I rarely saw them and often imagined them out there, sitting in their briefs before a noisy electric fan, grumpily polishing their CVs.

The Hills let me bunk with them in the main house, a sweet little bungalow with white clapboard, wooden steps leading to a wide porch, a front door that gave out a kittenish squeak every time you pulled it open and a loud bang every time you let it fly shut. The door had a tight screen, to keep out mosquitoes, which were big as birds. That first night, sitting over dinner, I couldn't hear anything but the rhythmic slap of bloodsuckers against mesh.

There wasn't much else to hear. We were all a bit awkward, trying to pretend that I was a jackaroo, not a prince, trying to pretend that we weren't thinking about Mummy, who'd loved Annie, and whom Annie had loved in turn. Annie clearly wanted to talk about Mummy, but as with Willy, I just couldn't. So I shoveled in the food, and praised it, and asked for seconds, and searched my brain for anodyne topics of conversation. But I couldn't think of any. The heat had already impaired my cognitive skills.

Falling asleep those first nights in the outback, I'd

conjure up the image of Marko and worriedly ask him: **Did we really think this through, mate?**

42.

THE REMEDY TO ALL problems, as always, was work. Hard, sweaty, nonstop labor, that was what the Hills had to offer, and plenty of it, and I couldn't get enough. The harder I worked, the less I felt the heat, and the easier it was to talk—or not talk— around the supper table.

But this wasn't merely work. Being a jackaroo required stamina, to be sure, but it also demanded a certain artistry. You had to be a whisperer with the animals. You had to be a reader of the skies, and the land.

You also had to possess a superior level of horse-manship. I'd come to Australia thinking I knew my way around horses, but the Hills were Huns, each born in a saddle. Noel was the son of a professional polo player. (He'd been Pa's former polo coach.) Annie could stroke a horse's nose and tell you what that beast was thinking. And George climbed into a saddle more easily than most people get into their beds.

A typical working day began in the middle of the night. Hours before dawn George and I would stumble outside, tackle the first chores, trying to get as much done as possible before the sun ascended. At first light we'd saddle up, gallop to the edges of the Hills' forty thousand acres (double the size of Balmoral) and begin to muster. That is, move the herd of cattle from here to there. We'd also search for individual cows that had strayed overnight, and drive them back into the herd. Or load some onto a trailer and take them to another section. I rarely knew exactly why we were moving these cows or those, but I got the bottom line:

Cows need their space.

I felt them.

Whenever George and I found a group of strays, a rebellious little cattle cabal, that was especially challenging. It was vital to keep them together. If they scattered, we'd be proper fucked. It would take hours to round them up and then the day would be wrecked. If one darted off, into a stand of trees, say, George or I would have to ride full speed after it. Every now and then, mid-chase, you'd get whipped out of the saddle by a low-hanging branch, maybe knocked cold. When you came to, you'd do a check for broken bones, internal bleeding, while your horse stood morosely over you.

The trick was never letting a chase last too long. Long chases wore out the cow, reduced its body fat, slashed its market value. Fat was money, and there was no margin for error with Aussie cattle, which had so little fat to begin with. Water was scarce, grass was scarce, and what little there was often got grubbed by kangaroos, which George and his family viewed as other people view rats.

I always flinched, and chuckled, at the way George spoke to errant cattle. He harangued them, abused them, cursed them, favoring one curse word in particular, a word many people go a lifetime without using. George couldn't go five minutes. Most people dive under a table when they hear this word, but for George it was the Swiss Army knife of language—endless applications and uses. (He also made it sound almost charming, with his Aussie accent.)

It was merely one of dozens of words in the complete George lexicon. For instance, a **fat** was a plump cow ready for slaughter. A **steer** was a young bull that should've been castrated but hadn't been yet. A **weaner** was a calf newly split from its mother. A **smoko** was a cigarette break. **Tucker** was food. I spent a lot of late 2003 sitting high in the saddle, watching a weaner while sucking a smoko and dreaming of my next tucker.

Sometimes hard, sometimes tedious, mustering could be unexpectedly emotional. Young females were easier, they went where you nudged them, but young males didn't care for being bossed around, and what they really didn't like was being split from their mums. They cried, moaned, sometimes charged you. A wildly swung horn could ruin a limb or sever an artery. But I wasn't afraid. Instead . . . I was empathetic. And the young males seemed to know.

The one job I wouldn't do, the one piece of hard work I shied from, was snipping balls. Every time George brought out that long shiny blade I'd raise my hands. **No, mate, can't do it.**

Suit yourself.

At day's end I'd take a scalding shower, eat a gargantuan supper, then sit with George on the porch, rolling cigarettes, sipping cold beers. Sometimes we'd listen to his small CD player, which made me think of Pa's wireless. Or Henners. **He and the other boy went to borrow another CD player . . .** Often we'd just sit gazing into the distance. The land was so tabletop flat you could see thunderstorms brewing hours ahead of when they arrived, the first spidery bolts flicking the far-off land. As the bolts got thicker, and closer, wind would race through the house, ruffling the curtains. Then the rooms would flutter with white light. The first thunderclaps would shake the furniture. Finally, the deluge. George would sigh. His parents would sigh. Rain was grass, rain was fat. Rain was money.

If it didn't rain, that also felt like a blessing, because after a windstorm the clear sky would be peppered with stars. I'd point out to George what the gang in Botswana had pointed out to me. **See that bright one next to the moon? That's Venus. And over there, that's Scorpius—best place to see it is the southern hemisphere. And there's Pleiades. And that's Sirius—brightest star in the sky. And there's Orion: the Hunter. All comes down to hunting, doesn't it? Hunters, hunted . . .**

What's that, Harry?

Nothing, mate.

The thing I found endlessly mesmerizing about the stars was how far away they all were. The light you saw was born hundreds of centuries ago. In other words, looking at a star, you were looking at the past, at a time long before anyone you knew or loved had lived.

Or died.

Or disappeared.

George and I usually hit the sack about eight thirty. Often we were too tired to take off our clothes. I was no longer afraid of the dark, I craved it. I slept as if dead, woke as if reborn. Sore, but ready for more.

There were no days off. Between the relentless work, the relentless heat, the relentless cows, I could feel myself being whittled down, lighter each morning by a kilo, quieter by a few dozen words. Even my British accent was being pared away. After six weeks I sounded nothing like Willy and Pa. I sounded more like George.

And dressed a bit like him as well. I took to wearing a slouchy felt cowboy hat like his. I carried one of his old leather whips.

Finally, to go with this new Harry, I acquired a new name. Spike.

It happened like this. My hair had never fully recovered after I'd let my Eton schoolmates shave it. Some strands shot up like summer grass, some lay flat, like lacquered hay. George often pointed at my head and said: **You look a right mess!** But on a trip to Sydney, to see the Rugby World Cup, I'd made an official appearance at the Taronga Zoo, and I'd been asked to pose for a photo with something called an echidna. A cross between a hedgehog and an anteater, it had hard spiky hair, which was why the zookeepers named it Spike. It looked, as George would say, a right mess.

More to the point, it looked like me. A lot like me. And when George happened to see a photo of me posing with Spike, he yelped.

Haz—that thing's got your hair!

Thereafter, he never called me anything but Spike. And then my bodyguards took up the chorus. Indeed, they made Spike my code name on the radio. Some even printed up T-shirts, which they wore while guarding me: **Spike 2003.**

Soon enough my mates at home got wind of this new nickname, and adopted it. I **became** Spike, when I wasn't Haz, or Baz, or Prince Jackaroo, or Harold, or Darling Boy, or Scrawny, a nickname given me by some Palace staff. Identity had always been problematic, but with a half dozen formal names and a full dozen nicknames it was turning into a hall of mirrors.

Most days I didn't care what people called me. Most days I thought: Don't care who I am, so long as it's someone new, someone other than Prince Harry. But then an official package would arrive from London, from the Palace, and the old me, the old life, the royal life, would come racing back.

The packet usually arrived in the everyday mail, though sometimes it was under the arm of a new bodyguard. (There was a constant changing of the guard, every couple of weeks, to keep them fresh and let them see their families.) Inside the packet would be letters from Pa, office paperwork, plus some briefs about charities in which I was involved. All stamped: ATT HRH PRINCE HENRY OF WALES.

One day the package contained a series of memos from the Palace comms team about a delicate matter. Mummy's former butler had penned a tell-all, which actually told nothing. It was merely one man's self-justifying, self-centering version of events. My mother once called this butler a dear friend, trusted him implicitly. We did too. Now this. He was milking her disappearance for money. It made my blood boil. I wanted to fly home, confront him. I phoned Pa, announced that I was getting on a plane. I'm sure it was the one and only conversation I had with him while I was in Australia. He—and then, in a separate phone call, Willy—talked me out of it.

All we could do, they both said, was issue a united condemnation.

So we did. Or they did. I had nothing to do with the drafting. (Personally, I'd have gone much further.) In measured tones it called out the butler for his treachery, and publicly requested a meeting with him, to uncover his motives and explore his so-called revelations.

The butler answered us publicly, saying he welcomed such a meeting. But not for any constructive purpose. To one newspaper he vowed: "I'd love to give them a piece of my mind."

He wanted to give **us** a piece of his mind?

I waited anxiously for the meeting. I counted the days.

Of course it didn't happen.

I didn't know why; I assumed the Palace quashed it. I told myself: Shame.

I thought of that man as the one errant **steer** that got away that summer.

43.

I DON'T RECALL HOW I learned about the first man trying to sneak onto the farm. Maybe from George? While we were out mustering?

I do remember that it was the local police who nabbed the intruder and got rid of him.

December 2003.

The police were pleased with themselves. But I was glum. I knew what was coming. Paps were like ants. There was never just one.

Sure enough, the very next day, two more crept onto the farm.

Time to go.

I owed so much to the Hills, I didn't want to repay them by ruining their lives. I didn't want to be the cause of them losing the one resource more precious than water—privacy. I thanked them for nine of the best weeks of my life, and flew home, arriving just before Christmas.

I went straight to a club my first night home. And the next night. And the next. The press thought I was still in Australia, and I decided their ignorance gave me carte blanche.

One night I met a girl, chatted with her over drinks. I didn't know she was a page-three girl. (That was the accepted, misogynistic, objectifying term for young topless women featured each day on page three of Rupert Murdoch's **The Sun**.) I wouldn't have cared if I'd known. She seemed smart and fun.

I left the club wearing a baseball cap. Paps everywhere. So much for carte blanche. I tried to blend into the crowd, walked casually down the road with my bodyguard. We went through St. James's Square and got into an unmarked police car. Just as we pulled away, a Mercedes with blacked-out windows jumped the pavement and swiped our car, nearly slamming head-on into the rear passenger door. We could see it coming, the driver not looking ahead, too busy trying to shoot photos. The story in the papers the next morning should've been about Prince Harry nearly being killed by a reckless pap. Instead it was about Prince Harry meeting and supposedly kissing a page-three girl, along with much frantic commentary about the horrors of the Spare dating . . . such a fallen woman.

Third in line to the throne . . . dating **her**?

The snobbery, the classism, was nauseating. The out-of-order priorities were baffling.

But it all greatly enhanced my sense of joy and relief at running away. Again.

Gap Year, Part Two.

Days later I was on a plane to Lesotho.

Better yet, it was decided that I could take along a mate.

The plan, once upon a time, had been to go with Henners.

In his stead I now asked George.

44.

LESOTHO WAS BEAUTIFUL. But also one of the grimmest places on earth. It was the epicenter of the global AIDS pandemic, and in 2004 the government had just declared a medical disaster. Tens of thousands had fallen to the disease, and the nation was turning into one vast orphanage. Here and there, you'd glimpse young children running about, lost looks on their faces.

Where's Daddy? Where's Mummy?

George and I signed up to help at several charities and schools. We were both bowled over by the lovely people we met, their resilience, their grace, their courage and good cheer in the face of so much suffering. We worked as hard as we'd worked on his farm, gladly and eagerly. We built schools. We repaired schools. We mixed gravel, poured cement, whatever was needed.

In this same spirit of service, I agreed one day to perform a task that might otherwise have been unthinkable—an interview. If I truly wanted to shine a light on conditions here, I had no choice: I'd have to cooperate with the dreaded press.

But this was more than cooperating. This would be my first-ever solo session with a reporter.

We met on a grassy hillside, early one morning. He started by asking: Why this place? Of all places?

I said that children in Lesotho were in trouble, and I loved children, understood children, so naturally I wanted to help.

He pressed. Why did I love children?

I gave my best guess: My incredible immaturity?

I was being glib, but the reporter chuckled and moved on to his next question. The subject of children had opened the door to the subject of my childhood, and that was the gateway to the only subject he, or anyone, really wanted to ask me about.

Do you think about . . . her . . . a lot through something like this?

I looked off, down the hillside, responded with a series of disjointed words: **Unfortunately it's been a long time now, um, not for me but for most people, it's been a long time since she's died, but the stuff that's come out has been bad, all the stuff that's come out, all these tapes . . .**

I was referring to recordings my mother had made before her death, a kind of quasi-confessional, which had just been leaked to the press, to coincide with release of the butler's memoir. Seven years after being hounded into hiding my mother was still being hounded, and libeled—it didn't make sense. In 1997 there'd been a nationwide reckoning, a period of collective remorse and reflection among all Britons. Everyone had agreed that the press was a pack of monsters, but consumers accepted blame as well. We all needed to do better, most people said. Now, many years later, all was forgotten. History was repeating itself daily, and I told the reporter it was "a shame."

Not a momentous declaration. But it represented the first time that either Willy or I had ever spoken publicly about Mummy. I was amazed to be the one going first. Willy always went first, in all things, and I wondered how this would go over—with him, with the world, but especially with Pa. (Not well, Marko told me later. Pa was dead-set against me addressing that topic; he didn't want either of his sons speaking about Mummy, for fear it would cause a stir, distract from his work, and perhaps shine an unflattering light on Camilla.)

Finally, with a completely false air of bravado, I shrugged and said to the reporter: **Bad news sells. Simple as that.**

Speaking of bad news . . . the reporter now referenced my most recent scandal.

The page-three girl, of course.

He mentioned that **some were wondering** if I'd really learned anything from my visit to the rehab clinic. Had I truly "converted"? I don't remember if he used that word, **converted**, but at least one paper had.

Did Harry need to be converted?

Harry the Heretic?

I could barely make out the reporter through the sudden red mist. How are we even talking about this? I blurted something about not being normal, which caused the reporter's mouth to fall open. **Here we go.** He was getting his headline, his news fix. Were his eyes rolling up into his head?

And **I** was supposed to be the addict?

I explained what I meant by normal. I didn't lead a normal life, because I couldn't lead one. **Even my**

father reminds me that unfortunately Willy and I can't be normal. I told the reporter that no one but Willy understood what it was like to live in this surreal fishbowl, in which normal events were treated as abnormal, and the abnormal was routinely normalized.

That was what I was trying to say, starting to say, but then I took another look down the hillside. Poverty, disease, orphans—death. It rendered everything else rubbish. In Lesotho, no matter what you were going through, you were well-off compared to others. I suddenly felt ashamed, and wondered if the journalist had sense enough to be ashamed too. Sitting here above all this misery and talking about page-three girls? Come on.

After the interview I went and found George and we drank beer. A lot of beer. Gallons of beer.

I believe that was also the night I smoked an entire shopping bag of weed.

I don't recommend it.

Then again, it might have been another night. Hard to be precise when it comes to a shopping bag full of weed.

45.

GEORGE AND I FLEW from Lesotho to Cape Town, to meet up with some mates, and Marko. March 2004.

We were staying at the home of the consulate

general, and one night we talked about having some people over. For dinner. Just one small problem. We didn't know anyone in Cape Town.

But wait—that wasn't completely true. I'd met someone years earlier, a girl from South Africa. At the Berkshire Polo Club.

Chelsy.

I remembered her being . . .

Different.

I went through my phone, found her number.

Give her a call, Marko said.

Really?

Why not?

To my shock, the number worked. And she answered.

Stammering, I reminded her who I was, said I was in her town, wondered if she might like to come over . . .

She sounded unsure. She sounded as if she didn't believe it was me. Flustered, I handed the phone to Marko, who promised that it was really me, and that the invitation was sincere, and that the evening would be very low-key—nothing to worry about. Pain-free. Maybe even fun.

She asked if she could bring her girlfriend. And her brother.

Of course! The more the merrier.

Hours later, there she was, sailing through the door. Turned out, my memory hadn't lied. She was . . . **different.** That was the word that had come to mind when I first met her, and it immediately came to mind now, and then again and again during the barbecue. Different.

Unlike so many people I knew, she seemed wholly unconcerned with appearances, with propriety, with royalty. Unlike so many girls I met, she wasn't visibly fitting herself for a crown the moment she shook my hand. She seemed immune to that common affliction sometimes called **throne syndrome**. It was similar to the effect that actors and musicians have on people, except with actors and musicians the root cause is talent. I had no talent—so I'd been told, again and again—and thus all reactions to me had nothing to do with me. They were down to my family, my title, and consequently they always embarrassed me, because they were so unearned. I'd always wanted to know what it might be like to meet a woman and not have her eyes widen at the mention of my title, but instead to widen them myself, using my mind, my heart. With Chelsy that seemed a real possibility. Not only was she uninterested in my title, she seemed bored by it. **Oh, you're a prince? Yawn.**

She knew nothing about my biography, less than nothing about my family. Granny, Willy, Pa—who're they? Better yet, she was remarkably incurious. She probably didn't even know about my mother; she was likely too young to recall the tragic events of August 1997. I couldn't be sure this was true, of course, because to Chelsy's credit we didn't talk about it. Instead we talked about the main thing we had in common— Africa. Chelsy, born and raised in Zimbabwe, now living in Cape Town, loved Africa with all her soul. Her father owned a big game farm, and that was the fulcrum of her world. Though she'd enjoyed her years at a British boarding school, Stowe, she'd always hurried home for the holidays. I told her I understood. I told her about my life-changing experiences in Africa, my first formative trips. I told her about the strange visitation from the leopard. She nodded. She got it. **Brilliant. Africa does offer moments like that, if you're ready. If you're worthy.**

At some point in the evening I told her I'd soon be entering the Army. I couldn't gauge her reaction. Maybe she had none? At least it didn't seem a deal-breaker.

Then I told her that George and Marko and I were all heading off the next day to Botswana. We were going to meet up with Adi, some others, float upriver. **Come with us?**

She smiled shyly, gave it a moment's thought. She and her girlfriend had other plans . . .

Oh. Too bad.

But they'd cancel them, she said. They'd love to come with us.

46.

WE SPENT THREE DAYS walking, laughing, drinking, mingling with the animals. Not just wild animals. By chance we met up with a snake wrangler, who showed us his cobra, his rattlesnake. He manipulated the snakes up and down his shoulders, his arms, giving us a private show.

Later that night, Chelsy and I had our first kiss under the stars.

George, meanwhile, fell head over heels in love with her girlfriend.

When the time came for Chelsy and her girlfriend to go home, and George to go back to Australia, and Marko to go back to London, there were sad good-byes all around.

Suddenly I found myself alone in the bush, with just Adi.

What now?

We heard about a camp nearby. Two filmmakers were doing a wildlife documentary and we were invited to go round and meet them.

We jumped into a Land Cruiser and soon found ourselves in the middle of a raucous bush party. Men and women drinking, dancing, all wearing bizarre animal masks made from cardboard and pipe cleaners. An Okavango Carnival.

The leaders of this mayhem were a couple in their thirties: Teej and Mike. They were the filmmakers, I gathered. In fact, they owned a whole film company, plus this camp. I introduced myself, complimented them on their ability to throw a truly epic bash. They laughed and said they were going to pay for it tomorrow.

Both had to get up early for work.

I asked if I could tag along. I'd love to see how the filmmaking was done.

They looked at me, then at each other. They knew who I was, and while it was surprising enough to meet me in the bush, the idea of hiring me as a helper was a lot to take in.

Mike said: **Course you can come. But you'll have to work. Lift heavy boxes, lug cameras around.**

I could see from their faces that they expected that to be the end of it.

I smiled and said: **Sounds great.**

They were shocked. And pleased.

It felt something like love at first sight. On both sides.

Teej and Mike were Africans. She was from Cape Town; he was from Nairobi. She'd been born in Italy, however, spent her first years in Milan, and took special pride in her Milanese roots, the source of her soulfulness, she said, which was as close to a boast as you'd ever hear from Teej. She'd even grown up speaking Italian, though she'd forgotten it, she said sadly. Except she hadn't. Any time she went into a hospital she shocked everyone by coming out of the anesthetic speaking fluent Italian.

Mike had grown up on a farm, learned to ride horses not long after he'd learned to walk. By chance his next-door neighbor was one of the first-ever wildlife filmmakers. Every time Mike got a free minute he'd run next door and sit with this neighbor, barrage him with questions. Mike had found his one true calling and the neighbor recognized it, fostered it.

Both Teej and Mike were talented, brilliant, and wholly devoted to wildlife. I wanted to spend as much time as possible with these two, not just on this trip but in general. The problem was, would they let me?

I'd often catch Teej looking in my direction, sizing me up, a curious smile on her face—as though I were something wild that had unexpectedly wandered into their camp. But instead of shooing me, or using me, as many would've done, she reached out and . . . petted me. Decades of observing wildlife had given her a feel for wildness, a reverence for it as a virtue and even a basic right. She and Mike were the first people ever to cherish whatever wildness was still inside me, whatever hadn't been lost to grief—and paps. They were outraged that others wanted to eliminate this last bit, that others were keen to put me into a cage.

On that trip, or perhaps the next, I asked Teej and Mike how they'd met. They smiled guiltily.

Mutual friend, Mike mumbled.

Blind date, Teej whispered.

The setting was a small restaurant. When Mike walked in, Teej was already at the table, her back to the door. She couldn't see Mike, she could only hear his voice, but even before turning around she knew, from the tone, the timbre, the change in room temperature, that she was in big trouble.

They got on beautifully over dinner, and the next day Teej went to Mike's place for coffee. She nearly fainted when she walked in. On the top shelf of his bookcase was a book by her grandfather, Robert Ardrey, a legendary scientist, essayist, writer. (He'd won an Oscar nomination for the screenplay of **Khartoum**.) In addition to her grandfather's books, Mike had all Teej's other favorites **arranged in the same order as they were arranged on her own shelves**. She put a hand to her mouth. This was synchronicity. This was a sign. She never went back to her apartment, except to pack her stuff. She and Mike had been together ever since.

They told me this story around the campfire. With Marko and that lot, the campfire was central, but with Teej and Mike it was sacrosanct. The same drinks went round, the same riveting stories, but it felt more ritualistic. There are few places where I've felt closer to truth, or more alive.

Teej saw it. She could tell how at home I felt with them. She said: **I think your body was born in Britain, but your soul was born here in Africa.**

Possibly the highest compliment I'd ever received.

After a few days of walking with them, eating with them, falling in love with them, I felt an overwhelming peace.

And an equally overwhelming need to see Chelsy again.

What to do? I wondered. How to make it happen? How to get into Cape Town without the press seeing and ruining it?

Adi said: Let's drive!

Drive? Huh. Yes. Brilliant!

It was only two days, after all.

We jumped into a car, drove without stopping, drinking whisky and gobbling chocolate for energy. I arrived at Chelsy's front door barefoot, scruffy, crowned with a filthy beanie, a huge smile creasing my dirty face.

She gasped . . . then laughed.

Then . . . opened the door a bit wider.

47.

CHELS AND I LEARNED an important lesson. Africa was Africa . . . but Britain was always Britain.

Soon after we arrived back at Heathrow we were papped.

Never fun for me, but not a shock either. There'd been a few years, after Mummy disappeared, when I'd hardly ever been papped, but now it was constant. I advised Chelsy to treat it like a chronic illness, something to be managed.

But she wasn't sure she wanted to have a chronic illness.

I told her I understood. Perfectly valid feeling. But this was my life, and if she wanted to share any part of it, she'd have to share this too.

You get used to it, I lied.

Thereafter, I put the chances at fifty-fifty, maybe sixty-forty, I'd ever see Chels again. Odds were, the press would cost me another person I cared about. I tried to reassure myself that it was fine, that I didn't really have time for a relationship just then.

I had work to do.

For starters, I was facing the entrance exams required for the Royal Military Academy at Sandhurst.

They took four days, and they were nothing like exams at Eton. There was **some** bookwork, **some** written stuff, but mostly they were tests for psychological toughness and leadership skills.

Turned out . . . I had both. I passed with flying colors.

I was delighted. My trouble concentrating, my trauma over my mother, none of that came into play. None of that counted against me with the British Army. On the contrary, I discovered, those things made me all the more ideal. The Army was **looking** for lads like me.

What's that you say, young man? Parents divorced? Mum's dead? Unresolved grief or psychological trauma? Step this way!

Along with news that I'd passed I received a report date, several months away. Which meant I'd have time to gather my thoughts, tie up loose ends. Even better, time to spend with Chels . . . if she'd have me?

She would. She invited me to come back to Cape Town, meet her parents.

I did. And liked them instantly. They were impossible not to like. They enjoyed funny stories, gin and tonics, good food, stalking. Her father was bear-sized, broad-shouldered, cuddly, but also a definite alpha. Her mother was petite, an amazing listener, and a frequent bestower of epic hugs. I didn't know what the future held, I didn't want to put any carts before any horses, but I thought: If you designed in-laws from the ground up, you couldn't do much better than these guys.

48.

THERE MUST HAVE BEEN something in the air. Just as I was embarking on my new romance, Pa announced that he'd decided to marry. He'd asked Granny's permission, and she'd granted it. Reluctantly, it was reported.

Despite Willy and me urging him not to, Pa was going ahead. We pumped his hand, wished him well. No hard feelings. We recognized that he was finally going to be with the woman he loved, the woman he'd always loved, the woman Fate might've intended for him in the first place. Whatever bitterness or sorrow we felt over the closing of another loop in Mummy's story, we understood that it was beside the point.

Also, we sympathized with Pa and Camilla as a couple. They'd taken star-crossed to new levels. After years of thwarted longing, they were now just a few steps from happiness . . . and new obstacles kept appearing. First there was the controversy over the nature of the ceremony. Courtiers insisted it would have to be a civil ceremony, because Pa, as future supreme governor of the Church of England, couldn't marry a divorcée in the church. That set off a furious debate about locations. If the civil ceremony were to be held at Windsor Castle, the couple's first choice, then Windsor would first need to be licensed for civil weddings, and if that were to happen then everyone in Britain would be allowed to have their civil weddings there. No one wanted that.

The decision was therefore made that the wedding would take place at Windsor Guildhall.

But then the Pope died.

Bewildered, I asked Willy: **What's the Pope got to do with Pa?**

Loads, it turned out. Pa and Camilla didn't want to get married on the same day the Pope was being laid to rest. Bad karma. Less press. More to the point, Granny wanted Pa to represent her at the funeral.

The wedding plans were changed yet again.

Delay after delay—if you listened carefully you could hear, wafting across the Palace grounds, the shrieks and groans of despair. You just couldn't tell whose they were: the wedding planner's or Camilla's (or Pa's).

Other than feeling sorry for them, I couldn't help but think that some force in the universe (Mummy?) was blocking rather than blessing their union. Maybe the universe delays what it disapproves of?

When the wedding did finally take place—without Granny, who chose not to attend—it was almost cathartic for everyone, even me. Standing near the altar I mostly kept my head bowed, eyes on the floor, just as I had during Mummy's funeral, but I did sneak several long peeks at the groom and the bride and each time I thought: Good for you.

Though, also: Goodbye.

I knew without question that this marriage would take Pa away from us. Not in any real sense, not in any deliberate or malicious way, but nevertheless—away. He was entering a new space, a closed space, a tightly insular space. Willy and I would see less of Pa, I predicted, and that left me with mixed feelings. I didn't relish losing a second parent, and I had complex feelings about gaining a step-parent who, I believed, had recently sacrificed me on her personal PR altar. But I saw Pa's smile and it was hard to argue with that, and harder still to deny the cause: Camilla. I wanted so many things, but I was surprised to discover at their wedding that one of the things I wanted most, still, was for my father to be happy.

In a funny way I even wanted Camilla to be happy. Maybe she'd be less dangerous if she was happy?

There are published reports that Willy and I snuck out of the church and hung JUST MARRIED signs on their car. I don't think so. I might've hung a sign: BE HAPPY. If I'd thought of it at the time.

I do remember watching them drive off and thinking: They're happy. They're really happy.

Damn, I'd like all of us to be happy.

49.

AROUND THIS TIME, just before the wedding, or perhaps just after, I went off with Willy to train with the British Special Boat Service. It wasn't official training. Just a bit of boys and toys, as we called it. Mostly a lark, though it did grow out of long-standing and solemn tradition.

Our family had always maintained close ties with the British military. Sometimes that meant an official visit, sometimes a casual lunch. Sometimes it meant a private chat with men and women home from the wars. But sometimes it meant taking part in rigorous exercises. Nothing showed respect for the military like doing, or trying to do, what they did.

Such exercises were always kept secret from the press. The military preferred it that way, and God knows the royals did too.

It was Mummy who took Willy and me on our first military exercise—a "killing house" in Herefordshire. The three of us were put into a room, told not to move. Then the room went dark. A squad kicked down the door. They threw flash bangs, scared the devil out of us, which was their aim. They wanted to teach us how to respond "if ever" our lives were in danger.

If ever? That made us laugh. **Have you seen our mail?**

But this day with Willy was different. Much more physical, more participatory. Less about teaching, more about adrenaline. We raced across Poole Harbour on speedboats, "attacked" a frigate, clambered up its cable ladders while shooting 9-mm MP5s loaded with paintball rounds. In one exercise we scurried down a flight of metal stairs into the frigate's hold. Someone cut the lights, to make it more interesting, I suppose. In the pitch-dark, four steps from the bottom, I fell, landed on my left knee, which was immediately impaled on a fixed bolt sticking out of the floor.

Blinding pain washed over me.

I managed to get up, keep going, finish the drill.

But at the end of the exercise we jumped off the boat's helipad, into the water, and I found my knee wasn't working. My whole leg wasn't working. When I got out of the water and stripped off the dry suit, Willy looked down and turned pale.

My knee was gushing blood.

Paramedics were there within minutes.

The Palace announced some weeks later that my entry into the Army would be postponed. Indefinitely.

Reporters demanded to know why.

The Palace comms team told them: **Prince Harry has injured his knee playing rugby.**

Reading the papers, my leg iced and elevated, I threw back my head and laughed. I couldn't help savoring one small particle of self-indulgent glee as the papers, for once, **unwittingly** printed a lie about me.

They soon got their revenge, however. They began pushing a story that I was **afraid** to go into the Army, that I was bunking off, using a fake knee injury as a way of stalling.

I was, they said, a coward.

50.

ONE OF WILLY'S friends was having a birthday party. In the countryside near Gloucestershire. More than a birthday party, it was a fancy-dress party, with a cringy theme. Natives and colonials. Guests were **required** to dress accordingly.

January 2005.

I didn't love fancy-dress parties. And I couldn't stand themes. For Willy's last birthday, or the one before, he'd had a fancy-dress party with a theme: **Out of Africa.** I found it irritating and baffling. Every time I'd gone to Africa I'd worn shorts and a T-shirt, maybe a **kikoi. Would that do, Willy?** But this was magnitudes worse.

Not one item of native or colonial garb hung in my wardrobe. I was crashing with Pa and Camilla, some days at St. James's, some days at Highgrove, largely living out of a suitcase, so I didn't give a damn about clothes. I looked most days as if I'd got dressed in a very dark and disordered room. A fancy-dress party, therefore, **with a theme,** was my nightmare.

Pass. Hard pass.

Willy, however, insisted. **We'll find you something to wear, Harold.**

His new girlfriend promised to help.

I liked his new girlfriend. She was carefree, sweet, kind. She'd done a gap year in Florence, knew about photography, art. And clothes. She loved clothes.

Her name was Kate. I forget what native or colonial thing she was wearing to the party, but with her help Willy had chosen for himself some kind of . . . feline outfit. Skintight leotard with (am I remembering this correctly?) a springy, bouncy tail. He tried it on for us and he looked like a cross between Tigger and Baryshnikov. Kate and I had a great time pointing our fingers at him and rolling around on the floor. It was ridiculous, especially in a three-way mirror.

But ridiculous, they both said, was the point of the upcoming party.

I liked seeing Kate laugh. Better yet, I liked making her laugh. And I was quite good at it. My transparently silly side connected with her heavily disguised silly side. Whenever I worried that Kate was going to be the one to take Willy from me, I consoled myself with thoughts of all our future laughing fits together, and I told myself how great everything would be when I had a serious girlfriend who could laugh along with us. Maybe it would be Chelsy.

Maybe, I thought, I can make Kate laugh with my costume.

But what would it be? What's Harold going to be? This became our constant topic.

On the day of the party it was decided that I'd go to a nearby village, Nailsworth, where there was a well-known costume shop. Surely I could find something there.

It's a bit blurry, though some things come back with total certainty. The shop had an unforgettable smell. I remember its musty, moldy funk, with an undercurrent of something else, something indefinable, some airborne by-product of a tightly sealed room, containing hundreds of pairs of trousers, shared over several decades, by thousands of humans.

I went up and down the rows, sifting through the racks, seeing nothing I liked. With time running out I narrowed my options to two.

A British pilot's uniform.

And a sand-colored Nazi uniform.

With a swastika armband.

And a flat cap.

I phoned Willy and Kate, asked what they thought. Nazi uniform, they said.

I rented it, plus a silly mustache, and went back to the house. I tried it all on. They both howled. Worse than Willy's leotard outfit! Way more ridiculous!

Which, again, was the point.

But the mustache needed trimming, so I snipped the long bits on the ends, made it a proper Hitler mouser. Then added in some cargo trousers.

Off we went to the party, where no one looked twice at my costume. All the natives and colonials were more focused on getting drunk and groping each other. No one took any notice of me, which I put down as a small win.

Someone, however, snapped photos. Days later this someone saw a chance to make some cash, or some trouble, and sought out a reporter. **How much for snaps from a recent party attended by young royals?** The crown jewel of the photos was thought to be Willy in his leotard.

But the reporter spotted something else. Hello, what's this? The Spare? As a Nazi?

There was some haggling over price, according to reports I've heard. A sum of five thousand pounds was agreed upon and weeks later the photo appeared in every paper in the known world, beneath titanic headlines.

Heil Harry!

Heir Aberrant.

Royal Heil to Pay.

What followed was a firestorm, which I thought at times would engulf me. And I felt that I deserved to be engulfed. There were moments over the course of the next several weeks and months when I thought I might die of shame.

The typical response to the photos was: What could he have been **thinking?** The simplest answer was: I wasn't. When I saw those photos, I recognized immediately that my brain had been shut off, that perhaps it had been shut off for some time. I wanted to go around Britain knocking on doors, explaining to people: **I wasn't thinking. I meant no harm.** But it wouldn't have made any difference. Judgment was swift, harsh. I was either a crypto Nazi or else a mental defective.

I turned to Willy. He was sympathetic, but there wasn't much to say. Then I phoned Pa. To my surprise he was serene. At first I was suspicious. I thought maybe he was seeing my crisis as another opportunity to bolster his PR. But he spoke to me with such tenderness, such genuine compassion, that I was disarmed. And grateful.

He didn't gloss over the facts. **Darling boy, how could you be so foolish?** My cheeks burned. **I know, I know.** But he quickly went on to say that it was the foolishness of youth, that he remembered being publicly vilified for youthful sins, and it wasn't fair, because youth is the time when you're, by definition, unfinished. You're still growing, still becoming, still learning, he said. He didn't specifically cite any of his youthful humiliations, but I knew. His most intimate conversations had been leaked, his most ill-conceived remarks had been trumpeted. Past girlfriends had been interrogated, their rating of his lovemaking spread across tabloids, even books. He knew all about humiliation.

He promised that the fury about this would blow over, the shame would fade. I loved him for that promise, even though—or maybe because—I knew it to be false. The shame would never fade. Nor should it.

Day after day the scandal grew. I was excoriated in newspapers, on radio, on TV. Members of Parliament called for my head on a spike. One said I should be barred from entering Sandhurst.

The blowing-over, therefore, according to Pa's staff, would need some help. I'd need to make some sort of public atonement.

Fine by me, I said. Sooner the better.

So Pa sent me to a holy man.

51.

BEARDED, BESPECTACLED, with a deeply lined face and dark, wise eyes, he was Chief Rabbi of Britain, that much I'd been told. But right away I could see he was much more. An eminent scholar, a religious philosopher, a prolific writer with more than two dozen books to his name, he'd spent many of his days staring out of windows and thinking about the root causes of sorrow, of evil, of hate.

He offered me a cup of tea, then dived straight in. He didn't mince words. He condemned my actions. He wasn't unkind, but it had to be done. There was no way round it. He also placed my stupidity in historical context. He spoke about the six million, the annihilated. Jews, Poles, dissenters, intellectuals, homosexuals. Children, babies, old people, turned to ash and smoke.

A few short decades ago.

I'd arrived at his house feeling shame. I now felt something else, a bottomless self-loathing.

But that wasn't the rabbi's aim. That certainly wasn't how he wanted me to leave him. He urged me not to be devastated by my mistake, but instead to be motivated. He spoke to me with the quality one often encounters in truly wise people—forgiveness. He assured me that people do stupid things, say stupid things, but it doesn't need to be their intrinsic nature. I was showing my true nature, he said, by seeking to atone. Seeking absolution.

To the extent that he was able, and qualified, he absolved me. He gave me grace. He told me to lift my head, go forth, use this experience to make the world better. To become a teacher of this event. Henners, I thought, would've liked the sound of that. Henners with his love of teaching.

No matter what I did, the calls grew louder for me to be barred from the Army. The top brass, however, were holding fast. If Prince Harry had been in the Army when he dolled himself up as the Führer, they said, he'd have been disciplined.

But he's not in the Army yet, they added.

So he's perfectly free to be a thicko.

52.

HE WAS TO BE OUR NEW private secretary: Jamie Lowther-Pinkerton was his name. But I don't remember Willy and me referring to him as anything other than JLP.

We should've just called him Marko II. Or maybe Marko 2.0. He was meant to be Marko's replacement, but also a more official, more detailed, more permanent version of our dear friend.

All the things Marko had been doing informally, the minding and guiding and advising, JLP would now do formally, we were told. In fact it was Marko who'd found JLP, and recommended him to Pa, and then trained him. So we already trusted the man, right from the start. He came with that all-important seal of approval. Marko said he was a good man.

Deeply calm, slightly stiff, JLP wore shiny gold cufflinks and a gold signet ring, symbols of his probity, constancy, and stalwart belief in a certain kind of steadfast style. You always got the sense that, even on the morning of Armageddon, JLP would button in these amulets before leaving the house.

Despite his spit and polish, however, his enameled exterior, JLP was a force, the product of Britain's finest military training, which meant, among other things, that he didn't deal in bullshit. He didn't give it, didn't take it, and everyone, far and wide, seemed to know. When British officials decided to launch a massive offensive against a Colombian drug cartel, they chose JLP to lead it. When the actor Ewan McGregor decided to take a three-month motorbike trip through Mongolia and Siberia and Ukraine, for which he'd require survival training, he turned to JLP.

To me, JLP's finest trait was his reverence for truth, his expertise in truth. He was the opposite of so many people in government and working in the Palace. So, not long after he started working for Willy and me, I asked him to get me some truth—in the form of the secret police files on Mummy's crash.

He looked down, looked away. Yes, he worked for Willy and me, but he cared about us too, and he cared about tradition, chain of command. My request seemed to jeopardize all three. He grimaced and furrowed his brow, an amorphous area, since JLP didn't have a lot of hair. Finally, he smoothed back the charcoal bristles remaining on each side and said that, were he to procure said files, it would be very upsetting for me. **Very upsetting indeed, Harry.**

Yes. I know. Sort of the point.

He nodded. **Ah. Hmm. I see.**

A few days later he brought me into a tiny office up a back staircase in St. James's Palace and handed me a brown Do Not Bend envelope. He said he'd decided against showing me **all** the police files. He'd gone through and removed the more . . . "challenging" ones. **For your sake.**

I was frustrated. But I didn't argue. If JLP didn't think I could handle them, then I probably couldn't.

I thanked him for protecting me.

He said he'd leave me to it, then walked out.

I took several breaths, opened the file.

Exterior photos. Outside the tunnel in which the crash occurred. Looking into the mouth of the tunnel.

Interior photos. A few feet inside the tunnel.

Deep interior photos. Well inside the tunnel. Looking down the tunnel, and out the other end.

Finally . . . close-ups of the smashed Mercedes, which was said to have entered the tunnel around midnight and never emerged in one piece.

All seemed to be police photos. But then I realized that many, if not most, were from paps and other photographers at the scene. The Paris police had seized their cameras. Some photos were taken moments after the crash, some much later. Some showed police officers walking about, others showed onlookers milling and gawping. All gave a sense of chaos, a disgraceful carnival atmosphere.

Now came more detailed photos, clearer, closer, inside the Mercedes. There was the lifeless body of Mummy's friend, whom I now knew to be her boyfriend. There was her bodyguard, who'd survived the crash, though it left him with gruesome injuries. And there was the driver, slumped over the wheel. He was blamed by many for the crash, because there was allegedly alcohol in his blood, and because he was dead and couldn't answer.

At last I came to the photos of Mummy. There were lights around her, auras, almost halos. How strange. The color of the lights was the same color as her hair—golden. I didn't know what the lights were, I couldn't imagine, though I came up with all sorts of supernatural explanations.

As I realized their true origin, my stomach clenched.

Flashes. They were flashes. And within some of the flashes were ghostly visages, and half visages, paps and reflected paps and refracted paps on all the smooth metal surfaces and glass windscreens. Those men who'd chased her . . . they'd never stopped shooting her while she lay between the seats, unconscious, or semiconscious, and in their frenzy they'd sometimes accidentally photographed each other. Not one of them was checking on her, offering her help, not even comforting her. They were just shooting, shooting, shooting.

I hadn't known. I hadn't dreamed. I'd been told that paps chased Mummy, that they'd hunted her like a pack of wild dogs, but I'd never dared to imagine that, like wild dogs, they'd also feasted on her defenseless body. I hadn't been aware, before this moment, that the last thing Mummy saw on this earth was a flashbulb.

Unless . . . Now I looked much closer at Mummy: no visible injuries. She was slumped, out of it, but generally . . . fine. Better than fine. Her dark blazer, her glowing hair, her radiant skin—doctors at the hospital where she was taken couldn't stop remarking how beautiful she was. I stared, trying to make myself cry, but I couldn't, because she was so lovely, and so alive.

Maybe the photos JLP held back were more definitive. Maybe they showed death in plainer terms. But I didn't consider that possibility too closely. I slammed the folder shut and said: **She's hiding**.

I'd requested this file because I sought proof, and the file proved nothing, except that Mummy was in a car crash, after which she looked generally unharmed, while those who chased her continued to harass her. That was all. Rather than proof, I'd discovered more reasons for rage. In that little office, seated before that wretched Do Not Bend envelope, the red mist came down, and it wasn't a mist, it was a torrent.

53.

I CARRIED A SMALL overnight bag containing a few personal items, plus one standard-size ironing board, slung jauntily under my arm like a surfboard. The Army had ordered me to bring it. From here on my shirts and trousers would need to be crease-free.

I knew as much about operating an ironing board as I did about operating a tank—less, actually. But that was now the Army's problem. I was now the Army's problem.

I wished them luck.

So did Pa. It was he who dropped me off in Camberley, Surrey, at the Royal Military Academy at Sandhurst.

May 2005.

He stood to one side and watched me put on my red name tag, WALES, then sign in. He told reporters how proud he was.

Then extended his hand. **Off you go, darling boy.** Photo op. Click.

I was assigned to a platoon of twenty-nine young men and women. Early the next day, after pulling on our new combats, we filed into an ancient room, hundreds of years old. You could smell the history— it seemed to come off the wood-paneled walls like steam. We recited an oath to the Queen. **I swear allegiance to Crown and country . . .** The lad beside me shot an elbow into my ribs. **Bet you say Granny rather than Queen!**

That was the last time, for the next five weeks, that he or anyone else would venture a joke. There was nothing funny about boot camp.

Boot camp—such a benign name for what happened. We were pushed to our limits, physically, mentally, spiritually. We were taken—or dragged— to a place beyond our limits, and then a bit further, by a stolid group of lovable sadists called color sergeants. Large, loud, extremely masculine men—and yet they all had tiny little dogs. I've never heard or read an explanation for this, and I can't venture one. I'll only say that it was odd to see these testosterone-rich, mostly bald ogres cooing at their poodles, shih tzus and pugs.

I'd say they treated us like dogs, except they treated their dogs so much better. With us they never said:

There's a good boy! They got up in our faces, shouted at us through the clouds of their aftershave, and never, ever let up. They belittled us, harassed us, shrieked at us, and made no secret of their intent. They meant to break us.

If they couldn't break us, brilliant. Welcome to the Army! If they could, even better. Better to know now. Better that **they** should break us than the enemy.

They used a variety of approaches. Physical duress, psychological intimidation—and humor? I remember one color sergeant pulling me aside. **Mr. Wales, I was on guard one day at Windsor Castle, wearing my bearskin, and along came a boy who kicked gravel on my boots! And that boy . . . was YOU!**

He was joking, but I wasn't sure I should laugh, and I wasn't sure it was true. I didn't recognize him, and I certainly didn't remember kicking gravel on any guardsmen. But if it **was** true, I apologized and hoped we could put it behind us.

Within two weeks several cadets had tapped out. We woke to find their beds made, their stuff gone. No one thought less of them. This shit wasn't for everybody. Some of my fellow cadets would confess, before lights out, that they feared being next.

I never did, however. I was, for the most part, fine. Boot camp was no picnic, but I never wavered in my belief that I was exactly where I was meant to be. They can't break me, I thought. Is it, I wondered, because I'm already broken?

Also, no matter what they did to us, it was done away from the press, so for me every day was a kind of holiday. The training center was like Club H. No matter what the color sergeants dished out, there was always, always the compensatory bonus of no paps. Nothing could really hurt me in a place where the press couldn't find me.

And then they found me. A reporter from **The Sun** sneaked onto the grounds and shambled around, holding a phony bomb, trying to prove—what? No one knew. **The Sun** said their reporter, this faux flâneur, was trying to expose the training center's lax security, to prove that Prince Harry was in danger.

The truly scary part was that some readers actually believed their rubbish.

54.

EVERY DAY, UPON waking at five A.M., we were forced to down a huge bottle of water. The bottle was Army-issued, black plastic, a leftover from the Boer War. Any liquid inside tasted of first-generation plastic. And piss. Plus, it was piss warm. So, after the guzzling, moments before setting out on our morning run, some of us would fall to the ground and vomit the water straight back up.

No matter. Next day, you had to guzzle that plastic piss water again, from the same water bottle, and then get out there for another post-vomit run.

Oh, the running. We ran constantly. We ran around a track. We ran along a road. We ran through deep woods. We ran across meadows. Sometimes we ran with 40 kilograms on our backs, sometimes carrying a huge log. We ran and ran and ran until we passed out, which we sometimes did while still running. We'd lie there, half conscious, legs still pumping, like sleeping dogs chasing squirrels.

In between the runs we'd drag our bodies up ropes, or hurl them at walls, or ram them against each other. At night something more than pain would creep into our bones. It was a deep, shuddering throb. There was no way to survive that throb except to dissociate from it, tell your mind that **you** were not **it**. Sunder yourself from yourself. The color sergeants said this was part of their Grand Plan. Kill the Self.

Then we'd all be on the same page. Then we'd truly be One Unit.

As the primacy of Self fades, they promised, the idea of Service takes over.

Platoon, country, that'll be all you know, cadets. And that'll bloody well be enough.

I couldn't tell how the other cadets felt about all this, but I bought in, all the way. Self? I was more than ready to shed that dead weight. Identity? Take it.

I could understand, for someone attached to their self, their identity, that this experience might be harsh. Not me. I rejoiced as slowly, steadily, I felt myself being reduced to an essence, the impurities removed, only the vital stuff remaining.

A little like what happened in Tooloombilla. Only more so.

It all felt like an enormous gift, from the color sergeants, from the Commonwealth.

I loved them for it. At night, before blacking out, I gave thanks.

55.

AFTER THOSE FIRST FIVE weeks, after the close of boot camp, the color sergeants eased up. Ever so slightly. They didn't shout at us quite so much. They treated us like soldiers.

As such, however, it was time to learn about war. How to make it, how to win it. Some of this involved stupefyingly boring classroom lessons. The better bits involved drills simulating different ways of being killed, or not, depending.

CBRN, they were called. Chemical, biological, radiological, nuclear. We practiced putting on protective gear, pulling it off, cleaning and wiping the poisons and other muck that might be thrown, dropped or sprayed on us. We dug countless trenches, donned masks, curled into the fetal position, rehearsed the Book of Revelation over and over.

One day the color sergeants assembled us outside a redbrick building, which had been turned into a CS gas chamber. They ordered us inside, activated the gas. We took off our gas masks, put them on again, took them off. If you weren't quick about it, you got a mouthful, a lungful. But you couldn't always be quick, and that was the point, so eventually everyone sucked gas. The exercises were supposed to be about war; to me they were about death. The whole leitmotif of Army training was death. How to avoid it, but also how to face it, head-on.

It felt natural, therefore, almost inevitable, that they put us on buses and took us to Brookwood Military Cemetery, to stand on graves, to listen as someone read a poem.

"For the Fallen."

The poem predated the ghastliest wars of the twentieth century, so it still had a trace of innocence.

They shall not grow old,
As we that are left grow old . . .

It was striking how much of our earliest training was intercut, leavened, with poetry. The glory of dying, the beauty of dying, the necessity of dying, these concepts were pounded into our heads along with the skills to avoid dying. Sometimes it was explicit, but sometimes it was right in our faces. Whenever we were herded into chapel we'd look up and see etched in stone: **Dulce et decorum est pro patria mori.**

Sweet and fitting it is to die for one's country.

Words first written by an ancient Roman, an exile, then repurposed by a young British soldier who'd died for his country. Repurposed ironically, but no one told us that. They certainly weren't etched ironically into that stone.

Poetry, for me, was slightly preferable to history. And psychology. And military strategy. I wince just remembering those long hours, those hard chairs in Faraday Hall and Churchill Hall, reading books and memorizing dates, analyzing famous battles, writing essays on the most esoteric concepts of military strategy. These, for me, were the ultimate trials of Sandhurst.

Given a choice, I'd have taken five more weeks of boot camp.

I fell asleep in Churchill Hall, more than once.

You there, Mr. Wales! You're sleeping!

We were advised, when feeling sleepy, to jump up, get the blood flowing. But that seemed overly confrontational. By standing you were informing the instructor that he or she was a bore. What sort of mood would they be in when it came time to mark your next paper?

Weeks ran together. In week nine—or was it ten?—we learned bayoneting. Wintry morning. A field in Castlemartin, Wales. The color sergeants put on head-splitting punk rock music, full volume, to rouse our animal spirits, and then we began running at sandbag dummies, bayonets high, slashing and shouting: **KILL! KILL! KILL!**

When the whistles blew, when the drill was "over," some guys couldn't turn it off. They kept stabbing and stabbing their dummies. A quick glimpse into the dark side of human nature. Then we all laughed and pretended we hadn't seen what we'd just seen.

Week twelve—or maybe thirteen?—was guns and grenades. I was a good shot. I'd been shooting rabbits and pigeons and squirrels with a .22 since I was twelve.

But now I got better.

So much better.

56.

IN LATE SUMMER WE were shipped to Wales and put through a punishing exercise called Long Reach. A nonstop march, yomp and run over several days, up and down barren countryside, with a load of gear strapped to our backs, equivalent to the weight of one young teenager. Worse, Europe was suffering a historic heat wave, and we set out at the crest of the wave, the hottest day of the year.

A Friday. We were told that the exercise would run through Sunday night.

Late Saturday, during our only enforced rest, we slept in bags on a dirt track. After two hours we were awakened by thunder and hard rain. I was in a team of five, and we stood up, held our faces to the rain, drinking the drops. It felt so good. But then we were wet. And it was time to march again.

Sopping wet, in driving rain, marching now became something altogether different. We were grunting, panting, groaning, slipping. Gradually I felt my resolve start to give way.

At a momentary stop, a checkpoint, I felt a burning in my feet. I sat on the ground, pulled off my right boot and sock, and the bottom of my foot peeled away.

Trench foot.

The soldier beside me shook his head. **Shit. You can't go on.**

I was gutted. But, I confess, also relieved.

We were on a country road. In a nearby field stood an ambulance. I staggered towards it. As I got close, medics lifted me onto the open tailgate. They examined my feet, said this march was over for me.

I nodded, slumped forward.

My team was getting ready to leave. **Goodbye, lads. See you back at camp.**

But then one of our color sergeants appeared. Color Sergeant Spence. He asked for a word. I hopped off the tailgate, limped with him over to a nearby tree.

His back to the tree, he spoke to me in a level tone. It was the first time in months he hadn't shouted at me.

Mr. Wales, you've got one last push. You've literally got six or eight miles left, that's all. I know, I know, your feet are shit, but I suggest you don't quit. I know you can do this. You know you can do this. Push on. You'll never forgive yourself if you don't.

He walked away.

I limped back to the ambulance, asked for all their zinc oxide tape. I wrapped my feet tightly and rammed them back into my boots.

Uphill, downhill, forward, I went on, trying to think of other things to distract myself from the agony. We neared a stream. The icy water would be a blessing, I thought. But no. All I could feel were the rocks in the bed pressing against the raw flesh.

The last four miles were among the most difficult steps I've ever taken on this planet. As we crossed the finish line I began to hyperventilate with relief.

One hour later, back in camp, everyone put on trainers. For the next several days we shuffled about the barracks like old men.

But proud old men.

At some point I limped up to Color Sergeant Spence, thanked him.

He gave a little smile and walked away.

57.

THOUGH EXHAUSTED, though a bit lonely, I felt radiant. I was in the shape of my life, I was thinking and seeing more clearly than ever before. The feeling was not unlike that described by people who enter monastic orders. Everything felt lit up.

As with monks, each cadet had his own cell. It had to be pristine at all times. Our small beds had to be made—tight. Our black boots had to be bulled—shiny as wet paint. Our cell doors had to be propped open—always. Even though you could close the door at night, color sergeants could—and often did—walk in at any time.

Some cadets complained bitterly. **No privacy!**

That made me laugh. Privacy? What's that?

At the end of each day I'd sit in my cell, bulling my boots, spitting on them, rubbing them, making them mirrors in which I could see my shorn head. No matter what institution I landed in, it seemed, a tragically bad haircut was the first order of business. Then I'd text Chels. (I was allowed to keep my mobile, for security reasons.) I might tell her how things were going, tell her I missed her. Then I'd loan my phone to any other cadets who might want to text their girlfriends or boyfriends.

Then it was lights-out.

No problem. I was no longer remotely afraid of the dark.

58.

IT WAS NOW OFFICIAL. I was no longer Prince Harry. I was Second Lieutenant Wales of the Blues and Royals, second oldest regiment of the British Army, part of the Household Cavalry, bodyguards to the Monarch.

The "passing out," as they called it, took place on April 12, 2006.

On hand were Pa and Camilla, Grandpa, Tiggy and Marko.

And, of course, Granny.

She hadn't attended a passing-out parade for decades, so her appearance was a dazzling honor. She smiled for all to see as I marched past.

And Willy saluted. He was at Sandhurst too now. A fellow cadet. (He'd started after me, because he'd gone to university first.) He couldn't resort to his typical attitude when we were sharing an

institution, couldn't pretend not to know me—
or he'd be insubordinate.

For one brief moment, Spare outranked Heir.

Granny inspected the troops. When she came to
me, she said: **Oh . . . hello.**

I smiled. And blushed.

The passing-out ceremony was followed by the
playing of "Auld Lang Syne," and then the college
adjutant rode his white horse up the steps of the Old
College.

Last, there was a lunch in the Old College. Granny
gave a lovely speech. As the day petered out, the adults
left, and the real partying began. A night of serious
drinking, raucous laughter. My date was Chels. There
was eventually a second passing out, as it were. I
woke the next morning with a wide grin and a slight
headache.

Next stop, I said to the shaving mirror, Iraq.

Specifically, southern Iraq. My unit would be
relieving another unit, which had spent months
doing advanced reconnaissance. Dangerous work,
constantly dodging roadside IEDs and snipers. In
that same month ten British soldiers had been killed.
In the previous six months, forty.

I searched my heart. I wasn't fearful. I was committed. I was eager. But also: war, death, whatever,
anything was better than remaining in Britain, which
was its own kind of battle. Just recently, the papers
had run a story about Willy leaving a voicemail for
me, pretending to be Chels. They'd also run a story
about me asking JLP for help on a Sandhurst research

project. Both stories, for once, were true. The question was—how could the papers have known such deeply private things?

It made me paranoid. Willy too. It made us reconsider Mummy's so-called paranoia, view it through a very different lens.

We began to examine our inner circle, to question our most trusted friends—and their friends. With whom had they been speaking? In whom had they confided? No one was above suspicion because no one could be. We even doubted our bodyguards, and we'd always worshipped our bodyguards. (Hell, officially I was now a bodyguard—the Queen's bodyguard.) They'd always been like big brothers to us. But now they were also suspects.

For a fraction of a second we even doubted Marko. That was how toxic the suspicion became. No one was above it. Some person, or persons, extremely close to me and Willy, was sneaking stuff to the newspapers, so everyone needed to be considered.

What a relief it will be, I thought, to be in a proper war zone, where none of this is part of my daily calculus.

Please, put me on a battlefield where there are clear rules of engagement.

Where there's some sense of honor.

part 2 bloody, but unbowed

1.

Britain's Ministry of Defence told the world in February 2007 that I was deploying, that I would be commanding a group of light tanks along the Iraqi border, near Basra. It was official. I was off to war.

Public reaction was peculiar. Half of Britons were furious, calling it dreadful to risk the life of the Queen's youngest grandson. Spare or not, they said, it's unwise to send a royal into a war zone. (It was the first time in twenty-five years that such a thing had been done.)

Half, however, said bravo. Why should Harry get special treatment? What a waste of taxpayers' money it would be to train the boy as a soldier and then not to use him.

If he dies, he dies, they said.

The enemy certainly felt that way. By all means, said the insurgents, who were trying to foment a civil war across Iraq, send us the boy.

One of the insurgent leaders extended a formal invitation worthy of high tea.

"We are awaiting the arrival of the young handsome spoiled prince with bated breath . . ."

There was a plan for me, the insurgent leader said. They were going to kidnap me, then decide what to do with me—torture, ransom, kill.

In seeming direct contradiction of this plan, he concluded by promising that the handsome prince would return to his grandmother "without ears."

I remember hearing that and feeling the tips of my ears grow warm. I flashed back to childhood, when a friend suggested my ears be surgically pinned back, to prevent or correct the family curse. I said, flatly, no.

Days later, another insurgent leader invoked my mother. He said that I should learn from her example, break away from my family. **Rebel against the imperialists, Harry.**

Or else, he warned, a prince's "blood will flow into our desert."

I would've worried about Chels hearing any of this, but since we'd begun dating she'd been so harassed by the press that she'd completely unplugged. The papers didn't exist for her. The internet was off-limits.

The British military, however, was very plugged in. Two months after announcing my deployment, the head of the Army, General Dannatt, abruptly called it off. Besides the public threats from insurgent leaders, British intelligence learned that my photo had been distributed among a group of Iraqi snipers, with instructions that I was the "mother of all targets." These snipers were elite: they'd recently cut down six British soldiers. So the mission had simply become too dangerous, for me, for anyone who might have the bad luck to be standing next to me. I'd become, in the assessment of Dannatt and others, a "bullet magnet." And the reason, he said, was the press. In his public statement canceling my deployment, he blasted journalists for their overwrought coverage, their wild speculations, which had "exacerbated" the threat level.

Pa's staff also issued a public statement, saying I was "very disappointed," which was untrue. I was crushed. When word first reached me I was at Windsor Barracks, sitting with my guys. I took a moment to collect myself, then told them the bad news. Though we'd just spent months traveling, training together, during which we'd become brothers in arms, they were now on their own.

It wasn't simply that I felt sorry for myself. I worried about my team. Someone else would have to do my job, and I'd have to live forever with the wondering, the guilt. What if they were no good?

The following week, several papers reported that I was in deep depression. One or two, however, reported that the abrupt about-face in my deployment had been my own doing. The coward story, again. They said that, behind the scenes, I'd pressed my superiors to pull the plug.

2.

I PONDERED QUITTING the Army. What was the point of staying if I couldn't actually be a soldier?

I talked it over with Chels. She was torn. On the

one hand she couldn't hide her relief. On the other she knew how much I wanted to be there for my team. She knew that I'd long felt persecuted by the press, and that the Army had been the one healthy outlet I'd found.

She also knew that I believed in the Mission.

I talked it over with Willy. He had complicated feelings as well. He sympathized, as a soldier. But as a sibling? A highly competitive older brother? He couldn't bring himself to totally regret this turn of events.

Most of the time Willy and I didn't have any truck with all that Heir-Spare nonsense. But now and then I'd be brought up short and realize that on some level it really did matter to him. Professionally, personally, he cared where I stood, what I was doing.

Not getting comfort from any quarter, I looked for it in vodka and Red Bull. And gin and tonic. I was photographed around this time going into or coming out of multiple pubs, clubs, house parties, at wee hours.

I didn't love waking to find a photo of myself on the front page of a tabloid. But what I really couldn't bear was the sound of the photo being taken in the first place. That click, that terrible noise, from over my shoulder or behind my back or within my peripheral vision, had always triggered me, had always made my heart race, but after Sandhurst it sounded like a gun cocking or a blade being notched open. And then, even a little worse, a little more traumatizing, came that blinding flash.

Great, I thought. The Army has made me more able to recognize threats, to **feel** threats, to become adrenalized in the face of those threats, and now it's casting me aside.

I was in a bad, bad place.

Paps, somehow, knew. Around this time they began hitting me with their cameras, deliberately, trying to incite me. They'd brush, smack, jostle, or just straight wallop me, hoping to get a rise, hoping I'd retaliate, because that would create a better photo, and thus more money in their pockets. A snap of me in 2007 fetched about thirty thousand pounds. Down payment on a flat. But a snap of me doing something **aggressive?** That might be a down payment on a house in the countryside.

I got into one scrap that became big news. I came away with a swollen nose, and my bodyguard was livid. **You made those paps rich, Harry! You happy?**

Happy? No, I said. No, I'm not happy.

The paps had always been grotesque people, but as I reached maturity they were worse. You could see it in their eyes, their body language. They were more emboldened, more radicalized, just as young men in Iraq had been radicalized. Their mullahs were editors, the same ones who'd vowed to do better after Mummy died. The editors promised publicly to never again send photographers chasing after people, and now, ten years later, they were back to their old ways. They justified it by no longer sending their own photographers, directly; instead they contracted with pap agencies, who sent the photographers, a distinction without a shred of difference. The editors were still inciting and handsomely rewarding thugs and losers to stalk the Royal Family, or anyone else unlucky enough to be deemed famous or newsworthy.

And no one seemed to give a shit. I remember leaving a club in London and being swarmed by twenty paps. They surrounded me, then surrounded the police car in which I was sitting, threw themselves across the bonnet, all wearing football scarves around their faces and hoods over their heads, the uniform of terrorists everywhere. It was one of the scariest moments of my life, and I knew no one cared. Price you pay, people would say, though I never understood what they meant.

Price for what?

I was particularly close to one of my bodyguards. Billy. I called him Billy the Rock, because he was so solid, so dependable. He once pounced on a grenade someone tossed at me from a crowd. Luckily, it turned out not to be a real one. I promised Billy I wouldn't push any more paps. But neither could I just stroll into their ambushes. So, when we left a club, I said, **You're going to have to stuff me into the boot of the car, Billy.**

He looked at me, wide-eyed. **Really?**

That's the only way I won't be tempted to have a go at them, and they won't be able to make any money out of me.

Win-win.

I didn't tell Billy that this was something my mother used to do.

Thus began a very strange routine between us. When leaving a pub or club in 2007, I'd have the car pull into a back alley or underground parking lot, climb into the boot and let Billy shut the lid, and I'd lie there in the dark, hands across my chest, while he and another bodyguard ferried me home. It felt like being in a coffin. I didn't care.

3.

To mark the tenth anniversary of our mother's death, Willy and I organized a concert in her honor. The proceeds would go to her favorite charities, and to a new charity I'd just launched— Sentebale. Its mission: the fight against HIV in Lesotho, particularly among children. (Sentebale is the Sesotho word for "forget-me-not," Mummy's favorite flower.)

While planning the concert Willy and I were emotionless. All business. **It's the anniversary, we need to do this, there are a million details, full stop.** The venue had to be big enough (Wembley Stadium) and the tickets had to be priced right (forty-five pounds) and the entertainers had to be A-list (Elton John, Duran Duran, P. Diddy). But on the night of the event, standing backstage, looking out at all those faces, feeling that pulsing energy, that pent-up love and longing for our mother, we crumpled.

Then Elton walked onstage. He seated himself at a grand piano and the place went mad. I'd asked him to sing "Candle in the Wind," but he said no, he didn't want to be morbid. He chose instead: "Your Song."

I hope you don't mind
That I put down in words
How wonderful life is while you're in the world

He sang it with a twinkle and a smile, aglow with good memories. Willy and I tried for that same energy, but then photos of Mummy began flashing on the screen. Each one more radiant. We went from being crumpled to being swept away.

As the song ended Elton jumped up, introduced us. **Their Royal Highnesses, Prince William and Prince Harry!** The applause was deafening, like nothing we'd ever heard. We'd been applauded in the streets, at polo games, parades, operas, but never in a place this cavernous, or in a context this charged. Willy walked out, I followed, each of us wearing a blazer and open shirt, as if going to a school dance. We were both frightfully nervous. On any topic, but especially on the topic of Mummy, we weren't accustomed to public speaking. (In fact, we weren't accustomed to **private** speaking about her.) But standing before 65,000 people, and another 500 million watching live in 140 countries, we were paralyzed.

Maybe that was the reason we didn't actually . . . say anything? I look at the video now and it's striking. Here was a moment, maybe **the** moment, for us to describe her, to dig down deep and find the words to remind the world of her sterling qualities, her once-a-millennium magic—her disappearance. But we didn't. I'm not suggesting a full-blown homage was in order, but maybe some small personal tribute?

We offered no such thing.

It was still too much, too raw.

The only thing I said that was real, that came from my heart, was a shout-out to my team. **I'd also like to take this opportunity to say hi to all the guys in A Squadron, Household Cavalry, who are serving out in Iraq at the moment! I wish I was there with you. I'm sorry I can't be! But to you and everybody else on operations at the moment, we'd both like to say: Stay safe!**

4.

DAYS LATER I WAS IN Botswana, with Chels. We went to stay with Teej and Mike. Adi was there too. The first convergence of those four special people in my life. It felt like bringing Chels home to meet Mum and Dad and big bro. Major step, we all knew.

Luckily, Teej and Mike and Adi loved her. And she saw how special they were too.

One afternoon, as we were all getting ready to go for a walk, Teej started nagging me.

Bring a hat!

Yeah, yeah.

And sunscreen! Lots of sunscreen! Spike, you're going to fry with that pale skin!

All right, all right.
Spike—
Okaaay, Mom.

It just flew out of my mouth. I heard it, and stopped. Teej heard it and stopped. But I didn't correct myself. Teej looked shocked, but also moved. I was moved as well. Thereafter, I called her Mom all the time. It felt good. For both of us. Though I made a point, always, to call her Mom, rather than Mum.

There was only one Mum.

A happy visit, overall. And yet there was a constant subtext of stress. It was evident in how much I was drinking.

At one point Chels and I took a boat, drifted up and down the river, and the main thing I remember is Southern Comfort and Sambuca. (Sambuca Gold by day, Sambuca Black by night.) I remember waking in the morning with my face stuck to a pillow, my head not feeling like it was fastened to my neck. I was having fun, sure, but also dealing in my own way with unsorted anger, and guilt about not being at war—not leading my lads. And I wasn't dealing well. Chels and Adi, Teej and Mike said nothing. Maybe they saw nothing. I was probably doing a pretty good job of covering it all up. From the outside my drinking probably looked like partying. And that was what I told myself it was. But deep down, on some level, I knew.

Something had to change. I knew I couldn't go on like this.

So the moment I got back to Britain I asked for

a meeting with my commanding officer, Colonel Ed Smyth-Osbourne.

I admired Colonel Ed. And I was fascinated by him. He wasn't put together like other men. Come to mention it, he wasn't put together like any other human I'd encountered. The basic ingredients were different. Scrap iron, steel wool, lion's blood. He **looked** different too. His face was long, like a horse's, but not equine smooth; he had a distinctive tuft of hair on each cheek. His eyes were large, calm, capable of wisdom and stoicism. My eyes, by contrast, were still bloodshot from my Okavango debauch, and darting all around as I delivered my pitch.

Colonel, I need to find a way of getting back onto operations, or else I'm going to have to quit the Army.

I'm not certain Colonel Ed believed my threat. I'm not certain I did. Still, politically, diplomatically, strategically, he couldn't afford to discount it. A prince in the ranks was a big public-relations asset, a powerful recruiting tool. He couldn't ignore the fact that, if I bolted, his superiors might blame him, and their superiors too, and up the chain it might go.

On the other hand, much of what I saw from him that day was genuine humanity. The guy got it. As a soldier, he felt for me. He shuddered at the thought of being kept from a scrap. He really did want to help.

Harry, there might be a way . . .

Iraq was permanently off the table, he said. Alas.

No two ways about that, I'm afraid. But maybe, he added, Afghanistan was an option.

I squinted. **Afghanistan?**

He muttered something about it being "the safer option."

Riiight . . . safer . . .

What on earth was he banging on about? Afghanistan was worlds more dangerous than Iraq. At that moment Britain had seven thousand soldiers in Afghanistan and each day found them engaged in some of the fiercest combat since the Second World War.

But who was I to argue? If Colonel Ed thought Afghanistan safer, and if he was willing to send me there, great.

What job would I do in Afghanistan, Colonel?

FAC. Forward air controller.

I blinked.

Highly sought-after job, he explained. FACs were tasked with orchestrating all air power, giving cover to lads on the ground, calling in raids—not to mention rescues, medevacs, the list went on. It wasn't a new job, certainly, but it was newly vital in this new sort of warfare.

Why's that, sir?

Because the bloody Taliban is everywhere! And nowhere!

You simply couldn't **find** them, he explained. Terrain was too rugged, too remote. Mountains and deserts honeycombed with tunnels and caves—it was like hunting goats. Or ghosts. You had to get the bird's-eye view.

Since the Taliban had no air force, not one plane, that was easy. We British, plus the Yanks, owned the air. But FACs helped us press that advantage. Say a squadron out on patrol needed to know about nearby threats. The FAC checked with drones, checked with fighter pilots, checked with helicopters, checked his high-tech laptop, created a 360-degree picture of the battlefield.

Say that same squadron suddenly came under fire. The FAC consulted a menu—Apache, Tornado, Mirage, F-15, F-16, A-10—and ordered up the aircraft best suited to the situation, or the best one available, then guided that aircraft onto the enemy. Using cutting-edge hardware, FACs didn't simply rain fire on the enemy's heads, they placed it there, like a crown.

Then he told me that all FACs get a chance to go up in a Hawk and experience being in the air.

By the time Colonel Ed stopped talking I was salivating. **FAC it is, sir. When do I leave?**

Not so fast.

FAC was a plum job. Everyone wanted it. So that would take some doing. Also, it was a complex job. All that technology and responsibility required loads of training.

First things first, he said. I'd have to go through a challenging certification process.

Where, sir?

At RAF Leeming.

In . . . the Yorkshire Dales?

5.

EARLY AUTUMN. DRYSTONE WALLS, patchwork fields, sheep snacking on grassy slopes. Dramatic limestone cliffs and crags and scree. In every direction, another beautiful purple moor. The landscape wasn't quite so famous as the Lake District, just over to the west, but it was still breathtaking, and still inspired some of the great artists in British history. Wordsworth, for one. I'd managed to avoid reading that old gent's stuff in school, but now I thought he must be pretty damn good if he spent time around these parts.

It felt like sacrilege to be standing on a cliff above this place and trying to obliterate it.

Of course it was pretend obliteration. I didn't actually blow up one single dale. Still, at the end of each day I felt I had. I was studying the Art of Destruction, and the first thing I learned was that destruction is partially creative. It begins with imagination. Before destroying something you have to imagine it destroyed, and I was getting very good at imagining the dales as a smoking hellscape.

The drill each day was the same. Rise at dawn. Glass of orange juice, bowl of porridge, then a full English, then head into the fields. As first daylight poured over the horizon I'd begin speaking to an aircraft, usually a Hawk. The aircraft would reach its IP, initial point, five to eight nautical miles away, and then I'd give the target, signal the run. The aircraft would turn and commence. I'd talk it through the sky, over the countryside, using different landmarks. L-shaped wood. T-shaped dike. Silver barn. In selecting landmarks I'd been instructed to start big, move on to something medium, then pick something small. Picture the world, I was told, as a hierarchy.

Hierarchy, you say? Think I can handle that.

Each time I called out a landmark, the pilot would say back: **Affirm.**

Or else: **I am visual.** I liked that.

I enjoyed the rhythms, the poetry, the meditative chant of it all. And I found deeper meanings in the exercise. I'd often think: It's the whole game, isn't it? Getting people to see the world as you see it? And say it all back to you?

Typically the pilot would be flying low, five hundred feet off the deck, level with the rising sun, but sometimes I'd send him lower and put him into a pop-up. As he streaked towards me at the speed of sound, he'd pull back, shoot upwards at a forty-five-degree angle. Then I'd begin a new series of descriptions, new details. As he reached the top of his climb and rolled his wings, as he leveled and started to feel negative g-force, he'd see the world just as I'd painted it, then swoop down.

Suddenly he'd cry out: **Tally target!** Then: **In dry!**

Then I'd say: **Clear dry.**

Meaning, his bombs were but spirits melting into air.

Then I'd wait, listening keenly for the pretend explosions.

The weeks just flew by.

6.

ONCE I WAS A TRAINED FAC, I had to become combat ready, which meant mastering twenty-eight different combat "controls."

A control was basically an interaction with an aircraft. Each control was a scenario, a little play. For instance, imagine two aircraft come into your airspace. **Good morning, this is Dude Zero One and Dude Zero Two. We're a pair of F-15s with two PGMs on board, plus one JDAM, we've got a playtime of ninety minutes and we are currently two nautical miles east of your location at Flight Level 150, waiting for talk-on . . .**

I needed to know precisely what they were saying, and how to respond to them precisely in their own jargon.

Sadly, I wouldn't be able to do this in a normal training area. The normal areas, like Salisbury Plain, were too out in the open. Someone would see me, and tip off the press, and my cover would be blown; I'd be back where I started. Instead, Colonel Ed and

I decided that I should learn the controls somewhere remote . . . somewhere like . . .

Sandringham.

We both smiled when the thought occurred. Then laughed.

The last place anyone would think of Prince Harry getting himself combat ready. Granny's country estate.

I got a room at a small hotel near Sandringham— Knights Hill. I'd known the place all my life, driven past it a million times. Whenever we visited Granny at Christmas, our bodyguards would sleep there. Standard room: hundred quid.

In summers, Knights Hill tended to be full of bird-watchers, wedding parties. But now, in the autumn, it was empty.

The privacy was thrilling, and would've been total, if not for the older lady in the pub connected to the hotel. She watched me, goggle-eyed, every time I passed.

Alone, **almost** anonymous, my existence narrowed to one interesting task, I was delirious. I tried not to say so to Chelsy when I phoned her in the evenings, but it was the kind of happiness that's hard to hide.

I recall one difficult chat. What were we doing? Where were we heading?

She knew I cared about her. But she felt unseen. **I am not visual.**

She knew how desperate I was to go to war. How could she not forgive my being a bit detached? I was taken aback.

I explained that this was what I needed to do, the thing I'd wanted to do all my life, and I needed to do it with all my heart and soul. If that meant there was less heart and soul left over for anything or anyone else, well . . . I was sorry.

7.

PA KNEW I WAS living at Knights Hill, knew what I was up to. And he was just down the road at Sandringham on an extended visit. And yet he never dropped in. Giving me space, I guess.

Also, he was still very much in his newlywed phase, even though the wedding was more than two years prior.

Then one day he looked up in the sky and saw a Typhoon aircraft doing low passes along the seawall and he figured it must be me. So he got into his Audi and hurried over.

He found me in the marshes, on a quad bike, talking to a Typhoon some miles off. While I waited for the Typhoon to appear in the sky overhead we had a quick chat. He said he could see how good I was getting at this new job. Above all, he could see how hard I was working at it, and that delighted him.

Pa had always been a worker. He believed in work. Everyone must **work,** he often said. But his own work was also a kind of religion, because he was furiously trying to save the planet. He'd been fighting for decades to alert people to climate change, never flagging, despite being cruelly mocked by the press as a Henny Penny. Countless times, late at night, Willy and I would find him at his desk amid mountains of bulging blue postbags—his correspondence. More than once we discovered him, face on the desk, fast asleep. We'd shake his shoulders and up he'd bob, a piece of paper stuck to his forehead.

But along with the importance of work, he also believed in the magic of flight. He was a helicopter pilot, after all, so he particularly loved seeing me steer these jets over the marshy flats at ungodly speeds. I mentioned that the good citizens of Wolferton didn't share his enthusiasm. A ten-thousand-kilo jet roaring just over their tiled roofs didn't exactly cause jubilation. RAF Marham had received dozens of complaints. Sandringham was supposed to be a no-fly zone.

All complainants were told: Such is war.

I loved seeing Pa, loved feeling his pride, and I felt buoyed by his praise, but I had to get back to work. I was mid-control, couldn't tell the Typhoon to please hold on a moment.

Yes, yes, darling boy, back to work.

He drove off. As he went down the track I told the Typhoon: **New target. Gray Audi. Headed southeast from my position down track. Towards a big silver barn oriented east-west.**

The Typhoon tracked Pa, did a low pass straight over him, almost shattering the windows of his Audi.

But ultimately spared him. On my orders.

It went on to blow a silver barn to smithereens.

8.

ENGLAND WAS IN THE semifinal of the 2007 Rugby World Cup. No one had predicted that. No one had believed England was any good this time round, and now they were on the verge of winning it all. Millions of Britons were swept away with rugby fever, including me.

So when I was invited to attend the semifinal, that October, I didn't hesitate. I said yes immediately.

Bonus: The semifinal was being held that year in Paris—a city I'd never visited.

The World Cup provided me with a driver, and on my first night in the City of Light I asked him if he knew the tunnel where my mother . . .

I watched his eyes in the rearview, growing large.

He was Irish, with a kindly, open face, and I could easily discern his thoughts: **What the feck? I didn't sign on for this.**

The tunnel is called Pont de l'Alma, I told him.

Yes, yes. He knew it.

I want to go through it.

You want to go through the tunnel?

At sixty-five miles per hour—to be precise.

Sixty-five?

Yes.

The exact speed Mummy's car had supposedly been driving, according to police, at the time of the crash. Not 120 miles per hour, as the press originally reported.

The driver looked over at the passenger seat. Billy the Rock nodded gravely. **Let's do it.** Billy added that if the driver ever revealed to another human that we'd asked him to do this, we'd find him and there would be hell to pay.

The driver gave a solemn nod.

Off we went, weaving through traffic, cruising past the Ritz, where Mummy had her last meal, with her boyfriend, that August night. Then we came to the mouth of the tunnel. We zipped ahead, went over the lip at the tunnel's entrance, the bump that supposedly sent Mummy's Mercedes veering off course.

But the lip was nothing. We barely felt it.

As the car entered the tunnel I leaned forward, watched the light change to a kind of watery orange, watched the concrete pillars flicker past. I counted them, counted my heartbeats, and in a few seconds we emerged from the other side.

I sat back. Quietly I said: **Is that all of it? It's . . . nothing. Just a straight tunnel.**

I'd always imagined the tunnel as some treacherous passageway, inherently dangerous, but it was just a short, simple, no-frills tunnel.

No reason anyone should ever die inside it.

The driver and Billy the Rock didn't answer.

I looked out of the window: **Again.**

The driver stared at me in the rearview. **Again?**

Yes. Please.

We went through again.

That's enough. Thank you.

It had been a very bad idea. I'd had plenty of bad

ideas in my twenty-three years, but this one was uniquely ill-conceived. I'd told myself that I wanted closure, but I didn't really. Deep down, I'd hoped to feel in that tunnel what I'd felt when JLP gave me the police files—disbelief. Doubt. Instead, that was the night all doubt fell away.

She's dead, I thought. **My God, she's really gone for good.**

I got the closure I was pretending to seek. I got it in spades. And now I'd never be able to get rid of it.

I'd thought driving the tunnel would bring an end, or brief cessation, to the pain, the decade of unrelenting pain. Instead it brought on the start of Pain, Part Deux.

It was close to one o'clock in the morning. The driver dropped me and Billy at a bar, where I drank and drank. Some mates were there, and I drank with them, and tried to pick fights with several. When the pub threw us out, when Billy the Rock escorted me back to the hotel, I tried to pick a fight with him too. I growled at him, swung on him, slapped his head.

He barely reacted. He just frowned like an ultra-patient parent.

I slapped him again. I loved him, but I was determined to hurt him.

He'd seen me like this before. Once, maybe twice. I heard him say to another bodyguard: **He's a handful tonight.**

Oh, you want to see a handful? Here you go, here's a handful.

Somehow Billy and the other bodyguard got me

up to my room, poured me onto my bed. But after they left I popped right up again.

I looked around the room. The sun was just coming up. I stepped outside, into the hall. There was a bodyguard on a chair beside the door, but he was sound asleep. I tiptoed past, got into the lift, left the hotel.

Of all the rules in my life, this was considered the most inviolate. Never leave your bodyguards. Never wander off by yourself, anywhere, but especially not in a foreign city.

I walked along the Seine. I squinted at the Champs-Élysées in the distance. I stood next to some big Ferris wheel. I went past little book stalls, past people drinking coffee, eating croissants. I was smoking, keeping my gaze unfocused. I have a dim recollection of a few people recognizing me, and staring, but thankfully this was before the age of smartphones. No one stopped me to take a photo.

Later, after I'd had a sleep, I rang Willy, told him about my night.

None of it came as news to him. Turned out, he'd driven the tunnel too.

He was coming to Paris for the rugby final. We decided to do it together.

Afterwards, we talked about the crash, for the first time ever. We talked about the recent inquest. A joke, we both agreed. The final written report was an insult. Fanciful, riddled with basic factual errors and gaping logical holes. It raised more questions than it answered.

After all these years, we said, and all that money—how?

Above all, the summary conclusion, that Mummy's driver was drunk and thereby the sole cause of the crash, was convenient and absurd. Even if the man had been drinking, even if he was shit-faced, he wouldn't have had any trouble navigating that short tunnel.

Unless paps had chased and blinded him.

Why were those paps not more roundly blamed?

Why were they not in jail?

Who sent them? And why were **they** not in jail?

Why indeed—unless corruption and cover-ups were the order of the day?

We were united on all these points, and also on next steps. We'd issue a statement, jointly call for the inquiry to be reopened. Maybe hold a press conference.

We were talked out of it by the powers that be.

9.

ONE MONTH LATER I WENT to RAF Brize Norton and boarded a C-17. There were dozens of other soldiers on the plane, but I was the only stowaway. With help from Colonel Ed and JLP, I boarded in secret, then crept into an alcove behind the cockpit.

The alcove had bunkbeds for the crew on overnight flights. As the big engines fired, as the plane roared down the runway, I lay down on a bottom bunk, my small rucksack as a pillow. Somewhere below, in the cargo hold, my Bergen was neatly packed with three pairs of camo trousers, three clean T-shirts, one pair of goggles, one air bed, one small notebook, one tube of sun cream. It felt like more than enough. I could honestly say that nothing I needed or wanted in life had been left behind, other than a few pieces of Mummy's jewelry, and the lock of her hair in the little blue box, and the silver-framed photo of her that used to sit on my desk at Eton, all of which I'd stashed in a safe place. And, of course, my weapons. My 9-mm and SA80A had been surrendered to a stern-faced clerk, who'd locked them in a steel box that also went into the hold. I felt their absence most acutely, since, for the first time in my life, other than that wobbly morning stroll in Paris, I was about to venture forth into the wide world without armed bodyguards.

The flight was eternal. Seven hours? Nine? I can't say. It felt like a week. I tried to sleep, but my head was too full. I spent most of the time staring. At the upper bunk. At my feet. I listened to the engines, listened to the other soldiers on board. I replayed my life. I thought about Pa and Willy. And Chels.

The papers reported that we'd broken up. (One headline: HOORAY HARRY'S DUMPED.) The distance, the different life goals were too much. It was hard enough maintaining a relationship in the same country, but with me going off to war, it just didn't seem feasible. Of course, none of this was true. We'd not broken up. She'd given me a touching, tender farewell, and promised to wait for me.

She knew, therefore, to disregard all the other stories in the papers, about how I'd reacted to the breakup. Reportedly, I'd gone on a pub crawl and guzzled a few dozen vodkas before staggering into a waiting car. One paper actually asked the mother of a soldier recently killed in action how she felt about my being publicly intoxicated.

(She was against it.)

If I die in Afghanistan, I thought, at least I'll never have to see another fake headline, read another shameful lie about myself.

I thought a lot on that flight about dying. What would it mean? Did I care? I tried to picture my funeral. Would it be a state funeral? Private? I tried to imagine the headlines: **Bye, Harry.**

How would I be remembered by history? For the headlines? Or for who I actually was?

Would Willy walk behind my coffin? Would Grandpa and Pa?

Before I'd shipped out, JLP sat me down, told me I needed to update my will.

My will? Really?

If anything happened, he said, the Palace needed to know what I wanted to be done with my few belongings, and where I wished to be . . . buried. He asked so plainly, so calmly, as you'd ask somebody where they'd like to have lunch. But that was his gift. The truth was the truth, no sense leaning away from it.

I looked away. I couldn't really think of a spot where I wanted to spend the hereafter. I couldn't think of any spot that felt sacred, besides Althorp, maybe, and that was out of the question. So I said: Frogmore Gardens?

It was beautiful, and slightly removed from things. Peaceful.

JLP gave a nod. He'd see to it.

Amid these thoughts and recollections I managed to doze off for a few minutes, and when I opened my eyes we were swooping down to Kandahar Airfield.

Time to put on the body armor. Time to put on the Kevlar.

I waited for everyone else to disembark, then some Special Forces guys appeared in the alcove. They returned my weapons and handed me a vial of morphine, to keep on my person at all times. We were now in a place where pain, injuries, trauma were commonplace. They hurried me off the plane into a four-by-four with blacked windows and dusty seats. We drove to a different part of the base, then hurried into a Portakabin.

Empty. Not a soul.

Where is everybody? Bloody hell, was peace declared while I was in the air?

No, the whole base was out on a mission.

I looked around. Apparently they'd left in the middle of a meal. Tables were covered with half-empty pizza boxes. I tried to remember what I'd eaten on the flight. Nothing. I began shoving cold pizza into my mouth.

I took my in theater test, one last barrier to entry, one last measure to prove that I knew how to do the job. Shortly after, I climbed into a Chinook and flew about fifty miles to a much smaller outpost. Forward Operating Base Dwyer. Long, unwieldy name for what was little more than a sandcastle made of sandbags.

I was met by a sand-covered soldier who said he'd been ordered to show me around.

Welcome to Dwyer.

Thanks.

I asked how the place got its name.

One of our lads. K-I-A. Vehicle hit a land mine.

The quick tour revealed Dwyer to be even more spartan than it looked from the Chinook. No heat, few lights, not much water. There was plumbing, of a sort, but the pipes were usually clogged or frozen. There was also a building that purported to be a "shower block," but I was advised: use at your peril.

Basically, my tour guide told me, just give up being clean. Focus instead on staying warm.

It gets that cold here?

He chortled.

Dwyer was home to about fifty soldiers, mostly artillery and Household Cavalry. I met them in twos and threes. They were all sandy-haired, by which I mean their hair was matted with sand. Their faces and necks and eyelashes—also encrusted. They looked like fillets of fish that'd been breadcrumbed before frying.

Within one hour, I did too.

Everyone and everything at Dwyer was either caked with sand or sprinkled with sand or painted the color of sand. And out beyond the sand-colored tents and sandbags and sand walls was an infinite ocean of . . . sand. Fine, fine sand, like talcum powder. The lads spent much of their day gazing at all that sand. So, after completing my tour, getting my cot and some chow, I did too.

We told ourselves we were scanning for the enemy, and we were, I suppose. But you couldn't stare at that many grains of sand without also thinking about eternity. All that shifting, swirling, whirling sand, you felt it saying something to you about your minuscule niche in the cosmos. Ashes to ashes. Sand to sand. Even when I retired, settled onto my metal cot, drifted off to sleep, sand was uppermost on my mind. I heard it out there, having whispery conversations with itself. I felt a grain on my tongue. On my eyeball. I dreamed of it.

And when I woke, there was a spoonful of it in my mouth.

10.

AT THE CENTER OF DWYER was a towering spike, a kind of makeshift Nelson's Column. Nailed to it were dozens of arrows, pointing every which way, each arrow painted with the name of a place some soldier at Dwyer called home.

Sydney Australia 7223 miles
Glasgow 3654 miles
Bridgwater Somerset 3610 miles

That first morning, walking past the spike, I had a thought. Maybe I should write my own home up there.

Clarence House 3456 miles

That'd get a laugh.

But no. Just as none of us was eager to draw the Taliban's attention, I was eager not to draw the attention of my fellow squaddies. My main goal was to blend in.

One of the arrows pointed towards "The Cannons," two enormous 105-mm guns at the back of the non-working shower block. Nearly every day, several times a day, Dwyer fired off those big guns, lobbed massive shells in a smoky parabola towards Taliban positions. The noise made your blood stop, fried your brains. (One day the guns were fired at least a hundred times.) For the rest of my life, I knew, I'd be hearing some vestige of that sound; it would echo forever in some part of my being. I would also never forget, when the guns finally stopped, that immense silence.

11.

DWYER'S OPS ROOM was a box wrapped in desert camo. The floor was thick black plastic made of interlinked pieces, like a jigsaw puzzle. It made a weird noise when you walked across it. The focal point of the room, indeed the whole camp, was the main wall, which featured a giant map of Helmand Province, with pins (yellow, orange, green, blue) representing units of the battle group.

I was greeted by Corporal of Horse Baxter. Older than me, but my coloring. We exchanged a few wry cracks, a rueful smile about involuntary membership in the League of Redheaded Gentlemen. Also, the Balding Brotherhood. Like me, Baxter was fast losing coverage on top.

I asked where he was from.

County Antrim.

Irish, eh?

Sure.

His lilting accent made me think he could be kidded. I gave him a hard time about the Irish, and he returned fire, laughing, but his blue eyes looked unsure. **Crikey, I'm taking the piss out of a prince.**

We got down to work. He showed me several radios stacked along a desk under the map. He showed me the Rover terminal, a pudgy little laptop with compass points stenciled along the sides. **These radios are your ears. This Rover is your eyes.** Through them I'd make a picture of the battlefield, then try to control what happened in and above it. In one sense I'd be no different from the air-traffic controllers at Heathrow: I'd spend my time guiding jets to and fro. But often the job wouldn't even be that glamorous: I'd be a security guard, blearily monitoring feeds from dozens of cameras, mounted on everything from recon aircraft to drones. The only fighting I'd be doing would be against the urge to sleep.

Jump in. Have a seat, Lieutenant Wales.

I cleared my throat, sat down. I watched the Rover. And watched.

Minutes passed. I turned up the volume on the radios. Turned it down.

Baxter chuckled. **That's the job. Welcome to the war.**

12.

THE ROVER HAD AN ALTERNATIVE NAME, because everything in the Army needed an alternative name.

Kill TV.

As in:

Whatcha doing?

Just watching a bit of Kill TV.

The name was meant to be ironic, I figured. Or else it was just blatantly fake advertising. Because the only thing getting killed was time.

You watched an abandoned compound thought to have been used by the Taliban.

Nothing happened.

You watched a tunnel system suspected to have been used by the Taliban.

Nothing happened.

You watched a sand dune. And another sand dune.

If there's anything duller than watching paint dry, it's watching desert . . . **desert**. I wondered how Baxter hadn't gone mad.

So I asked him.

He said that after hours of nothing, there'd be something. The trick was staying alert for **that**.

If Kill TV was dull, Kill Radio was mad. All the

handsets along the desk gave off a constant babble, in a dozen accents, British, American, Dutch, French, to say nothing of the various personalities.

I began trying to match the accents with the call signs. American pilots were Dude. Dutch pilots were Rammit. French were Mirage, or Rage. Brits were Vapor.

Apache helicopters were called Ugly.

My personal call sign was Widow Six Seven.

Baxter told me to grab a handset, say hello. **Introduce yourself.** When I did, the voices all perked up, turned their attention to me. They were like baby birds demanding to be fed. Their food was information.

Who are you? What's happening down there? Where am I going?

Besides information, the thing they wanted most often was permission. To enter my air space or to leave it. Rules forbade pilots to pass overhead without assurance that it was safe, that a battle wasn't raging, that Dwyer wasn't blasting away its heavy guns. In other words, was it a hot ROZ (restricted operating zone)? Or cold? Everything about the war revolved around this binary question. Hostilities, weather, water, food—hot or cold?

I liked this role, keeper of the ROZ. I liked the idea of working closely with top guns, being the eyes and ears for such highly skilled men and women, their last link to terra firma, their alpha and omega. I was . . . Earth.

Their need for me, their dependency, created instant bonds. Strange emotions flowed, weird intimacies took shape.

Hey there, Widow Six Seven.

Hey, Dude.

How's your day?

Quiet so far, Dude.

We were mates instantly. Comrades. You could feel it.

After they checked in with me, I'd hand them over to the FAC in Garmsir, a little river town nearby.

Thanks, Widow Six Seven. Goodnight.

Roger, Dude. Stay safe.

13.

AFTER RECEIVING PERMISSION to cross my airspace, a pilot wouldn't always cruise on through, he'd arrow through, and sometimes his need to know conditions on the ground would be urgent. Every second mattered. Life and death were in my hands. I was calmly seated at a desk, holding a fizzy drink and a biro (**Oh. A biro. Wow.**) but I was also in the middle of the action. It was exhilarating, the thing I'd trained for, but terrifying. Shortly before my arrival an FAC got one number wrong when reading out the geo coordinates to an American F-15; the result was an errant bomb landing on British forces instead of the enemy. Three soldiers killed, two horribly maimed. So every word and digit I spoke would have consequences.

We were "providing support," that was the phrase used constantly, but I realized how euphemistic it was. No less than the pilots, we were sometimes delivering death, and when it came to death, more so than life, you had to be precise.

I confess: I was happy. This was important work, patriotic work. I was using skills honed in the Dales, and at Sandringham, and all the way back to boyhood. Even to Balmoral. There was a bright line connecting my stalking with Sandy and my work here now. I was a British soldier, on a battlefield, at last, a role for which I'd been preparing all my life.

I was also Widow Six Seven. I'd had plenty of nicknames in my life, but this was the first nickname that felt more like an alias. I could really and truly **hide** behind it. For the first time I was **just** a name, a random name, and a random number. No title. And no bodyguard. **Is this what other people feel like every day?** I savored the normality, wallowed in it, and also considered how far I'd journeyed to find it. Central Afghanistan, the dead of winter, the middle of the night, the midst of a war, while speaking to a man fifteen thousand feet above my head—how abnormal is your life if that's the first place you ever feel normal?

After every action there would be a lull, which was sometimes harder to deal with psychologically. Boredom was the enemy and we fought it by playing rugby, our ball a heavily taped-up roll of loo paper, or by jogging on the spot. We also did a thousand press-ups, and built primitive weightlifting equipment, taping wooden crates to metal bars. We made punch bags out of duffels. We read books, organized marathon chess matches, slept like cats. I watched grown men log twelve hours a day in bed.

We also ate and ate. Dwyer had a full kitchen. Pasta. Chips. Beans. We were given thirty minutes each week on the sat phone. The phone card was called Paradigm, and it had a code on the back, which you punched into the keypad. Then a robot, a nice-sounding woman, told you how many minutes you had left. Next thing you knew . . .

Spike, that you?

Chels.

Your old life, down the line. The sound always made you catch your breath. To think of home was never easy, for a complex set of reasons. To **hear** home was a stab in the chest.

If I didn't call Chels, I called Pa.

How are you, darling boy?

Not bad. You know.

But he asked me to write rather than call. He loved my letters.

He said he'd much prefer a letter.

14.

AT TIMES I WORRIED that I was actually missing out on the real war. Was I perhaps sitting in the war's waiting room? The real war, I feared, was just down the valley; I could see the thick puffs of smoke, the plumes from explosions, mostly in and around Garmsir. A place of tremendous strategic importance. Critical gateway, river port through which supplies, especially guns, flowed to the Taliban. Plus, an entry point for new fighters. They'd be issued an AK-47, a fistful of bullets, and told to head towards us through their maze of trenches. This was their initiation test, which the Taliban called their "blooding."

Were Sandy and Tiggy working for the Taliban?

It happened often. A Taliban recruit would pop up, fire at us, and we'd return fire with twenty times the force. Any Taliban recruit who survived that barrage would then be promoted, sent to fight and die in one of the bigger cities, like Gereshk, or Lashkar Gah, which some called Lash Vegas. Most, however, didn't survive. The Taliban left their bodies to rot. I watched dogs the size of wolves chew many a recruit off the battlefield.

I began pleading with my commanding officers: Get me out of here. A few guys made the same plea, but for different reasons. I was begging to go closer to the front. **Send me to Garmsir.**

Finally, on Christmas Eve 2007, my request was approved. I was to replace an outgoing FAC at Forward Operating Base Delhi, which was inside an abandoned Garmsir school.

Small gravel courtyard, corrugated tin roof. Someone said the school had been an agricultural university. Someone else said it had been a madrassa. For the moment, however, it was a part of the British Commonwealth. And my new home.

It was also home to a company of Gurkhas.

Recruited from Nepal, from the remotest villages along the foothills of the Himalayas, the Gurkhas had fought in every British war of the last two centuries, and distinguished themselves in each one. They scrapped like tigers, never gave up, and as a result they held a special place in the British Army—and in my heart. I'd been hearing about the Gurkhas since I was a boy: one of the first uniforms I'd ever worn was a Gurkha uniform. At Sandhurst the Gurkhas always played the enemy in military exercises, which always felt a bit ridiculous because they were beloved.

After the exercises a Gurkha would invariably walk up to me and offer me a cup of hot chocolate. They had a solemn reverence for royalty. A king, to their minds, was divine. (Their own king was believed to be the reincarnated Hindu god Vishnu.) A prince, therefore, wasn't far off. I'd felt this growing up, but now felt it again. As I walked through Delhi, the Gurkhas all bowed. They called me **saab**.

Yes, saab. No, saab.

I pleaded: Don't. I'm just Lieutenant Wales. I'm just Widow Six Seven.

They laughed. **No chance, saab.**

Neither would they have dreamed of allowing me to go anywhere by myself. Royal persons required royal escort. Often I'd be headed to the mess, or the loo, and suddenly become aware of a shadow on my right. Then another on my left. **Hello, saab.** It was embarrassing, albeit touching. I adored them, as did the local Afghans, who sold the Gurkhas many chickens and goats and even bantered with them about recipes. The Army talked a lot about winning Afghan "hearts and minds," meaning converting locals to democracy and freedom, but only the Gurkhas seemed to be actually doing it.

When they weren't escorting me, the Gurkhas were intent on fattening me up. Food was their love language. And while each Gurkha thought himself a five-star chef, they all had the same speciality. Goat curry.

I remember one day hearing rotors overhead. I looked up. Everyone on the base looked up. A chopper slowly descending. And hanging from the skids, wrapped in a net, was a goat. Christmas present for the Gurkhas.

In a great burst of dust the helicopter touched down. Out jumped a man, bald, blondish, the picture of a British officer.

He was also vaguely familiar.

I know this bloke, I said aloud.

I snapped my fingers. **It's good old Bevan!**

He'd worked for Pa for a few years. He'd even chaperoned us one winter in Klosters. (I recalled him skiing in a Barbour jacket, so quintessentially aristocratic.) Now, apparently, he was the brigade commander's number two. And thus, delivering goats on behalf of the commander to the beloved Gurkhas.

I was floored to bump into him, but he was only

mildly surprised—or interested. He was too preoccu-
pied with those goats. Besides the one in the net, he'd
cradled one between his knees on the whole flight,
and he now guided this little fellow on a lead, like a
cocker spaniel, over to a Gurkha.

Poor Bevan. I could see how he'd bonded with that
goat, how unprepared he was for what was coming.

The Gurkha took out his kukri and lopped off
its head.

The tan, bearded face dropped to the ground like
one of the taped-up loo rolls we used for rugby balls.

The Gurkha then neatly, expertly collected the
blood in a cup. Nothing was to be wasted.

As for the second goat, the Gurkha handed me
the kukri, asked if I'd like to do the honors.

Back home I had several kukris. They'd been gifts
from Gurkhas. I knew how to handle one. But no, I
said, no, thank you, not here, not just now.

I wasn't sure why I said no. Maybe because there
was enough killing all around me without adding
more. I flashed back to telling George that I absolutely didn't want to snip off any balls. Where did I
draw the line?

At suffering, that's where. I didn't want to go all
Henry VIII on that goat mainly because I wasn't
skilled in the art, and if I missed or miscalculated the
poor thing would suffer.

The Gurkha nodded. **As you wish, saab.**

He swung the kukri.

Even after the goat's head hit the ground, I remember, its yellow eyes kept blinking.

15.

MY JOB AT DELHI WAS similar to the one I'd had at Dwyer. Only the hours were different. Constant. At Delhi I was on call, day and night.

The ops room was a former classroom. Like seemingly everything else in Afghanistan, the school that housed Delhi had been bombed—dangling wood beams, tipped-over desks, floors scattered with spilled papers and books—but the ops room looked as if it had been ground zero. A disaster area. On the plus side, during night shifts, the many holes in the walls gave a stunning view of the stars.

I recall one shift, around one A.M. I asked a pilot overhead for his code, so I could key it into my Rover and see his feed.

The pilot answered sourly that I was doing it wrong.

Doing what wrong?

It's not the Rover, it's the Longhorn.

The Long what?

You're new, huh?

He described the Longhorn, a machine no one had bothered to tell me about. I looked around, found it. Big black briefcase covered with dust. I brushed it off, turned it on. The pilot talked me through getting it operational. I didn't know why the Longhorn was required for him instead of the Rover, but I wasn't about to ask and irritate him even more.

Especially since the experience had been bonding. Thereafter he and I were mates.

His call sign was Magic.

I'd often pass an entire night chatting to Magic. He and his crew liked to talk, to laugh, eat. (I dimly recall them feasting one night on fresh crabs.) Above all they loved practical jokes. After one sortie, Magic zoomed out his camera, told me to look. I leaned into my screen. From twenty thousand feet his view of the curvature of Earth was astonishing.

Slowly, he turned his camera.

My screen filled with breasts.

Porn magazine.

Ah, you got me, Magic.

Some pilots were women. Exchanges with them went very differently. One night I found myself speaking to a British pilot who mentioned how gorgeous the moon was.

It's full, she said. **You should see it, Widow Six Seven.**

I see it. Through one of the holes in my wall. Lovely.

Suddenly the radio burst to life: a shrill chorus. The guys back at Dwyer told us to "get a room." I felt myself blushing. I hoped the pilot hadn't thought I was flirting. I hoped she wouldn't think so now. Above all, I hoped she, and all other pilots, wouldn't work out who I was, and tell the British press that I was using the war as a way to meet women. I hoped the press wouldn't then treat her as they'd treated every other girl I'd ever had anything to do with.

Before that shift ended, however, the pilot and I

overcame this brief awkwardness and did some solid work together. She helped me monitor a Taliban bunker, right in the heart of no-man's-land, not far beyond Delhi's walls. There were thermals around the bunker . . . human forms. A dozen, I guessed. Maybe fifteen.

Taliban, for sure, we said. Who else would be moving in those trenches?

I went through the Checklist to make sure. Pattern of life, the Army called it. Can you see women? Can you see children? Can you see dogs? Cats? Is there anything to indicate that this target might be next door to a hospital? A school?

Any civvies (civilians) whatsoever?

No. All no.

It added up to Taliban, and nothing but Taliban.

I planned a strike for the next day. I was assigned to work it out with two American pilots, Dude Zero One and Dude Zero Two. I briefed them on the target, told them I wanted a 2,000-pound JDAM (Joint Direct Attack Munition). I wondered why we used that clunky name. Why not just call it a bomb? Maybe because this was no ordinary bomb; it had radar-controlled guidance systems. And it was heavy. It weighed as much as a black rhino.

Typically, with a smattering of Taliban fighters, the standard request would be a 500-pounder. But I didn't think that would be enough force to penetrate the fortified bunkers I was seeing on my screen.

Granted, FACs never thought 500 pounds was enough. We always wanted 2,000-pounders. Go big or go home, we always said. But in this case I felt strongly that only big would do the job. The bunker system would withstand anything less. Not only did I want a 2,000-pound JDAM on top of the bunker, I wanted the second aircraft to follow up with a 20-mm, strafe the trenches running from the bunker, pick off guys as they "ex-filled."

Negative, said Dude Zero One.

The Americans saw no need for a 2,000-pound bomb.

We prefer to drop two 500-pound bombs, Widow Six Seven.

How very un-American.

I felt strongly that I was right, and I wanted to argue, but I was new and lacked self-confidence. This was my first airstrike. So I just said:

Roger that.

New Year's Eve. I held the F-15s at bay, about eight kilometers, so the noise of their engines wouldn't spook the targets. When conditions looked to be just right, all calm, I summoned them.

Widow Six Seven, we're in hot.

Dude Zero One, Dude Zero Two, you're cleared hot.

Cleared hot.

They went streaking towards the target.

On my screen I watched the pilot's crosshair settle over the bunker.

One second.

Two.

White flash. Loud bang. The wall of the ops room

shuddered. Dust and pieces of stone rained down from the ceiling.

I heard Dude Zero One's voice: **Delta Hotel** (direct hit). Stand by for BDA (battle damage assessment).

Plumes of smoke rose from the desert.

Moments later . . . just as I'd feared, Taliban came running out of the trench. I groaned at my Rover, then stomped outside.

The air was cold, the sky pulsing blue. I could hear Dude Zero One and Dude Zero Two way above, tailing off. I could hear the echo of their bombs. Then all was silent.

Not all of them got away, I consoled myself. Ten, at least, didn't make it out of that trench.

Still—a bigger bomb would've really done the trick.

Next time, I told myself. Next time, I'll trust my gut.

16.

I GOT PROMOTED, SORT OF. To a small lookout high above the battlefield. For quite some time the lookout had been driving the Taliban mad. We had it, they wanted it, and if they couldn't get it then they were bound to destroy it. They'd attacked the lookout scores of times in the months before I got there.

Hours after my arrival at the lookout, here they came again.

AK-47s rattling, bullets whizzing by. It sounded like someone throwing beehives through our window.

There were four Gurkhas with me, and they unleashed a Javelin missile in the direction of the incoming fire.

Then they told me to take a seat behind the 50-cal. **Jump on, saab!**

I climbed into the gun nest, grabbed the big handles. I shoved in my earplugs, took aim through the mesh hanging from the window. I squeezed the trigger. The feeling was like a train through the middle of my chest. The sound was locomotive-like as well. **Chugga chugga chugga.** The gun spat bullets across the desert, and shell casings flew around the lookout like popcorn. It was the first time I'd ever fired a 50-cal. I simply couldn't believe the power.

In my direct line of sight was abandoned farmland, ditches, trees. I lit it all up. There was an old building with two domes that looked like a frog's eyes. I peppered those domes.

Meanwhile, Dwyer began lobbing its big guns.

All was mayhem.

I don't remember much after that, but I don't need to—there's video. The press was there, by my side, filming. I hated them being there, but I'd been ordered to take them on an outing. In return they'd agreed to sit on any images or information they gathered until I was out of the country.

How many did we kill? the press wanted to know.

We couldn't be sure.

Indeterminate, we said.

I thought I'd be in that lookout for a long time. But soon after that day I was summoned up north to FOB Edinburgh. I boarded a Chinook full of mailbags, lay down among them to hide. Forty minutes later I was hopping off, into knee-deep mud. **When the hell did it rain?** I was shown to my quarters in a sandbag house. A tiny bed.

And a roommate. Estonian signals officer.

We hit it off. He gave me one of his badges as a welcome gift.

Five miles away was Musa Qala, a town that had once been a Taliban fortress. In 2006 we'd seized it, after some of the worst fighting British soldiers had seen in half a century. More than a thousand Taliban had been subdued. After paying such a price, however, the town was quickly, carelessly, lost again. Now we'd won it a second time, and we aimed to keep it.

And a nasty job it was. One of our lads had just been blown up by an IED.

Plus, we were despised in and around the town. Locals who'd cooperated with us had been tortured, their heads put on spikes along the town walls.

There would be no winning of either hearts or minds.

17.

I WENT ON PATROL. I drove with a convoy of Scimitar tanks from FOB Edinburgh through Musa Qala, and beyond. The road took us down through a wadi, in which we soon came upon an IED.

The first one I'd encountered.

It was my job to call in the bomb experts. One hour

later the Chinook arrived. I found it a secure location for landing, threw a smoke grenade to indicate the best spot, and to show which way the wind was blowing.

A team quickly hopped out, approached the IED. Slow, painstaking work. It took them forever. Meanwhile, we were all totally exposed. We expected Taliban contact any second; around us we heard whizzing motorbikes. Taliban scouts, no doubt. Clocking our location. When the motorbikes got too close, we fired flare guns, warning them off.

In the distance were poppy fields. I looked off, thought of the famous poem. **In Flanders fields the poppies blow . . .** In Britain the poppy was a symbol of remembrance, but here it was just the coin of the realm. All those poppies would soon be processed into heroin, sales of which would pay for the Taliban bullets fired at us, and the IEDs left for us under roads and wadis.

Like this one.

At last the bomb experts blew up the IED. A mushroom cloud shot into the air, which was so dust-saturated you didn't think there could be room for any more.

Then they packed up and left, and we continued north, deeper and deeper into the desert.

18.

WE MADE A SQUARE of our vehicles, which we called a harbor. The next day, and the day after, and so on, we ventured out to do patrols around the town.

Show of presence, we were told.

Keep moving, we were told.

Keep the Taliban wondering, we were told. Keep 'em off balance.

Overall, however, the base mission was to support an ongoing American offensive. There was a constant roar of American jets overhead, and explosions in a nearby village. We worked in very close concert with the Americans, engaging the Taliban in frequent firefights.

A day or two after we'd established our harbor, we were sitting on high ground, watching shepherds in the distance. All we could see for miles around were these men and their sheep. The scene looked innocent enough. But the shepherds were getting too close to the Americans, making them nervous. The Americans fired several warning shots. Inevitably, they hit one of the shepherds. He'd been riding a motorbike. We couldn't tell from our distance if it had been an accident or deliberate. We watched the sheep scatter, then saw the Americans swoop in and pick up the shepherds.

When they'd gone I went out into the field, with a few Fijian soldiers, and picked up the motorbike. I wiped it down, put it aside. Took care of it. After the Americans had questioned the shepherd, bandaged and released him, he came to us.

He was shocked that we'd retrieved his motorbike.

He was more shocked that we'd cleaned it.

And he nearly passed out when we gave it back.

19.

THE NEXT DAY, OR PERHAPS the day after, our convoy was joined by three journalists. I was ordered to take them into the battlefield, give them a tour—with an explicit understanding that the news embargo was still in effect.

I was in a Spartan, up front of the convoy, the journalists stowed inside. They kept popping up, nagging me. They wanted to get out, take some photos, get some film. But it wasn't safe. The Americans were still clearing the area.

I was standing in the turret when one journalist tapped my leg, asked yet again for permission to get out.

I sighed: **OK. But be careful of mines. And stay close.**

They all piled out of the Spartan, started setting up their camera.

Moments later, the guys ahead of us came under attack. Rounds went sizzling over our heads.

The journalists froze, looked at me, helpless.

Don't just stand there! Get back in!

I didn't want them there in the first place, but I especially didn't want anything happening to them on my watch. I didn't want any journalist's life on my ledger. I couldn't handle the irony.

Was it hours later, or days, that we learned the Americans had dropped a Hellfire missile on the nearest village? There were many injured. A boy was brought out of the village, up the ridge, in a wheelbarrow, his legs hanging over the side. They were ripped to pieces.

Two men were pushing the barrow, straight towards us. I couldn't tell who they were to the boy. Family? Friends? When they reached us, they weren't able to explain. None spoke English. But the boy was in a shit state, that was clear, and I watched as our medics quickly began treating him.

One terp (interpreter) tried to calm the boy, while also trying to learn the facts from his escorts.

How did this happen?

Americans.

I was edging closer, but I was stopped by a sergeant on his sixth tour. **No, boss, you don't wanna see this. You'll never be able to get it out of your head if you do.**

I backed off.

Minutes later, a whistle, then a zip. A huge explosion behind us.

I felt it in my brain.

I looked around. Everyone was on their stomachs. Except me, and two others.

Where did that come from?

A few of our guys pointed into the distance. They were desperate to return fire, and asked me for permission.

Yes!

But the Taliban who fired were already gone. We'd missed our chance.

We waited for the adrenaline to fade, for the ringing

in our ears to stop. It took a long time. I remember one of our guys whispering over and over: **Fuck me that was close.**

We tried for hours to piece it all together, what happened. Some of us believed the Americans wounded that boy; others felt that the boy had been a pawn in a classic Taliban feint. The wheelbarrow thing had been a little charade designed to keep us on the hill, distracted, immobile, so the Taliban could fix our position. The enemy had messed up that boy in the barrow, then used him as bait.

Why did the boy and the men go along with it?

Because if they didn't, they'd be killed.

Along with everyone they loved.

20.

W E COULD SEE THE LIGHTS of Musa Qala in the distance. February 2008.

Our tanks were in a harbor and we were eating dinner out of bags, talking in low voices.

After the meal, around midnight, I went on radio stag. Sitting in the back of a Spartan, the big door open, I had the desk pulled down and I was taking notes off the radio. My only light was a dim bulb overhead in a wire cage. The stars in the desert sky were brighter than that bulb, and seemed closer.

I was running the radio off the Spartan's battery, so every now and then I'd start the engine to give the battery a charge. I didn't like making noise, for fear of attracting the Taliban's attention, but I had no choice.

After a while I tidied up the Spartan, poured myself a cup of hot chocolate from a thermos, which didn't warm me. Nothing could. The desert could get so cold. I was wearing desert combats, desert boots, a green puffer, a wool beanie—and still shivering.

I tweaked the radio's volume, tried to pick up the voices between its crackles and squelches. Mission reports being sent in. Info about mail deliveries. Messages being passed through battle group net, none of which related to my squadron.

I think it was about one A.M. when I heard several people talking about Red Fox.

Zero Alpha, the officer in command, was telling someone that Red Fox this and Red Fox that . . . I jotted a few notes, but stopped writing and looked up at the stars when I heard them mention . . . C Squadron.

The voices were saying that this Red Fox was in trouble, no doubt about it.

I made out that Red Fox was a person. Had he done something wrong?

No.

Were others planning to do him wrong?

Yes.

Judging from the tone of the voices, Red Fox was about to be murdered. I swallowed a mouthful of hot chocolate and blinked at the radio and knew with total certainty that Red Fox was me.

Now the voices were saying more explicitly that

Red Fox's cover had been blown, that he was exposed to the enemy, that he needed to be extracted immediately.

Fuck, I said. Fuck fuck **fuck**.

My mind flashed back to Eton. The fox I'd glimpsed, when stoned, from the window of the loo. So, he really had been a messenger from the future after all. **One day you'll be alone, late at night, in the darkness, hunted like me . . . see how you like it.**

Next day we went on patrol and I was full-on paranoid, worried I'd be recognized. I wore a **shemagh** tightly over my face, with blacked-out ski goggles, while keeping my head on a swivel and my finger tight on the trigger of my machine gun.

After dusk Special Forces collected me, their Chinook escorted by two Apaches I was chatting with over the radio. They flew me across the valley, back to FOB Edinburgh. We landed in darkness and I couldn't see a thing. I ran into the FOB, then into a green canvas tent, where it was even darker.

I heard a squeak.

A soft light came on.

A man stood before me, screwing a small lightbulb into a socket dangling from the roof.

Colonel Ed.

His long face seemed longer than I remembered, and he was wearing a long green overcoat, like something straight out of the First World War. He filled me in on what happened. An Australian magazine had outed me, told the world I was in Afghanistan. The magazine was inconsequential, so no one noticed at first, but then some bell-end in America picked up the story, posted it on his worthless website, and that got picked up by the crawlers. Now the news was everywhere. The worst-kept secret in the Milky Way was the presence of one Prince Harry in Helmand Province.

So—you're out.

Colonel Ed apologized. He knew this wasn't when or how I wanted to end my tour of duty. On the other hand, he wanted me to know that his superiors had been pressing for weeks to pull me, so I was lucky the tour hadn't been shorter. I'd eluded the powers that be, and the Taliban, and managed to put together a respectably long stint with a sterling record. Bravo, he said.

I was on the verge of begging to stay, but I could see there was no chance. My presence would put everyone around me in grave peril. Including Colonel Ed. Now that the Taliban knew I was in the country, and roughly where, they'd throw everything they had into killing me. The Army didn't want me dying, but it was the same story as one year earlier: The Army was extra keen that others not die because of me.

I shared that sentiment.

I shook Colonel Ed's hand, left the tent. I grabbed my few belongings, said a few quick goodbyes, then jumped back on the Chinook, which was still turning and burning.

Within an hour I was back in Kandahar.

I showered, shaved, got ready to catch a big plane

bound for England. There were other soldiers milling about, waiting to board as well. Their mood was very different. They were all jubilant. Going home.

I stared at the ground.

Eventually we all began to realize that the boarding process was taking an inordinately long time.

What's the holdup? we asked, impatiently.

A crew member said we were waiting on one last passenger.

Who?

A Danish soldier's coffin was being loaded into the cargo hold.

We all fell silent.

When we eventually got on, and took off, the curtain at the front of the plane swung open briefly. I could see three guys on hospital beds. I unbuckled my seatbelt, walked up the aisle and discovered three gravely injured British soldiers. One, I recall, had gruesome injuries from an IED. Another was wrapped head to toe in plastic. Despite being unconscious, he was clutching a test tube containing bits of shrapnel removed from his neck and head.

I spoke with the doctor caring for them, asked if the lads would live. He didn't know. But even if they did, he said, they faced a very tough road.

I felt angry with myself for having been so self-absorbed. I spent the rest of that flight thinking about the many young men and women going home in similar shape, and all the ones not going home at all. I thought about the people at home who didn't know the first thing about this war—by choice. Many opposed it, but few knew a damned thing about it. I wondered why. Whose job was it to tell them?

Oh, yes, I thought. The press.

21.

I LANDED ON MARCH 1, 2008. The obligatory press conference stood between me and a proper meal. I held my breath, went before the chosen reporter, answered his questions. He used the word **hero**, which I wouldn't stand for. **The heroes are the guys on the plane. Not to mention the guys still back at Delhi and Dwyer and Edinburgh.**

I walked out of the room, straight into Willy and Pa. I think Willy hugged me. I think I gave Pa a kiss on each cheek. He might also have . . . squeezed my shoulder? It would've appeared, to anyone at a distance, a normal family greeting and interaction, but for us it was a flamboyant, unprecedented demonstration of physical affection.

Then they both stared at me, wide-eyed. I looked exhausted. Haunted.

You look older, Pa said.

I am.

We piled into Pa's Audi and zoomed off towards Highgrove. Along the way we spoke as if we were in a library. Very hushed.

How are you, Harold?

Oh, I dunno. How are you?

Not bad.

How's Kate?

Good.

I miss anything?

No. Same old.

I rolled down the window, watched the countryside fly by. My eyes couldn't quite absorb all that color, all that green. I breathed in the fresh air and wondered which was the dream, the months in Afghanistan or this trip in the car? The guns of Dwyer, the beheaded goats, the boy in the wheelbarrow—was that reality? Or was reality these soft leather seats and Pa's cologne?

22.

I WAS GIVEN A MONTH OFF. I spent the first part of it with mates. They heard I was home, rang me up, asked me out for a drink.

OK, but just one.

A place called the Cat and Custard Pot. Me: sitting in a dark corner, nursing a gin and tonic. Them: laughing and chatting and making all sorts of plans for trips and projects and holidays.

Everyone seemed so loud. Had they always been so loud?

They all said I seemed quiet. Yeah, I said, yeah, I guess so.

How come?

No reason.

I just felt like being quiet.

I felt out of place, a bit distant. At times I felt sort

of panicky. At other times I felt angry. **Do you folks know what's happening on the other side of the world right now?**

After a day or two I rang Chels, asked to see her. Begged. She was in Cape Town.

She invited me to come.

Yes, I thought. That's what I need right now. A day or two with Chels and her folks.

After, she and I ran off to Botswana, met up with the gang. We started at Teej and Mike's house. Big hugs and kisses at the door; they'd been worried sick about me. Then they fed me, and Mike kept handing me drinks, and I was in the place I loved most, under the sky I loved most, so happy that at one point I wondered if I might not have tears in my eyes.

A day or two later Chels and I drifted upriver on a rented houseboat. The **Kubu Queen**. We cooked simple meals, slept on the upper deck of the boat, under the stars. Gazing at Orion's Belt, the Little Dipper, I'd try to decompress, but it was hard. The press got wind of our trip, and they were papping us constantly, every time the boat neared the shore.

After a week or so we went back to Maun, ate a farewell dinner with Teej and Mike. Everyone turned in early, but I sat up with Teej, told her a bit about the war. Just a bit. It was the first time I'd spoken of it since arriving home.

Willy and Pa had asked. But they hadn't asked the way Teej asked.

Nor had Chelsy. Did she tiptoe around the subject because she still disliked my going? Or because she knew it would be hard for me to talk about it? I wasn't sure, and I felt that she wasn't sure, that neither of us was sure about anything.

Teej and I talked about that too.

She likes me, I said. Loves me, I guess. But she doesn't like the baggage that comes with me, doesn't like everything that comes with being royal, the press and so forth, and none of that is ever going away. So what hope is there?

Teej asked point-blank if I could see myself married to Chels.

I tried to explain. I cherished Chels's carefree and authentic spirit. She never worried about what other people thought. She wore short skirts and high boots, danced with abandon, drank as much tequila as I did, and I cherished all those things about her . . . but I couldn't help worrying how Granny might feel about them. Or the British public. And the last thing I wanted was for Chels to change to accommodate them.

I wanted so badly to be a husband, a father . . . but I just wasn't sure. **It takes a certain kind of person to withstand the scrutiny, Teej, and I don't know if Chels can handle it. I don't know that I want to ask her to handle it.**

23.

THE PRESS REPORTED BREATHLESSLY on our return to Britain, how we dashed to Chelsy's off-campus flat in Leeds, where she lived with two girls, whom I trusted, and who, more important, trusted me, and how I snuck into their flat disguised in a hoodie and baseball cap, giving her flatmates a laugh, and how I loved pretending to be a university student, going for pizza and hanging out in pubs, even wondering if I'd made the right choice in skipping university—not one word of which was true.

I went to Chels's Leeds flat twice.

I barely knew her flatmates.

And I never once regretted my decision to skip university.

But the press was getting worse. They were now just peddling fantasies, phantasms, while physically stalking and harassing me and everyone in my inner circle. Chels told me that paps had been following her to and from lectures—she asked me to do something about it.

I told her I'd try. I told her how sorry I was.

When she was back in Cape Town she phoned me and said people were tailing her everywhere and it was driving her crazy. She couldn't imagine how they always knew where she was and where she'd be. She was freaking out. I talked it over with Marko, who advised me to ask Chels's brother to check the underside of the car.

Sure enough: tracking device.

Marko and I were able to tell her brother exactly what to check for, and where, because it had happened to so many other people around me.

Chels said again that she just wasn't sure if she was up for this. A lifetime of being stalked?

What could I say?

I'd miss her, so much. But I completely understood her desire for freedom.

If I had a choice, I wouldn't want this life either.

24.

FLACK, THEY CALLED HER.

She was funny. And sweet. And cool. I met her at a restaurant with some mates, months after Chels and I had gone our separate ways.

Spike, this is Flack.

Hi. What do you do, Flack?

She was on TV, she explained. She was a presenter.

Sorry, I said. **I don't watch much TV.**

She wasn't taken aback that I didn't recognize her, which I liked. She didn't have a big ego.

Even after she explained who she was and what she did, I still wasn't certain. **What's your full name again?**

Caroline Flack.

Days later we met for dinner and games. Poker night at Marko's flat, Bramham Gardens. After an hour or so I stepped outside, disguised in one of Marko's cowboy hats, to speak with Billy the Rock. As I exited the building I lit a cigarette and looked right. There, behind a parked car . . . two sets of feet.

And two bobbing heads.

Whoever it was didn't recognize me in Marko's

hat. So I was able to stroll casually down to Billy and lean into his police car and whisper: **Bogey at three o'clock.**

What? No!

Billy, how could they have known?

Search me.

No one knows I'm here. Are they tracking me? Are they getting into my phone? Or Flack's?

Billy bolted from the car, ran around the corner, surprised the two paps. He screamed at them. But they screamed right back. Entitled. Emboldened.

They didn't get their photo that night—small victory. But very soon after they papped me and Flack, and those photos set off a frenzy. Within hours a mob was camped outside Flack's parents' house, and all her friends' houses, and her grandmother's house. She was described in one paper as my "bit of rough," because she'd once worked in a factory or something.

Jesus, I thought, are we really such a country of insufferable snobs?

I continued to see Flack on and off, but we didn't feel free anymore. We kept on, I think, because we genuinely enjoyed each other's company, and because we didn't want to admit defeat at the hands of these arseholes. But the relationship was tainted, irredeemably, and in time we agreed that it just wasn't worth the grief and harassment.

Especially for her family.

Goodbye, we said. Goodbye and good luck.

25.

I WENT WITH JLP to Kensington Palace for a cocktail with General Dannatt.

As we knocked at the door to the general's apartment I felt jumpier than I had when leaving for war.

The general and his wife, Pippa, greeted us warmly, congratulated me on my service.

I smiled, but then frowned. Yes, they said. They were sorry about my deployment being cut short.

The press—they ruin everything, don't they?

They do, they surely do.

The general poured me a gin and tonic. We gathered in chairs, a sitting area, and I took a big gulp and felt the gin go down and blurted that I needed to get back. I needed to do a full and proper tour.

The general stared. **Oh. I see. Well, if that's the case . . .**

He began thinking aloud, running through different options, analyzing all the politics and ramifications of each.

What about . . . becoming a helicopter pilot?

Wow. I leaned back. Hadn't ever considered that. Maybe because Willy and my father—and Grandpa and Uncle Andrew—were pilots. I was always keen on following my own line, doing my own thing, but General Dannatt said this would be the best way. The only way. I'd be safer, so to speak, above the fray, among the clouds. So would everyone else serving with me. Even if the press were to find out I'd gone back to Afghanistan, even if they did something stupid again—even **when** they did something stupid again—so what? The Taliban might know where I was, but good luck to them tracking me in the air.

How long until I can qualify as a pilot, General?

About two years.

I shook my head. **Too long, sir.**

He shrugged. **It takes what it takes. And for good reason.**

There was a great deal of schoolwork involved, he explained.

Bloody hell. At every turn, life was determined to drag me back into a classroom.

I thanked him, told him I'd think about it.

26.

BUT I SPENT THAT SUMMER of 2008 not thinking about it.

I didn't think much about anything, besides the three wounded soldiers who'd been with me on the plane home. I wanted other people to think about them too, and talk about them. Not enough people were thinking and talking about British soldiers coming back from the battlefield.

With every free minute I was trying to work out a way I could change that.

In the meantime, the Palace was keeping me busy. I was sent to America, my first official working trip there. (I'd been to Colorado once, white-water rafting, and touring Disney World with Mummy.) JLP was involved in drafting the itinerary, and he knew exactly the kinds of things I wanted to do. I wanted to visit wounded soldiers, and I wanted to lay a wreath at the site of the World Trade Center. And I wanted to meet the families of those who'd died on September 11, 2001. He made it all happen.

I remember little else of that trip besides those moments. I look back and read stories of the hullaba-loo, everywhere I went, the giddy discussions of my mother, much of it due to her love of America and her historic visits there, but what I remember most is sitting with wounded soldiers, visiting military gravesites, talking to families swamped in grief.

I held their hands, I nodded and told them: **I know.** I think we all made each other feel better. Grief is a thing best shared.

I returned to Britain firmer in my belief that more needed to be done for everyone affected by the war on terror. I pushed myself hard—too hard. I was burned out, and didn't know it, and many mornings I woke feeling weak with fatigue. But I didn't see how I could slow down, because so many were asking for help. So many were suffering.

Around this time I learned about a new British organization: Help for Heroes. I loved what they were doing, the awareness they were bringing to the plight of soldiers. Willy and I reached out to them. **What can we do?**

There is something, said the founders, parents of a British soldier. **Would you wear our wristband?**

Of course! We wore one at a football game, with Kate, and the effect was electrifying. Demand for the wristband skyrocketed, donations began rolling in. It was the start of a long, meaningful relationship. More, it was a visceral reminder of the power of our platform.

Still, I did most of my work behind the scenes. I spent many days at Selly Oak Hospital, and Headley Court, chatting with soldiers, listening to their stories, trying to give them a moment of peace or a laugh. I never alerted the press and only let the Palace do so once, I think. I didn't want a reporter within a mile of those encounters, which might look casual on the surface, but were in reality searingly intimate.

You were in Helmand Province too?

Oh, yes.

Lose any guys out there?

Yeah.

Anything I can do?

You're doing it, mate.

I stood by the bedsides of men and women in a terrible state, and often with their families. One young lad was wrapped in bandages, head to foot, in an induced coma. His mum and dad were there, and they told me they'd been keeping a diary about his recovery; they asked me to read it. I did. Then, with their permission, I wrote something in it for him to read when he woke. Afterwards, we all hugged, and when we said goodbye it felt like family.

Finally, I went to a physical rehab center for an official engagement and met with one of the soldiers from the flight home. Ben. He told me how the IED had taken off his left arm and right leg. Boiling hot day, he said. He was running, heard a blast, then felt himself flying twenty feet into the air.

He remembered **seeing** his leg leaving his body.

He told me this with a faint, brave smile.

The day before my visit he'd received his new prosthetic leg. I glanced down. **Very sleek, mate. Looks quite strong!** We'll soon see, he said. His rehab regime called for him to go up and down a climbing wall that day.

I hung around, watched.

He settled into a harness, grabbed a rope, shimmied up the wall. He gave a rousing whoop and cheer at the top, then a wave, then climbed back down.

I was astounded. I'd never been so proud—to be British, to be a soldier, to be his brother in arms. I told him so. I told him I wanted to buy him a beer for getting to the top of that wall. No, no, a crate of beer.

He laughed. **Wouldn't say no to that, mate!**

He said something about wanting to run a marathon.

I said if he ever did, when he did, he'd find me waiting at the finish line.

27.

TOWARDS THE END OF that summer I went to Botswana, met up with Teej and Mike. They'd recently done masterwork on the David Attenborough series **Planet Earth**, and a few other BBC films, and now they were shooting an important film about elephants. Several herds, stressed by habitat encroachment and drought, were stampeding into Namibia in search of food, running straight into the arms of poachers—hundreds, armed with AK-47s. Teej and Mike hoped their film might shine a light on this rolling massacre.

I asked if I could help. They didn't hesitate. **Course, Spike.**

In fact, they offered to hire me as a credited, though unpaid, cameraman.

From Day One they talked about how **different** I seemed. Not that I wasn't always a hard worker, but clearly I'd learned from the Army how to take direction. They never had to tell me anything twice.

Many times during that shoot we'd be riding around the bush in their flatbed truck and I'd gaze off and think: How bizarre. My whole life I've despised photographers, because they specialize in stealing your freedom, and now I'm a working photographer, fighting to preserve the freedom of these majestic animals. And feeling freer in the process.

More ironic, I was filming veterinarians as they put tracking devices on the animals. (The devices would help researchers better understand the herd's migration patterns.) Until now, I didn't have the happiest associations with tracking devices.

One day we filmed a vet dart a big bull elephant, then wrap a tracking collar around his neck. But the dart only nicked the elephant's tough skin, so he was able to gather himself and charge away.

Mike yelled: **Grab the camera, Spike! Run!**

The elephant was tearing through thick bush, mostly along a sandy path, though sometimes there was no path. The vet and I tried to stay in his footprints. I couldn't believe the animal's speed. He went eight kilometers before slowing, then stopping. I kept my distance, and when the vet caught up, I watched him put another dart into the elephant. Finally the big fella went down.

Moments later Mike came roaring up in his truck. **Good job, Spike!**

I was panting, hands on my knees, bathed in sweat.

Mike looked down in horror. **Spike. Where are your shoes?**

Oh. Yeah. Left them on the truck. Didn't think there was time to grab them.

You ran eight kilometers . . . through the bush . . . in no shoes?

I laughed. **You told me to run. Like you said, the Army taught me how to take direction.**

28.

RIGHT AT THE TURN OF the new year, 2009, a video went viral.

Me, as a cadet, three years earlier, sitting with other cadets.

At an airport. Cyprus, perhaps? Or else maybe waiting to fly to Cyprus?

The video was shot by me. Killing time before our flight, messing around, I panned the group, gave a running commentary on each lad, and when I came to my fellow cadet and good friend Ahmed Raza Kahn, a Pakistani, I said: **Ah, our little Paki friend . . .**

I didn't know that Paki was a slur. Growing up, I'd heard many people use that word and never saw anyone flinch or cringe, never suspected them of being racist. Neither did I know anything about unconscious bias. I was twenty-one, awash in isolation and privilege, and if I thought anything about this word at all, I thought it was like Aussie. Harmless.

I'd sent the footage to a fellow cadet, who was making an end-of-year video. Since then, it had circulated, flitted from computer to computer, and ultimately ended up in the hands of someone who sold it to the **News of the World**.

Heated condemnations began rolling in.

I'd learned nothing, people said.

I'd not matured one bit after the Nazi debacle, people said.

Prince Harry is worse than a thicko, they said, worse than a party boy—he's a racist.

The Tory leader denounced me. A cabinet minister went on TV to flog me. Ahmed's uncle condemned me to the BBC.

I was sitting in Highgrove, watching this furor rain down, barely able to process it.

My father's office issued an apology on my behalf.

I wanted to issue one as well, but courtiers advised against it.

Not the best strategy, sir.

To hell with strategy. I didn't care about strategy. I cared about people not thinking I was a racist. I cared about **not being** a racist.

Above all, I cared about Ahmed. I connected with him directly, apologized. He said he knew I wasn't a racist. No big deal.

But it was. And his forgiveness, his easy grace, only made me feel worse.

29.

AS THAT CONTROVERSY CONTINUED to spread, I shipped off to RAF Barkston Heath. Strange time to begin flight training, to begin any kind of training. My congenitally weak powers of concentration were never weaker. But maybe, I told myself, it's also the best time. I wanted to hide from humanity, flee the planet, and since a rocket wasn't available, maybe an aeroplane would do.

Before I could climb into any aircraft, however, the Army would need to make sure I had the right stuff. For several weeks they poked my body, probed my mind.

Drug-free, they concluded. They seemed surprised.

Also, videos to the contrary notwithstanding, not a total thicko.

So . . . proceed.

My first aircraft would be a Firefly, they said. Bright yellow, fixed wing, single prop.

Simple machine, according to my first flight instructor, Sergeant Major Booley.

I got in and thought: Really? Didn't look simple to me.

I turned to Booley, studied him. He wasn't simple either. Short, solid, tough, he'd fought in Iraq and the Balkans and should've been a hard case, given all he'd seen and been through, but in fact he seemed to suffer no ill-effects from his tours of combat. On the contrary, he was all gentleness.

He needed to be. With so much on my mind, I entered our sessions wildly distracted, and it showed. I kept expecting Booley to lose patience, to begin shouting at me, but he never did. In fact, after one session, he invited me for a motorbike ride in the country. **Let's go and clear our heads, Lieutenant Wales.**

It worked. Like a charm. And the motorbike, a gorgeous Triumph 675, was a timely reminder of what I was after in these flight lessons. Speed and power.

And freedom.

Then we discovered we weren't free: the press had followed us the whole way and papped us outside Booley's house.

After a period of acclimatizing to the Firefly's cockpit, becoming familiar with the control panel, we finally took her up. On one of our first flights together, with no warning, Booley threw the aircraft into a stall. I felt the left wing dip, a sickening feeling of disorder, of entropy, and then, after several seconds that felt like decades, he recovered the aircraft and leveled the wings.

I stared at him. **What in the absolute—?**

Was this an aborted suicide attempt?

No, he said gently. This was the next stage in my training. Countless things can go wrong in the air, he explained, and he needed to show me what to do— but also how to do it.

Stay. Cool.

Our next flight, he pulled the same stunt. But this time he didn't recover the aircraft. As we went spinning and pirouetting towards Earth he said: **It's time.**

For what?

For YOU to . . . DO IT.

He looked at the controls. I grabbed them, stuck the boot in, regained the aircraft in what felt like the nick of time.

I looked at Booley, waited for congratulations.

Nothing. Barely any reaction at all.

Over time Booley would do this again and again, cut the power, put us into freefall. As the creaking metal and roaring white noise of the stilled engine became deafening he'd turn calmly to his left: **It's time.**

Time?

You have control.

I have control.

After I restored the power, after we returned to base safely, there was never any fanfare. Not even much chatter. No medals in Booley's cockpit for simply doing your job.

At last, one clear morning, after a routine handful of circuits over the airfield, we landed softly and Booley jumped out as if the Firefly were on fire.

What's the matter?

It's time, Lieutenant Wales.

Time?

For you to solo.

Oh. OK.

Up I went. (After first making sure my parachute was strapped on.) I did one or two circuits round the airfield, talking to myself all the while: **Full power. Keep the wheel on the white line. Pull up . . . slowly! Dip the nose. Don't stall! Turn in the climb. Level off. OK, now you're downwind. Radio the tower. Check your ground markers.**

Pre-landing checks.

Reduce power!

Start to descend in the turn.

There you go, steady now.

Roll out there, line up, line it up.

Three-degree flight path, get the nose on the piano keys.

Request clearance to land.

Point the aircraft where you want it to land . . .

I made an uneventful one-bounce landing and taxied off the runway. To the average person it would've looked like the most mundane flight in the history of aviation. To me it was one of the most wonderful moments of my life.

Was I a pilot now? Hardly. But I was on my way.

I jumped out, marched up to Booley. My God, I

wanted to high-five him, take him out for drinks, but it was out of the question.

The one thing I absolutely didn't want to do was say goodbye to him, but that was what needed to happen next. Now that I'd soloed, I needed to embark on the next phase of my training.

As Booley was so fond of saying, it was time.

30.

I SHIPPED OFF TO RAF Shawbury and discovered that helicopters were much more complex than Fireflys.

Even the preflight checks were more extensive.

I stared at the galaxy of toggles and switches and thought: **How am I going to memorize all this?**

Somehow I did. Slowly, under the watchful eyes of my two new instructors, Sergeant Majors Lazel and Mitchell, I learned them all.

In no time we were lifting off, rotors beating the frothy clouds, one of the great physical sensations anyone can experience. The purest form of flying, in many ways. The first time we ascended, straight vertical, I thought: I was born for this.

But **flying** the helicopter, I learned, wasn't the hard part. Hovering was. At least six long lessons were devoted to this one task, which sounded easy at first and quickly came to seem impossible. In fact, the more you practiced hovering, the more impossible it seemed.

The main reason was a phenomenon called "hover monkeys." Just above the ground a helicopter falls prey to a fiendish confluence of factors: air flow, downdraft, gravity. First it wobbles, then it rocks, then it pitches and yaws—as if invisible monkeys are hanging from both its skids, yanking. To land the helicopter you have to shake off those hover monkeys, and the only way to do that is by . . . ignoring them.

Easier said. Time and time again the hover monkeys got the better of me, and it was small consolation that they also got the better of every other pilot training with me. We talked among ourselves about these little bastards, these invisible gremlins. We grew to hate them, to dread the shame and rage that came with being bested by them yet again. None of us could work out how to restore the aircraft's equilibrium and put it on the deck without denting the fuselage. Or scraping the skids. To walk away from a landing with a long, crooked mark on the tarmac behind you— that was the ultimate humiliation.

Come the day of our first solos we were all basket cases. **The hover monkeys, the hover monkeys,** that was all you heard around the kettle and the coffee pot. When it was my turn I climbed into the helicopter, said a prayer, asked the tower for clearance. **All clear.** I started her up, lifted off, did several laps around the field, no problem, despite strong winds.

Now it was zero hour.

On the apron were eight circles. You had to land inside one. Left of the apron was an orange brick building with huge glass windows where the other pilots and students waited their turn. I knew they were all standing at those windows, watching, as I felt the hover monkeys take hold. The aircraft was rocking. **Get off**, I shouted, **leave me alone.**

I fought the controls and managed to set the helicopter inside one of the circles.

Walking inside the orange building, I threw out my chest and proudly took my place at the windows to watch the others. Sweaty but smiling.

Several student pilots had to abort their landings that day. One had to set down on a nearby patch of grass. One landed so hot and wobbly, fire trucks and an ambulance rushed to the scene.

When he walked into the orange building I could see in his eyes that he felt as I would've felt in his shoes.

Part of him honestly wished he'd crashed and burned.

31.

DURING THIS TIME I WAS LIVING in Shropshire, with Willy, who was also training to become a pilot. He'd found a cottage ten minutes from the base, on someone's estate, and invited me to stay with him. Or maybe I invited myself?

The cottage was cozy, charming, just up a narrow country lane and behind some thickly canopied trees. The fridge was stuffed with vacuum-packed meals sent by Pa's chefs. Creamy chicken and rice, beef curry. At the back of the house there were beautiful stables, which explained the horse smell in every room.

Each of us enjoyed the arrangement: our first time living together since Eton. It was fun. Better yet, we were together for the decisive moment, the triumphal unraveling of Murdoch's media empire. After months of investigation, a gang of reporters and editors at Murdoch's trashiest newspaper were finally being identified, handcuffed, arrested, charged with harassment of politicians, celebrities—and the Royal Family. Corruption was being exposed, finally, and punishments were forthcoming.

Among the soon-to-be-exposed villains was the Thumb, that same journalist who'd long ago published an absurd non-story about my thumb injury at Eton. I'd healed up nicely, but the Thumb had never mended his ways. On the contrary he'd got a whole lot worse. He'd moved up the ranks of the newspaper world, becoming a boss, with a whole team of Thumbs at his command (under his thumb?), many of them hacking willy-nilly into people's phones. Blatant criminality, which the Thumb claimed, laughably, to know nothing about.

Also going down? Rehabber Kooks! The same loathsome editor who'd cooked up my rehab charade—she'd been "resigned." Two days later the cops arrested her.

Oh, the relief we felt when we heard. For us and our country.

A similar fate was soon to befall the others, all the plotters and stalkers and liars. Soon enough they would all lose their jobs, and their ill-gotten fortunes, amassed during one of the wildest crime sprees in British history.

Justice.

I was overjoyed. So was Willy. More, it was glorious to finally have our suspicions validated and our circle of closest friends vindicated, to know that we hadn't been stark, staring paranoid. Things really had been amiss. We'd been betrayed, as we'd always suspected, but not by bodyguards or best mates. It was those Fleet Street weasels yet again. And the Metropolitan Police, who'd inexplicably failed to do their jobs, refusing time and again to investigate and arrest obvious lawbreakers.

The question was why? Pay-offs? Collusion? Fear?

We'd soon find out.

The public was horrified. If journalists could use the mighty powers vested in them for evil, then democracy was in sorry shape. More, if journalists were allowed to probe and foil the security measures that notable figures and government officials required to stay safe, then they'd ultimately show terrorists how to do it too. And then it would be a free-for-all. No one would be safe.

For generations Britons had said with a wry laugh: Ah, well, of course our newspapers are shit— but what can you do? Now they weren't laughing. And there was general agreement: We need to do something.

There were even death rattles coming from the most popular Sunday newspaper, Murdoch's **News of** the World. The leading culprit in the hacking scandal, its very survival was in doubt. Advertisers were talking about fleeing, readers were talking about boycotts. Was it possible? Murdoch's baby—his grotesque two-headed circus baby—might finally expire?

A new era was at hand?

Strange. While all this put Willy and me in a chipper mood, we didn't talk much about it explicitly. We had loads of laughs in that cottage, passed many happy hours talking about all kinds of things, but seldom that. I wonder if it was just too painful. Or maybe still too unresolved. Maybe we didn't want to jinx it, didn't dare pop the cork on the champagne until we saw photos of Rehabber Kooks and the Thumb sharing a cell.

Or maybe there was some tension under the surface between us, which I wasn't fully comprehending. While sharing that cottage we agreed to a rare joint interview, in an airplane hangar at Shawbury, during which Willy griped endlessly about my habits. Harry's a slob, he said. Harry snores.

I turned and gave him a look. Was he joking?

I cleaned up after myself, and I didn't snore. Besides, our rooms were separated by thick walls, so even if I did snore there was no way he heard. The reporters were having fits of giggles about it all, but I cut in: **Lies! Lies!**

That only made them laugh harder. Willy too.

I laughed as well, because we often bantered like that, but when I look back on it now, I can't help but wonder if there wasn't something else at play. I was training to get to the front lines, the same place Willy had been training to get, but the Palace had scuttled his plans. The Spare, sure, let him run around a battlefield like a chicken with its head cut off, if that's what he likes.

But the Heir? No.

So Willy was now training to be a search and rescue pilot, and perhaps feeling quietly frustrated about it. In which case, he was seeing it all wrong. He was doing remarkable, vital work, I thought, saving lives every week. I was proud of him, and full of respect for the way he was dedicating himself wholeheartedly to his preparation.

Still, I should've figured out how he might have been feeling. I knew all too well the despair of being pulled from a fight for which you've spent years preparing.

32.

FROM SHAWBURY I MOVED ON to Middle Wallop. I now knew how to fly a helicopter, the Army conceded, but next I needed to learn how to fly one **tactically**. While doing other things. Many other things. Like reading a map and locating a target and firing missiles and talking on the radios and peeing into a bag. Multitasking in the air at 140 knots—not for everyone. To accomplish this Jedi mind trick, my brain would first need to be reshaped, my synapses rewired, and my Yoda in this massive neuro-reengineering would be Nigel.

A.k.a. Nige.

It was he who drew the unenviable task of becoming my fourth, and arguably most important, flight instructor.

The aircraft on which we'd be conducting our sessions was the Squirrel. That was the colloquial name for the little French-made single-engine helicopter on which most British students trained. But Nige was less focused on the actual Squirrel in which we sat than the squirrels inside my head. Head squirrels were the ancient enemies of human concentration, Nige assured me. Without my being aware of it they'd taken up residence in my consciousness. More devious than the hover monkeys, he said, they were also far more dangerous.

The only way to get rid of head squirrels, Nige insisted, was iron discipline. A helicopter is easily mastered, but the head takes more time and more patience.

Time and patience, I thought impatiently. I don't have much of either, Nige, so let's crack on . . .

It also takes a kind of self-love, Nige said, and this manifests as confidence. **Confidence, Lieutenant Wales. Believe in yourself—that's everything.**

I saw the truth in his words, but I couldn't imagine ever putting that truth into practice. The fact was, I **didn't** believe in myself, didn't believe in much of anything, least of all me. Whenever I made a mistake, which was often, I was quite harsh with Harry. It felt as if my mind were seizing up like an overheated engine, the red mist would come down, and I'd stop thinking, stop functioning.

No, Nige would say softly whenever this happened. **Don't let one mistake destroy this flight, Lieutenant Wales.**

But I let one mistake ruin many a flight.

Sometimes my self-loathing would spill onto Nige. After having a go at me, I'd have a go at him. **Fuck it, you fly the damn thing!**

He'd shake his head. **Lieutenant Wales, I'm not touching the controls. We are going to get down on the ground and you're going to get us there and then we'll talk about it all afterwards.**

He had a herculean will. You'd never have guessed it from his appearance. Average height, average build, steel-gray hair combed neatly to one side. He wore spotless green overalls, spotless clear spectacles. He was a Navy civvie, a kindly grandpa who loved sailing— a top bloke. But he had the heart of a fucking ninja.

And at that moment I needed a ninja.

33.

OVER SEVERAL MONTHS NIGE the Ninja managed to show me how to fly a helicopter while doing other things, countless other things, and, what was more, to do so with something approaching self-love. These were flying lessons, but I think back on them as life lessons, and gradually there were more good ones than bad.

Good or bad, however, every ninety-minute session in Nige's Squirrel Dojo left me hooped. Upon landing I'd think: **I need a nap.**

But first: the debrief.

This was where Nige the Ninja really put me through it, because he sugarcoated nothing. He spoke bluntly and wounded blithely. There were things I needed to hear, and he didn't care about his tone when he told me.

I got defensive.

He pressed on.

I shot him hate-you-forever stares.

He pressed on.

I said, **Yeah, yeah, I get it.**

He pressed on.

I stopped listening.

Poor Nige . . . He pressed on.

He was, I realize now, one of the most truthful people I've ever known, and he knew a secret about truth that many people are unwilling to accept: it's **usually** painful. He wanted me to believe in myself, but that belief could never be based on false promises or fake compliments. The royal road to mastery was paved with facts.

Not that he was categorically opposed to compliments. One day, almost in passing, he said that I appeared to lack any . . . fear. **You're not terribly concerned, if I may say, Lieutenant Wales, with dying.**

That's true.

I explained that I hadn't been afraid of death since the age of twelve.

He nodded once. He got it. We moved on.

34.

NIGE EVENTUALLY RELEASED ME, set me free like a wounded bird restored to health, and with his certification the Army pronounced me ready to fly Apaches.

But nope—it was a trick. I wasn't going to fly Apaches. I was going to sit in a windowless classroom and **read** about Apaches.

I thought: Could anything be crueler? Promise me a helicopter, hand me a stack of homework?

The course lasted three months, during which I nearly went insane. Every night I'd slump back to my cell-like room in the officers' mess and vent to a mate on the phone, or else to my bodyguard. I considered leaving the course altogether. I'd never even wanted to fly Apaches, I said to everyone, petulantly. I wanted to fly the Lynx. It was simpler to learn, and I'd get back to the war faster. But my commanding officer, Colonel David Meyer, quashed that idea. **Not a chance, Harry.**

Why, Colonel?

Because you've had operational ground experience in reconnaissance, you were a very fine FAC, and you're a bloody good pilot. You're going to fly Apaches.

But—

I can tell from the way you fly, the way you read the ground, this is what you were meant to do.

Meant to do? The course was torture!

And yet I was on time every day. I showed up with my three-ring binders full of info about the Apache engines, and listened to the lectures, and fought like crazy to keep up. I tried to draw on everything I'd learned from my flight instructors, from Booley to Nige, and treated the classroom as an aircraft going down. My job was to regain control.

And then one day . . . it was over. They said I'd be permitted at long last to strap myself into an honest-to-God Apache.

For . . . ground taxiing.

Are you joking?

Four lessons, they said.

Four lessons . . . on taxiing?

As it turned out, four lessons was barely enough to absorb all there was to know about ground taxiing that massive bird. I felt, while taxiing, as if the aircraft was on stilts, set on a bed of jelly. There were moments when I truly wondered if I'd ever be able to do it, if this whole journey might be at an end here, before it had even begun.

I blamed part of my struggle on the seating arrangement. In the Firefly, in the Squirrel, the instructor was always right next to me. He could reach over, fix my mistakes straightaway, or else model the correct way. Booley would put his hand on the controls, or Nige would do the pedals, and I'd do the same.

I realized that much of what I'd learned in life had come through this sort of modeling. More than most people I needed a guide, a guru—a partner.

But in the Apache the instructor was either way up front or way in the back—unseen.

I was all alone.

35.

THE SEATING ARRANGEMENT eventually became less of an issue. Day by day the Apache felt less alien, and some days it even felt good.

I learned to be alone in there, to think alone, function alone. I learned to communicate with this big, fast, nasty, beautiful beast, to speak its language, to listen when it talked. I learned to perform one set of skills with my hands, while doing another with my feet. I learned to appreciate how phenomenal this machine was: unthinkably heavy, yet capable of ballet-like suppleness. The most technologically complex helicopter in the world, and also the most nimble. I could see why only a handful of people on earth knew how to fly Apaches, and why it cost millions of dollars to train each of those people.

And then . . . it was time to do it all at night.

We started with an exercise called "the bag," which was just what it sounded like. The Apache's windows were covered and you felt as if you were inside a brown-paper bag. You had to take all data about conditions outside the aircraft through instruments and gauges. Eerie, unnerving—but effective. You were forced to develop a kind of second sight.

Then we took the Apache up into the actual night sky, made our way around the base, slowly expanded beyond. I was a bit trembly the first time we sailed across Salisbury Plain, over those desolate valleys and woods where I'd crawled and dragged my arse through those first exercises. Then I was flying over more populated areas. Then: London. The Thames glistening in the darkness. The Millennium Wheel winking at the stars. The Houses of Parliament, and Big Ben, and the palaces. I wondered if Granny was in, and if she was awake. Were the corgis settling down while I did these graceful whirls over their fuzzy heads?

Was the flag up?

In darkness I became fully proficient with the monocle, the most astonishing and iconic part of the Apache's technology. A sensor in the Apache's nose transmitted images through a cable, up to the cockpit, where it fed into the monocle, which was clipped to my helmet, in front of my right eyeball. Through that monocle I got all my knowledge of the outside world. All my senses were reduced to that one small portal. It felt at first like writing with my toe or breathing through my ear, and then it became second nature. And then it became mystical.

Circling London one night, I was suddenly blinded, and thought for half a second that I might drop into the Thames. I saw bright colors, mostly emerald green, and after a few seconds I realized: someone on the ground had hit us with a laser pen. I was disoriented. And furious. But I told myself to be grateful for the experience, for the practice. I was also perversely grateful for the stray memory it knocked loose. Mohamed Al Fayed, giving Willy and me laser pens from Harrods, which he owned. He was the father of Mummy's boyfriend, so maybe he was trying to win us over. If so, job done. We thought those lasers were genius.

We whipped them around like light sabers.

36.

NEAR THE TAIL END OF my Apache training, at Wattisham Airfield in Suffolk, I got one more instructor.

It was his job to put on the finishing touches.

Upon meeting, shaking hands, he gave me a knowing smile.

I smiled back.

He kept smiling.

I smiled back, but started to wonder: What?

I thought he was about to pay me a compliment. Or ask a favor.

Instead he asked if I recognized his voice.

No.

He was part of the team that extracted me, he said.

Oh, back in 2008?

Yes.

We'd talked briefly over the radio that night, I recalled.

I remember how gutted you were.

Yeah.

I could hear it in your voice.

Yeah. I was devastated.

He smiled wider. **Now look at you.**

37.

I WAS TURNING TWENTY-FIVE in a few days, and it felt like more than just another birthday. Mates told me twenty-five was the Watershed Age, the moment when many young men and women come to a fork in their personal road. At twenty-five you take a concrete step forward . . . or else begin to slide backwards. I was ready to move forward. I felt, in many ways, that I'd been bag-flying for years.

I reminded myself that it ran in the family, that twenty-five had been a big year for many of us. Granny, to name one. At twenty-five she'd become the sixty-first monarch in the history of England.

So I decided to mark this milestone birthday with a trip.

Botswana again.

The whole gang was there, and in between cake and cocktails they said how different I seemed— again. I had seemed older, harder, after my first combat tour. But now, they said, I seemed more . . . grounded.

Odd, I thought. Through flight training . . . I've become more grounded?

No one gave me more praise or love than Teej and Mike. Late one night, however, Mike sat me down for a somber heart-to-heart. At their kitchen table he spoke at length about my relationship with Africa. The time's come, he said, for that relationship to change. Until then the relationship had been all take, take, take—a fairly typical dynamic for Brits in Africa. But now I needed to give back. For years I'd heard him and Teej and others lamenting the crises facing this place. Climate change. Poaching. Drought. Fires. I was the only person they knew who had any kind of influence, any kind of global megaphone—the only person who might actually be able to do something.

What can I do, Mike?

Shine a light.

38.

A GROUP OF US piled into flat-bottomed boats and steered upriver.

We camped for a few days, explored some remote islands. No one for miles and miles around.

One afternoon we stopped off on Kingfisher Island, and mixed up some drinks, and watched the sunset. Rain was falling, which made the light look pink. We listened to music, everything mellow, dreamy, and lost all track of time. As we were pushing off, getting back onto the river, we suddenly ran into two big problems.

Darkness.

And a major storm.

Each was a problem you never wanted to encounter on the Okavango. But both at the same time? We were in trouble.

Now came the wind.

In the dark, in the maelstrom, the river was impossible to navigate. The water pitched and rolled. Plus the driver on our boat was wasted. We kept plowing into sandbars.

I thought: We might end up in this river tonight.

I shouted that I was taking the wheel.

I recall brilliant flashes of lightning, seismic claps of thunder. There were twelve of us on two boats and no one was saying a word. Even the most experienced Africa hands were tight-faced, though we tried to pretend we were in control by continuing to blast the music.

Suddenly the river narrowed. Then bent sharply. We were desperate to get back, but we had to be patient. Obey the river. Go where it led us.

Just then, a massive flash. Everything bright as noon for about two seconds, long enough to see, standing directly before us, in the middle of the river, a group of enormous elephants.

In the flare-up I locked eyes with one. I saw her snow-white tusks swooping up, I saw every wrinkle in her dark wet skin, the hard water line above her shoulders. I saw her giant ears, shaped like an angel's wings.

Someone whispered: **Holy shit.**

Someone cut the music.

Both drivers killed the engines.

In total silence we floated on the swollen river, waiting for the next lightning flash. When it came, there they were again, those majestic creatures. This time, when I stared at the elephant closest to me, when I looked deep into her eyeball, when she looked back into mine, I thought of the all-seeing eye of the Apache, and I thought of the Koh-i-Noor diamond, and I thought of a camera's lens, convex and glassy like the elephant's eye, except that a camera lens always made me nervous and this eye made me feel safe. This eye wasn't judging, wasn't taking—it just **was**. If anything, the eye was slightly . . . tearful? Was that possible?

Elephants have been known to weep. They hold funerals for loved ones, and when they come upon an elephant lying dead in the bush they stop and pay their respects. Were our boats intruding on some such ceremony? Some sort of gathering? Or maybe we'd interrupted some kind of rehearsal. From antiquity comes a story of one elephant who was observed privately practicing complicated dance steps he'd need to perform in an upcoming parade.

The storm was getting worse. We had to go. We restarted the boats, cruised away. Goodbye, we whispered to the elephants. I eased into the middle of the current, lit a cigarette, told my memory to hold on to this encounter, this unreal moment when the line between me and the external world grew blurry or disappeared outright.

Everything, for one half second, was one. Everything made sense.

Try to remember, I thought, how it felt to be that close to the truth, the real truth:

That life isn't all good, but it isn't all bad either.

Try to remember how it felt, finally, to understand what Mike had been trying to say.

Shine a light.

39.

I GOT MY WINGS. Pa, as Army Air Corps Colonel-in-Chief, pinned them to my chest.

May 2010.

Happy day. Pa, wearing his blue beret, officially presented me with mine. I put it on and we saluted each other. It felt almost more intimate than a hug.

Camilla was on hand. And Mummy's sisters. And Chels. We were back together.

Then broke up soon after.

We had no choice—yet again. We had all the same old problems, nothing had been solved. Also, Chels wanted to travel, have fun, be young, but I was once again on a path to war. I'd soon be shipping off. If we stayed together, we'd be lucky to see each other a handful of times over the next two years, and that was no kind of relationship. Neither of us was surprised when we found ourselves in the same old emotional cul-de-sac.

Goodbye, Chels.

Goodbye, Hazza.

The day I got my wings, I figured she got hers.

We went to Botswana one last time. One last trip upriver, we said. One last visit to Teej and Mike.

We had great fun, and naturally wavered about our decision. I tried now and then, and talked now and then, of different ways this might still work. Chels played along. We were being so obviously, willfully delusional, that Teej felt the need to step in.

It's over, kids. You're postponing the inevitable. And making yourselves crazy in the process.

We were staying in a tent in her garden. She sat with us in the tent, delivering these difficult truths while holding hands with each of us. Looking us in the eyes, she urged us to let this breakup be final.

Don't waste the most precious thing there is. Time.

She was right, I knew. As Sergeant Major Booley said: It's time.

So I forced myself to put the relationship out of my mind—in fact, all relationships. Stay busy, I told myself as I flew away from Botswana. In the short while left before you ship to Afghanistan, just stay busy.

To that end, I went to Lesotho with Willy. We visited several schools built by Sentebale. Prince Seeiso was with us; he'd co-founded the charity with me back in 2006, shortly after losing his own mother. (His mother had also been a fighter in the war against HIV.) He took us to meet scores of children, each with a wrenching story. The average life expectancy in Lesotho at that time was forty-something, while in Britain it was seventy-nine for men, eighty-two for women. Being a child in Lesotho was like being middle-aged in Manchester, and while there were various complicated reasons for this, the main one was HIV.

A quarter of all Lesotho adults were HIV-positive.

After two or three days we set off with Prince Seeiso towards more remote schools, off the grid. Way off. As a gift Prince Seeiso gave us wild ponies, to ride part of the way, and tribal blankets for the cold. We wore them as capes.

Our first stop was a frozen village in the clouds: Semonkong. Some seven thousand feet above sea level, it lay between snow-tipped mountains. Plumes of warm air spurted from the horses' noses as we pushed them up, up, but when the climb got too steep, we switched to trucks.

Upon arriving we went straight into the school. Shepherd boys would come here twice a week, have a hot meal, go to a class. We sat in semi-darkness, beside a paraffin lamp, watching a lesson, and then we sat on the ground with a dozen boys, some as young as eight. We listened to them describe their daily trek to our school. It defied belief: after twelve hours of tending their cattle and sheep, they'd walk for two hours through mountain passes just to learn maths, reading, writing. Such was their hunger to learn. They braved sore feet, bitter cold—and far worse. They were so vulnerable on the road, so exposed to the elements, several had died from lightning strikes. Many had been attacked by stray dogs. They dropped their voices and told us that many had also been sexually abused by wanderers, rustlers, nomads, and other boys.

I felt ashamed to think of all my bitching about school. About anything.

Despite what they'd suffered, the boys were still boys. Their joy was irrepressible. They thrilled at the gifts we'd brought—warm coats, wool beanies. They put on the clothes, danced, sang. We joined them.

One boy kept to the side. His face was round, open, transparent. There was obviously a terrible burden on his heart. I felt it would be prying to ask. But I had one more gift in my bag, a torch, and I gave it to him.

I said I hoped it would light his way each day to school.

He smiled.

I wanted to tell him that his smile would light mine. I tried.

Alas, my Sesotho wasn't very good.

40.

Soon after we returned to Britain the Palace announced that Willy was going to marry.

November 2010.

News to me. All that time together in Lesotho, he'd never mentioned it.

The papers published florid stories about the moment I realized Willy and Kate were well matched, the moment I appreciated the depth of their love and thus decided to gift Willy the ring I'd inherited from Mummy, the legendary sapphire, a tender moment between brothers, a bonding moment for all three of us, and absolute rubbish: none of it ever happened. I never gave Willy that ring because it wasn't mine to give. He already had it. He'd asked for it after Mummy died, and I'd been more than happy to let it go.

Now, as Willy focused on wedding preparations, I wished him well and turned sharply inward. I thought long and hard about my singlehood. I'd always assumed I'd be the first to be married, because I'd wanted it so badly. I'd always assumed that I'd be a young husband, a young father, because I'd resolved not to become my father. He'd been an older dad, and I'd always felt that this created problems, placed barriers between us. In his middle years he'd become more sedentary, more habitual. He liked his routines. He wasn't the kind of father who played endless rounds of tag, or tossed a ball until long after dark. He'd been so once. He'd chased us all over Sandringham, making up wonderful games, like the one where he wrapped us in blankets, like hot dogs, until we screamed with helpless laughter, and then yanked the blanket and shot us out of the other end. I don't know if Willy or I have ever laughed harder. But, long before we were ready, he stopped engaging in that kind of physical fun. He just didn't have the enthusiasm—the puff.

But I would, I always promised myself. I would.

Now I wondered: Will I?

Was that the real me who made that promise to become a young father? Or was this the real me, struggling to find the right person, the right partner, while also struggling to work out who I was?

Why is this thing, which I supposedly want so badly, not happening?

And what if it never happens? What will my life mean? What will my ultimate purpose be?

War, I reckoned. When all else failed, as it usually did, I still had soldiering. (If only I had a deployment date.)

And after the wars, I thought, there will always be charitable work. Since the Lesotho trip, I'd felt more passionate than ever about continuing Mummy's causes. And I was determined to take up the cause Mike gave me at his kitchen table. That's enough for a full life, I told myself.

It seemed like serendipity, therefore, like a synthesis of all my thinking, when I heard from a group of wounded soldiers planning a trek to the North Pole. They were hoping to raise millions for Walking With The Wounded, and also to become the first amputees ever to reach the Pole unsupported. They invited me to join them.

I wanted to say yes. I was dying to say yes. Just one problem. The trek was in early April, dangerously close to Willy's announced wedding date. I'd have to get there and back with no hitches, or risk missing the ceremony.

But the North Pole wasn't a place you could ever be sure of getting to and from without hitches. The North Pole was a place of infinite hitches. There were always variables, usually related to weather. So

I was nervous at the prospect, and the Palace was doubly nervous.

I asked JLP for his advice.

He smiled. **It's a once-in-a-lifetime opportunity.**

Yes. It is.

You've got to go.

But first, he said, there was one other place I needed to go.

In a direct continuation of conversations he and I had begun five years earlier, after my Nazi debacle, he'd organized a trip to Berlin.

And so. December 2010. A bitterly cold day. I put my fingertips to the bullet holes in the city's walls, the still-fresh scars from Hitler's insane vow to fight to the last man. I stood at the former site of the Berlin Wall, which had also been the site of SS torture chambers, and swore I could hear the echoes of agonized screams on the wind. I met a woman who'd been sent to Auschwitz. She described her confinement, the horrors she saw, heard, smelt. Her stories were as difficult to hear as they were vital. But I won't retell them. They're not mine to retell.

I'd long understood that the photo of me in a Nazi uniform had been the result of various failures—failure of thinking, failure of character. But it had also been a failure of education. Not just school education, but self-education. I hadn't known enough about the Nazis, hadn't taught myself enough, hadn't asked enough questions of teachers and families and survivors.

I'd resolved to change that.

I couldn't become the person I hoped to be until I changed that.

41.

M Y PLANE LANDED on an archipelago called Svalbard. March 2011.

Stepping off the plane I did a slow turn, taking it all in. White, white, and more white. As far as the eye could see, nothing but ivory, snowy whiteness. White mountains, white snowdrifts, white hills, and threaded through it were narrow white roads, and not many of those. Most of the two thousand local residents had a snowmobile, not a car. The landscape was so minimalist, so spare, I thought: Maybe I'll move here.

Maybe **this** is my purpose.

Then I found out about the local law forbidding anyone to leave town **without** a gun, because the hills beyond were patrolled by desperately hungry polar bears, and I thought: Maybe not.

We drove into a town called Longyearbyen, the northernmost town on earth, a mere eight hundred miles from the apex of the planet. I met my fellow trekkers. Captain Guy Disney, a cavalryman who'd lost the lower part of his right leg to an RPG. Captain Martin Hewitt, a paratrooper whose arm became paralyzed after he'd been shot. Private Jaco Van Gass, another paratrooper, who'd lost much of his left leg and half his left arm to an RPG. (He gave the remaining nib of his arm a jaunty nickname, Nemo, which always cracked us up.) Sergeant Steve Young, a Welshman, whose back had been broken by an IED. Doctors said he'd never walk again, and now he was about to tug a 200-pound sledge to the North Pole.

Inspiring lot. I told them I was honored to join them, honored just to be in their company, and it didn't matter that the temperature was thirty below. In fact, the weather was so bad we were delayed in setting off.

Ugh, Willy's wedding, I thought, my face in my hands.

We spent several days waiting, training, eating pizza and chips at the local pub. We did some exercises to acclimatize to the harsh temperatures. We pulled on orange immersion suits, jumped into the Arctic Ocean. Shocking how much warmer the water was than the brutally cold air.

But mostly we got to know each other, bonded.

When the weather finally cleared we hopped onto an Antonov and flew up to a makeshift ice camp, then switched to helicopters and flew to within two hundred miles of the Pole. It was about one A.M. when we landed, but bright as midday in a desert. There was no darkness up there: darkness had been banished. We waved goodbye to the helicopters and began.

Experts on Arctic conditions had urged the team to avoid sweating, because any moisture freezes instantly at the North Pole, which causes all kinds of problems. But no one told me. I'd missed those training sessions with the experts. So there I was, after the first day's walk, after the pulling of heavy sledges, absolutely gushing perspiration, and sure enough my clothes were turning to solid ice. More alarming, I was beginning to notice the first spots of trouble on my fingers and ears.

Frostnip.

I didn't complain. How could I, among that bunch? But I also didn't feel like complaining. Despite the discomfort, I felt only gratitude at being with such heroes, at serving such a worthy cause, at seeing a place so few people ever get to see. In fact, on Day Four, when it came time to leave, I didn't want to. Also, we hadn't yet reached the Pole.

Alas, I had no choice. It was leave now or miss my brother's wedding.

I got onto a helicopter, bound for Barneo Airfield, from which my plane was to take off.

The pilot hesitated. He insisted that I needed to see the Pole before leaving. **You can't come all this way and not see it,** he said. So he flew me there and we hopped out into total whiteout. Together, we located the exact spot with GPS.

Standing on top of the world.

Alone.

Holding the Union Jack.

Back on the helicopter, off to Barneo. But just then, a powerful storm came sweeping across the top of the earth, canceling my flight, canceling all flights. Hurricane winds battered the area, growing so intense that they cracked the runway.

Repairs would be required.

While waiting, I hung out with an assortment of

engineers. We drank vodka, sat in their makeshift sauna, then jumped into the ice-cold ocean. Many times I tipped back my head, downed another shot of delicious vodka, told myself not to stress about the runway, the wedding, anything.

The storm passed, the runway got rebuilt, or moved, I forget which. My plane went roaring down the ice and lifted me into the blue sky. I waved out the window. Goodbye, my brothers.

42.

ON THE EVE OF THE wedding Willy and I had dinner at Clarence House with Pa. Also present were James and Thomas—Willy's best men.

The public had been told that I was to be best man, but that was a bare-faced lie. The public expected me to be best man, and thus the Palace saw no choice but to say that I was. In truth, Willy didn't want me giving a best-man speech. He didn't think it safe to hand me a live mic and put me in a position to go off script. I might say something wildly inappropriate.

He wasn't wrong.

Also, the lie gave cover to James and Thomas, two civilians, two innocents. Had they been outed as Willy's best men, the rabid press would've chased them, tracked them, hacked them, investigated them, ruined their families' lives. Both chaps were shy, quiet. They couldn't handle such an onslaught, and shouldn't be expected to.

Willy explained all this to me and I didn't blink. I understood. We even had a laugh about it, speculating about the inappropriate things I might've said in my speech. And so the pre-wedding dinner was pleasant, jolly, despite Willy visibly suffering from standard groom jitters. Thomas and James forced him to down a couple of rum and Cokes, which did seem to settle his nerves. Meanwhile I regaled the company with tales of the North Pole. Pa was very interested, and sympathetic about the discomfort of my frostnipped ears and cheeks, and it was an effort not to overshare and tell him also about my equally tender penis. Upon arriving home I'd been horrified to discover that my nether regions were frostnipped as well, and while the ears and cheeks were already healing, the todger wasn't.

It was becoming more of an issue by the day.

I don't know why I should've been reluctant to discuss my penis with Pa, or all the gentlemen present. My penis was a matter of public record, and indeed some public curiosity. The press had written about it extensively. There were countless stories in books, and papers (even **The New York Times**) about Willy and me not being circumcised. Mummy had forbidden it, they all said, and while it's absolutely true that the chance of getting penile frostbite is much greater if you're not circumcised, all the stories were false. I was snipped as a baby.

After dinner we moved to the TV room and watched the news. Reporters were interviewing folks who'd camped just outside Clarence House, in hopes of getting a front-row seat at the wedding. We went to the window and looked at the thousands of them, in tents and bedrolls, up and down the Mall, which runs between Buckingham Palace and Trafalgar Square. Many were drinking, singing. Some were cooking meals on portable stoves. Others were wandering about, chanting, celebrating, as if **they** were getting married in the morning.

Willy, rum-warmed, shouted: **We should go and see them!**

He texted his security team to say he wanted to do so.

The security team answered: **Strongly advise against.**

No, he shot back. **It's the right thing to do. I want to go out there. I need to see them!**

He asked me to come. He begged.

I could see in his eyes that the rum was really hitting hard. He needed a wingman.

Painfully familiar role for me. But all right.

We went out, walked the edge of the crowd, shaking hands. People wished Willy well, told him they loved him, loved Kate. They gave us both the same teary smiles, the same looks of fondness and pity we'd seen that day in August 1997. I couldn't help but shake my head. Here it was, the eve of Willy's Big Day, one of the happiest of his life, and there was simply no avoiding the echoes of his Worst Day. Our Worst Day.

I looked at him several times. His cheeks were bright crimson, as if he was the one with frostnip.

Maybe that was the reason we bade farewell to the crowd, turned in early. He was tipsy.

But also, emotionally, physically, we were both all in. We needed rest.

I was shocked, therefore, when I went to collect him in the morning and he looked as if he hadn't slept a wink. His face was gaunt, his eyes red.

You OK?

Yeah, yeah, fine.

But he wasn't.

He was wearing the bright red uniform of the Irish Guards, not his Household Cavalry frock coat uniform. I wondered if that was the matter. He'd asked Granny if he could wear his Household Cavalry kit and she'd turned him down. As the Heir, he must wear the Number One Ceremonial, she decreed. Willy was glum at having so little say in what he wore to get married, at having his autonomy taken from him on such an occasion. He'd told me several times that he felt frustrated.

I assured him that he looked bloody smart in the Harp of Ireland, with the Crown Imperial and the forage cap with the regimental motto: **Quis Separabit? Who shall separate us?**

It didn't seem to make an impression.

I, on the other hand, did not look smart, nor did I feel comfortable, in my Blues and Royals uniform, which protocol dictated that I wear. I'd never worn it before and hoped not to wear it again anytime soon. It had huge shoulder pads, and huge cuffs, and I could imagine people saying: **Who's this idiot?** I felt like a kitsch version of Johnny Bravo.

We climbed into a plum-colored Bentley. Neither of us said anything as we waited for the driver to pull out.

As the car pulled away, finally, I broke the silence. **You reek.**

The aftermath of last night's rum.

I jokingly cracked a window, pinched my nose— offered him some mints.

The corners of his mouth bent slightly upward.

After two minutes, the Bentley stopped. **Short trip,** I said.

I peered out of the window:

Westminster Abbey.

As always, my stomach lurched. I thought: Nothing like getting married in the same place where you did your mum's funeral.

I shot a glance at Willy. Was he thinking the same thing?

We went inside, shoulder to shoulder. I looked again at his uniform, his cap. **Who shall separate us?** We were soldiers, grown men, but walking with that same tentative, boyish gait as when we'd trailed Mummy's coffin. **Why did the adults do that to us?** We marched into the church, down the aisle, made for a side room off the altar—called the Crypt. Everything in that building spoke of death.

It wasn't just the memories of Mummy's funeral. More than three thousand bodies lay beneath us, behind us. They were buried under the pews, wedged into the walls. War heroes and poets, scientists and saints, the cream of the Commonwealth. Isaac Newton, Charles Dickens, Chaucer, plus thirteen kings and eighteen queens, they were all interred there.

It was still so hard to think of Mummy in the realm of Death. Mummy, who'd danced with Travolta, who'd quarreled with Elton, who'd dazzled the Reagans—could she really be in the Great Beyond with the spirits of Newton and Chaucer?

Between these thoughts of Mummy and death and my frostnipped penis, I was in danger of becoming as anxious as the groom. So I started pacing, shaking my arms, listening to the crowd murmuring in the pews. They'd been seated two hours before we arrived. **You just know many of them need a pee**, I said to Willy, trying to break the tension.

No reaction. He stood up, started pacing too.

I tried again. **The wedding ring! Oh, no—where is it? Where did I put the bloody thing?**

Then I pulled it out. **Phew!**

He gave a smile, went back to his pacing.

I couldn't have lost that ring if I'd wanted to. A special kangaroo pouch had been sewn inside my tunic. My idea, actually, that was how seriously I took the solemn duty and honor of bearing it.

Now I took the ring from its pouch, held it to the light. A thin band of Welsh gold, shaved off a hunk given to the Royal Family nearly a century before. The same hunk had provided a ring for Granny when she married, and for Princess Margaret, but it was nearly exhausted now, I'd heard. By the time I got married, if I ever got married, there might be none left.

I don't recall leaving the Crypt. I don't recall walking out to the altar. I have no memory of the readings, or removing the ring, or handing it to my brother. The ceremony is mostly a blank in my mind. I recall Kate walking down the aisle, looking incredible, and I recall Willy walking her back up the aisle, and as they disappeared through the door, into the carriage that would convey them to Buckingham Palace, into the eternal partnership they'd pledged, I recall thinking: Goodbye.

I loved my new sister-in-law, I felt she was more **sister** than in-law, the sister I'd never had and always wanted, and I was pleased that she'd forever be standing by Willy's side. She was a good match for my older brother. They made each other visibly happy, and therefore I was happy too. But in my gut I couldn't help feeling that this was yet another farewell under this horrid roof. Another sundering. The brother I'd escorted into Westminster Abbey that morning was gone—forever. Who could deny it? He'd never again be first and foremost Willy. We'd never again ride together across the Lesotho countryside with capes blowing behind us. We'd never again share a horsey-smelling cottage while learning to fly. **Who shall separate us?**

Life, that's who.

I'd had the same feeling when Pa got married, the same presentiment, and hadn't it come true? In the Camilla era, as I'd predicted, I saw him less and less. Weddings were joyous occasions, sure, but they were also low-key funerals, because after saying their vows people tended to disappear.

It occurred to me then that identity is a hierarchy. We are primarily one thing, and then we're primarily another, and then another, and so on, until death—**in succession.** Each new identity assumes the throne of Self, but takes us further from our original self, perhaps our core self—the child. Yes, evolution, maturation, the path towards wisdom, it's all natural and healthy, but there's a purity to childhood, which is diluted with each iteration. As with that hunk of gold, it gets whittled away.

At least, that was the thought I had that day. My big brother Willy had moved on, moved up the line, and thereafter he'd be first a husband, then a father, then grandfather, and so on. He'd be a new person, many new persons, and none of them would be Willy. He'd be The Duke of Cambridge, the title chosen for him by Granny. Good for him, I thought. Great for him. But a loss for me all the same.

I think my reaction was also somewhat reminiscent of what I'd felt the first time I climbed inside an Apache. After being accustomed to having someone at my side, someone to model, I found myself terrifyingly alone.

And a eunuch to boot.

What was the universe out to prove by taking my penis at the same moment it took my brother?

Hours later, at the reception, I made a few quick

remarks. Not a speech, just a brief two-minute intro to the real best men. Willy told me several times that I was to act as "compère."

I had to look the word up.

The press reported extensively on my preparations for this intro, how I phoned Chels and tested some of the lines on her, bristling but ultimately caving when she urged me not to reference "Kate's killer legs," all of which was horseshit. I never phoned Chels about my remarks; she and I weren't in regular touch, which was why Willy checked with me before inviting her to the wedding. He didn't want either of us to feel uncomfortable.

The truth is, I road-tested a few lines on JLP, but mostly I winged it. I told a few jokes about our childhood, a silly story about Willy's days playing water polo, and then I read a few hilarious snippets culled from letters of support sent in by the general public. One American bloke wrote to say that he'd wanted to make something special for the new Duchess of Cambridge, so he'd set out to capture a ton of ermine, traditional fur of royalty. This overenthusiastic Yank explained that he'd intended to catch **one thousand ermines** for the item of clothing he had in mind (God, was it a tent?) but unfortunately he'd only managed to scare up . . . two.

Rough year for ermine, I said.

Still, I added, the Yank improvised, made the best of things, as Yanks do, and cobbled together what he had, which I now held aloft.

The room let out a collective gasp.

It was a thong.

Soft, furry, a few silken strings attached to a V-shaped ermine pouch no larger than the ring pouch inside my tunic.

After the collective gasp came a warm, gratifying wave of laughter.

When it died away I closed on a serious note. Mummy: **How she'd have loved to have been here. How she'd have loved Kate, and how she'd have loved seeing this love you've found together.**

As I spoke these words I didn't look up. I didn't want to risk making eye contact with Pa or Camilla—and above all with Willy. I hadn't cried since Mummy's funeral, and I wasn't going to break that streak now.

I also didn't want to see anyone's face but Mummy's. I had the clearest vision in my mind of her beaming on Willy's Big Day, and having a proper laugh about that dead ermine.

43.

UPON REACHING THE TOP OF the world, the four wounded soldiers uncorked a bottle of champagne and drank to Granny. They were kind enough to phone me and let me listen to their joy.

They'd set a world record, raised a truckload of cash for wounded veterans, and reached the bloody North Pole. What a coup. I congratulated them, told them I missed them, wished I could've been there.

A white lie. My penis was oscillating between

extremely sensitive and borderline traumatized. The last place I wanted to be was Frostnipistan.

I'd been trying some home remedies, including one recommended by a friend. She'd urged me to apply Elizabeth Arden cream.

My mum used that on her lips. You want me to put that on my todger?

It works, Harry. Trust me.

I found a tube, and the minute I opened it the smell transported me through time. I felt as if my mother was right there in the room.

Then I took a smidge and applied it . . . down there.

"Weird" doesn't really do the feeling justice.

I needed to see a doctor, ASAP. But I couldn't ask the Palace to find me one. Some courtier would get wind of my condition and leak it to the press and the next thing I knew my todger would be all over the front pages. I also couldn't just call a doctor on my own, at random. Under normal circumstances that would be impossible, but now it was doubly so. **Hi, Prince Harry here—listen, I seem to be having a spot of bother with my nether regions and I was just wondering if I could pop around and . . .**

I asked another mate to find me, very discreetly, a dermatologist who specialized in certain appendages . . . and certain personages. Tall order.

But the mate came back and said his father knew just the bloke. He gave me a name and address and I jumped into a car with my bodyguards. We sped to a nondescript building on Harley Street, where lots of doctors were housed. One bodyguard snuck me through a back door, into an office. I saw the doctor, seated behind a big wooden desk, making notes, presumably about the previous patient. Without looking up from his notes he said, **Yes, yes, do come in.**

I walked in, watched him writing for what seemed an inordinately long time. The poor chap who went before me, I thought, must have had a lot going on.

Still not looking up, the doctor ordered me to step behind the curtain, take off my clothes, he'd be with me in a moment.

I went behind, stripped, hopped onto the examination table. Five minutes passed.

At last the curtain pulled back and there was the doctor.

He looked at me, blinked once, and said: **Oh. I see. It's you.**

Yes. I thought you'd been warned, but I get the sense you hadn't.

Right. So, you're here. Riiight. OK. It's you. Hm. Remind me of the problem?

I showed him my todger, softened by Elizabeth Arden.

He couldn't see anything.

Nothing to see, I explained. It was an invisible scourge. For whatever reason, my particular case of frostnip manifested as greatly heightened **sensation** . . .

How did this happen? he wanted to know.

North Pole, I told him. I went to the North Pole and now my South Pole is on the fritz.

His face said: Curiouser and curiouser.

I described the cascading dysfunctions. **Everything's difficult, Doctor. Sitting. Walking.** Sex, I added, was out of the question. Worse, my todger constantly felt like it was **having** sex. Or ready to. I was sort of losing it, I told him. I'd made the mistake of googling this injury, and I'd read horror stories about **partial penectomies**, a phrase you never want to come across when googling your symptoms.

The doctor assured me it was unlikely I'd need one of those.

Unlikely?

He said he was going to try to rule out other things. He gave me a full examination, which was more than invasive. No stone unturned, so to speak.

The likeliest cure, he announced at last, would be time.

What do you mean? Time?

Time, he said, **heals.**

Really, Doc? That hasn't been my experience.

44.

IT WAS HARD SEEING CHELS at Willy's wedding. There were loads of feelings still there, feelings I'd suppressed, feelings I hadn't suspected. I also felt a certain way about the hungry-looking men trailing after her, circling her, nagging her to dance.

Jealousy got the better of me that night, and I told her so, which made me feel worse. And a bit pathetic.

I needed to move on, meet someone new. Time, as the doctor predicted, would fix my todger. When would it work its magic on my heart?

Mates tried to help. They mentioned names, arranged meetings, dates.

Nothing ever panned out. So I was barely listening when they mentioned another name in the summer of 2011. They told me a bit about her—brilliant, beautiful, cool—and mentioned her relationship status. She'd just recently become single, they said. And she won't be single long, Spike!

She's free, man. You're free.

Am I?

And you're well matched! No doubt you two will hit it off.

I rolled my eyes. When does that prediction ever pan out?

But then, wonder of wonders, it did. We did. We sat at the bar, chatted and laughed, while the friends with us melted away, along with the walls and the drinks and the barman. I suggested the whole group go back to Clarence House for a nightcap.

We sat around talking, listened to music. Lively group. Merry group. When the party broke up, when everybody cleared out, I gave Florence a lift home. That was her name. Florence. Though everyone called her Flea.

She lived in Notting Hill, she said. Quiet street. When we pulled up outside her flat she invited me up for a cup of tea. Sure, I said.

I asked my bodyguard to drive around the block a few hundred times.

Was it that night or another that Flea told me about her distant ancestor? Actually, it was probably neither. A mate told me later, I think. In any event, he'd led the Charge of the Light Brigade, the doomed advance on Russian guns in Crimea. Incompetent, possibly mad, he'd caused the deaths of a hundred men. A shameful chapter, the polar opposite of Rorke's Drift, and now I was taking a page from his book, bullishly charging full steam ahead. Over that first cup of Earl Grey, I was asking myself: Could she be my person?

The connection was that strong.

But I was also that mad. And I could see she knew it, read it all over my non–poker face. I hoped she found it charming.

Apparently she did. The weeks that followed were idyllic. We saw each other often, laughed a lot, and no one knew.

Hope got the better of me.

Then the press found out and down came the curtain on our idyll.

Flea phoned me in tears. **There were eight paps outside her flat.** They'd chased her halfway across London.

She'd just seen herself described by one paper as "an underwear model." Based on a photoshoot done years and years before! Her life boiled down to one photo, she said. It was so reductive, so degrading.

Yes, I said quietly. **I know what that feels like.**

They were digging, digging, ringing up everyone she'd ever known. They were already after her family. They were giving her the full Caroline Flack treatment, while still giving it to Caroline as well.

Flea just kept saying: **I can't do this.**

She said she was under twenty-four-hour surveillance. Like some kind of criminal. I could hear sirens in the background.

She was upset, crying, and I felt like crying, but of course I didn't.

She said one last time: **I can't do this anymore, Harry.**

I had the phone on speaker. I was on the second floor of Clarence House, standing by the window, surrounded by beautiful furnishings. Lovely room. The lamps were low, the rug at my feet was a work of art. I pressed my face against the window's cold polished glass and asked Flea to see me one last time, at least talk it over.

Soldiers went marching past the house. Changing of the guard.

No.

She was firm.

Weeks later I got a call from one of the friends who'd set us up at the bar. **Didja hear? Flea's got back with the old boyfriend!**

Has she?

Wasn't meant to be, I guess.

Right.

The friend told me he'd heard that it was Flea's

mother who told her to end things, who warned her that the press would destroy her life. **They'll hound you to the gates of Hell**, her mother said.

Yeah, I told the friend. **Mums do know best.**

45.

I STOPPED SLEEPING.
I simply stopped. I was so disappointed, so profoundly dejected, that I just stayed up night after night, pacing, thinking. Wishing I had a TV.

But I was living on a military base now, in a cell-like room.

Then, mornings, on zero sleep, I'd try to fly an Apache.

Recipe for disaster.

I tried herbal remedies. They helped, a bit, I was able to get an hour or two of sleep, but they left me feeling brain-dead most mornings.

Then the Army informed me I'd be hitting the road—a series of maneuvers and exercises.

Maybe just the thing, I thought. Snap me out of it.

Or it might be the last straw.

First they sent me to America. The southwest. I spent a week or so hovering over a bleak place called Gila Bend. Conditions were said to be similar to Afghanistan. I became more fluid with the Apache, more lethal with its missiles. More at home in the dust. I blew up a lot of cacti. I wish I could say it wasn't fun.

Next I went to Cornwall. A desolate place called Bodmin Moor.

January 2012.

From blazing hot to bitter cold. The moors are always cold in January, but I arrived just as a fierce winter storm was blowing in.

I was billeted with twenty other soldiers. We spent the first few days trying to acclimatize. We rose at five A.M., got the blood flowing with a run and a vomit, then bundled into classrooms and learned about the latest methods that bad actors had devised for snatching people. Many of these methods would be put to use against us over the next few days, as we tried to navigate a long march across the frigid moor. The exercise was called Escape and Evasion, and it was one of the last hurdles for flight crews and pilots before deployment.

Trucks took us to an isolated spot, where we did some field lessons, learned some survival techniques. We caught a chicken, killed it, plucked it, ate it. Then it started to rain. We were instantly soaked. And exhausted. Our superiors looked amused.

They grabbed me, and two others, loaded us onto a truck, drove us to a place even more remote.

Out.

We squinted at the terrain, the skies. **Really? Here?**

Colder, heavier rain started to come down. The instructors shouted that we should imagine our helicopter had just crash-landed behind enemy lines, and our only hope of survival was to go by foot from one end of the moor to the other, a distance of ten miles.

We'd been given a meta narrative, which we now recalled: We were a Christian army, fighting a militia sympathetic to Muslims.

Our mission: Evade the enemy, escape the forbidding terrain.

Go.

The truck roared away.

Wet, cold, we looked around, looked at each other. **Well, this sucks.**

We had a map, a compass, and each man had a bivvy bag, essentially a body-length waterproof sock, to sleep in. No food was allowed.

Which way?

This way?

OK.

Bodmin was desolate, allegedly uninhabited, but here and there in the distance we saw farmhouses. Lighted windows, smoke curling from brick chimneys. How we longed to knock on a door. In the good old days people would help out the soldiers on exercise, but now things were different. Locals had been scolded many times by the Army; they knew not to open their doors to strangers with bivvy bags.

One of the two men on my team was my mate Phil. I liked Phil, but I started to feel something like unbounded love for the other man, because he told us he'd visited Bodmin Moor as a summer walker and he knew where we were. More, he knew how to get us out.

He led, we followed like children, through the dark and into the next day.

At dawn we found a wood of fir trees. The temperature approached freezing, the rain fell even harder. We said to hell with our solitary bivvy bags, and curled up together, spooned actually, each trying to get into the middle, where it was warmer. Because I knew him, spooning Phil felt less awkward, and at the same time much more. But the same went for spooning the third man. **Sorry, that your hand?** After a few hours of something vaguely approximating sleep we peeled ourselves apart and began the long march again.

The exercise required that we stop at several checkpoints. At each one we had to complete a task. We managed to hit every checkpoint, perform every task, and at the last checkpoint, a kind of safe house, we were told the exercise was over.

It was the middle of the night. Pitch-black. The directing staff appeared and announced: **Well done, guys! You made it.**

I nearly passed out on my feet.

They loaded us onto a truck, told us we were headed back to the base. Suddenly a group of men in camo jackets and black balaclavas appeared. My first thought was Lord Mountbatten being ambushed by the IRA—I don't know why. Entirely different circumstance, but maybe some vestigial memory of terrorism, deep in my DNA.

There were explosions, gunshots, guys storming the truck and screaming at us to look down at the ground. They wrapped blacked-out ski goggles over our eyes, zip-tied our hands, dragged us off.

We were pushed into what sounded like an underground bunker system. Damp, wet walls. Echoey. We were taken from room to room. The bags over our heads were ripped off, then put back on. In some rooms we were treated well, in others we were treated like dirt. Emotions went up and down. One minute we'd be offered a glass of water, the next we'd be shoved to our knees and told to keep our hands above our heads. Thirty minutes. An hour. From one stress position to another.

We hadn't really slept in seventy-two hours.

Much of what they did to us was illegal under the rules of the Geneva Conventions, which was the goal.

At some point I was blindfolded, moved into a room, where I could sense that I wasn't alone. I had a feeling it was Phil in there with me, but maybe it was the other guy. Or a guy from one of the other teams. I didn't dare ask.

Now we could hear faint voices somewhere above or below, inside the building. Then a strange noise, like running water.

They were trying to confuse, disorient us.

I was terrifyingly cold. I'd never been so cold. Far worse than the North Pole. With the cold came numbness, drowsiness. I snapped to attention when the door burst open and our captors barged in. They took off our blindfolds. I was right, Phil was there. Also the other guy. We were ordered to strip. They pointed at our bodies, our flaccid cocks. They went on and on about how small. I wanted to say: You don't know the half of what's wrong with this appendage.

They interrogated us. We gave them nothing.

They took us into separate rooms, interrogated us some more.

I was told to kneel. Two men walked in, screamed at me.

They left.

Atonal music was piped in. A violin being scraped by an angry two-year-old.

What is that?

A voice answered: **Silence!**

I became convinced that the music wasn't a recording, but an actual child, perhaps also being held prisoner. What in heaven's name was that kid doing to that violin? More—what were they doing to that kid?

The men returned. Now they had Phil. They'd gone through his social media, studied him, and they began saying things about his family, his girlfriend, which scared him. It was astonishing how much they knew. How can perfect strangers know so much?

I smiled: Welcome to the party, pal.

I wasn't taking this seriously enough. One of the men grabbed me, shoved me against a wall. He wore a black balaclava. He pressed his forearm into my neck, spitting every word from his mouth. He pressed my shoulders against the concrete. He ordered me to stand three feet from the wall, arms above my head, all ten fingertips against the wall.

Stress position.

Two minutes.

Ten minutes.

My shoulders started to seize.

I couldn't breathe.

A woman entered. She was wearing a **shemagh** over her face. She went on and on about something, I didn't understand. I couldn't keep up.

Then I realized. Mummy. She was talking about my mother.

Your mother was pregnant when she died, eh? With your sibling? A Muslim baby!

I fought to turn my head, to look at her. I said nothing but I screamed at her with my eyes. **You doing this for my benefit now—or yours? Is this the exercise? Or you getting a cheap thrill?**

She stormed out. One of the captors spat in my face.

We heard the sound of gunshots.

And a helicopter.

We were dragged into a different room and some-one called out, **OK, that's it. End exercise!**

There was a debrief, during which one of the instructors offered a half-arsed apology about the stuff to do with my mother.

Hard for us to find something about you that you'd be shocked we knew.

I didn't answer.

We felt you needed to be tested.

I didn't answer.

But that took it a bit too far.

Fair enough.

Later I learned that two other soldiers in the exercise had gone mad.

46.

I'D BARELY RECOVERED from Bodmin Moor when word came down from Granny. She wanted me to go to the Caribbean. A two-week tour to commemorate her sixtieth year on the throne, my first official royal tour representing her.

It was strange to be called away so suddenly, with a finger snap, from my Army duties, especially so close to deployment.

But then I realized it wasn't strange at all.

She was, after all, my commander.

March 2012. I flew to Belize, drove from the airport to my first event along roads thronged with people, all waving signs and flags. At my first stop, and every stop thereafter, I drank toasts to Granny and my hosts with homemade alcohol, and performed many rounds of a local dance called the punta.

I also had my first taste of cow-foot soup, which had more of a kick than the homemade alcohol.

At one stop I told a crowd: **Unu come, mek we goo paati.** In Creole that means: **Come on, let's party.** The crowd lost it.

People cheered my name, and shouted my name, but many shouted my mother's name. At one stop a lady hugged me and cried: **Diana's baby!** Then fainted.

I visited a lost city called Xunantunich. Thriving Mayan metropolis, centuries ago, a guide told me.

I climbed a stone temple, El Castillo, which was intricately carved with hieroglyphs, friezes, faces. At the top someone said this was the highest point in the whole nation. The view was stunning, but I couldn't help looking down at my feet. Below were the bones of untold numbers of dead Mayan royals. A Mayan Westminster Abbey.

In the Bahamas I met ministers, musicians, journalists, athletes, priests. I attended church services, street festivals, a state dinner, and drank more toasts. I rode out to Harbour Island in a speedboat that broke down and began to sink. As we took on water, along came the press boat. I wanted to say no thanks, never, but it was either join them or swim for it.

I met India Hicks, Pa's goddaughter, one of Mummy's bridesmaids. She took me along the Harbour Island beach. The sand was bright pink. **Pink sand?** It made me feel stoned. Not altogether unpleasant. She told me why the sand was pink, a scientific explanation, which I didn't understand.

At some point I visited a stadium full of children. They lived in abject poverty, faced daily challenges, and yet they greeted me with jubilant cheers and laughter. We played, danced, did a little boxing. I'd always loved children, but I felt an even keener connection to this group because I'd just become a godfather—to Marko's son Jasper. Deep honor. And an important signpost, I thought, I hoped, in my evolution as a man.

Towards the end of the visit the Bahamian children

gathered around me and presented me with a gift. A gigantic silver crown and an enormous red cape.

One of them said: **For Her Majesty.**

I'll see that she gets it.

I hugged many of them on my way out of the stadium, and on the plane to the next stop I donned their crown proudly. It was the size of an Easter basket and my staff dissolved into fits of hysterical laughter.

You look a perfect idiot, sir.

That may be. But I'm going to wear it at the next stop.

Oh, sir, no, sir, please!

I still don't know how they talked me out of it.

I went to Jamaica, bonded with the prime minister, ran a footrace with Usain Bolt. (I won, but cheated.) I danced with a woman to Bob Marley's "One Love."

> **Let's get together to fight this holy**
> **Armagiddyon (one love)**

At every stop, it seemed, I planted a tree, or several. Royal tradition—though I added a twist. Normally, when you arrive at a tree planting, the tree is already in the ground, and you just throw a ceremonial bit of soil into the hole. I insisted on actually planting the tree, covering the roots, giving it some water. People seemed shocked by this break with protocol. They treated it as radical.

I told them: **I just want to make sure the tree will live.**

47.

WHEN I GOT HOME, the reviews were raves. I'd represented the Crown well, according to courtiers. I reported back to Granny, told her about the tour.

Marvelous. Well done, she said.

I wanted to celebrate, felt I deserved to celebrate. Also, with war in the offing, it was celebrate now or maybe never.

Parties, clubs, pubs, I went out a lot that spring, and tried not to care that, no matter where I went, two paps were always present. Two sorry-looking, extremely terrible paps: Tweedle Dumb and Tweedle Dumber.

For much of my adult life there had been paps waiting for me outside public places. Sometimes a mob of them, sometimes a handful. The faces always varied, and often I couldn't even see the faces. But now there were always these two faces, and always clearly visible. When there was a mob, they were right in the middle. When there was no one else, they were there all by themselves.

But it wasn't just public places. I'd be walking down a side street, which I'd only decided to walk down seconds before, and they'd leap from a phone box or from under a parked car. I'd leave a friend's apartment, certain that no one knew I'd been there, and they'd be standing outside the building, in the middle of the street.

Besides being everywhere, they were ruthless, much more aggressive than other paps. They'd block my path, they'd chase me to my police car. They'd block me from getting into the car, then chase the car down the street.

Who were they? How were they doing this? I didn't think they had any kind of sixth sense or extrasensory perception. On the contrary, they looked as if they didn't possess one full frontal cortex between them. So, what hidden trick were they leveraging? An invisible tracker? A source inside the police?

They were after Willy too. He and I talked about them a lot that year, talked about their unsettling appearance, their complementary ruthlessness and idiocy, their take-no-prisoners approach. But mainly we discussed their omnipresence.

How do they know? How do they always know?

Willy had no idea, but was determined to find out.

Billy the Rock was determined as well. He walked up to the Tweedles several times, interrogated them, looked deep into their eyes. He managed to get a sense of them. The older, Tweedle Dumb, was doughy, he reported, with close-cropped black hair and a smile that chilled the blood. Tweedle Dumber, on the other hand, never smiled, and rarely spoke. He seemed to be some sort of apprentice. Mostly he just stared.

What was their game? Billy didn't know.

Following me everywhere, tormenting me, getting rich off me, even that wasn't enough for them. They also liked to rub my nose in it. They'd run alongside me, taunt me, while pressing the buttons on their cameras, reeling off two hundred photos in ten seconds. Many paps wanted a reaction, a tussle, but what Tweedle Dumb and Tweedle Dumber seemed to want was a fight to the death. Blinded, I'd fantasize about punching them. Then I'd take deep breaths, remind myself: Don't do it. That's just what they want. So they can sue and become famous.

Because, in the end, I decided **that** was their game. That was what it was all about: two fellas who weren't famous, thinking it must be fabulous to be famous, trying to become famous by attacking and ruining the life of someone famous.

Why did they want to be famous? That was the thing I never understood. Because fame is the ultimate freedom? What a joke. Some kinds of fame provide extra freedom, maybe, I suppose, but royal fame was fancy captivity.

The Tweedles couldn't fathom this. They were children, incapable of understanding anything nuanced. In their simplified cosmology: You're royal. So. This is the price you pay for living in a castle.

Sometimes I wondered how it might go if I could just talk to them, calmly, explain that I didn't live in a castle, my grandmother lived in a castle, that in fact Tweedle Dumb and Tweedle Dumber both had far grander lifestyles than mine. Billy had done a deep dive on their finances, so I knew. Each Tweedle owned multiple houses, and several luxury cars, purchased with proceeds from their photos of me and my family. (Offshore bank accounts too, like their sponsors, the media barons who funded them, chiefly Murdoch and the impossibly Dickensian-sounding Jonathan Harmsworth, 4th Viscount Rothermere.)

It was around this time that I began to think Murdoch was evil. No, strike that. I began to know that he was. Firsthand. Once you've been chased by someone's henchmen through the streets of a busy modern city you lose all doubt about where they stand on the Great Moral Continuum. All my life I'd heard jokes about the links between royal misbehavior and centuries of inbreeding, but it was then that I realized: Lack of genetic diversity was nothing compared to press gaslighting. Marrying your cousin is far less dicey than becoming a profit center for Murdoch Inc.

Of course I didn't care for Murdoch's politics, which were just to the right of the Taliban's. And I didn't like the harm he did each and every day to Truth, his wanton desecration of objective facts. Indeed, I couldn't think of a single human being in the 300,000-year history of the species who'd done more damage to our collective sense of reality. But what really sickened and frightened me in 2012 was Murdoch's ever-expanding circle of flunkies: young, broken, desperate men willing to do whatever was necessary to earn one of his Grinchy smiles.

And at the center of that circle . . . were these two mopes, the Tweedles.

There were so many nightmarish run-ins with Tweedle Dumb and Tweedle Dumber, but one stands out. A friend's wedding. Walled garden, totally secluded. I was chatting with several guests, listening to the birdsong, the whoosh of wind in the leaves. Within these soothing sounds, however, I became aware of one small . . . **click**.

I turned. There, in the hedgerow. One eye. And one glassy lens.

Then: that chubby face.

Then: that demonic rictus.

Tweedle Dumb.

48.

THE ONE GOOD THING about Tweedle Dumb and Tweedle Dumber was that they made me ready for war. They filled me with choking rage, always a good precursor for battle. They also made me want to be anywhere but England. **Where are my goddamned orders?**

Please send my orders.

And then, of course, as so often happens . . .

I was at a music festival and my cousin tapped me on the shoulder. **Harry, this is my friend Cressida.**

Oh. Um. Hello.

The setting was inauspicious. Lots of people, zero privacy. Also, I was still suffering a broken heart. On the other hand, the landscape was lovely, the music was good, the weather was fine.

There were sparks.

Soon after that day we went to dinner. She told me about her life, her family, her dreams. She wanted to be an actress. She was so soft-spoken and shy, acting was the last profession I'd have imagined for her, and I said so. But she confessed that it made her feel alive. Free. She made it sound like flying.

Weeks later, at the end of another date, I gave her a lift home. **I'm just off the King's Road.** We pulled up to a large house on a well-kept street.

You live here? This is your house?

No.

She explained that she was staying for a few days with an aunt.

I walked her up the steps. She didn't invite me in. I didn't expect her to, didn't want her to. Take it slow, I thought. I leaned in to give her a kiss, but my aim was off. I could take out a cactus from three miles away with a Hellfire missile but I couldn't quite find her lips. She turned, I tried again on the return trip, and we managed something like a graze. Painfully awkward.

The next morning I phoned my cousin. Discouraged, I told her the date had gone well, but the ending had left something to be desired. She didn't disagree. She'd already spoken to Cressida. She sighed. **Awkward.**

But then came the good news. Cressida was game to try again.

We met days later for another dinner.

As it happened, her flatmate was dating my longtime mate Charlie. Brother of my late friend Henners.

I joked: **Obviously this is meant to be. The four of us could have so much fun.**

But I wasn't totally joking.

We tried another kiss. Not so awkward.

I had hope.

For our next date she and her flatmate had Charlie and me over. Drinks, laughs. Before I knew what was happening, we were a thing.

Sadly, however, I could only see Cress at weekends. I was busier than ever, doing my final preps for deployment. And then I got my official orders, my actual deployment date, and the clock was now loudly ticking. For the second time in my life I needed to tell a young woman I'd just met that I'd soon be going off to war.

I'll wait, she said. **But not forever**, she added quickly. **Who knows what's going to happen, Haz?**

Right. Who knows?

Easier to just tell myself, and others, that we're not together.

Yes. That is easier, I suppose.

But when you're back . . .

When. She'd said **when**. Not **if**.

I was grateful.

Some people said if.

49.

MY MATES CAME TO me and reminded me of the Plan.

The Plan?

You know, Spike. The Plan?

Oh, right? The Plan.

We'd talked about this before, months earlier. But now I wasn't sure.

They gave me the hard sell. **You're going to war. Staring death in the face.**

Right, thanks.

You have a duty to live. Now. Seize the day.

Seize the—?

Carpe diem.

OK . . . what?

Carpe diem. Seize the day.

Ah, so it's two ways of saying the same thing then—

Vegas, Spike! Remember? The Plan.

Yes, yes, The Plan, but . . . seems risky.

Seize the—!

Day. Got it.

I'd had an experience, recently, that made me think they weren't altogether wrong, that **carpe diem** was more than empty words. Playing polo that spring in Brazil, to raise money for Sentebale, I'd seen a player take a hard fall from his horse. As a boy, I'd seen Pa take that same fall, the horse giving way, the ground simultaneously smacking and swallowing him. I remembered thinking: Why's Pa snoring? And then someone yelling: **He's swallowed his tongue!** A quick-thinking player jumped from his horse and saved Pa's life. Recalling that moment, subconsciously, I'd done likewise: jumped off my horse, run to the man, pulled out his tongue.

The man coughed, began to breathe again.

I'm fairly sure he wrote a sizable check later that afternoon to Sentebale.

But equally valuable was the lesson. Carpe your diems while ye may.

So I told my mates: **OK. Vegas. Let's go**.

A year before, after exercises in Gila Bend, my mates and I had rented Harleys, ridden from Phoenix to Vegas. Most of the trip went unnoticed. So now, after a farewell weekend with Cressida, I flew to Nevada to do it again.

We even went to the same hotel, and all chipped in on the same suite.

It had two levels, connected by a grand staircase of white marble, which looked as if Elvis and Wayne Newton were about to descend arm in arm. You didn't need to take the stairs, however, since the suite also had a lift. And a billiard table.

The best part was the living room: six massive windows looking onto the Strip, and arranged before the windows was a low L-shaped sofa where you could gaze at the Strip, or the distant mountains, or the massive wall-mounted plasma TV. Such opulence. I'd been inside a few palaces in my time, and this was palatial.

That first night, or the next—it's a bit of a neon blur—someone ordered food, someone else ordered cocktails, and we all sat around and had a loud chat, catching up. What happened to everyone since we'd last been in Vegas?

So, Lieutenant Wales, raring to go back to war?

I am, I really am.

Everyone looked taken aback.

For dinner we hit a steakhouse, and ate like kings. New York strips, three kinds of pasta, really nice red wine. Afterwards, we went to a casino, played blackjack and roulette, lost. Tired, I excused myself, went back to the suite.

Yes, I thought with a sigh, sliding under the covers, I'm that guy, turning in early, telling everyone to please keep it down.

The next morning we ordered breakfast, Bloody Marys. We all headed off to the pool. It was pool-party season in Vegas, so a big blowout was raging. We bought fifty beach balls and handed them out, as a way of breaking the ice.

We really were that nerdy. And needy.

That is, my mates were. I wasn't looking to make new friends. I had a girlfriend, and I aimed to keep it that way. I texted her several times from the pool, to reassure her.

But people kept handing me drinks. And by the time the sun was dipping over the mountains I was in rough shape, and filling up with . . . ideas.

I need something to commemorate this trip, I decided. Something to symbolize my sense of freedom, my sense of carpe diem.

For instance . . . a tattoo?

Yes! Just the thing!

Maybe on my shoulder?

No, too visible.

Lower back?

No, too . . . racy.

Maybe my foot?

Yes. The sole of my foot! Where the skin had once peeled away. Layers upon layers of symbolism!

Now, what would the tattoo be?

I thought and thought. What's important to me? What's sacred?

Of course—Botswana.

I'd seen a tattoo parlor down the block. I hoped they'd have a good atlas, with a clear map of Botswana.

I went to find Billy the Rock to tell him where we were going. He smiled.

No way.

My mates backed him up. **Absolutely not.**

In fact, they promised to physically stop me. I was not going to get a tattoo, they said, not on their watch, least of all a foot tattoo of Botswana. They promised to hold me down, knock me out, whatever it took.

A tattoo is permanent, Spike! It's forever!

Their arguments and threats are one of my last clear memories from that evening.

I gave in. The tattoo could wait till the next day.

Instead, we trooped off to a club, where I curled into the corner of a leather banquette and watched a procession of young women come and go, chatting up my mates. I talked to one or two, and encouraged them to focus on my mates. But mostly I stared into space and thought about being forced to forgo my tattoo dream.

Around two A.M. we went back to our suite. My mates invited four or five women who worked at the hotel to join us, along with two women they'd met at the blackjack tables. Soon someone suggested we play pool, and that did sound fun. I racked the balls, started playing eight-ball with my bodyguards.

Then I noticed the blackjack girls hovering. They looked dodgy. But when they asked if they could play I didn't want to be rude. Everyone took turns, and no one was very good.

I suggested we up the stakes. How about a game of strip pool?

Enthusiastic cheers.

Ten minutes later I was the big loser, reduced to my skivvies. Then I lost my skivvies. It was harmless, silly, or so I thought. Until the next day. Standing outside the hotel in the blinding desert sun I turned and saw one of my mates staring at his phone, his mouth falling open. He told me: Spike, one of those blackjack girls secretly snapped a few photos . . . and sold them.

Spike . . . you're everywhere, mate.

Specifically what was everywhere was my arse. I was naked before the eyes of the world . . . seizing my diem.

Billy the Rock, now studying his phone, kept saying: **This isn't good, H.**

He knew this was going to be hard for me. But he also knew it wasn't going to be any fun for himself and the other bodyguards. They could easily lose their jobs over this.

I berated myself: How had I let it happen? How had I been so stupid? Why had I trusted other people? I'd counted on strangers having goodwill, I'd counted on those dodgy girls showing some **basic** decency, and now I was going to pay the price forever. These photos would never go away. They were permanent. They'd make a foot tattoo of Botswana look like a splodge of Indian ink.

My sense of guilt and shame made it hard at moments to draw a clean breath. Meanwhile, the papers back home had already begun skinning me alive. **The Return of Hooray Harry. Prince Thicko Strikes Again.**

I thought of Cress reading the stories. I thought of my superiors in the Army.

Who would give me the heave-ho first?

While waiting to find out, I fled to Scotland, met up with my family at Balmoral. It was August and they were all there. Yes, I thought, yes, the one thing missing from this Kafkaesque nightmare is Balmoral, with all its complicated memories and the pending anniversary of Mummy's death just days away.

Soon after my arrival I met Pa at nearby Birkhall. To my surprise, to my relief, he was gentle. Even bemused. He felt for me, he said, he'd been there, though he'd never been naked on a front page. Actually, that was untrue. When I was about eight years old a German newspaper had published naked photos of him, taken with a telephoto lens while he was holidaying in France.

But he and I had both put those photos out of our minds.

Certainly he'd **felt** naked many times before the world, and that was our common ground. We sat by a window and talked for quite a long time about this strange existence of ours, while watching Birkhall's red squirrels frolic on the lawn.

Carpe diem, squirrels.

50.

MY ARMY SUPERIORS, LIKE PA, were nonplussed. They didn't care about me playing billiards in the privacy of a hotel room, naked or not. My status remained unchanged, they said. All systems go.

My fellow soldiers stood up for me too. Men and women in uniform, all around the world, posed naked, or nearly so, covering their privates with helmets, weapons, berets, and posted the photos online, in solidarity with Prince Harry.

As for Cress: After hearing my careful and abashed explanation, she came to the same conclusion. I'd been a dummy, not a debaucher.

I apologized for embarrassing her.

Best of all, none of my bodyguards were dismissed or even disciplined—mainly because I kept it a secret that they'd been with me at the time.

But the British papers, even knowing I was off to war, continued to vent and fume as if I'd committed a capital offense.

It was a good time to leave.

September 2012. The same eternal flight, but this time I wasn't a stowaway. This time there was no hidden alcove, no secret bunkbeds. This time I was allowed to sit with all the other soldiers, to feel part of a team.

As we touched down at Camp Bastion, however, I realized I wasn't quite one of the lads. Some looked nervous, their collars tighter, their Adam's apples larger. I remembered that feeling, but for me this was coming home. After more than four years, and against all odds, I was finally back. As a Captain. (I'd been promoted since my first tour.)

My accommodation this time was better. In fact, compared to my last tour, it was Vegas-esque. Pilots were treated like—the word was unavoidable, everybody used it—royalty. Soft beds, clean rooms. More, the rooms were actual rooms, not trenches or tents. Each even had its own air-con unit.

We were given a week to learn our way around Bastion, and to recover from jet lag. Other Bastionites were helpful, more than happy to show us the ropes.

Captain Wales, this is where the latrines are!

Captain Wales, over here is where you'll find hot pizza!

It felt a bit like a field trip, until, on the eve of my twenty-eighth birthday, I was sitting in my room, organizing my stuff, and sirens started going off. I opened my door, peered out. All down the hall other doors were flying open, other heads popping out.

Now both my bodyguards came running. (Unlike the last tour of duty, I had bodyguards this time, mainly because there was proper accommodation for them, and because they could blend in: I was living with thousands of others.) One said: **We're under attack!**

We heard explosions in the distance, near the aircraft hangars. I started to run for my Apache but my bodyguards stopped me.

Way too dangerous.

We heard shouting outside. **Make ready! MAKE READY!**

We all got into body armor and stood in the doorway to await the next instructions. As I double-checked my vest and helmet one bodyguard kept up a constant patter: **I knew this was going to happen, I just knew it, I told everyone, but no one would listen. Shut up, they said, but I told them, I told them, Harry's going to get hurt! Fuck off, they said, and now here we are.**

He was a Scot, with a thick burr, and often sounded like Sean Connery, which was charming under normal circumstances, but now he just sounded like Sean Connery having a panic attack. I cut off his long story about being an unappreciated Cassandra and told him to put a sock in it.

I felt naked. I had my 9-mm, but my SA80A was locked up. I had my bodyguards, but I needed my Apache. That was the only place I'd feel safe—and useful. I needed to rain fire down on our attackers, whoever they were.

More explosions, louder explosions. The windows flickered. Now we saw flames. American Cobras came thumping overhead and the whole building shuddered. The Cobras fired. The Apaches fired. An awesome roar filled the room. We all felt dread, and adrenaline. But we Apache pilots were especially agitated, itching to get into our cockpits.

Someone reminded me that Bastion was about the size of Reading. How could we ever navigate our way from here to the helicopters without a map, while taking fire?

That was when we heard the all-clear.

The sirens stopped. The thump of rotors faded.

Bastion was secure again.

But at a terrible price, we learned. Two American soldiers were killed. Seventeen British and American soldiers were injured.

Throughout that day and the next we pieced together what happened. Taliban fighters had got hold of American uniforms, cut a hole in the fence, and slipped in.

They cut a hole in the fence?

Yep.

Why?

In short, me.

They were looking for Prince Harry, they said.

The Taliban actually issued a statement: Prince Harry was our target. And the date of the attack had been carefully chosen as well.

They'd timed it, they proclaimed, to coincide with my birthday.

I didn't know if I believed that.

I didn't want to believe it.

But one thing was beyond dispute. The Taliban

had learned about my presence on the base, and the granular details of my tour, through the nonstop coverage that week in the British press.

51.

THERE WAS SOME TALK, after the attack, about pulling me off the battlefield. Again.

I couldn't bear to think about that. It was too awful to contemplate.

To keep my mind off the possibility, I fell to my work, got into the rhythm of the job.

My schedule was helpfully rigid: two days of planned ops, three days of VHR (very high readiness). In other words, sitting around a tent, waiting to be summoned.

The VHR tent had the look and feel of a student room at university. The collegiality, the boredom— the mess. There were several cracked-leather couches, a big Union Jack on the wall, snack foods everywhere. We'd pass the time playing FIFA, drinking gallons of coffee, flipping through lad mags. (**Loaded** was quite popular.) But then the alarm would sound and my student days, along with every other era of my life, would feel a million miles away.

One of the lads said we were glorified firefighters. He wasn't wrong. Never fully asleep, never fully relaxed, always ready to go. We could be sipping a cup of tea, eating an ice cream, crying about a girl, having a chat about football, but our senses were always tuned and our muscles were always taut, awaiting that alarm.

The alarm itself was a phone. Red, plain, no buttons, no dial, just a base and handset. Its ringer was antique, consummately British. **Brrrang.** The sound was vaguely familiar; I couldn't place it at first. Eventually I realized. It was exactly like Granny's phone at Sandringham on her big desk, in the huge sitting room where she took calls between games of bridge.

There were always four of us in the VHR tent. Two flight crews of two men each, a pilot and a gunner. I was a gunner and my pilot was Dave—tall, lanky, built like a long-distance marathoner, which in fact he was. He had short dark hair and an epic desert tan.

More glaringly, he possessed a deeply enigmatic sense of humor. Several times a day I'd ask myself: Is Dave serious? Is he being sarcastic? I could never tell. It's going to take me a while to solve this guy, I'd think. But I never did.

Upon hearing the red phone ring, three of us would drop everything, bolt for the Apache, while the fourth would answer the phone and gather details of the op from a voice at the other end. Was it a medevac? (Medical evacuation.) A TIC? (Troops in contact.) If the latter, how far were the troops, how quickly could we get to them?

Once inside the Apache we'd fire up the air-con, strap on harnesses and body armor. I'd click on one of the four radios, get more details on the mission, punch the GPS coordinates into the onboard computer. The first time you ever start an Apache, going through preflight checks takes one hour, if not more. After a few weeks at Bastion, Dave and I had it down to eight minutes. And it still felt like an eternity.

We were always heavy. Brimming with fuel, bristling with a full complement of missiles, plus enough 30-mm rounds to turn a concrete apartment building into Swiss cheese—you could feel all that **stuff** holding you down, tying you to Earth. My first-ever mission, a TIC, I **resented** the feeling, the contrast between our urgency and Earth's gravity.

I remember clearing Bastion's sandbag walls with inches to spare, not flinching, not giving that wall a second thought. There was work to do, lives to save. Then, seconds later, a cockpit warning light began flashing. **ENG CHIPS.**

Meaning: Land. Now.

Shit. We're going to have to put down in Taliban territory. I started thinking of Bodmin Moor.

Then I thought . . . maybe we could just ignore the warning light?

No, Dave was already turning us back to Bastion.

He was the more experienced flier. He'd already done three tours, he knew all about those warning lights. Some you could ignore—they blinked all the time and you pulled out the fuses to make them shut up—but not this one.

I felt cheated. I wanted to go, go, go. I was willing to risk crashing, being taken prisoner—whatever. Ours not to reason why, as Flea's great-granddad said, or Tennyson. Whoever. The point was: Unto the breach.

52.

I NEVER FULLY GOT OVER how fast the Apache was. We'd usually cruise above a target area at a civilized 70 knots. But often, hurrying to the target area, we'd open her up, push her all the way to 145. And since we were barely off the ground, it felt three times faster. What a privilege, I thought, to experience this kind of raw power, and to put it to work for our side.

Flying super low was standard operating procedure. Harder for Taliban fighters to see you coming. Alas, easier for local kids to throw rocks at us. Which they did all the time. Children throwing rocks was about all the Taliban had in the way of anti-aircraft capability, other than a few Russian SAMs.

The problem wasn't evading the Taliban but finding them. In the four years since my first tour, they'd got much better at escaping. Humans are adaptable, but never more so than in war. The Taliban had worked out exactly how many minutes they had from first contact with our troops until the cavalry came over the horizon, and their internal clocks were finely calibrated: they'd shoot at as many guys as possible, then bolt.

They'd got better at hiding too. They could effortlessly melt into a village, blend into the civilian population, or vaporize into their network of tunnels. They didn't run away—it was far more diffuse than that, more mystical.

We didn't give up the search easily. We'd circle, sweep back and forth, sometimes for two hours. (The Apache ran out of fuel after two hours.) Sometimes, at the end of two hours, we'd still be unwilling to give up. So we'd refuel.

One day we refueled three times, spending a total of eight hours in the air.

When we finally returned to base the situation was dire: I'd run out of piss bags.

53.

I WAS THE FIRST in my squadron to pull the trigger in anger.

I remember the night as well as any in my life. We were in the VHR tent, the red phone rang, we all sprinted to the aircraft. Dave and I raced through preflight checks, I gathered the mission details: One of the control points closest to Bastion had come under small arms fire. We needed to get there, ASAP, and find out where the fire was coming from. We took off, swept over the wall, went vertical, climbed to fifteen hundred feet. Moments later I swung the night sight onto the target area. **There!**

Eight hot spots, eight kilometers away. Thermal smudges—walking from where the contact had been.

Dave said: **That's got to be them!**

Yeah—there's no friendly forces out here on patrol! Especially not at this hour.

Let's make sure. Confirm no patrols outside the wall.

I called the J-TAC. Confirmed: no patrols.

We flew above the eight hot spots. They quickly broke into two groups of four. Evenly spaced, they went slowly along a track. That was our patrolling technique—were they mimicking us?

Now they hopped on mopeds, some two-up, some one-up. I told Control we were visual on all eight targets, asked for clearance, permission to fire. Permission was a must before engaging, always, unless it was a case of self-defense or imminent danger.

Beneath my seat was a 30-mm cannon, plus two Hellfires on the wing, 50-kg guided missiles that could be fitted with different warheads, one of which was excellent for obliterating high-value targets. Besides Hellfires we had a few unguided air-to-ground rockets, which on our particular Apache were flechette. To shoot the flechette you had to tip the helicopter down at a precise angle; only then would the flechette fly out like a cloud of darts. That's what the flechette was, in fact, a lethal burst of eighty 5-inch tungsten darts. I remembered in Garmsir hearing about our forces having to pick pieces of Taliban guys out of trees after a direct hit from flechette.

Dave and I were ready to fire that flechette. But permission still hadn't come.

We waited. And waited. And watched the Taliban speeding off in different directions.

I said to Dave: **If I find out later that one of these guys has injured or killed one of our guys after we let them go . . .**

We stayed with two motorbikes, followed them down a windy road.

Now they separated.

We picked one, followed it.

Finally Control got back to us.

The persons you're following . . . what's their status?

I shook my head and thought: **Most of them are gone, because you've been so slow.**

I said: **They've split up and we're down to one bike. Permission to fire.**

Dave said to use the Hellfire. I was nervous about using it, however; I shot the 30-mm cannon instead.

Mistake. I hit the motorbike. One man down, presumably dead, but one hopped off and ran into a building.

We circled, called in ground troops.

You were right, I told Dave. **Should've used the Hellfire.**

No worries, he said. **It was your first time.**

Long after returning to base, I did a sort of mental scan. I'd been in combat before, I'd killed before, but this was my most direct contact with the enemy— ever. Other engagements felt more impersonal. This one was eyes on target, finger on trigger, fire away.

I asked myself how I felt.

Traumatized?

No.

Sad?

No.

Surprised?

No. Prepared in every way. Doing my job. What we'd trained for.

I asked myself if I was callous, perhaps desensitized. I asked myself if my non-reaction was connected to a long-standing ambivalence towards death.

I didn't think so.

It was really just simple maths. These were bad people doing bad things to our guys. Doing bad things to the world. If this guy I'd just removed from the battlefield hadn't already killed British soldiers, he soon would. Taking him meant saving British lives, sparing British families. Taking him meant fewer young men and women wrapped like mummies and shipped home on hospital beds, like the lads on my plane four years earlier, or the wounded men and women I'd visited at Selly Oak and other hospitals, or the brave team with whom I'd marched to the North Pole.

And so my main thought that day, my only thought, was that I wished Control had got back to us sooner, had given us permission to fire more quickly, so we'd got the other seven.

And yet, and yet. Much later, speaking about it with a mate, he asked: **Did it factor into your feeling that these killers were on motorbikes? The chosen vehicle of paps all over the world?** Could I honestly say that, while chasing a pack of motorbikes, not one particle of me was thinking about the pack of motorbikes that chased one Mercedes into a Paris tunnel?

Or the packs of motorbikes that had chased me a thousand times?

I couldn't say.

54.

ONE OF OUR DRONES had been watching the Taliban school its fighters.

Despite popular assumptions, the Taliban had good equipment. Nothing like ours, but good, effective—when used correctly. So they often needed to bring their soldiers up to speed. There were frequent tutorials in the desert, instructors demonstrating the newest gear from Russia and Iran. That was what this lesson captured by the drones seemed to be. A shooting lesson.

The red phone rang. Down went the coffee mugs and PlayStation controls. We ran to the Apaches, flew north at a good clip, twenty-five feet off the ground.

Darkness was starting to fall. We were ordered by controllers to hold off, about eight kilometers.

In the deepening twilight we could barely see the target area. Just shadows moving about.

Bikes leaning against a wall.

Wait, we were told.

We circled and circled.

Wait.

Shallow breaths.

Now came the signal: The shooting lesson is over. Giddyup. Go, go, go.

The instructor, the high-value target, was on a motorbike, one of his students on the back. We screamed towards them, clocked them moving along at 40 k.p.h., one of them carrying a hot-barreled PKM machine gun. I held my thumb over the cursor, watched the screen, waited. **There!** I pulled one trigger to fire the pointing laser and another to fire the missile.

The thumbstick I fired was remarkably similar to the thumbstick for the PlayStation game I'd just been playing.

The missile hit just short of the motorbike's spokes. Textbook. Exactly where I'd been taught to aim. Too high, you might send it over the top of his head. Too low, you'd take out nothing but dirt and sand.

Delta Hotel. Direct hit.

I followed up with the 30-mm.

Where the motorbike had been was now a cloud of smoke and flames.

Well done, Dave said.

We swooped back to camp, critiqued the video.

Perfect kill.

We played some more PlayStation.

Turned in early.

55.

IT CAN BE HARD TO BE precise with Hellfires. Apaches fly with such tremendous speed that it's hard to take steady aim. Hard for some anyway. I developed pinpoint accuracy, as if I was throwing darts in a pub.

My targets were moving fast too. The speediest motorbike I shot was going about 50 k.p.h. The driver, a Taliban commander who'd been calling in fire all day on our forces, was hunched over the handlebars, looking back as we gave chase. He was purposely speeding between villages, using civilians for cover. Old people, children, they were mere props to him.

Our windows of opportunity were those one-minute spans when he was between villages.

I remember Dave calling out: **You've got two hundred meters till it's a no-go.**

Meaning, two hundred meters until this Taliban commander was hiding behind another child.

I heard Dave again: **You've got trees coming on the left, wall on the right.**

Roger.

Dave moved us into the five o'clock position, dropped to six hundred feet. **Now—**

I took the shot. The Hellfire smacked the motorbike, sent it flying into a small thatch of trees. Dave flew us over the trees, and through plumes of smoke we saw a ball of fire. And the bike. But no body.

I was ready to follow up with the 30-mm, strafe the area, but I couldn't see anything to strafe.

We circled and circled. I was getting nervous. **Did he get away, mate?**

There he is!

Fifty feet to the right of the motorbike: body on the ground.

Confirmed.

Away we flew.

56.

THREE TIMES WE WERE called to this same forlorn place: a string of bunkers overlooking a busy highway. We had intel that Taliban fighters were routinely gathering there. They came in three cars, jalopies, carrying RPGs and machine guns, took up positions and waited for lorries to come down the road.

Controllers had seen them blow up at least one convoy.

There were sometimes half a dozen men, sometimes as many as thirty. Taliban, clear as day.

But three times we flew there to engage, and three times we failed to get permission to fire. We never knew why.

This time we were determined things would be different.

We got there fast, saw a lorry coming down the road, saw the men taking aim. Bad things were about to happen. That lorry's doomed, we said, unless we do something.

We requested permission to engage.

Permission denied.

We asked again. **Ground Control, request permission to engage hostile target—!**

Stand by . . .
Boom. A huge flash and an explosion on the road.
We screamed for permission.
Stand by . . . waiting for ground commander clearance.

We went screaming in, saw the lorry blown to pieces, saw the men jumping into their jalopies and onto motorbikes. We followed two motorbikes. We begged for permission to fire. Now we were requesting a different kind of permission: not permission to stop an act, but permission to address an act just witnessed.

This kind of permission was called 429 Alpha.

Do we have Four Two Nine Alpha to engage?
Stand by . . .

We kept following the two motorbikes through several villages, while griping about the bureaucracy of war, the reluctance of higher-ups to let us do what we'd been trained to do. Maybe, in our griping, we were no different from soldiers in every war. We wanted to fight: we didn't understand larger issues, underlying geopolitics. Big picture. Some commanders often said, publicly and privately, that they feared every Taliban killed would create three more, so they were extra cautious. At times we felt the commanders were right: we **were** creating more Taliban. But there had to be a better answer than floating nearby while innocents got slaughtered.

Five minutes became ten became twenty.

We never did get permission.

57.

EVERY KILL WAS ON VIDEO.

The Apache saw all. The camera in its nose recorded all. So, after every mission, there would be a careful review of that video.

Returning to Bastion, we'd walk into the gun tape room, slide the video into a machine, which would project the kill onto wall-mounted plasma TVs. Our squadron commander would press his face against the screens, examining, murmuring—wrinkling his nose. He wasn't merely looking for errors, this chap, he was hungry for them. He wanted to catch us in a mistake.

We called him awful names when he wasn't around. We came close to calling him those names to his face. **Look, whose side are you on?**

But that was what he wanted. He was trying to provoke us, to get us to say the unspeakable.

Why?

Jealousy, we decided.

It ate him up inside that he'd never pulled a trigger in battle. He'd never attacked the enemy.

So he attacked us.

Despite his best efforts, he never found anything irregular in any of our kills. I was part of six missions that ended in the taking of human life, and they were all deemed justified by a man who wanted to crucify us. I deemed them the same.

What made the squadron commander's attitude so execrable was this: He was exploiting a real and legitimate fear. A fear we all shared. Afghanistan was a war of mistakes, a war of enormous collateral damage—thousands of innocents killed and maimed, and that always haunted us. So my goal from the day I arrived was never to go to bed doubting that I'd done the right thing, that my targets had been correct, that I was firing on Taliban and only Taliban, no civilians nearby. I wanted to return to Britain with all my limbs, but more, I wanted to go home with my conscience intact. Which meant being aware of what I was doing, and why I was doing it, at all times.

Most soldiers can't tell you precisely how much death is on their ledger. In battle conditions, there's often a great deal of indiscriminate firing. But in the age of Apaches and laptops, everything I did in the course of two combat tours was recorded, time-stamped. I could always say precisely how many enemy combatants I'd killed. And I felt it vital never to shy away from that number. Among the many things I learned in the Army, accountability was near the top of the list.

So, my number: Twenty-five. It wasn't a number that gave me any satisfaction. But neither was it a number that made me feel ashamed. Naturally, I'd have preferred not to have that number on my military CV, on my mind, but by the same token I'd have preferred to live in a world in which there was no Taliban, a world without war. Even for an occasional practitioner of magical thinking like me, however, some realities just can't be changed.

While in the heat and fog of combat, I didn't think of those twenty-five as people. You can't kill people if you think of them as people. You can't really harm people if you think of them as people. They were chess pieces removed from the board, Bads taken away before they could kill Goods. I'd been trained to "other-ize" them, trained well. On some level I recognized this learned detachment as problematic. But I also saw it as an unavoidable part of soldiering.

Another reality that couldn't be changed.

Not to say that I was some kind of automaton. I never forgot being in that TV room at Eton, the one with the blue doors, watching the Twin Towers melt as people leaped from the roofs and high windows. I never forgot the parents and spouses and children I met in New York, clutching photos of the moms and dads who'd been crushed or vaporized or burned alive. September 11 was vile, indelible, and all those responsible, along with their sympathizers and enablers, their allies and successors, were not just our enemies, but enemies of humanity. Fighting them meant avenging one of the most heinous crimes in world history, and preventing it from happening again.

As my tour neared its end, around Christmas 2012, I had questions and qualms about the war, but none of these was moral. I still believed in the Mission, and the only shots I thought twice about were the ones I hadn't taken. For instance, the night we were called in to help some Gurkhas. They were pinned down by a nest of Taliban fighters, and when we arrived there was a breakdown in communications, so we simply weren't able to help. It haunts me still: hearing my Gurkha brothers calling out on the radio, remembering every Gurkha I'd known and loved, being prevented from doing anything.

As I fastened my bags and said my goodbyes I was honest with myself: I acknowledged plenty of regrets. But they were the healthy kind. I regretted the things I **hadn't** done, the Brits and Yanks I hadn't been able to help.

I regretted the job not being finished.

Most of all, I regretted that it was time to leave.

58.

I STUFFED MY BERGEN FULL of dusty clothes, plus two souvenirs: a rug bought in a bazaar, a 30-mm shell casing from the Apache.

The first week of 2013.

Before I could get onto the plane with my fellow soldiers I went into a tent and sat in the one empty chair.

The obligatory exit interview.

The chosen reporter asked what I'd done in Afghanistan.

I told him.

He asked if I'd fired on the enemy.

What? Yes.

His head went back. Surprised.

What did he think we were doing over here? Selling magazine subscriptions?

He asked if I'd killed anyone.

Yes . . .

Again, surprised.

I tried to explain: **It's a war, mate, you know?**

The conversation came around to the press. I told the reporter that I thought the British press was crap, particularly with regard to my brother and sister-in-law, who'd just announced that they were pregnant, and were subsequently being besieged.

They deserve to have their baby in peace, I said.

I admitted that my father had begged me to stop thinking about the press, to not read the papers. I admitted that I felt guilty every time I did, because it made me complicit. **Everyone's guilty for buying the newspapers. But hopefully no one actually believes what's in them.**

But of course they did. People did believe, and that was the whole problem. Britons, among the most literate people on the planet, were also the most credulous. Even if they didn't believe every word, there was always that residue of wonder. **Hmm, where there's smoke there must be fire . . .** Even if a falsehood was disproved, debunked beyond all doubt, that residue of initial belief remained.

Especially if the falsehood was negative. Of all human biases, "negativity bias" is the most indelible. It's baked into our brains. Privilege the negative, prioritize the negative—that's how our ancestors survived. That's what the bloody papers count on, I wanted to say.

But didn't. It wasn't that kind of discussion. Wasn't a discussion at all. The reporter was keen to move on, to ask about Vegas.

Naughty Harry, eh? Hooray Harry.

I felt a mix of complicated emotions about saying goodbye to Afghanistan, but I couldn't wait to say goodbye to this chap.

First, I flew with my squadron to Cyprus, for what the Army called "decompression." I hadn't had any mandated decompression after my last tour, so I was excited, though not as much as my bodyguards. **Finally! We can have a bloody cold beer!**

Everyone was issued exactly two cans. No more. I didn't like beer, so I handed mine over to a soldier who looked like he needed it more than me. He reacted as if I'd given him a Rolex.

We were then taken to a comedy show. Attendance was quasi-mandatory. Whoever organized it had had good intentions: a bit of levity after a tour of hell. And, to be fair, some of us did laugh. But most didn't. We were struggling and didn't know we were struggling. We had memories to process, mental wounds to heal, existential questions to sort. (We'd been told that a padre was available if we needed to talk, but I remember no one going near him.) So we just sat at the comedy show in the same way we'd sat in the VHR tent. In a state of suspended animation. Waiting.

I felt bad for those comedians. One tough gig.

Before we left Cyprus someone told me I was all over the papers.

Oh yeah?

The interview.

Shit. I'd completely forgotten.

Apparently I'd caused quite a stir by admitting that I'd killed people. In a war.

I was criticized up and down for being . . . a killer?

And being blithe about it.

I'd mentioned, in passing, that the Apache controls were reminiscent of video-game controls. And thus:

Harry compares killing to video game!

I threw down the paper. Where was that padre?

59.

I TEXTED CRESS, TOLD HER I was home.

She texted back, said she was relieved, which made me relieved.

I hadn't been sure what to expect.

I wanted to see her. And yet we didn't make a plan. Not in that first exchange. There was some distance there, some stiffness.

You sound different, Harry.

Well, I don't feel different.

I didn't want her to think I was different.

A week later, some mates gave a dinner party. Welcome home, Spike! At my mate Arthur's place. Cress turned up with my cousin Eugenie—a.k.a.

Euge. I hugged them both, saw the shock on their faces.

They said I looked like a completely different person.

Stockier? Bigger? Older?

Yes, yes, all that. But also something else they couldn't name.

Whatever it was, it seemed frightening or off-putting to Cressida.

We agreed, therefore, that this wasn't a reunion. Couldn't be. Can't have a reunion with someone you don't know. If we wanted to keep seeing each other—and I certainly did—we'd have to start again.

Hello, I'm Cress.

Hello, I'm Haz. Nice to meet you.

60.

I GOT UP EACH day, went to the base, did my work, enjoyed none of it. It felt pointless.

And boring. I was bored to tears.

More, for the first time in years, I was without a purpose. A goal.

What's next? I asked myself every night.

I begged my commanding officers to send me back.

Back where?

To the war.

Oh, they said, **ha-ha, no**.

In March 2013 word came down that the Palace

wanted to send me on another royal tour. My first since the Caribbean. This time: America.

I was glad for the break in the monotony. On the other hand I was also worried about returning to the scene of the crime. I imagined days and days of questions about Vegas.

No, Palace courtiers assured me. Impossible. Time and the war had eclipsed Vegas. This was strictly a goodwill tour, to promote the rehabilitation of wounded British and American soldiers. **No one is going to mention Vegas, sir.** Cut to May 2013, me touring the devastation caused by Hurricane Sandy, alongside New Jersey governor Chris Christie. The governor gifted me a blue fleece, which the press spun . . . **as his way of keeping me clothed.** Actually, Christie spun it that way too. A reporter asked him what he thought of my time in Las Vegas, and Christie vowed that if I spent the whole day with him, "nobody's going to get naked." The line got a big laugh, because Christie is famously stout.

Before Jersey I'd gone to Washington, D.C., met with President Barack Obama and First Lady Michelle Obama, visited Arlington National Cemetery, laid a wreath at the Tomb of the Unknown Soldier. I'd laid dozens of wreaths before, but the ritual was different in America. You didn't place the wreath on the grave yourself; a white-gloved soldier placed it with you, and then you laid your hand singly, for one beat, upon the wreath. This extra step, this partnering with another living soldier, moved me. Holding my hand to the wreath for that extra second, I found myself a bit wobbly, my mind flooding with images of all the men and women with whom I'd served. I thought about death, injury, grief, from Helmand Province to Hurricane Sandy to the Alma tunnel, and I wondered how other people just got on with their lives, whereas I felt such doubt and confusion—and something else.

What? I wondered.

Sadness?

Numbness?

I couldn't name it. And without being able to give it a name, I felt a kind of vertigo.

What was happening to me?

The whole American tour lasted only five days— a true whirlwind. So many sights, and faces, and remarkable moments. But on the flight home I was thinking about only one part.

A stop-off in Colorado. Something called the Warrior Games. A kind of Olympiad for wounded soldiers, with two hundred men and women taking part, each of whom inspired me.

I watched them closely, saw them having the time of their lives, saw them competing to the hilt, and I asked them . . . how?

Sport, they said. The most direct route to healing.

Most were natural athletes, and they told me these games had given them a rare chance to rediscover and express their physical talents, despite their wounds. As a result it made their wounds, both mental and physical, disappear. Maybe only for a moment, or a day, but that was enough. More than enough. Once you've made a wound disappear for any length of time, it's no longer in control—you are.

Yes, I thought. I get that.

And so, on the flight back to Britain, I kept going over those games in my mind, wondering if we could do something similar in Britain. A version of those Warrior Games, but perhaps with more soldiers, more visibility, more benefits to participants. I scribbled some notes on a sheet of paper and by the time my plane touched down I had the essential idea sketched out.

A Paralympics for soldiers from all over the world! In London's Olympic Park! Where the London Olympics had just happened!

With full support and cooperation from the Palace. Maybe?

Big ask. But I felt that I'd accrued some political capital. Despite Vegas, despite at least one article that made me out to be some kind of war criminal, despite my whole checkered history as the naughty one, Britons seemed to have a generally positive view of the Spare. There was a feeling that I was coming into my own. Plus, most Brits had a positive view of the military community overall, despite the unpopularity of the war. Surely they'd be supportive of an effort to help soldiers and their families.

The first step would be pitching the Royal Foundation Board, which oversaw my charitable projects and Willy's and Kate's. It was **our** foundation, so I told myself: No problem.

Also, the calendar was on my side. This was early

summer 2013. Willy and Kate, weeks from having their first child, were going to be out of commission for a while. The foundation therefore didn't have any projects in the pipeline. Its roughly seven million pounds was just sitting there, doing nothing. And if these International Warrior Games worked, they'd enhance the foundation's profile, which would energize donors and replenish the foundation's accounts many times over. There'd be that much more to go around when Willy and Kate came back full-time. So I was feeling supremely confident in the days leading up to my pitch.

But when the actual day came, not so much. I realized how badly I wanted this, for the soldiers and their families, and if I'm being honest: for myself. And this sudden attack of nerves kept me from being at my best. Still, I got through it, and the board said yes.

Thrilled, I reached out to Willy, expecting him to be thrilled as well.

He was sorely irritated. He wished I'd run all this by him first.

My assumption, I said, was that other people had done so.

He complained that I'd be using up all the funds in the Royal Foundation.

That's absurd, I spluttered. I was told only a half-million-pound grant would be needed to get the games going, a fraction of the foundation's money. Besides, it was coming from the Endeavour Fund, an arm of the foundation I'd created specifically for veterans' recovery. The rest would come from donors and sponsors.

What was going on here? I wondered.

Then I realized: My God, sibling rivalry.

I put a hand over my eyes. Had we not got past this yet? The whole Heir versus Spare thing? Wasn't it a bit late in the day for that tired childhood dynamic?

But even if it wasn't, even if Willy insisted on being competitive, on turning our brotherhood into some kind of private Olympiad, hadn't he built up an insurmountable lead? He was married, with a baby on the way, while I was eating takeaway alone over the sink.

Pa's sink! I still lived with Pa!

Game over, man. You win.

61.

I EXPECTED MAGIC. I thought this challenging, en-nobling task of creating an International Warrior Games would propel me into the next phase of my postwar life. It didn't work out like that. Instead, day by day, I felt more sluggish. More hopeless. More lost.

By the late summer of 2013 I was in trouble, toggling between bouts of debilitating lethargy and terrifying panic attacks.

My official life was all about being in public, standing up in front of people, giving speeches and talks, doing interviews, and now I found myself nearly incapable of fulfilling these basic functions. Hours before a speech or public appearance I'd be soaked with sweat. Then, during the event itself, I'd be unable to think, my mind buzzing with fear and fantasies of running away.

Time and again I just managed to stave off the urge to flee. But I could envisage a day when I wouldn't be able to, when I'd actually sprint off a stage or burst out of a room. Indeed, that day seemed to be coming fast, and I could already picture the blaring headlines, which always made the anxiety three times worse.

The panic often started with putting on a suit first thing in the morning. Strange—that was my trigger: The Suit. As I buttoned up my shirt I could feel my blood pressure soaring. As I knotted my tie I could feel my throat closing. By the time I was pulling on the jacket, lacing the smart shoes, sweat was running down my cheeks and back.

I'd always been sensitive to heat. Like Pa. He and I would joke about it. We're not made for this world, we said. Bloody snowmen. The dining room at Sandringham, for instance, was our version of Dante's **Inferno**. Much of Sandringham was balmy, but the dining room was subtropical. Pa and I would always wait for Granny to look away, then one of us would jump up, sprint to a window, crack it an inch. **Ah, blessed cool air.** But the corgis always betrayed us. The cool air would make them whimper, and Granny would say: **Is there a draft?** And then a footman would promptly shut the window. (That loud thump, unavoidable because the windows were so old, always felt like the door of a jail cell being slammed.) But now, every time I was about to make any kind of public appearance, no matter the venue, it felt like the Sandringham dining room. During one speech I became so overheated that I felt sure everyone was noticing and discussing it. During one drinks reception I searched frantically for anyone else who might be experiencing the same heatstroke. I needed some assurance that it wasn't just me.

But it was.

As is so often true of fear, mine metastasized. Soon it wasn't merely public appearances, but all public venues. All crowds. I came to fear simply being around other human beings.

More than anything else I feared cameras. I'd never liked cameras, of course, but now I couldn't abide them. The telltale click of a shutter opening and closing . . . it could knock me sideways for a whole day.

I had no choice: I began staying home. Day after day, night after night, I sat around eating takeaway, watching **24**. Or **Friends**. I think I might've watched every episode of **Friends** in 2013.

I decided I was a Chandler.

My **actual** friends would comment in passing that I didn't seem myself. As if I had flu. Sometimes I'd think, Maybe I'm **not** myself. Maybe that's what's going on here. Maybe this is some kind of metamorphosis. A new self is emerging, and I'm just going to have to be this new person, this frightened person, for the rest of my days.

Or maybe this had always been me, and it was only now becoming evident? My psyche, like water, had found its level.

I ransacked Google for explanations. I plugged my symptoms into various medical search engines. I kept trying to self-diagnose, to put a name to what was wrong with me . . . when the answer was right under my nose. I'd met so many soldiers, so many young men and women suffering from post-traumatic stress, and I'd heard them describe how hard it was to leave the house, how uncomfortable it was to be around other people, how excruciating it was to enter a public space—especially if it was loud. I'd heard them talk about timing their visit to a shop or supermarket carefully, making sure to arrive minutes before closing time, to avoid the crowds and noise. I'd empathized with them, deeply, and yet never made the connection. It never occurred to me that I, too, was suffering from post-traumatic stress. Despite all my work with wounded soldiers, all my efforts on their behalf, all my struggles to create a games that would spotlight their condition, it never dawned on me that I was a wounded soldier.

And my war didn't begin in Afghanistan.

It began in August 1997.

62.

I PHONED MY FRIEND Thomas one evening. Thomas, brother of my beloved mate Henners.

Thomas, so funny and witty. Thomas, with the in-
fectious laugh.

Thomas, living reminder of better days.

I was at Clarence House, sitting on the floor of the
TV room. Probably watching **Friends**.

Hey, Boose, what're you up to?

He laughed. No one else called him Boose.

Harr-eese! Hello!

I smiled. No one else called me Harr-eese.

He said he was just leaving a business dinner.
He was pleased to have someone to chat with while
he was making his way home.

His voice, so much like his brother's, was an instant
comfort. It made me happy, even though Thomas
wasn't happy. He, too, was struggling, he said. Going
through a divorce, other challenges.

The conversation went inexorably to that original
challenge, the wellspring of all challenges, Henners.
Thomas missed his brother so much. Me too, I said.
Man, me too.

He thanked me for speaking at an event to raise
money for Henners's charity.

Wouldn't miss it. That's what friends are for.

I thought of the event. And the pre-event panic
attack.

Then we reminisced, randomly. Thomas and
Henners, Willy and me, Saturday mornings, lounging around with Mummy, watching telly—having
burping contests.

She was like a teenage boy!

She was, mate.

Going with Mummy to see Andrew Lloyd Webber.

Me and Henners mooning the security cameras at Ludgrove.

We both started laughing.

He reminded me that Henners and I were so close, people called us Jack and Russell. Maybe that was because Willy and I had Jack Russells? Oh I wondered where Henners might be. Was he with Mummy? Was he with the dead from Afghanistan? Was Gan-Gan there too? I was jolted from this train of thought by the sound of Thomas screaming.

Boose, mate, you OK?

Angry voices, a scuffle, a struggle. I put the phone on speaker, shot down the corridor, up the stairs, burst into the police room. I shouted that my mate was in trouble. We leaned over the phone, listening, but the line had already gone dead.

It was obvious: Thomas was being mugged. Luckily he'd just happened to mention the name of the restaurant where he'd had dinner. It was in Battersea. Plus, I knew where he lived. We checked a map: there was only one logical route between those two points. Several bodyguards and I raced there and found Thomas on the side of the road. Near Albert Bridge. Beaten, shaken. We took him to the nearest police station, where he signed a statement. Then we drove him home.

Along the way he kept thanking me for coming to his rescue.

I hugged him tightly. **What friends are for.**

63.

I WAS GIVEN A DESK AT Wattisham Airfield, which I hated. I'd never wanted a desk. I couldn't bear sitting at a desk. My father loved his desk, seemed pinned to it, enamored of it, surrounded by his books and mailbags. That was never me.

I was also given a new task. Refine my knowledge of the Apache. Perhaps on the way to becoming an instructor. That **was** a job I thought **might** be fun. Teaching others to fly.

But it wasn't. It just didn't feel like my calling.

Once again I broached the idea of going back to the war. Once again the answer was a hard no. Even if the Army was inclined to send me, Afghanistan was winding down.

Libya was heating up, though. **How about that?**

No, the Army said—in every way they knew how, officially and unofficially, they denied my request.

Everyone has had quite enough of Harry in a war zone.

At the end of a typical working day I'd leave Wattisham, drive back to Kensington Palace. I was no longer staying with Pa and Camilla: I'd been assigned my own place, a flat on KP's "lower ground floor," in other words, halfway underground.

The flat had three tall windows, but they admitted little light, so the differences between dawn, dusk and midday were nominal at best. Sometimes the question was rendered moot by Mr. R, who lived directly upstairs. He liked to park his massive gray Discovery hard against the windows, blotting out all light entirely.

I wrote him a note, politely asking if he might perhaps pull his car forward a few inches. He fired back a reply telling me to suck eggs. Then he went to Granny and asked her to tell me the same.

She never did speak to me about it, but the fact that Mr. R felt secure enough, supported enough, to denounce me to the monarch showed my true place in the pecking order. He was one of Granny's equerries.

I should fight, I told myself. I should confront the man face-to-face. But I figured—no. The flat actually suited my mood. Darkness at noon suited my mood.

Also, it was the first time I was living on my own, somewhere other than Pa's, so on balance I really had no complaints.

I invited a mate over one day. He said the flat reminded him of a badger sett. Or maybe I said that to him. Either way, it was true, and I didn't mind.

We were chatting, my mate and I, having a drink, when suddenly a sheet dropped down in front of my windows. Then the sheet began to shake. My mate stood, went to the window and said: **Spike . . . what in the . . . ?** Falling from the sheet was a cascade of what looked to be—brown confetti?

No.

Glitter?

No.

My mate said: **Spike, is that hair?**

It was. Mrs. R was giving a trim to one of her sons,

shaking out the sheet in which she'd collected the clippings. The real problem, however, was that my three windows were open and it was a breezy day. Gusts of fine hair blew into the flat. My mate and I coughed, laughed, picked strands off our tongues.

What didn't come into the flat landed like summer rain on the shared garden, which just then was blooming with mint and rosemary.

For days I went around composing a harsh note to Mrs. R in my head. I never sent it. I knew I was being unfair: she didn't know she was hairing me out. More, she didn't know the real source of my antipathy towards her. She was guilty of an even more egregious vehicular crime than her husband. Every day Mrs. R parked her car in Mummy's old spot.

I can still see her gliding into that space, right where my mother's green BMW used to be. It was wrong of me, and I knew it was wrong, but on some level I condemned Mrs. R for it.

64.

I WAS AN UNCLE. Willy and Kate had welcomed their first child, George, and he was beautiful. I couldn't wait to teach him about rugby and Rorke's Drift, flying and corridor cricket—and maybe give him a few pointers about how to survive life in the fishbowl.

Reporters, however, used this joyous occasion as an opportunity to ask me . . . if I was miserable.

What?

The baby had moved me one link down the chain of succession, making me fourth from the throne instead of third. So reporters said, Bad luck, eh?

You must be joking.

There must be some misgivings.

Couldn't be happier.

A half-truth.

I was delighted for Willy and Kate, and I was indifferent to my place in the order of succession.

But nothing to do with either thing, I wasn't anywhere close to happy.

65.

ANGOLA. I traveled to that war-torn country, an official visit, and went specifically to several places where daily life had been poisoned by land mines, including one town believed to be the most heavily mined place in all of Africa.

August 2013.

I wore the same protective gear my mother had worn when she visited Angola on her historic trip. I even worked with the same charity that had invited her: Halo Trust. I was deeply frustrated to learn from the charity's executives and fieldworkers that the job she'd spotlighted, indeed the entire global crusade my mother had helped launch, was now stalled. Lack of resources, lack of resolve.

This had been Mummy's most passionate cause

at the end. (She'd gone to Bosnia three weeks before she'd gone to Paris in August 1997.) Many could still remember her walking alone into a live minefield, detonating a mine via remote control, announcing bravely: "One down, seventeen million to go." Her vision of a world rid of land mines seemed within reach back then. Now the world was going backwards.

Taking up her cause, detonating a land mine myself, made me feel closer to her, and gave me strength, and hope. For a brief moment. But overall I felt that I was walking each day through a psychological, emotional minefield. I never knew when the next explosion of panic might be.

Upon returning to Britain, I did another dive into the research. I was desperate to find a cause, a treatment. I even spoke to Pa, took him into my confidence. **Pa, I'm really struggling with panic attacks and anxiety.** He sent me to a doctor, which was kind of him, but the doctor was a general practitioner with no knowledge or new ideas. He wanted to give me pills.

I didn't want to take pills.

Not until I'd exhausted other remedies, including homeopathic ones. In my research I came across many people recommending magnesium, which was said to have a calming effect. True, it did. But in large quantities it also had unpleasant side effects—loosens the bowels—which I learned the hard way at a mate's wedding.

Over dinner one night at Highgrove, Pa and I spoke at some length about what I'd been suffering.

I gave him the particulars, told him story after story. Towards the end of the meal he looked down at his plate and said softly: **I suppose it's my fault. I should've got you the help you needed years ago.**

I assured him that it wasn't his fault. But I appreciated the apology.

As autumn neared my anxiety was heightened, I think, by my impending birthday, the last of my twenties. Dregs of my youth, I thought. I was beset by all the traditional doubts and fears, asked myself all the basic questions people ask when they get older. Who am I? Where am I going? Normal, I told myself, except that the press was abnormally echoing my self-questioning.

Prince Harry . . . Why Won't He Marry?

They dredged up every relationship I'd ever had, every girl I'd ever been seen with, put it all into a blender, hired "experts," a.k.a. quacks, to try to make sense of it. Books about me dived into my love life, homed in on each romantic failure and near miss. I seem to recall one detailing my flirtation with Cameron Diaz. Harry just couldn't see himself with her, the author reported. Indeed I couldn't, since we'd never met. I was never within fifty meters of Ms. Diaz, further proof that if you like reading pure bollocks then royal biographies are just your thing.

Behind all this hand-wringing about me was something more substantive than "tittle-tattle." It went to the whole underpinning of the monarchy, which was **based** on marriage. The great controversies about kings and queens, going back centuries, generally centered on whom they married, and whom they didn't, and the children who issued from those unions. You weren't a fully vested member of the Royal Family, indeed a true human being, until you were wed. No coincidence that Granny, head of state in sixteen countries, started every speech: "My husband and I . . ." When Willy and Kate married they became The Duke and Duchess of Cambridge, but more important they became a Household, and as such were entitled to more staff, more cars, bigger home, grander office, extra resources, engraved letterheads. I didn't care about such perks, but I did care about respect. As a confirmed bachelor I was an outsider, a nonperson within my own family. If I wanted that to change, I had to get hitched. That simple.

All of which made my twenty-ninth birthday a complex milestone, and some days a complex migraine.

I shuddered to think of how I might feel on the next birthday: thirty. Truly over-the-hill. To say nothing of the inheritance it would trigger. Upon reaching thirty I'd receive a large sum left to me by Mummy. I scolded myself for being gloomy about that: most people would kill to inherit money. To me, however, it was another reminder of her absence, another sign of the void she'd left, which pounds and euros could never fill.

The best thing, I decided, was to get away from birthdays, get away from everything. I decided to mark the anniversary of my arrival on Earth by traveling to its end. I'd already been to the North Pole. Now I'd walk to the South.

Another trek in the company of Walking With The Wounded.

People warned me that the South Pole was even colder than the North. I laughed. How could that be possible? I'd already frozen my penis, mate—wasn't that the very definition of worst-case scenario?

Also, this time I'd know how to take proper precautions—snugger underwear, more padding, etc. Better yet, one very close mate hired a seamstress to make me a bespoke cock cushion. Square, supportive, it was sewn from pieces of the softest fleece and . . .

Enough said.

66.

IN BETWEEN PREPARATIONS for the assault on the Pole I sat down with my new private secretary, Ed Lane Fox, whom we all called Elf.

November 2013.

A onetime captain in the Household Cavalry, Elf was trim, smart, sleek. He often reminded people of Willy, but that was down to his hairline more than his personality. He reminded me less of my older brother than of a racing dog. Like a greyhound, he wouldn't ever stop. He'd chase that rabbit to the end of time. In other words, he was wholly dedicated to the Cause, whatever it might be at any given moment.

His greatest gift, though, might've been his knack

for seeing to the heart of things, for sizing up and simplifying situations and problems, which made him the perfect man to help enact this ambitious idea of an International Warrior Games.

Now that some of the money was in hand, Elf advised, next order of business was finding someone with the uncommon organizational skills, the social and political connections, to take on a job this size. He knew of just the man.

Sir Keith Mills.

Of course, I said. Sir Keith had organized the 2012 Olympics, in London, which had been such a smash.

Indeed, who else could there be?

Let's invite Sir Keith to Kensington Palace for a cup of tea.

67.

I COULD BUILD A SCALE REPLICA of that sitting room. Two big windows, small red sofa, chandelier shining softly on an oil painting of a horse. I'd been there for meetings before. But when I walked in that day, I felt that this would be the setting for one of the more crucial meetings of my life, and every detail of the scene impressed itself on me.

I tried to stay calm as I pointed Sir Keith to a chair and asked how he took his tea.

After a few minutes of chitchat, I made my pitch.

Sir Keith listened respectfully, raptor-eyed, but when I'd finished he ummed and aahed.

All sounded very wonderful, he said, but he was semi-retired. Trying to cut back on projects, you know. He wanted to streamline his life, focus on his passions, chiefly sailing. America's Cup, and so forth.

In fact he was scheduled to begin a holiday the very next day.

How to talk to a man who's just hours away from starting a holiday into rolling up his sleeves and taking on an impossible project?

There's no way, I thought.

But the whole point of these games was: Never give up.

So I kept on. I went at him, and at him, and told him about the soldiers I'd met, their stories, and also a bit of mine. One of the first and fullest accounts I'd ever given anyone of my time at war.

Slowly I could see that my passion, my enthusiasm, were making dents in Sir Keith's defenses.

Brow furrowed, he said: **Well . . . Who have you got so far on this project?**

I looked at Elf. Elf looked at me.

That's the beauty of it, Sir Keith. You see . . . you're the first.

He chuckled. **Clever.**

No, no, really. You can get the band back together, if you wish. Hire anyone you want.

Despite the overt and obvious salesmanship, there was a great deal of truth in what I was saying. We hadn't yet managed to trick anyone else into joining us, so he'd have carte blanche. He could organize a staff however he wished, bring on every single person who'd helped him pull off such a successful Olympics.

He nodded. **When are you thinking of doing this?**

September.

What?

September.

You mean ten months from now?

Yes.

No way.

Has to be.

I wanted the games to coincide with the centenary commemorations of the First World War. I felt that connection was vital.

He sighed, promised to consider it.

I knew what that meant.

68.

A FEW WEEKS LATER I flew to the Antarctic, landed at a research station called Novolazarevskaya, a tiny village of huts and Portakabins. The few hardy souls living there were fabulous hosts. They housed me, fed me—their soups were amazing. I couldn't get enough.

Maybe because it was thirty-five degrees below zero?

More piping-hot chicken noodle, Harry?

Yes, please.

The team and I spent a week or two carb-loading, gearing up. And, of course, quaffing vodka. At last, one bleary morning . . . off we went. We climbed into a plane, flew up to the ice shelf, stopped to refuel. The plane landed on a field of solid, flat white, as in a dream. There was nothing to be seen in any direction but a handful of giant fuel barrels. We taxied over to them and I got out while the pilots filled up. The silence was holy—not a bird, not a car, not a tree—but it was only one part of the larger, all-encompassing nothingness. No smells, no wind, no sharp corners or distinct features to distract from the endless and insanely beautiful vista. I walked off to be by myself for a few moments. I'd never been anywhere half so peaceful. Overcome with joy, I did a headstand. Months and months of anxiety passed away . . . for a few minutes.

We got back onto the plane, flew to the starting point of the trek. As we began walking, at last, I remembered: Oh, yeah, my toe's broken.

Just recently, in fact. A boys' weekend in Norfolk. We drank and smoked and partied till dawn, and then, while trying to reassemble one of the rooms we'd rearranged, I dropped a heavy chair with brass wheels onto my foot.

Silly injury. But debilitating. I could barely walk. No matter, I was determined not to let the team down.

Somehow I kept pace with my fellow walkers, nine hours each day, pulling a sledge that weighed about two hundred pounds. It was hard for everyone to gain traction on the snow, but for me the particular challenge was the slick, undulating patches carved out by the wind. Sastrugi, that was the Norwegian word for these patches. Trekking across sastrugi with a broken toe? Maybe this could be an event at the International Warrior Games, I thought. But any time I felt tempted to complain—about my toe, my fatigue, anything—I had only to glance at my fellow walkers. I was directly behind a Scottish soldier named Duncan, who had no legs. Behind me, an American soldier named Ivan was blind. So not one whinge would be heard from me, I vowed.

Also, an experienced polar guide had advised me before I left Britain to use this trek to "clean the hard drive." That was his phrase. **Use** the repetitive motion, he said, **use** the biting cold, **use** that nothingness, that landscape's unique blankness, to narrow your focus until your mind falls into a trance. It will become a meditation.

I followed his advice to the letter. I told myself to stay present. **Be** the snow, **be** the cold, **be** each step, and it worked. I fell into the loveliest trance, and even when my thoughts were dark I was able to stare at them, watch them float away. Sometimes it would happen that I'd watch my thoughts connect to other thoughts and all at once the whole chain of thoughts would make some sense. For instance, I considered all of the previous challenging walks of my life—the North Pole, the Army exercises, following Mummy's coffin to the grave—and while the memories were painful, they also provided continuity, structure, a kind of narrative spine that I'd never suspected. Life was one long walk. It made sense. It was wonderful. All was interdependent and interconnected . . .

Then came the dizzies.

The South Pole, counterintuitively, is high above sea level, roughly three thousand meters, and so altitude sickness is a real danger. One walker had already been taken off our trek; now I understood why. The feeling started slowly and I brushed it off. Then it knocked me flat. Head spins, followed by crushing migraine, pressure building in both lobes of my brain. I didn't want to stop but it wasn't up to me. My body said, Thanks, this is where we get off. The knees went. The upper torso followed.

I hit the snow like a pile of rocks.

Medics pitched a tent, laid me flat, gave me some sort of anti-migraine injection. In my buttocks, I think. Steroids, I heard them say. When I came to, I felt semi-revived. I caught up with the group, searched for a way back into the trance.

Be the cold, **be** the snow . . .

As we neared the Pole we were all in sync, all elated. We could see it there, **just over there**, through our ice-crusted eyelashes. We began running to it.

Stop!

The guides told us it was time to make camp.

Camp? What the—? But the finish line's just there.

You're not allowed to camp at the Pole! So we'll all have to camp here tonight, then strike out for the Pole in the morning.

Camped in the shadow of the Pole, none of us could sleep, we were too excited. And thus we had a party. There was some drinking, horseplay. The underside of the world rang with our giggles.

Finally, at first light, December 13, 2013, we took off, stormed the Pole. On or near the exact spot was a huge circle of flags representing the twelve signatories of the Antarctic treaty. We stood before the flags, exhausted, relieved, disoriented. **Why's there a Union Jack on the coffin?** Then we hugged. Some press accounts say one of the soldiers took off his leg and we used it as a tankard to guzzle champagne, which sounds right, but I can't remember. I've drunk booze out of multiple prosthetic legs in my life and I can't swear that was one of the times.

Beyond the flags stood a huge building, one of the ugliest I'd ever seen. A windowless box, built by the Americans as a research center. The architect who designed this monstrosity, I thought, must've been filled with hate for his fellow humans, for the planet, for the Pole. It broke my heart to see a thing so unsightly dominate a land so otherwise pristine. Nevertheless, along with everyone else, I hurried inside the ugly building to warm up, have a pee, drink some cocoa.

There was a huge café and we were all starving. Sorry, we were told, café's closed. **Would you like a glass of water?**

Water? Oh. OK.

Each of us was handed a glass.

Then a souvenir. A test tube.

With a tiny cork in the top.

On the side was a printed label: CLEANEST AIR IN THE WORLD.

69.

I WENT DIRECTLY FROM the South Pole to Sandringham.

Christmas with the family.

Hotel Granny was full that year, overrun by family, so I was given a mini room in a narrow back corridor, among the offices of Palace staff. I'd never stayed there before. I'd rarely even set foot there before. (Not so unusual; all Granny's residences are vast— it would take a lifetime to see every nook and cranny.) I liked the notion of seeing and exploring uncharted territory—I was a grizzled polar explorer, after all!— but I also felt a bit unappreciated. A bit unloved. Relegated to the hinterlands.

I told myself to make the best of it, use this time to protect the serenity I'd achieved at the Pole. My hard drive was cleaned.

Alas, my family at that moment was infected with some very scary malware.

It was largely to do with the Court Circular, that annual record of "official engagements" done by each member of the Royal Family in the preceding calendar year. Sinister document. At the end of the year, when all the numbers got tallied, comparisons would be made in the press.

Ah, this one's busier than that one.

Ah, this one's a lazy shit.

The Court Circular was an ancient document, but it had lately morphed into a circular firing squad.

It didn't **create** the feelings of competitiveness that ran in my family, but it amplified them, weaponized them. Though none of us ever spoke about the Court Circular directly, or mentioned it by name, that only created more tension under the surface, which built invisibly as the last day of the calendar year approached. Certain family members had become **obsessed,** feverishly striving to have the highest number of official engagements recorded in the Circular each year, no matter what, and they'd succeeded largely by including things that weren't, strictly speaking, engagements, recording public interactions that were mere blips, the kinds of things Willy and I wouldn't dream of including. Which was essentially why the Court Circular was a joke. It was all self-reported, all subjective. Nine private visits with veterans, helping with their mental health? Zero points. Flying via helicopter to cut a ribbon at a horse farm? Winner!

But the main reason the Court Circular was a joke, a scam, was that none of us was deciding in a vacuum how much work to do. Granny or Pa decided, by way of how much support (money) they allocated to our work. Money determined all. In the case of Willy and me, Pa was the sole decider. It was he alone who controlled our funds; we could only do what we could do with whatever resources and budget we got from him. To be publicly flogged for how much Pa permitted us to do—that felt grossly unfair. Rigged.

Maybe the stress around all this stuff stemmed from the overarching stress about the monarchy itself. The family was feeling the tremors of global change, hearing the cries of critics who said the monarchy was outdated, costly. The family tolerated, even **leaned into,** the nonsense of the Court Circular for the same reason it accepted the ravages and depredations of the press—fear. Fear of the public. Fear of the future. Fear of the day the nation would say: OK, shut it down. So, by the time Christmas Eve 2013 rolled around, I was actually quite content in my back corridor, in my micro room, looking at photos of the South Pole on my iPad.

Staring at my little test tube.

CLEANEST AIR IN THE WORLD.

I took off the cork stopper, downed it in one.

Ah.

70.

I MOVED OUT of the badger sett, into Nottingham Cottage, a.k.a. Nott Cott. Willy and Kate had been living there, but they'd outgrown it. After moving into Princess Margaret's old place, just across the way, they'd passed me their keys.

It felt good to be out of the badger sett. But even better to be just across the way from Willy and Kate. I looked forward to popping in all the time.

Look! It's Uncle Harry!

Ello! Just thought I'd stop by.

Holding a bottle of wine and an armful of kiddie presents. Dropping to the floor and wrestling with little George.

Will you stay for supper, Harold?

Love to!

But it didn't work out that way.

They were half a football pitch away, just beyond a stone courtyard, so close that I could see their nanny pass by all the time with the pram, and I could hear their elaborate renovations. I assumed they'd have me over any minute now. Any day.

But day after day it didn't happen.

I get it, I thought. They're busy! Building a family!

Or maybe . . . they don't want a third wheel?

Maybe if I get married, things will be different?

They'd both mentioned, pointedly, repeatedly, how much they liked Cressida.

71.

MARCH 2014. A CONCERT at Wembley Arena. Walking onstage I suffered the typical panic attack. I made my way to the center, clenched my fists, spat out the speech. There were fourteen thousand young faces before me, gathered for We Day. Maybe I'd have been less nervous if I'd concentrated more on them, but I was having a proper Me Day, thinking about the last time I'd given a speech under this roof.

Tenth anniversary of Mummy's death.

I'd been nervous then too. But not like this.

I hurried off. Wiping the shine from my face, and staggering up to my seat to join Cress.

She saw me and blanched. You OK?

Yeah, yeah.

But she knew.

We watched the other speakers. That is, she watched, I tried to catch my breath.

The next morning our photo was in all the papers and splashed online. Someone tipped off the royal correspondents to where we were sitting, and at long last we were outed. After nearly two years of secretly dating, we were revealed to be a couple.

Odd, we said, that it should be such big news. We'd been photographed before, skiing in Verbier. But these photos landed differently, maybe because this was the first time she'd joined me at a royal engagement.

As a result, we became less clandestine, and that felt like a plus. Several days later we went to Twickenham, watched England play Wales, got papped, and didn't even bother to talk about it. Soon after, we left on a skiing holiday with friends, to Kazakhstan, got papped again, and didn't even know. We were too distracted. Skiing was so sacred for us, so symbolic, especially after our previous skiing holiday, in Switzerland, when she'd miraculously opened me up.

It happened late one night, after a long day on the slopes, and a fun time at après-ski. We'd gone back to my cousin's chalet, where we were staying, and Cress was washing her face, brushing her teeth, while I was sitting on the edge of the bath. We were talking about nothing special, as I recall, but suddenly she asked about my mother.

Unique. A girlfriend asking about my mother. But it was also the way she asked. Her tone was just the right blend of curiosity and compassion. The way she reacted to my answer was just right too. Surprised, concerned, with no judgment.

Maybe other factors were at play as well. The alchemy of physical fatigue and Swiss hospitality. The fresh air and alcohol. Maybe it was the softly falling snow outside the windows, or the culmination of seventeen years of suppressed grief. Maybe it was maturity. Whatever the reason or combination of reasons, I answered her, straight-out, and then started to cry.

I remember thinking: Oh, I'm crying.

And saying to her: **This is the first time I've . . .**

Cressida leaned towards me: **What do you mean . . . first time?**

This is the first time I've been able to cry about my mum since the burial.

Wiping my eyes, I thanked her. She was the first person to help me across that barrier, to help me unleash the tears. It was cathartic, it accelerated our bond, and added an element rare in past relationships: immense gratitude. I was indebted to Cress, and that was the reason why, when we got home from Kazakhstan, I felt so miserable, because at some point during that ski trip I'd realized that we weren't a match.

I just knew. Cress, I think, knew as well. There was massive affection, deep and abiding loyalty—but not love everlasting. She was always clear about not wanting to take on the stresses of being a royal, and I was never sure I wanted to ask her to do so, and this unalterable fact, though it had been lurking in the background for some time, became undeniable on those Kazakh slopes.

Suddenly it was clear. **This can't work.**

How odd, I thought. Every time we go skiing . . . a revelation.

The day after we got home from Kazakhstan I phoned a mate, who was also close with Cress. I told him about my feelings and asked for advice. Without hesitation the mate said that if it was done it must be done quickly. So I drove straight over to see Cress.

She was staying with a friend. Her bedroom was on the ground floor, windows looking onto the street. I heard cars and people going by as I sat gingerly on the bed and told her my thinking.

She nodded. None of it seemed to surprise her. These things had been on her mind as well.

I've learned so much from you, Cress.

She nodded. She looked at the floor, tears running down her cheeks.

Damn, I thought.

She helped me cry. And now I'm leaving her in tears.

72.

M<small>Y MATE,</small> G<small>UY,</small> was getting married. I wasn't exactly in the mood for a wedding. But it was Guy. All-round good bloke. Longtime mate of Willy and me. I loved him. And owed him.

He'd been dragged through the muck by the press, more than once, in my name.

The wedding was in America, in the Deep South.

My arrival there set off a torrent of talk about . . . what else?

Vegas.

I thought: After all this time? Really? Is my bare arse that memorable?

So be it, I told myself. Let them bang on about Vegas, I'm going to focus on Guy's Big Day.

On the way to Guy's stag party a group of us stopped off in Miami. We ate a fabulous meal, visited a few clubs, danced until well past midnight. Toasted Guy. Next day we all flew to Tennessee. I remember, despite the crowded wedding schedule, finding time to tour Graceland, erstwhile home of Elvis Presley. (Actually, he originally bought it for his mother.)

Everyone kept saying: Well, well, so this is where the King lived.

Who?

The King. Elvis Presley.

Oh. The King. Right.

People variously called the house a castle, a mansion, a palace, but it reminded me of the badger sett. Dark, claustrophobic. I walked around saying: The King lived here, you say? Really?

I stood in one tiny room with loud furniture and shag carpet and thought: The King's interior designer must've been on acid.

In honor of Elvis, every member of the bridal party wore blue suede shoes. At the reception there was much kicking up of those shoes, young British men and women dancing drunkenly and singing gleefully without pitch or rhythm. It was riotous, ridiculous, and Guy looked happier than I'd ever seen him.

He'd always been cast as our sidekick, but not now. He and his bride were the stars of this show, the center of attention, and my old mate was rightly savoring it. It made me so happy to see him so happy, though now and then, as couples paired off, as lovers drifted into corners or swayed to songs by Beyoncé and Adele, I'd wander over to the bar and think: When's it going to be my turn? The one person who might want it most, to be married, to have a family, and it's never going to happen. More than a little petulantly, I thought: It's just not fair of the universe.

73.

B UT THE UNIVERSE was just getting warmed up. Soon after I got back to Britain, the main villain in the phone-hacking scandal, Rehabber Kooks, was acquitted at trial.

June 2014.

The evidence had been strong, everybody said.

Not strong enough, the jury said. They believed what Rehabber Kooks testified on the witness stand, even though she'd strained credulity. No, she'd abused credulity. She'd treated credulity as she'd once treated a redheaded teenage royal.

Likewise her husband. He'd been caught on video throwing black bin liners full of computers and thumb drives and other personal belongings, including his porn collection, into a garage dustbin, just hours before the police searched their place. But he swore it was all a silly coincidence, sooo . . . no evidence-tampering here, sayeth the justice system. Carry on. As you were. I never believed what I read, but now I truly couldn't believe what I was reading. They were letting this woman walk? And there was no furor from the general public? Did people not realize that this was about more than privacy, more than public safety—more than the Royal Family? Indeed, the phone-hacking case first broke wide open because of poor Milly Dowler, a teenager who'd been abducted and murdered. Rehabber Kooks's minions broke into Milly's phone after she'd been declared missing—they'd violated her parents at the moment of their worst pain and given them false hope **that their little girl might be alive, because her messages were listened to.** Little did the parents know that it was Team Rehabber listening. If these journalists were villainous enough to go after the Dowlers in their darkest hour, and get away with it, was anyone safe?

Did people not care?

They didn't. They did not care.

My faith in the whole system took a serious hit when that woman got off scot-free. I needed a reset, a faith refresher. So I went where I always went.

The Okavango.

To spend a few restorative days with Teej and Mike. It helped.

But when I returned to Britain, I barricaded myself into Nott Cott.

74.

I DIDN'T GO OUT much at all. Maybe a dinner party now and then. Maybe the odd house party.

Sometimes I'd duck in and out of a club.

But it wasn't worth it. When I went out, it was always the same scene. Paps here, paps there, paps everywhere. Groundhog Day.

The dubious pleasure of a night out was never worth the pain.

But then I'd think: How am I going to meet someone if I don't go out?

So I'd try it again.

And: Groundhog Day.

One night, leaving a club, I saw two men come racing around a corner. They were headed straight for me and one had a hand on his hip.

Someone yelled: **Gun!**

I thought: Well, everyone, we had a good run.

Billy the Rock leaped forward, hand on his gun, and nearly shot the two men.

But it was just Tweedle Dumb and Tweedle Dumber. They didn't have guns, and I don't know what one of them was reaching for on his hip. But Billy held him and screamed into his face: **How many** times do we have to tell you? You're going to get someone fucking killed.

They didn't care. They did not care.

75.

THE TOWER OF LONDON. With Willy and Kate. August 2014.

The reason for our visit was an art installation. Across the dry moat were spread tens of thousands of bright red ceramic poppies. Ultimately, the plan was for 888,246 of these poppies to be spread there, one for each Commonwealth soldier who'd died in the Great War. The hundredth anniversary of the war's start was being marked all over Europe.

Apart from its extraordinary beauty, the art installation was a different way of visualizing war's carnage—indeed, of visualizing death itself. I felt stricken. All those lives. All those families.

It didn't help that this visit to the Tower was also three weeks before the anniversary of Mummy's death, or that I always connected her to the Great War, because her birthday, July 1, the start of the Battle of the Somme, was the war's bloodiest day, the bloodiest day in the history of the British Army.

In Flanders fields the poppies blow . . .

All these things were converging in my heart and mind outside the Tower as someone stepped forward, handed me a poppy and told me to place it. (The artists behind the installation wanted every poppy to be placed by a living person; thousands of volunteers had pitched in thus far.) Willy and Kate were also handed poppies and told to place them on any spot of their choosing.

After we'd finished, all three of us stood back, lost in our private thoughts.

I believe it was just then that the constable of the Tower appeared, greeted us, told us about the poppy, how it had come to be the British symbol of war. It was the only thing that bloomed on those blood-soaked battlefields, said the constable, who was none other than . . . General Dannatt.

The man who'd sent me back to war.

Truly, everything was converging.

He asked if we'd like a quick tour of the Tower.

Course, we said.

We walked up and down the Tower's steep stairs, peered into its dark corners, and soon found ourselves before a case of thick glass.

Inside were dazzling jewels, including . . . the Crown.

Holy shit. The Crown.

The one that had been placed upon Granny's head at her 1953 coronation.

For a moment I thought it was also the same crown that sat on Gan-Gan's coffin as it went through the streets. It looked the same, but someone pointed out several key differences.

Ah, yes. So this was Granny's crown, and hers alone, and now I remembered her telling me how unbelievably heavy it had been the first time they set it upon her head.

It looked heavy. It also looked magical. The more we stared, the brighter it got—was that possible? And the glow was seemingly internal. The jewels did their part, but the crown seemed to possess some inner energy source, something beyond the sum of its parts, its jeweled band, its golden fleurs-de-lis, its crisscrossing arches and gleaming cross. And of course its ermine base. You couldn't help but feel that a ghost, encountered late at night inside the Tower, might have a similar glow. I moved my eyes slowly, appreciatively, from the bottom to the top. The crown was a wonder, a transcendent and evocative piece of art, not unlike the poppies, but all I could think in that moment was how tragic that it should remain locked up in this Tower.

Yet another prisoner.

Seems a waste, I said to Willy and Kate, to which, I recall, they said nothing.

Maybe they were looking at that band of ermine, remembering my wedding remarks.

Maybe not.

76.

A FEW WEEKS LATER, after more than a year of talking and planning, thinking and worrying, seven thousand fans packed into the Queen Elizabeth

Olympic Park for the opening ceremony. The Invictus Games were born.

It had been decided that the International Warrior Games was a tongue twister, a mouthful. A clever Royal Marine had then come up with this far better alternative.

As soon as he suggested it we all said: Of course! After the William Ernest Henley poem!

Every Brit knew that poem. Many had the first line by heart.

Out of the night that covers me . . .

And what schoolboy or schoolgirl didn't encounter at least once those sonorous final lines?

I am the master of my fate,
I am the captain of my soul.

Minutes before my speech at the opening ceremony, I stood in the wings, holding notecards in my hands, which were visibly shaking. Before me, the podium looked like a gallows. I read my cards over and over, while nine Red Arrows did a flypast, streaming smoke colored red, white and blue. Then Idris Elba read "Invictus," maybe as well as anyone ever has, and then Michelle Obama, via satellite, said some eloquent words about the meaning of the games. Finally, she introduced me.

Long walk. Through a red-carpeted labyrinth. My cheeks looked red-carpeted as well. My smile was frozen, the fight-or-flight response in full effect. I scolded myself under my breath for being this way. These games were celebrating men and women who'd lost limbs, pushed their bodies to the limit and beyond, and here I was freaking out about a little speech.

But it wasn't my fault. Anxiety, by this point, was controlling my body, my life. And this speech, which I believed meant so much to so many, couldn't help but exacerbate my condition.

Plus, the producer told me as I walked onstage that we were running behind on time. **Ah, great, something else to think about. Thanks.**

As I reached the lectern, which I'd personally and carefully positioned, I berated myself, because it afforded a perfect view of all the competitors. All those trusting, wholesome, expectant faces—counting on me. I forced myself to look away, to look at nothing. Hurrying, hyper-conscious of the clock, I bleated out: **For some of those taking part this will be a stepping-stone to elite sport. But for others it will mark the end of a chapter in their recovery and the beginning of a new one.**

I went and found my seat, down front, beside Pa, who put a hand on my shoulder. **Well done, darling boy.** He was being kind. He knew I'd rushed the speech. For once I was glad not to hear the raw truth from him.

Just on the numbers, Invictus was a hit. Two million people watched on TV, thousands filled the arenas for each event. Among the highlights, for me, was the wheelchair rugby final, Britain versus America, thousands of fans cheering Britain on to victory in the Copper Box.

Wherever I went that week, people came up to me, shook my hand, told me their stories. Children, parents, grandparents, always with tears in their eyes, told me that these games had restored something they'd feared forever lost: the true spirit of a son, a daughter, a brother, a sister, a mum, a dad. One woman tapped me on the shoulder and told me I'd resurrected her husband's smile.

Oh, that smile, she said. **I hadn't seen it since he got injured.**

I knew Invictus would do some good in the world, I always **knew**, but I was caught off guard by this wave of appreciation and gratitude. And joy.

Then came the emails. Thousands, each more moving than the last.

I've had a broken back for five years, but after watching these brave men and women I've got off the sofa today and I'm ready to begin again.

I've been suffering depression since returning from Afghanistan but this demonstration of human courage and resilience has made me see . . .

At the closing ceremony, moments after I introduced Dave Grohl and the Foo Fighters, a man and woman approached, their young daughter between them. The daughter was wearing a pink hoodie and orange ear defenders. She looked up at me: **Thank you for making my daddy . . . Daddy again.**

He'd won a gold medal.

Just one problem, she said. She couldn't see the Foo Fighters.

Ah well, we can't have that!

I lifted her onto my shoulders and together the four of us watched, danced, sang, and celebrated being alive.

It was my thirtieth birthday.

77.

SHORTLY AFTER THE GAMES I informed the Palace that I'd be leaving the Army. Elf and I worked on the public announcement; it was hard to get the wording just right, to explain it to the public, maybe because I was having trouble explaining it to myself. In hindsight I see that it was a hard decision to explain because it wasn't a decision at all. It was just time.

But time for what, exactly, besides leaving the Army? From now on I'd be something I'd never been: a full-time royal.

How would I even do that?

And was that what I wanted to be?

In a lifetime of existential crises, this was a bugger. Who are you when you can no longer be the thing you've always been, the thing you've trained to be?

Then one day I thought I glimpsed the answer.

It was a crisp Tuesday, near the Tower of London. I was standing in the middle of the street and suddenly here he came, yomping down the road—young Ben, the soldier with whom I'd flown back from Afghanistan in 2008, the soldier I'd visited and cheered as he climbed a wall with his new prosthetic leg. Six years after that flight, as promised, he was running a marathon. Not the London marathon, which would've been miraculous on its own. He was running **his own marathon**, along a route he'd designed himself, in the outline of a poppy laid over the city of London.

A staggering thirty-one miles, he'd done the full circuit to raise money and awareness—and heart rates.

I'm in shock, he said on finding me there.

You're in shock? I said. **That makes two of us.**

Seeing him out there, still being a soldier, despite no longer being a soldier—that was the answer to the riddle with which I'd been struggling so long.

Question: How do you stop being a soldier, when a soldier is all you've ever been or wanted to be?

Answer: You don't.

Even when you stop being a soldier, you don't have to stop being a soldier. Ever.

78.

AN AFGHANISTAN WAR SERVICE at St. Paul's Cathedral, and then a reception at the Guildhall hosted by the City of London Corporation, and then the launch of Walking With The Wounded's Walk Of Britain, and then a visit to England's rugby team, and then watching them practice for a match against France, and then following them to Twickenham and cheering them on, and then a memorial for the Olympian Richard Meade, the most successful equestrian in British history, and then a trip with Pa to Turkey to attend ceremonies marking the hundredth anniversary of Gallipoli, and then a meeting with descendants of the men who fought in that epic battle, and then back to London to hand out medals to runners at the London Marathon.

That was the start of my 2015.

Just the highlights.

The papers were awash with stories about Willy being lazy, and the press had taken to calling him "Work-shy Wills," which was obscene, grossly unfair, because he was busy having children and raising a family. (Kate was pregnant again.) Also, he was still beholden to Pa, who controlled the purse strings. He did as much as Pa wanted him to do, and sometimes that wasn't much, because Pa and Camilla didn't want Willy and Kate getting loads of publicity. Pa and Camilla didn't like Willy and Kate drawing attention away from them or their causes. They'd openly scolded Willy about it many times.

Case in point: Pa's press officer berated Willy's team when Kate was scheduled to visit a tennis club on the same day Pa was doing an engagement. Told that it was too late to cancel the visit, Pa's press officer warned: **Just make sure the Duchess doesn't hold a tennis racquet in any of the photos!**

Such a winning, fetching photo would undoubtedly wipe Pa and Camilla off the front pages. And that, in the end, couldn't be tolerated.

Willy told me that both he and Kate felt trapped, and unfairly persecuted, by the press and by Pa and Camilla, so I felt some need to carry the banner for all three of us in 2015. But selfishly, I also didn't want the press coming for me. To be called lazy? I shuddered. I never wanted to see that word attached to my name. The press had called me stupid for most of my life, and naughty, and racist, but if they dared to call me lazy . . . I couldn't guarantee I wouldn't go down to Fleet Street and start pulling people out from behind their desks.

I didn't understand until months later that there were even more reasons why the press was gunning for Willy. First, he'd got them all worked up by ceasing to play their game, denying them unfettered access to his family. He'd refused several times to trot Kate out like a prized racehorse, and that was considered a bridge too far.

Then he'd had the temerity to go out and give a vaguely anti-Brexit speech, which really galled them. Brexit was their bread and butter. How dare he suggest it was bullshit.

79.

I WENT TO AUSTRALIA FOR a round of military exercises and while there I got word: Willy and Kate had welcomed their second child. Charlotte. I was an uncle again, and very happy about it.

But, predictably, during one interview that day or

the next a journalist questioned me about it as though I'd received a terminal diagnosis.

No, mate. Thrilled to bits.

But you're further down the line of succession.

Couldn't be happier for Willy and Kate.

The journalist pressed: Fifth in line—hm. No longer even the Spare of the Spare.

I thought: First of all, it's a good thing to be farther from the center of a volcano. Second, what kind of monster would think of himself and his place in the line of succession at such a time, rather than welcoming a new life into the world?

I'd once heard a courtier say that when you were fifth or sixth in line you were "only a plane crash away." I couldn't imagine living that way.

The journalist persisted. Didn't the birth make me question my choices?

Choices?

Isn't it time you settled down?

Well, uh—

People are starting to compare you to Bridget Jones.

I thought: Are they really? Bridget Jones, ay?

The journalist waited.

It'll happen, I assured him, or her, I can't recall the face, only the preposterous line of questioning. **When, kind sir, do you plan to wive?** It will happen when it happens, I said, the way you'd assure a naggy auntie.

The faceless journalist stared with abject . . . pity.

Will it, though?

80.

PEOPLE OFTEN SPECULATED THAT I was clinging to my bachelor life because it was so glamorous. Many evenings I'd think: If only they could see me now.

Then I'd go back to folding my underwear and watching "The One with Monica and Chandler's Wedding."

Besides my own laundry (often laid out to dry on my radiators) I did my own chores, my own cooking, my own food shopping. There was a supermarket by the Palace and I went there, casually, at least once a week.

Of course I'd plan each trip as carefully as a patrol around Musa Qala. I'd arrive at different times, randomly, to throw off the press. I'd wear a disguise: low baseball cap, loose coat. I'd run along the aisles at warp speed, grabbing the salmon fillets I liked, the brand of yogurt I liked. (I'd memorized a map of the store.) Plus a few Granny Smith apples and bananas. And, of course, some crisps.

Then I'd sprint to the checkout.

Just as I'd honed my preflight checks in the Apache, I now honed my grocery shopping time down to ten minutes. But one night I got to the shop and began to run up and down the aisles and everything . . . had **moved.**

I hurried over to an employee: **What's happened? Excuse me?**

Where is everything?

Where is—?

Why has everything moved?

Honestly?

Yes, honestly.

To keep people here longer. So they'll buy more stuff.

I was gobsmacked. You can do that? By law?

A bit panicky, I resumed running up and down the aisles, filling my trolley as best I could, keeping an eye on the clock, then rushed to the checkout. That was always the trickiest part, because there was no honing the checkout: it all depended on others. More, the checkout counter stood right beside the news racks, which held every British tabloid and magazine, and half the front pages and magazine covers were photos of my family. Or my mum. Or me.

More than once I watched customers read about me, overheard them debating me. In 2015 I overheard them frequently discussing whether or not I'd ever marry. Whether or not I was happy. Whether or not I might be gay. I was always tempted to tap them on the shoulder . . . **Ello.**

One night, in disguise, watching some people discuss me and my life choices, I became aware of raised voices at the front of the queue. An older married couple, abusing the cashier. It was unpleasant at first, then intolerable.

I stepped forward, showed my face, cleared my throat: **Excuse me. Not sure what's going on here,** but I don't think you should be speaking to her like that.

The cashier was on the verge of tears. The couple abusing her turned and recognized me. They weren't in the least surprised, however. Just offended to be called out on their abuse.

When they left, when it came my turn to pay, the cashier tried to thank me as she bagged my avocados. I wouldn't hear of it. I told her to hang in there, scooped up my things and ran, like the Green Hornet.

Shopping for clothes was so much less complicated. As a rule I didn't think about clothing. I didn't fundamentally believe in fashion, and I couldn't understand why anybody would. I often got mocked on social media for my mismatched outfits, my ratty shoes. Writers would flag a photo of me and wonder why my trousers were so long, my shirts so crumpled. (They didn't dream that I'd dried them on the radiator.)

Not very princely, they'd say.

Right you are, I'd think.

My father tried. He gave me an absolutely gorgeous pair of black brogues. Works of art. Weighed as much as bowling balls. I wore them until the soles developed holes, and when I was mocked for wearing holey shoes I finally got them fixed.

Each year I received from Pa an official clothing allowance, but that was strictly for formal wear. Suits and ties, ceremonial outfits. For my everyday casual clothes I'd go to T.K. Maxx, the discount store. I was particularly fond of their once-a-year sale, when they'd be flush with items from Gap or J.Crew, items that had just gone out of season or were slightly damaged. If you timed it just right, got there on the first day of the sale, you could snag the same clothes that others were paying top prices for down the high street! With two hundred quid you could look like a fashion plate.

Here, too, I had a system. Get to the shop fifteen minutes before closing time. Grab a red bucket. Hurry to the top floor. Begin systematically working up one rack and down another.

If I found something promising I'd hold it up to my chest or legs, standing in front of a mirror. I never dawdled over color or style and certainly never went anywhere near a changing room. If it looked nice, comfortable, into the bucket it went. If I was on the fence about it, I'd ask Billy the Rock. He delighted in moonlighting as my stylist.

At closing time we'd run out with two giant shopping bags, feeling triumphant. Now the papers wouldn't call me a slob. At least for a little while.

Far better, I wouldn't have to think about clothes again for another six months.

81.

OTHER THAN THE occasional shopping, I stopped going out in 2015.

Stopped entirely.

No more occasional dinners with mates. No more house parties. No clubs. No nothing.

Every night I'd go straight home from work, eat over the sink, then catch up on paperwork, **Friends** on low in the background.

Pa's chef would sometimes stock my freezer with chicken pies, cottage pies. I was grateful not to have to venture to the supermarket quite as much . . . though the pies sometimes put me in mind of the Gurkhas and their goat stew, mainly because they were so unspicy. I missed the Gurkhas, missed the Army. I missed the war.

After dinner I'd smoke a joint, trying to make sure the smoke didn't waft into the garden of my neighbor, The Duke of Kent.

Then I'd turn in early.

Solitary life. Strange life. I felt lonely, but lonely was better than panicky. I was just beginning to discover a few healthy remedies to my panic, but until I felt surer of them, until I felt on more solid ground, I was leaning on this one decidedly unhealthy remedy.

Avoidance.

I was an agoraphobe.

Which was nearly impossible given my public role.

After one speech, which couldn't be avoided or canceled, and during which I'd nearly fainted, Willy came up to me backstage. Laughing.

Harold! Look at you! You're drenched.

I couldn't fathom his reaction. Him of all people. He'd been present for my very first panic attack. With Kate. We were driving out to a polo match in Gloucestershire, in their Range Rover. I was in the back and Willy peered at me in the rearview. He saw me sweating, red-faced. **You all right, Harold?** No, I wasn't. It was a trip of several hours and every few miles I wanted to ask him to pull over so I could jump out and try to catch my breath.

He knew something was up, something bad. He'd told me that day or soon after that I needed help. And now he was teasing me? I couldn't imagine how he could be so insensitive.

But I was at fault too. Both of us should've known better, should've recognized my crumbling emotional and mental states for what they were, because we'd just started to discuss the launching of a public campaign to raise awareness around mental health.

82.

I WENT TO EAST LONDON, to Mildmay Mission Hospital, to commemorate its 150th anniversary and recent renovations. My mother once paid the place a famous visit. She held the hand of a man who was HIV-positive, and thereby changed the world. She proved that HIV wasn't leprosy, that it wasn't a curse. She proved that the disease didn't disqualify people from love or dignity. She reminded the world that respect and compassion aren't gifts, they're the least we owe each other.

I learned that her famous visit had actually been one of many. A Mildmay worker pulled me aside, told me that Mummy would slip in and out of the hospital all the time. No fanfare, no photos. She'd just drop in, make a few people feel better, then run home.

Another woman told me she'd been a patient during one of those pop-ins. Born HIV-positive, this woman remembered sitting on Mummy's lap. She was only two at the time, but she remembered.

I cuddled her. Your mum. I did.

My face flushed. I felt such envy.

Did you?

I did, I did, and oh, it was so nice. She gave a great cuddle!

Yes, I remember.

But I didn't.

No matter how I tried, I barely remembered a thing.

83.

I VISITED BOTSWANA, spent a few days with Teej and Mike. I felt a craving for them, a physical need to go on a wander with Mike, to sit once more with my head in Teej's lap, talking and feeling safe.

Feeling home.

The very end of 2015.

I took them into my confidence, told them about my battles with anxiety. We were by the campfire, where such things were always best discussed. I told them I'd just recently found a few things that were sort of working.

So . . . there was hope.

For instance, therapy. I'd followed through on Willy's suggestion, and while I hadn't found a therapist I liked, simply speaking to a few had opened my mind to possibilities.

Also, one therapist said off-handedly that I was clearly suffering from post-traumatic stress, and that rang a bell. It got me moving, I thought, in the right direction.

Another thing that seemed to work was meditation. It quietened my racing mind, brought a degree of calm. I wasn't one to pray, Nature was still my God, but in my worst moments I'd shut my eyes and be still. Sometimes I'd also ask for help, though I was never sure whom I was asking.

Now and then I felt the presence of an answer.

Psychedelics did me some good as well. I'd experimented with them over the years, for fun, but now I'd begun to use them therapeutically, medicinally. They didn't simply allow me to escape reality for a while, they let me **redefine** reality. Under the influence of these substances I was able to let go of rigid preconcepts, to see that there was another world beyond my heavily filtered senses, a world that was equally real and doubly beautiful—a world with no red mist, no reason for red mist. There was only truth.

After the psychedelics wore off my memory of that world would remain: **This is not all there is.** All the great seers and philosophers say our daily life is an illusion. I always felt the truth in that. But how reassuring it was, after nibbling a mushroom, or ingesting ayahuasca, to experience it for myself.

The one remedy that proved most effective, how-ever, was work. Helping others, doing some good in the world, looking outward rather than in. That was the path. Africa and Invictus, these had long been the causes closest to my heart. But now I wanted to dive in deeper. Over the last year or so I'd spoken to helicopter pilots, veterinary surgeons, rangers, and they all told me that a war was on, a war to save the planet. War, you say?

Sign me up.

One small problem: Willy. Africa was **his** thing, he said. And he had the right to say this, or felt he did, because he was the Heir. It was ever in his power to veto **my** thing, and he had every intention of exercis-ing, even flexing, that veto power.

We'd had some real rows about it, I told Teej and Mike. One day, we almost came to blows in front of our childhood mates, the sons of Emilie and Hugh. One of the sons asked: **Why can't you both work on Africa?**

Willy had a fit, flew at this son for daring to make such a suggestion. **Because rhinos, elephants, that's mine!**

It was all so obvious. He cared less about finding his purpose or passion than about winning his life-long competition with me.

Over several more heated discussions, it emerged that Willy, when I'd gone to the North Pole, had sadly been resentful. He'd felt slighted that **he** hadn't been the one invited. At the same time he also said that he'd stepped aside, gallantly, that he'd permitted me to go, indeed that he'd permitted all my work with wounded soldiers. **I let you have veterans, why can't you let me have African elephants and rhinos?**

I complained to Teej and Mike that I'd finally seen my path, that I'd finally hit upon the thing that could fill the hole in my heart left by soldiering, in fact a thing even more sustainable—and Willy was standing in my way.

They were aghast. Keep fighting, they said. **There's room for both of you in Africa. There's need for you both.**

So, with their encouragement, I embarked on a four-month fact-finding trip, to educate myself about the truth of the ivory war. Botswana. Namibia. Tanzania. South Africa. I went to Kruger National Park, a vast stretch of dry, barren land the size of Israel. In the war on poachers, Kruger was the absolute front line. Its rhino populations, both black and white, were plummeting, due to armies of poachers being incentivized by Chinese and Vietnamese crime syndicates. One rhino horn fetched enormous sums, so for every poacher arrested, five more were ready to take their place.

Black rhinos were rarer, thus more valuable. They were also more dangerous. As browsers, they lived in thick bush, and wading in after them could be fatal. They didn't know you were there to help. I'd been charged a few times, and I was lucky to get away without being gored. (Tip: Always know the location of the nearest tree branch, because you might need to jump onto it.) I had friends who'd not been so lucky.

White rhinos were more docile, and more plentiful, but perhaps wouldn't be for long, because of that docility. As grazers, they also lived in open grassland. Easier to see, easier to shoot.

I went along on countless anti-poaching patrols. Over several days in Kruger, we always got there too late. I must have seen forty bullet-riddled rhino carcasses.

Poachers in other parts of South Africa, I learned, didn't always shoot the rhinos. Bullets were expensive, and gunshots gave away their position. So they'd dart a rhino with a tranquilizer, then take the horn while the rhino was asleep. The rhino would wake up with no face, then stumble into the bush to die.

I assisted on one long surgery, on a rhino named Hope, repairing her face, patching the exposed membranes inside the hole that once cradled her horn. It left me and the whole surgical team traumatized. We all wondered if this was the right thing for the poor girl. She was in so much pain.

But we just couldn't let her go.

84.

IN A HELICOPTER OVER KRUGER one morning, we flew in long loopy circles, searching for the telltale signs. Suddenly I spotted the most telltale sign of all.

There, I said.

Vultures.

We quickly descended.

Clouds of vultures took flight as we touched the ground.

We jumped out, saw frantic footprints in the dust, shell casings glinting in the sun. Blood everywhere. We followed the trail into the bush and found a huge white rhino, a gaping hole where her horn had been hacked. There were wounds all along her back. Fifteen craters, by my count.

Her six-month-old baby lay beside her, dead.

We pieced together what had happened. Poachers had shot the mother. She and her baby had run. The poachers chased them to this spot. The mother was still able to defend or shield her baby, so the poachers hacked her spine with axes, immobilizing her. While she was still alive, bleeding out, they'd taken her horn.

I couldn't speak. The sun beat down from a hot blue sky.

My bodyguard asked the ranger: Which was killed first, the baby or the mother?

Hard to say.

I asked: **Do you think the poachers are close by? Can we find them?**

Impossible.

Even if they were in the area—needle, haystack.

85.

IN NAMIBIA, CROSSING the northern desert in search of desert rhinos, I met an amiable doctor who was tracking desert lions. They were heavily persecuted in that part of Namibia, because they often encroached on farmland. The doctor was darting some, to study their health and movements. He took our number, told us he'd call if he found one.

That night we made camp by a dry stream. Everyone else was in tents, in trucks, but I unrolled my mat by the fire and covered myself with a thin blanket.

Everyone on my team thought I was joking. **This area is full of lions, boss.**

I told them I'd be fine. **Done it a million times.**

Around midnight the radio buzzed. The doctor. He was four kilometers away and he'd just darted two lions.

We jumped into the Land Cruiser, raced down the track. Namibian soldiers assigned to us by the government insisted on coming as well. As did local police in the area. Despite the pitch-dark, we found the doctor easily. He was standing beside two enormous lions. Both were lying on their bellies, heads resting heavily on their giant paws. He aimed his torch. We could see the lions' chests rising and falling. Quiet breathing.

I knelt beside the female, touched her skin, looked at her half-closed amber eyes. I can't explain it, and I can't defend it . . . but I felt that I knew her.

As I stood, one of the Namibian soldiers brushed past me, crouched beside the other lion. A big male. The soldier held up his AK-47, asked one of his buddies to get a photo. As if he'd made a kill.

I was about to say something, but Billy the Rock beat me to it. He told the Namibian soldier to get the fuck away from the lions.

Sullen, the soldier slunk away.

I turned now to say something to the doctor. There was a flash. I turned again, to see where it had come from, which soldier had shot his phone camera, and heard the men gasp.

I looked back: The lioness was standing before me. Resurrected.

She stumbled forward.

It's OK, the doctor said. **It's OK.**

She fell again, right at my feet.

Goodnight, sweet princess.

I looked left, right. No one was near me. The soldiers had all raced back to their trucks. The one with the AK-47 was rolling up the window. Even Billy the Rock had taken a half-step back.

The doctor said, **Sorry about that.**

Don't be.

We returned to camp. Everyone climbed into their tents, their trucks, except me.

I returned to my mat by the fire.

You're joking, they all said. **What about the lions? We just saw proof that there are lions out here, boss.**

Pff. Trust me. That lioness isn't going to hurt anybody.

In fact she's probably watching over us.

86.

B ACK TO AMERICA. With two good mates. January 2016.

My mate Thomas was dating a woman who lived in Los Angeles, so our first stop was her house. She gave a welcome party, invited a small group of friends over. Everyone was on the same page about alcohol—in other words, committed to consuming large amounts in a short time.

Where we didn't agree was which type.

The typical Brit, I asked for a gin and tonic.

Hell no, the Americans said, laughing. **You're in the States now, pal, have a real drink. Have a tequila.**

I was familiar with tequila. But mostly club tequila. Late-night tequila. What I was being offered now was proper tequila, fancy schmancy tequila, and I was being schooled in all the many ways of drinking it. Glasses were floating towards me containing tequila in every form. Neat. Rocks. Margarita. Splash of soda and lime.

I drank it all, every drop, and started feeling very bloody good.

I thought: I like these Americans. I like them a lot.

Strange time to be pro-American. Most of the world wasn't. Certainly not Britain. Many Brits despised the American war in Afghanistan, and resented being dragged into it. With some the anti-American sentiment ran very hot. I was reminded of my childhood, when people warned me all the time about Americans. Too loud, too rich, too happy. Too confident, too direct, too honest.

Nah, I always thought. Yanks didn't beat about the bush, didn't fill the air with polite snorts and throat clearings before coming to the point. Whatever was on their mind, they'd spit it out, like a sneeze, and while that could be problematic at times, I usually found it preferable to the alternative:

No one saying what they truly felt.

No one wanting to hear how you felt.

I'd experienced that at twelve years old. I experienced it even more now that I was thirty-one.

I floated through that day on a pink cloud of tequila fumes. No—floated is wrong. I **piloted** the pink cloud, and after I landed it—textbook landing, by the way—I woke with no hangover. Miracle.

The next day, or the day after, we moved for some reason. We went from the home of Thomas's girlfriend to the home of Courteney Cox. She was a friend of Thomas's girlfriend, and had more room. Also, she was traveling, on a job, and didn't mind if we crashed at her place.

No complaints from me. As a **Friends** fanatic, the idea of crashing at Monica's was highly appealing. And amusing. But then . . . Courteney turned up. I was very confused. Was her job canceled? I didn't think it was my place to ask. More: **Does this mean we have to leave?**

She smiled. **Of course not, Harry. Plenty of room.**

Great. But I was still confused because . . . she was Monica. And I was a Chandler. I wondered if I'd ever work up the courage to tell her. Was there enough tequila in California to get me that brave?

Soon after arriving home, Courteney invited more

people over. Another party began. Among the new-comers was a bloke who looked familiar.

Actor, my mate said.

Yes, I know he's an actor. What's his name?

My mate couldn't remember.

I went over and talked to the actor. He was a friendly sort, and I liked him straightaway. I still couldn't place his face or call up his name, but his voice was even more vexingly familiar.

I whispered to my mate: **Where do I know this guy from?**

My mate laughed. **Batman.**

Sorry?

Batman.

I was into my third or fourth tequila, so I was having trouble understanding and processing this remarkable bit of new information.

Fuck—yes! Batman LEGO movie. I turned back to the actor and asked: **Zit true?**

Is . . . what true?

Are you Him?

Am I—?

Batman.

He smiled. **Yes.**

What a thing to be able to say!

I begged: **Do it.**

Do what?

The voice.

He shut his eyes. He wanted to say no, but he didn't want to be impolite. Or else he recognized that I wouldn't stop. He fixed me with his ice-blue eyes and cleared his throat and in perfect gravelly Batmanese said: **Hello, Harry.**

Oh, I loved it. **Again!**

He did it again. I loved it even more.

We shared a big laugh.

Then, maybe to get rid of us, he led my mate and me to the fridge, from which he extracted a soft drink. While the door was open we spotted a huge box of black diamond mushroom chocolates.

Someone behind me said they were for everybody. **Help yourself, boys.**

My mate and I grabbed several, gobbled them, washed them down with tequila.

We waited for Batman to indulge as well. But he didn't. Not his thing, or something. Howdya like that? we said. This bloke's just sent us by ourselves into the fucking Batcave!

We took ourselves outside, sat down by a firepit, and waited.

I remember after a time standing up and wandering back into the house to use the loo.

It was hard to navigate the house, with its angular modern furniture and clean glass surfaces. Also, there weren't many lights on. But in time I managed to find a loo.

Lovely room, I thought, shutting the door.

I looked all around.

Beautiful hand soaps. Clean white towels. Exposed wood beams.

Mood lighting.

Leave it to the Yanks.

Beside the toilet was a round silver bin, the kind with a foot pedal to open the lid. I stared at the bin. It stared back.

What—staring?

Then it became . . . a head.

I stepped on the pedal and the head opened its mouth. A huge open grin.

I laughed, turned away, took a piss.

Now the loo became a head too. The bowl was its gaping maw, the hinges of the seat were its piercing silver eyes.

It said: **Aaah.**

I finished, flushed, closed its mouth.

I turned back to the silver bin, stepped on the pedal, fed it an empty packet of cigarettes from my pocket.

Open wide.

Aaah. Thank you, mate.

You're welcome, mate.

I left the bathroom, giggling, and walked straight into my mate.

What's so funny?

I told him he needed to walk into that loo right now and have the experience of a lifetime.

What experience?

Can't describe it. You have to see for yourself. Meeting Batman pales by comparison.

He was wearing a big puffer jacket with a furry collar, exactly like the one I'd worn to the North and South Poles. Without taking it off he walked into the loo.

I went to make myself another tequila.

Minutes later my mate appeared at my side. His face was white as a sheet.

What happened?

Don't want to talk about it.

Tell me.

My puffer jacket . . . became a dragon.

A dragon? In the loo?

And tried to eat me.

Oh dear.

You sent me into a dragon's lair.

Shit. Sorry, mate.

My delightful trip had been his hell.

How unfortunate. How interesting.

I led him outside gently, told him it would all be OK.

87.

THE NEXT DAY WE WENT to another house party. Inland, though the air still smelt like ocean.

More tequila, more names thrown at me.

And more mushrooms.

We all started playing some kind of game, some kind of charades—I think? Someone handed me a joint. Lovely. I took a hit, looked at the rinsed creamy blue of the California sky. Someone tapped me on the shoulder, said they wanted me to meet Christina Aguilera. Oh, hello, Christina. She looked rather mannish. No, apparently I'd misheard, it wasn't

Christina Aguilera, it was the guy who co-wrote one of her songs.

"Genie in a Bottle."

Did I know the lyrics? Did he tell me the lyrics?

I'm a genie in a bottle
You gotta rub me the right way

Anyway, he'd made a boatload from those lyrics, and now lived in high style.

Good for you, mate.

I left him, set off across the yard, and the memory trails away for a time. I seem to remember yet another house party . . . that day? The next?

Eventually, somehow, we made our way back to Monica's. That is, Courteney's. It was night. I walked down some stairs to her beachfront and stood with my toes in the ocean, watching the lacy surf come forward, recede, come forward, for what felt like ages. I looked from the water to the sky, back and forth.

Then I stared directly at the moon.

It was speaking to me.

Like the bin and the toilet.

What was it saying?

That the year ahead would be good.

Good how?

Something big.

Really?

Big.

Not more of the same?

No, something special.

Really, Moon?

Promise.

Please don't lie to me.

I was nearly the age Pa had been when he'd got married, and he'd been considered a tragically late bloomer. At thirty-two he'd been ridiculed for his inability or unwillingness to find a partner.

I was staring thirty-two in the face.

Something has to change. Please?

It will.

I opened my mouth to the sky, to the moon.

To the future.

Aaaah.

part 3   captain of my soul

1.

I WAS SITTING around Nott Cott, scrolling through Instagram. In my feed I saw a video: My friend Violet. And a young woman.

They were playing with a new app that put silly filters on your photos. Violet and the woman had dog ears, dog noses, long red dog tongues hanging out.

Despite the canine cartoon overlay, I sat up straighter.

This woman with Violet . . . my God.

I watched the video several times, then forced myself to put down the phone.

Then picked it up again, watched the video again.

I'd traveled the world, from top to bottom, literally. I'd hopscotched the continents. I'd met hundreds of thousands of people, I'd crossed paths with a ludicrously large cross-section of the planet's seven billion residents. For thirty-two years I'd watched a conveyor-belt of faces pass by and only a handful ever made me look twice. This woman stopped the conveyor-belt. This woman smashed the conveyor-belt to bits.

I'd never seen anyone so beautiful.

Why should beauty feel like a punch in the throat?

Does it have something to do with our innate human longing for order? Isn't that what scientists say? And artists? That beauty is symmetry and therefore represents a relief from the chaos? Certainly my life to that point had been chaotic. I can't deny hungering for order, can't deny seeking a bit of beauty. I'd just come back from a trip with Pa, Willy and Kate to France, where we'd marked the anniversary of the Battle of the Somme, honored the British dead, and I'd read a haunting poem, "Before Action." It was published by a soldier two days before he'd died in action. It ended: **Help me to die, O Lord.**

Reading it out, I realized I didn't want to die. I wanted to live.

A fairly staggering revelation for me just then.

But this woman's beauty, and my response to it, wasn't based merely on symmetry. There was an energy about her, a wild joy and playfulness. There was something in the way she smiled, the way she interacted with Violet, the way she gazed into the camera. Confident. Free. She believed life was one grand adventure, I could see that. What a privilege it would be, I thought, to join her on that journey.

I got all of that from her face. Her luminous, angelic face. I'd never had a firm opinion on that burning question: Is there just one person on this earth for each of us? But in that moment I felt there might be only one **face** for me.

This one.

I sent Violet a message. **Who . . . is . . . this . . . woman?**

She answered straightaway. **Yeah, I've had six other guys ask me.**

Great, I thought.

Who is she, Violet?

Actress. She's in a TV show called Suits.

It was a drama about lawyers; the woman played a young paralegal.

American?

Yeah.

What's she doing in London?

Here for the tennis.

What's she doing at Ralph Lauren?

Violet worked for Ralph Lauren.

She's doing a fitting. I can connect you guys, if you like.

Um, yes. Please?

Violet asked if it would be all right to give the young woman, the American, my Instagram handle.

Of course.

It was Friday, July 1. I was due to leave London the next morning, heading to the home of Sir Keith Mills. I was to take part in a sailing race on Sir Keith's yacht, around the Isle of Wight. Just as I was stuffing the last few things into my overnight bag I glanced at my phone.

A message on Instagram.

From the woman.

The American.

Hello!

She said she'd got my info from Violet. She complimented my Instagram page. Beautiful photographs.

Thank you.

It was mostly photos of Africa. I knew she'd been there, because I'd studied her Instagram page too; I'd seen photos of her hanging out with gorillas in Rwanda.

She said she'd done some aid work there as well. With children. We shared thoughts about Africa, photography, travel.

Eventually we exchanged phone numbers, and migrated the conversation over to text, going late into the night. In the morning I moved from Nott Cott to the car, without a pause in the texting. I texted with her throughout the long drive to Sir Keith's place, continued through Sir Keith's hall—**How you doing, Sir Keith?**—and up the stairs and into his guestroom, where I locked the door and remained holed up, texting. I sat on the bed texting like a teenager until it was time to have dinner with Sir Keith and his family. Then, after dessert, I quickly returned to the guestroom and resumed texting.

I couldn't type fast enough. My thumbs were cramping. There was so much to say, we had so much in common, though we came from such different worlds. She was American, I was British. She was well-educated, I was decidedly not. She was free as a bird, I was in a gilded cage. And yet none of these differences felt disqualifying or even important. On the contrary, they felt organic, energizing. The contradictions created a sense of:

Hey . . . I know you.

But also: I need to know you.

Hey, I've known you forever.

But also: I've been searching for you forever.

Hey, thank God you've arrived.

But also: What took you so long?

Sir Keith's guestroom looked out onto an estuary. Many times, mid-text, I'd walk over to the window and gaze out. The view made me think of the Okavango. It made me think also of destiny, and serendipity. That convergence of river and sea, land and sky reinforced a vague sense of big things coming together.

It occurred to me how uncanny, how surreal, how bizarre, that this marathon conversation should have begun on July 1, 2016.

My mother's fifty-fifth birthday.

Late into the night, while waiting for her next text, I'd tap the American's name into Google. Hundreds of photos, each more dazzling. I wondered if she was googling me too. I hoped not.

Before turning out the light I asked how long she was going to be in London. Damn—she was leaving soon. She had to get back to Canada to resume filming her show.

I asked if I could see her before she left.

I watched the phone, waiting for the answer, staring at the endlessly fluttering ellipsis.

. . .

Then: **Sure!**

Great. Now: Where to meet?

I suggested my place.

Your place? On a first date! I don't think so.

No, I didn't mean it like that.

She didn't realize that being royal meant being radioactive, that I was unable to just meet at a coffee shop or pub. Reluctant to give her a full explanation, I tried to explain obliquely about the risk of being seen. I didn't do a good job.

She suggested an alternative. Soho House at 76 Dean Street. It was her headquarters whenever she came to London. She'd reserve us a table in a quiet room.

No one else would be around.

The table would be under her name.

Meghan Markle.

2.

AFTER TEXTING half the night, into the wee hours, I groaned when that alarm rang at dawn. Time to get on Sir Keith's boat. But I also felt grateful. A sailing race was the only way I'd be able to put down my phone.

And I needed to put it down, just for a spell, to collect my wits.

To pace myself.

Sir Keith's boat was called **Invictus**. Homage to the games, God love him. That day it had a crew of eleven, including one or two athletes who'd actually competed in the games. The five-hour race took us around the Needles, and into the teeth of a gale. The wind was so fierce, many other boats dropped out of the race.

I'd sailed before, many times—I recalled one golden holiday, with Henners, trying to capsize our little Laser boat for laughs—but never like this, on open sea, in conditions so squally. The waves were towering. I'd never feared death before, and now I found myself thinking: Please don't let me drown before my big date. Then another fear took hold. The fear of no onboard loo. I held it in for as long as I possibly could, until I had no choice. I swung my body over the side, into the tossing sea . . . and still couldn't pee, mainly thanks to stage fright. The whole crew looking.

Finally I went back to my post, sheepishly hung from the ropes, and peed my pants.

Wow, I thought, if Ms. Markle could see me now.

Our boat won our class, came in second overall. Hooray, I said, barely pausing to celebrate with Sir Keith and the crew. My only concern was jumping into that water, washing the pee off my trousers, then racing back to London, where the bigger race, the ultimate race, was about to begin.

3.

THE TRAFFIC WAS TERRIBLE. It was Sunday night, people were streaming back into London from their weekends in the country. Plus I had to get through Piccadilly Circus, a nightmare at the best of times. Bottlenecks, construction, accidents, gridlock, I ran into every conceivable obstacle. Again and again my bodyguards and I would come to a full stop in the road and we'd just sit. Five minutes. Ten.

Groaning, sweating, mentally shouting at the mass of unmoving cars. **Come! On!**

Finally it couldn't be avoided. I texted: **Running a bit late, sorry.**

She was already there.

I apologized: **Horrible traffic.**

Her reply: **OK.**

I told myself: She might leave.

I told my bodyguards: **She's gonna leave.**

As we inched towards the restaurant I texted again: **Moving, but still slow.**

Can't you just get out?

How to explain? No, I couldn't. I wasn't able to go running through the streets of London. It would be like a llama running through the streets. It would make a scene, cause security nightmares; never mind the press it might attract. If I was spotted high-stepping towards Soho House, that would be the end of whatever privacy we might briefly enjoy.

Also, I had three bodyguards with me. I couldn't ask them suddenly to take part in a track-and-field event.

Texting wasn't the way to convey this, however. So I just . . . didn't answer. Which surely irritated her.

At last I arrived. Red-cheeked, puffing, sweaty, half an hour late, I ran into the restaurant, into the quiet room, and found her at a small sitting area on a low velvet sofa in front of a low coffee table.

She looked up, smiled.

I apologized. Profusely. I couldn't imagine many people had been late for this woman.

I settled into the sofa, apologized again.

She said she forgave me.

She was having a beer, some sort of IPA. I asked for a Peroni. I didn't want beer, but it seemed easier.

Silence. We took it all in.

She was wearing a black sweater, jeans, heels. I knew nothing about clothes, but I knew she was chic. Then again, I knew she could make anything look chic. Even a bivvy bag. The main thing I noticed was the chasm between internet and reality. I'd seen so many photos of her from fashion shoots and TV sets, all glam and glossy, but here she was, in the flesh, no frills, no filter . . . and even more beautiful. Heart-attack beautiful. I was trying to process this, struggling to understand what was happening to my circulatory and nervous systems, and as a result my brain couldn't handle any more data. Conversation, pleasantries, the Queen's English, all became a challenge.

She filled the gap. She talked about London. She was here all the time, she said. Sometimes she just left her luggage at Soho House for weeks. They stored it without question. The people there were like family.

I thought: You're in London all the time? How have I never seen you? Never mind that nine million people lived in London, or that I rarely left my house, I felt that if she was here, I should've known. I should've been informed!

What brings you here so often?

Friends. Business.

Oh? Business?

Acting was her main job, she said, the thing she was known for, but she had several careers. Lifestyle writer, travel writer, corporate spokesperson, entrepreneur, activist, model. She'd been all over the world, lived in various countries, worked for the US embassy in Argentina—her CV was dizzying.

All part of the plan, she said.

Plan?

Help people, do some good, be free.

The waitress reappeared. She told us her name. Mischa. East European accent, shy smile, many tattoos. We asked about them; Mischa was more than happy to explain. She provided a needed buffer, a tapping of the brakes, a moment to take a breath, and I think she knew she was filling this role, and embraced it. I loved her for it.

Mischa left us and the conversation started to really flow. The initial awkwardness was gone, the warmth from our texting returned. We'd each had first dates on which there was nothing to talk about, and now we both felt that special thrill when there's too much to talk about, when there isn't enough time to say all that needs to be said.

But speaking of time . . . ours was up. She gathered her stuff.

Sorry, I have to go.

Go? So soon?

I have dinner plans.

If I hadn't been late, we'd have had more time. I cursed myself, got to my feet.

A brief goodbye hug.

I said I'd take care of the bill and she said in that case she'd foot the bill for thank-you flowers to Violet.

Peonies, she said.

I laughed. OK. Bye.

Goodbye.

Poof, she was gone.

Compared to her, Cinderella was the queen of long goodbyes.

4.

I'D MADE PLANS TO MEET my mate after. Now I phoned him, told him I was on my way, and half an hour later I was barging into his house off the King's Road.

He took one look at my face and said: What's happened?

I didn't want to tell him. I kept thinking: Do not tell him. Do not tell him. Do not tell him.

I told him.

I recounted the entire date, then pleaded: Shit, mate, what am I going to do?

Out came the tequila. Out came the weed. We drank and smoked and watched . . . Inside Out.

An animated movie . . . about emotions. Perfect. I was thoroughly inside out.

Then I was peacefully numb. **Good weed, dude.**

My phone rang. **Oh, shit.** I held it up to my mate. **It's her.**

Who?

HER.

She wasn't just calling. She was FaceTiming.

Hello?

Hello.

What are you up to?

Uh, I'm with my mate.

What's that in the background?

Oh, er—

Are you watching cartoons?

No. I mean, yeah. Kinda. It's . . . Inside Out?

I moved to a quiet corner of the flat. She was back at her hotel. She'd washed her face. I said: **God, I love your freckles.**

She took a quick breath. Every time she was photographed, she said, they airbrushed out her freckles.

That's insane. They're beautiful.

She said she was sorry she'd had to run. She didn't want me to think she hadn't enjoyed meeting me.

I asked when I could see her again. **Tuesday?**

I leave Tuesday.

Oh. Tomorrow?

Pause.

OK.

Fourth of July.

We set another date. Back at Soho House.

5.

SHE SPENT THAT WHOLE DAY at Wimbledon, cheering on her friend Serena Williams, from Serena's box. She texted me after the final set as she raced back to her hotel, then texted again while she changed, then texted me as she was rushing to Soho House.

This time I was already there—waiting. Smiling. Proud of myself.

She walked in, wearing a pretty blue sundress with white pinstripes. She was aglow.

I stood and said: **I bear gifts.**

A pink box. I held it forward.

She shook it. **What's this?**

No, no, don't shake it! We both laughed.

She opened the box. Cupcakes. Red, white and blue cupcakes, to be exact. In honor of Independence Day. I said something about the Brits having a very different view of Independence Day from the Yanks, but, oh, well.

She said they looked amazing.

Our waitress from Date One appeared. Mischa. She seemed genuinely happy to see us, to discover that there was a Date Two. She could tell what was happening, she got that she was an eyewitness, that she'd forever be part of our personal mythology. After bringing us a round of drinks she went away and didn't return for a long time.

When she did, we were deep in the middle of a kiss.

Not our first.

Meghan, holding my shirt collar, was pulling me towards her, holding me close. When she saw Mischa she released me immediately and we all laughed.

Excuse us.

No problem. Another round?

Again the conversation flowed, crackled. Burgers came and went, uneaten. I felt an overwhelming sense of Overture, Prelude, Kettle Drums, Act I. And yet also a sense of ending. A phase of my life—the first half?—was coming to a close.

As the night neared its end we had a very frank discussion. There was no way round it.

She put a hand to her cheek and said: **What're we gonna doooo?**

We have to give this a proper go.

What does that even mean? I live in Canada. I'm going back tomorrow!

We'll meet. A long visit. This summer.

My summer's already planned.

Mine too.

Surely in the whole summer we could find one small spot of time.

She shook her head. She was doing the full **Eat Pray Love**.

Eat what now?

The book?

Ah. Sorry. Not really big on books.

I felt intimidated. She was so the opposite of me. She read. She was cultured.

Not important, she said with a laugh. The point

was, she was going with three girlfriends to Spain, and then with two girlfriends to Italy, and then—

She looked at her calendar. I looked at mine.

She raised her eyes, smiled.

What is it? Tell me.

Actually, there's one small window . . .

Recently, she explained, a castmate had advised her not to be so structured about her summer of eating, praying and loving. Keep one week open, this castmate said, leave room for magic, so she'd been saying no to all kinds of things, reserving one week, even turning down a very dreamy bike trip through the lavender fields of southern France . . .

I looked at my calendar and said: **I have one week open as well.**

What if they're the same week?

What if?

Is it possible?

How crazy would that be?

It was the same week.

I suggested we spend it in Botswana. I gave her my best Botswana pitch. Birthplace of all humankind. Most sparsely populated nation on earth. True garden of Eden, with 40 percent of the land given over to Nature.

Plus, the largest number of elephants of any nation on earth.

Above all, it was the place where I'd found myself, where I always re-found myself, where I always felt close to—magic? If she was interested in magic, she should come with me, experience it with me. Camp under the stars, in the middle of nowhere, which is actually Everywhere.

She stared.

I realize it's crazy, I said. **But all of this is obviously crazy.**

6.

WE COULDN'T FLY TOGETHER. For one thing, I was already going to be in Africa. I was scheduled to be in Malawi, doing conservation work with African Parks.

But I didn't tell her the other reason: We couldn't risk being seen together, the press finding out about us. Not yet.

So, she finished her **Eat Pray Love** thing, then flew from London to Johannesburg, then to Maun, where I'd asked Teej to meet her. (I wanted to do it myself, of course, but couldn't without creating a scene.) After an eleven-hour odyssey, including a three-hour layover in Johannesburg, and a hot car ride to the house, Meghan had every right to be grumpy. But she wasn't. Bright-eyed, eager, she was ready for anything.

And looking like . . . perfection. She wore cut-off jean shorts, well-loved hiking boots, a crumpled Panama hat that I'd seen on her Instagram page.

As I opened the gate to Teej and Mike's house, I handed her a chicken-salad sandwich, wrapped in clingfilm. **Thought you might be hungry**. I suddenly wished I had flowers, a present, something besides this measly sandwich. We hugged, and it was awkward, not just because of the sandwich but the unavoidable suspense. We'd talked and FaceTimed countless times since our first dates, but this was all new and different. And a bit strange.

We were both thinking the same things. **Is it going to translate? To another continent?**

And what if it doesn't?

I asked about the flight. She laughed about the Air Botswana crew. They were big fans of **Suits**, so they'd asked her to pose for a photo.

Yay, I said, thinking: Shit. If one member of the crew posted that photo, the cat would be out of the bag.

We all jumped into a three-bench truck, Mike driving, my bodyguards trailing, and set off. Straight into the sun. After an hour of tarmac roads, we were facing four hours of dirt tracks. To make the time go faster I pointed out every flower, plant, bird. **That's a francolin. That's a hornbill. It's like Zazu from** The Lion King. **That's a lilac-breasted roller, and he seems to be doing his mating display.**

After a respectful period of time, I held her hand.

Next, when the road got flatter, I ventured a kiss.

Just as we both remembered.

My bodyguards, fifty meters behind us, pretended not to see.

As we got further into the bush, as we neared the Okavango, the fauna began changing.

There! Look!

Oh, my God. Is that . . . giraffes!
And over there, look!
A family of warthogs.
We saw a breeding herd of elephants. Dads, mums, babies. **Hi, guys.** We started along a firebreak road and the birds were going nuts, which sent a weird shiver down my spine. **Lions in the area.**

No way, she said.

Something told me to look back. Sure enough, a flickering tail. I shouted for Mike to stop. He hit the brakes, threw the truck into reverse. There—standing right before us, a big fella. Daddy. And there, four youngsters, lounging under a shady bush. With their mums.

We admired them for a while, then drove on.

Shortly before dusk we arrived at a small satellite camp Teej and Mike had made up. I carried our bags to a bell tent beside a huge sausage tree. We were on the edge of a big forest, looking down a gentle slope to the river, and beyond: a floodplain teeming with life.

Meghan—whom I was now calling Meg, or sometimes just M—was stunned. The vivid colors. The pure, fresh air. She'd traveled, but she'd never seen anything like this. This was the world before the world was made.

She opened her small suitcase—she needed to get something. Here it comes, I thought. The mirror, the hairdryer, the makeup kit, the fluffy duvet, the dozen pairs of shoes. I was shamefully stereotyping:

American actress equals diva. To my shock, and delight, there was nothing in that suitcase but bare essentials. Shorts, ripped jeans and snacks. And a yoga mat.

We sat in canvas chairs, watched the sun set and the moon rise. I whipped up some bush cocktails. Whisky with a splash of river water. Teej offered Meg a glass of wine and showed her how to cut the end off a plastic water bottle and turn it into a goblet. We told stories, laughed a lot, then Teej and Mike cooked us a lovely dinner.

We ate around the fire, staring at the stars.

At bedtime I guided Meg through the darkness to the tent.

Where's the flashlight? Meg asked.

You mean the torch?

We both laughed.

The tent was very small, and very Spartan. If she'd been expecting some glamping trip, she was now fully divested of that fantasy. We lay down inside, on our backs, feeling the moment, reckoning with the moment.

There were separate bedrolls, the result of much worry and many conversations with Teej. Didn't want to be presumptuous.

We pushed them together, lay shoulder to shoulder. We stared at the roof, listening, talking, watching moon shadows flutter across the nylon.

Then, a loud munching sound.

Meg bolted upright. **What's that?**

Elephant, I said.

Just one, from what I could tell. Just outside. Eating peacefully from the shrubs around us.

She won't hurt us.

She won't?

Soon after, the tent shook from a loud roar.

Lions.

Are we going to be OK?

Yes. Don't worry.

She lay down, put her head on my chest.

Trust me, I told her. **I'll keep you safe.**

7.

I WOKE JUST BEFORE DAWN, unzipped the tent quietly, tiptoed out. The stillness of a Botswana morning. I watched a flock of pygmy geese fly upriver, watched impala and lechwe having their morning drink at the water's edge.

The birdsong was incredible.

As the sun came up I gave thanks for this day, then walked down to the main camp for a piece of toast. When I returned I found Meg stretched on a yoga mat beside the river.

Warrior pose. Downward dog. Child's pose.

When she finished I announced: **Breakfast is served.**

We ate under an acacia tree, and she asked excitedly what the plan was.

I have surprises.

Beginning with a morning drive. We hopped into Mike's old doorless truck, went barreling into the bush. Sun on our cheeks, wind in our hair, we cruised through streams, bounced over hills, flushed lions out of deep grass. **Thanks for making such a racket last night, boys!** We came upon a large group of giraffes grazing the treetops, their eyelashes like rakes. They nodded good morning.

Not everyone was so friendly. Strolling by a vast watering hole, we saw a cloud of dust just up ahead. A grumpy warthog confronted us. He retreated when we stood our ground.

Hippos also snorted belligerently. We waved, retreated, jumped back into the truck.

We interrupted a pack of wild dogs trying to filch a dead buffalo from two lionesses. It wasn't going well. We left them to it.

The grass was golden, swaying in the wind. **Dry season,** I said to Meg. The air was warm, clean, a joy to breathe. We broke out a picnic lunch, washed it down with a couple of Savannah ciders. Afterwards we went for a swim in an estuary off the river, keeping our distance from the crocs. **Stay away from the dark water**.

I told her this was the cleanest, purest water in the world, because it was filtered by all that papyrus. Even sweeter than the water in the ancient bath at Balmoral, though . . . better not to think of Balmoral.

The anniversary was only weeks away.

At dusk we lay across the bonnet of the truck, watching the sky. When the bats came out, we went to find Teej and Mike. We turned on music, laughed and talked and sang and ate dinner again around the fire. Meg told us a bit about her life, about growing up in Los Angeles, about her struggles to become an actress, doing quick changes between auditions in her rundown SUV on which the doors didn't always work. She was forced to enter through the boot. She talked about her growing portfolio as an entrepreneur, her lifestyle website, which had tens of thousands of readers. In her free time she did philanthropic work—she was especially fierce about women's issues.

I was fascinated, hanging on every word, while in the background I heard a faint drumbeat: **She's perfect, she's perfect, she's perfect.**

Chels and Cress often mentioned my Jekyll-and-Hyde existence. Happy Spike in Botswana, tightly wound Prince Harry in London. I'd never been able to synthesize the two, and it bothered them, bothered me, but with this woman, I thought, I could do it. I could be Happy Spike all the time.

Except she didn't call me Spike. By now Meg had taken to calling me Haz.

Every moment of that week was a revelation and a blessing. And yet every moment also dragged us closer to the wrenching minute when we'd have to say goodbye. There was no way around it: Meg had to get back. I had to fly to the capital, Gaborone, to meet the president of Botswana, to discuss conservation issues, after which I was embarking on a three-phase lads' trip, months in the planning.

I would cancel, I told Meg, but my mates would never forgive me.

We said goodbye; Meg began to cry.

When will I see you again?

Soon.

Not soon enough.

No. Not nearly.

Teej put an arm around her and promised to take good care of her until her flight, several hours away.

Then one last kiss. And a wave.

Mike and I jumped into his white cruiser and headed to Maun airport, where we climbed into his small prop plane and, though it broke my heart, flew away.

8.

THERE WERE ELEVEN OF US. Marko, of course. Adi, of course. Two Mikes. Brent. Bidders. David. Jakie. Skippy. Viv. The whole gang. I met up with them in Maun. We loaded three silver flat-bottomed boats and set off. Days of floating, drifting, fishing, dancing. In the evenings we got fairly loud and very naughty. In the mornings we cooked bacon and eggs over open fires, went for cold swims. I drank bush cocktails, and African beer, and ingested certain controlled substances.

When the weather got really hot, we decided to break out the Jet Ski. I had the presence of mind, beforehand, to remove my iPhone from my pocket and stow it in the Jet Ski console. I congratulated myself on being so prudent. Then Adi jumped on the back of the Jet Ski, followed by a very anarchic Jakie.

So much for prudent.

I told Jakie to get off. **Three's too many.** He wouldn't hear me.

What could I do?

Away we went.

We were cruising around, laughing, trying to avoid the hippos. We roared past a sandbar on which a ten-foot crocodile was sleeping in the sun. Just as I curved the Jet Ski to the left I saw the croc open its eyes and slither into the water.

Moments later, Adi's hat flew off.

Go back, go back, he said.

I did a U-turn, not easy with three onboard. I brought us alongside the hat, and Adi leaned over to snatch it. Then Jakie leaned over to help. We all fell into the river.

I felt my sunglasses slip from my face, saw them plunk into the water. I dived after them. The moment I came up, I remembered the croc.

I could see Adi and Jakie thinking the same thing. Then I looked at the Jet Ski. Floating on its side. Shit.

My iPhone!

With all my photos! And phone numbers!

MEG!

The Jet Ski came to rest on the sandbar. We flipped it right and I grabbed my phone from the console. Soaked. Ruined. All the photos Meg and I had taken! Plus all our texts!

I'd known this lads' trip would be wild, so I'd sent some photos to Meg and other mates before leaving, as a precaution. Still, the rest were surely lost.

More, how was I going to be in touch with her?

Adi said not to worry, we'd put the phone in rice, a surefire way to dry it out.

Hours later, the moment we got back to camp, that was just what we did. We submerged the phone in a big bucket of uncooked white rice.

I looked down, highly dubious. **How long will this take?**

Day or two.

No good. I need a solution now.

Mike and I worked out a plan. I could write a letter to Meg, which he'd take home with him to Maun. Teej could then photograph the letter and text it to Meg. (She had Meg's number on her phone: I'd given it to her when she first went to collect Meg from the airport.)

Now I just had to write that letter.

The first challenge was finding a pen among that bunch of muppets.

Does anyone have a pen?

A what?

A pen.

I've got an EpiPen!

No! A pen. A biro! My kingdom for a biro!

Oh. A biro. Wow.

Somehow I found one. The next challenge was finding a place to compose.

I went off under a tree.

I thought. I stared into space. I wrote:

Hey Beautiful. OK you got me—can't stop thinking about you, missing you, LOTS. Phone went in river. Sad face . . . Apart from that, having an amazing time. Wish u were here.

Mike left, letter in hand.

Days later, wrapping up the boat part of the lads' trip, we returned to Maun. We met up with Teej, who immediately said: **Relax, I've already had a reply.**

So it hadn't been a dream. Meg was real. All of it was real.

Among other things, Meg said in her reply that she was eager to speak to me.

Jubilant, I went off on the second part of the lads' trip, into the Moremi forest. This time I brought a sat phone. While everyone was finishing dinner I found a clearing and climbed the tallest tree, thinking the reception might be better.

I dialed Meg. She answered.

Before I could speak she blurted: **I shouldn't say this but I miss you!**

I shouldn't say this as well but I miss you too!

And then we just laughed and listened to each other breathe.

9.

I FELT ENORMOUS PRESSURE, the next day, sitting down to write the next letter. A paralyzing case of writer's block. I just couldn't find the words to express my excitement, my contentment, my longing. My hopes.

The next best thing, I figured, in the absence of lyricism, would be to make the letter physically beautiful.

Alas, I wasn't in a location conducive to arts and crafts. The lads' trip was now moving into phase three—an eight-hour game drive into the arse end of nowhere.

What to do?

At a break I jumped out of the truck, ran into the bush.

Spike, where you going?

I didn't answer.

What's with him?

Wandering wasn't advisable in these parts. We were deep in lion country. But I was hell-bent on finding . . . something.

I stumbled, staggered, saw nothing but endless brown grass. **Are we in the bloody Outback?**

Adi had taught me how to look for flowers in the desert. When it came to thornbushes, he always said, check the highest branches. So I did. And sure enough: Bingo! I climbed the thornbush, picked the flowers, put them into a little bag slung over my shoulder.

Later in our drive we came into a mopani forest, where I spotted two bright pink impala lilies.

I picked them too.

Soon enough I'd assembled a small bouquet.

We now came to a part of the forest scorched by recent fires. Within the charred landscape I spotted an interesting piece of bark from a leadwood. I grabbed it, nestled it into my bag.

We got back to camp at sunset. I wrote the second letter, singed the paper's edges, surrounded it with my flowers and placed it inside the burned bark, then took a photo of it with Adi's phone. I sent this to Meg and counted the seconds until I got a reply, which she signed "Your girl."

By means of improvisation, and sheer determination, I managed somehow, throughout that lads' trip, to stay in constant contact. When I finally returned to Britain I felt a huge sense of accomplishment. I hadn't let soaked phones, drunken mates, lack of mobile reception, or a dozen other obstacles, scuttle the beginning of this beautiful . . .

What to call it?

Sitting in Nott Cott, bags all around me, I stared at the wall and quizzed myself. What is this? What's the word?

Is it . . .

The One?

Have I found her?

At long, long last?

I'd always told myself that there were firm rules about relationships, at least when it came to royalty, and the main one was that you absolutely must date a woman for three years before taking the plunge. How else could you know about her? How else could **she** know about you—and your royal life? How else could both of you be sure that this was what you wanted, that it was a thing you could endure together?

It wasn't for everybody.

But Meg seemed the shining exception to this rule. All rules. I knew her straightaway, and she knew me. The true me. Might seem rash, I thought, might seem illogical, but it's true: For the first time, in fact, I felt myself to be living in truth.

10.

A FRENZY OF TEXTING AND FaceTiming. Though we were thousands of miles apart, we were never actually apart. I'd wake up to a text. Instantly reply. Then: text, text, text. Then, after lunch: FaceTime. Then, throughout the afternoon: text, text, text. Then, late at night, another marathon FaceTime.

And still it wasn't enough. We were desperate to see each other again. We circled the last days of August, about ten days away, for our next meeting.

We agreed it would be best if she came to London.

On the big day, just after her arrival, she phoned as she was walking into her room at Soho House.

I'm here. Come see me!

I can't, I'm in the car . . .

Doing what?

Something for my mum.

Your mum? Where?

Althorp.

What's Althorp?

Where my uncle Charles lives.

I told her I'd explain later. We still hadn't talked about . . . all that.

I felt pretty sure she hadn't googled me, because she was always asking questions. She seemed to know almost nothing—so refreshing. It showed that she wasn't impressed by royalty, which I thought the first step to surviving it. More, since she hadn't done a deep dive into the literature, the public record, her head wasn't filled with disinformation.

After Willy and I had laid flowers at Mummy's grave, we drove together back to London. I phoned Meg, told her I was on my way. I tried to keep my voice nonchalant, not wanting to give myself away to Willy.

There's a secret way into the hotel, she said. **Then a freight lift.**

Her friend Vanessa, who worked for Soho House, would meet me and usher me in.

All went according to plan. After I'd met the friend and navigated a sort of maze through the bowels of Soho House, I finally reached Meg's door.

I knocked and suspended breathing while I waited.

The door flew open.

That smile.

Her hair was partly covering her eyes. Her arms were reaching for me. She pulled me inside and thanked her friend in one fluid motion, then slammed the door quickly before anyone saw.

I want to say we hung a Do Not Disturb sign on the door.

But I don't think there was time.

11.

IN THE MORNING WE NEEDED SUSTENANCE. We phoned room service. When they knocked at the door, I looked around frantically for a place to hide.

The room had nothing. No cubbyhole or wardrobes, no armoire.

So I lay flat on the bed and pulled the duvet over my head. Meg whispered to go into the bathroom but I preferred my hiding place.

Alas, our breakfast wasn't delivered by just any anonymous waiter. It was brought by a hotel assistant manager who loved Meg, and whom she loved, so he wanted to chat. He didn't notice that there were two breakfasts on the tray. He didn't notice the prince-shaped lump under the duvet. He talked and talked, and caught her up on all the latest, while I, in my duvet cave, started to run out of air.

Thank goodness for all that practice riding in the boot of Billy's police car.

When the man finally left, I sat up, gasping.

Then we both gasped, we were laughing so hard.

We decided to have dinner that night at my place, invite some friends over. We'd cook. Fun, we said, but it would mean food shopping first. There was nothing in my fridge besides grapes and cottage pies.

We could go to Waitrose, I said.

Of course we couldn't actually go to Waitrose **together**: that would cause a riot. So we drew up a plan to shop **simultaneously**, in parallel, and in disguise, without visibly acknowledging each other.

Meg got there minutes before me. She wore a flannel shirt, a bulky overcoat and a beanie, but I was still surprised that no one was recognizing her. Plenty of Brits watched **Suits**, surely, yet no one was staring. I'd have spotted her in a crowd of thousands.

Also, no one looked twice at her trolley, which was filled with her suitcases, and two large Soho House bags containing fluffy dressing-gowns she'd bought for us on checking out.

Equally anonymous, I grabbed a basket, walked casually up and down the aisles. Beside the fruit and veg I felt her stroll past me. Actually, it was more a saunter than a stroll. Very saucy. We slid our eyes towards each other, just an instant, then quickly away.

Meg had cut out a roasted-salmon recipe from **Food & Wine** and with that we'd made a list and divided it in two. She was in charge of finding a baking sheet, while I was tasked with finding parchment paper.

I texted her: **What the F is parchment paper?**

She talked me onto the target.

Above your head.

I spun around. She was a few feet away, peering from behind a display.

We both laughed.

I looked back to the shelf.

This?

No, the one next to it.

We were cackling.

When we'd got through our list, I paid at the checkout, then texted Meg about where to meet. **Down the parking ramp, under the shop, people-carrier with blacked-out windows.** Moments later, our shopping snug in the boot, Billy the Rock at the wheel, we roared out of the car park, heading for Nott Cott. I watched the city going past, all the houses and people, and I thought: **I can't wait for you all to meet her.**

12.

I WAS EXCITED TO welcome Meg to my home, but also embarrassed: Nott Cott was no palace. Nott Cott was palace adjacent—that was the best you could say for it. I watched her as she walked up the front path, through the white picket fence. To my relief she made no sign of dismay, gave no indication of disillusionment.

Until she got inside. Then she said something about a frat house.

I glanced around. She wasn't far off.

Union Jack in the corner. (The one I'd waved at the North Pole.) Old rifle on the TV stand. (A gift from Oman, after an official visit.) Xbox console.

Just a place to keep my stuff, I explained, moving around some papers and clothes. **I'm not here much.**

It was also constructed for smaller people, humans of a bygone era. Thus the rooms were tiny and the ceilings were doll's house low. I gave her a quick tour, which took thirty seconds. **Mind your head!**

I'd never noticed until then just how shabby the furniture was. Brown sofa, browner beanbag chair. Meg paused before the beanbag.

I know. I know.

Our dinner guests were my cousin Euge, her boyfriend Jack, and my mate Charlie. The salmon turned out perfectly and everyone complimented Meg on her culinary talents. They also devoured her stories. They wanted to hear all about **Suits**. And her travels. I was grateful for their interest, their warmth.

The wine was as good as the company, and there was plenty of it, and after dinner we moved into the snug, put on music and silly hats, and danced. I have a fuzzy memory, and a grainy video on my phone, of Charlie and me rolling on the floor while Meg sat nearby laughing.

Then we got into the tequila.

I remember Euge hugging Meg, as if they were sisters. I remember Charlie giving me a thumbs-up. I remember thinking: If meeting the rest of my family goes like this, we're home free. But then I noticed that Meg was feeling poorly. She complained of an upset stomach and looked terribly pale.

I thought: Uh-oh, lightweight.

She took herself off to bed. After a nightcap I saw our guests out and tidied up a bit. I got into bed around midnight and crashed out, but I woke at two A.M. to hear her in the bathroom, being sick, truly sick, not the drunken sick I'd imagined. Something else was going on.

Food poisoning.

She revealed that she'd had squid for lunch at a restaurant.

British calamari! Mystery solved.

From the floor she said softly: **Please tell me you're not having to hold back my hair while I'm vomiting.**

Yes. I am.

I rubbed her back and eventually put her to bed. Weak, near tears, she said she'd imagined a very different end to Date Four.

Stop, I said. Taking care of each other? That's the point.

That's love, I thought, though I managed to keep the words inside.

13.

Just before Meg returned to Canada we went to Frogmore gardens for a walk.

It was on the way to the airport.

A favorite spot of mine, I said. It spoke to her as well. She especially loved the swans, and especially one that was very grumpy. (We named him Steve.) Most swans are grumpy, I said. Majestic, but sourpusses. I always wondered why, since every British swan was the property of Her Majesty, and any abuse of them, thereby, was a criminal offense.

We chatted about Euge and Jack, whom she loved. We talked about Meg's work. We talked about mine. But mostly we talked about this relationship, a subject so immense it seemed inexhaustible. We continued the talk as we got back into the car and drove to the airport, and kept talking in the car park, where I dropped her on the sly. We agreed that if we were serious about giving ourselves a chance, a real chance, we'd need a serious plan. Which meant, among other things, making a vow never to let more than two weeks pass without seeing each other.

We'd both had long-distance relationships, and they'd always been hard, and part of the reason had always been lack of serious planning. Effort. You had to fight the distance, defeat that distance. Meaning, travel. Lots and lots of travel.

Alas, my movements attracted more attention, more press. Governments had to be alerted when I crossed international borders, local police had to be notified. All my bodyguards had to be shuffled. The burden therefore would fall on Meg. In the early days, it would have to be her spending time on planes, her crisscrossing the ocean—while still working full-time on **Suits**. Many days the car came for her at 4:15 A.M. to take her to set.

It wasn't fair for her to shoulder the burden, but

she was willing, she said. No choice, she said. The alternative was not seeing me, and that, she said, wasn't feasible. Or bearable.

For the hundredth time since July 1, my heart cracked open.

Then we said goodbye again.

See you in two weeks.

Two weeks. God. Yes.

14.

SOON AFTER THAT DAY, Willy and Kate invited me over to dinner.

They knew something was going on with me and they wanted to find out what it was.

I wasn't sure I was ready to tell them. I wasn't sure I wanted anyone else to know just yet. But then, as we sat around their TV room, both kids tucked into bed, the moment felt right.

I casually mentioned that there was . . . a new woman in my life.

They surged forward. **Who is she?**

I'll tell you, but please, please, please, I need you both to keep it a secret.

Yes, Harold, yes, yes—who is it?

She's an actress.

Oh?

She's American.

Oh.

On a show called Suits.

Their mouths fell open. They turned to each other.

Then Willy turned to me and said: **Fuck off!**

What?

No way.

Sorry?

Impossible!

I was baffled, until Willy and Kate explained that they were regular—nay, religious—viewers of **Suits**.

Great, I thought, laughing. I've been worrying about the wrong thing. All this time I'd thought Willy and Kate might not welcome Meg into the family, but now I had to worry about them hounding her for an autograph.

They barraged me with questions. I told them a bit of how we'd met, told them about Botswana, told them about Waitrose, told them I was smitten, but overall what I told them was heavily redacted. I just didn't want to give away too much.

I also said I couldn't wait for them to meet her, that I looked forward to the four of us spending lots of time together, and I confessed, for the umpteenth time, that this had long been my dream—to join them with an equal partner. To become a foursome. I'd said this to Willy so many times, and he'd always replied: **It might not happen, Harold! And you've got to be OK with that.** Well, now I felt that it **was** going to happen, and I told him so—but he still said to slow down.

She's an American actress after all, Harold. Anything might happen.

I nodded, a bit hurt. Then hugged him and Kate and left.

15.

MEG CAME BACK TO London a week later. October 2016.

We lunched with Marko and his family, and I introduced her to a few other close mates. All good. Everyone loved her.

Emboldened, I felt the time had come for her to meet my family.

She agreed.

First stop, Royal Lodge. To meet Fergie, because Meg already knew Fergie's daughter Euge, and Jack, so this seemed a logical baby step. But as we neared Royal Lodge I got word on my phone.

Granny was there.

She'd popped in.

On her way from church back to the castle.

Meg said: **Fun! I love grandmas.**

I asked if she knew how to curtsy. She said she thought so. But she also couldn't tell if I was serious.

You're about to meet the Queen.

I know, but it's your grandma.

But she's the Queen.

We pulled into the driveway, drove across the gravel, parked next to the big green box hedge.

Fergie came outside, somewhat aflutter, and said: **Do you know how to curtsy?**

Meg shook her head.

Fergie demonstrated once. Meg imitated her.

There wasn't time for a more advanced tutorial. We couldn't keep Granny waiting.

As we walked towards the door Fergie and I both leaned into Meg, whispering quick reminders. **When you first meet the Queen it's Your Majesty. Thereafter it's just Ma'am. Rhymes with ham.**

Just, whatever you do, don't talk over her, we both said, talking over each other.

We entered the large front sitting room and there she was. Granny. The monarch. Queen Elizabeth II. Standing in the middle of the room. She turned slightly. Meg went straight to her and dropped a deep, flawless curtsy.

Your Majesty. Pleasure to meet you.

Euge and Jack were near Granny and they almost seemed to pretend not to know Meg. They were very quiet, very proper. Each gave Meg a quick kiss on the cheek, but it was pure royal. Pure British.

There was some bloke standing to the other side of Granny and I thought: Bogey at twelve o'clock. Meg looked to me for a clue as to his identity, but I couldn't help—I'd never seen him before. Euge whispered into my ear that he was a friend of her mum's. Ah, OK. I looked at him hard: **Brilliant. Congratulations on being present for one of the most consequential moments of my life.**

Granny was dressed for church: a brightly colored dress and matching hat. I can't recall the color, I wish

I could, but it was bright. Fancy. I could see Meg regretting her jeans and black sweater.

I was also regretting my shabby trousers. We didn't plan, I wanted to tell Granny, but she was busy asking about Meg's visit.

Great, we said. **Wonderful.**

We asked about the church service.

Lovely.

It was all very pleasant. Granny even asked Meg what she thought of Donald Trump. (This was just before the November 2016 election, so everyone in the world seemed to be thinking and talking about the Republican candidate.) Meg thought politics a no-win game, so she changed the subject to Canada.

Granny squinted. **I thought you were American.**

I am, but I've been living in Canada for seven years for work.

Granny looked pleased. Commonwealth. Good, fine.

After twenty minutes Granny announced she had to be going. My uncle Andrew, seated beside her, holding her handbag, began to escort her out. Euge went with her too. Before reaching the door Granny looked back to say goodbye to Jack, and to Fergie's friend.

She locked eyes with Meg, gave a wave and a warm smile. **Bye.**

Bye. Lovely to meet you, Ma'am, as she dipped into a curtsy again.

Everyone flooded into the room after she'd driven

away. The whole vibe changed. Euge and Jack were their old selves, and someone suggested drinks.

Yes, please.

Everyone complimented Meg on her curtsy. So good! So deep!

After a moment Meg asked me something about the Queen's assistant.

I asked who she was talking about.

That man holding the purse. That man who walked her to the door.

That wasn't her assistant.

Who was it?

That was her second son. Andrew.

She definitely hadn't googled us.

16.

NEXT WAS WILLY. I knew he'd kill me if I let it go another minute. So Meg and I popped over one afternoon, shortly before he and I were due to leave on a shooting trip. Walking up to apartment 1A, under the huge arch, through the courtyard, I felt more nervous than I had before the meeting with Granny.

I asked myself why.

No answer came to mind.

We climbed the gray stone steps, rang the bell.

No reply.

After a wait the door opened and there was my big brother, a bit dressed up. Nice trousers, nice shirt, open collar. I introduced Meg, who leaned in and gave him a hug, which completely freaked him out.

He recoiled.

Willy didn't hug many strangers. Whereas Meg hugged most strangers. The moment was a classic collision of cultures, like flashlight-torch, which felt to me both funny and charming. Later, however, looking back, I wondered if it was more than that. Maybe Willy expected Meg to curtsy? It would've been protocol when meeting a member of the Royal Family for the first time, but she didn't know, and I didn't tell her. When meeting my grandmother, I'd made it clear—this is the Queen. But when meeting my brother, it was just Willy, who loved **Suits**.

Whatever, Willy got over it. He exchanged a few warm words with Meg, just inside the door, on the checkered floor of their hall. We were then interrupted by his spaniel, Lupo, barking as if we were burglars. Willy hushed Lupo.

Where's Kate?

Out with the kids.

Ah, too bad. Next time.

Then it was time to say goodbye. Willy needed to finish packing and we needed to go. Meg gave me a kiss and told us both to have fun on our shooting weekend, and off she went to spend her first night alone at Nott Cott.

Over the next few days I couldn't stop talking about her. Now that she and Granny had met, now that she and Willy had met, now that she was no longer a secret within the family, I had so much to say. My brother listened, attentive, always smiling thinly. Boring to hear someone besotted go on and on, I know, but I couldn't stop myself.

To his credit, he didn't tease, didn't tell me to shut up. On the contrary, he said what I'd hoped he'd say, even needed him to say.

Happy for you, Harold.

17.

WEEKS LATER, MEG AND I drove through the gate, into the lush gardens of Clarence House, which made Meg gasp.

You should see them in the spring. Pa designed them himself.

I added: **In honor of Gan-Gan, you know. She lived here before him.**

I'd mentioned Gan-Gan to Meg. I'd also mentioned that I used to live here at Clarence House, from when I was nineteen until I was about twenty-eight. After I moved out, Camilla turned my bedroom into her dressing room. I tried not to care. But, especially the first time I saw it, I cared.

We paused at the front door. Five o'clock, on the dot. Wouldn't do to be late.

Meg looked beautiful and I told her so. She was wearing a black-and-white dress, with a full skirt, patterned with flowers, and when I put my hand on her back I could feel how delicate the material was.

Her hair was down, because I suggested she wear it that way. **Pa likes it when women wear their hair down.** Granny too. She often commented on "Kate's beautiful mane."

Meg was wearing little makeup, which I'd also suggested. Pa didn't approve of women who wore a lot.

The door opened and we were greeted by Pa's Gurkha butler. And by Leslie, his long-time house manager, who'd also worked for Gan-Gan. They led us down the long corridor, past the big paintings and gilt-edged mirrors, along the crimson carpet with the crimson runner, past the big glass cabinet filled with gleaming porcelain and exquisite heirlooms, up the creaky staircase, which rose three steps before jogging right, up another twelve steps, then jogged right again. There, at last, on the landing above us, stood Pa.

Beside him stood Camilla.

Meg and I had rehearsed this moment several times. **For Pa, curtsy. Say, Your Royal Highness, or Sir. Maybe a kiss on each cheek if he leans in, otherwise a handshake. For Camilla, no curtsy. Not necessary. Just a quick kiss or handshake.**

No curtsy? You sure?

I didn't think it appropriate.

We all went into a large sitting room. Along the way Pa asked Meg if it was true, as he'd been told, that she was the star of an American soap opera! She smiled. I smiled. I desperately wanted to say: **Soap opera? No, that's our family, Pa.**

Meg said she was in a cable drama that aired in the evening. About lawyers. Called **Suits.**

Marvelous, Pa said. **How splendid.**

We came to a round table laid with a white cloth. Beside it stood a trolley with tea: honey cake, flapjacks, sandwiches, warm crumpets, crackers with some creamy spread, shredded basil—Pa's favorite. All surgically laid out. Pa sat with his back to an open window, as far as possible from the popping fire. Camilla sat across from him, her back to the fire. Meg and I sat between them, across from one another.

I wolfed down a crumpet with Marmite; Meg had two smoked-salmon tea sandwiches. We were starving. We'd been so nervous all day that we hadn't eaten.

Pa offered her some flapjacks. She loved them.

Camilla asked how Meg took her tea, dark or light, and Meg apologized for not knowing. **I thought tea was tea.** This sparked a rollicking discussion about tea, and wine, and other libations, and Britishisms versus Americanisms, and then we were onto the larger subject of Things We All Like, which led straight to dogs. Meg talked about her two "fur babies," Bogart and Guy, both of whom were rescues. Guy had a particularly sad story. Meg found him at a Kentucky kill shelter after someone abandoned him in deep woods, without food or water. Beagles, she explained, were put down in Kentucky more than in any other state, and when she saw Guy on the shelter's website she fell in love.

I watched Camilla's face darken. She was the patron of Battersea Dogs & Cats Home, so these kinds of stories always hit her hard. Pa too. He couldn't bear to think of any animal suffering. He was undoubtedly reminded of the time his beloved dog, Pooh, got lost on the grouse moor in Scotland—probably down a rabbit hole—never to be seen again.

The conversation was easy, all four of us talking at once, but then Pa and Meg fell into a quiet chat, and I turned to Camilla, who seemed keener on eavesdropping than talking to her stepson but, alas, she was stuck with me.

Soon, we all switched. How weird, I thought, that we're just instinctively observing the same protocol as we would at a state dinner with Granny.

Eventually the conversation broadened again to include everyone. We talked about acting and the arts generally. What a struggle it could be to make your way in such a trade, Pa said. He had a lot of questions about Meg's career, and he looked impressed by the way she answered. Her confidence, her intelligence, I thought, caught him unawares.

And then our time was up. Pa and Camilla had another engagement. Royal life. Heavily regimented, overscheduled, so forth.

I made a note to explain all this later to Meg.

We all stood. Meg leaned towards Pa. I flinched; like Willy, Pa wasn't a hugger. Thankfully, she gave him a standard British cheek-to-cheek, which he actually seemed to enjoy.

I walked Meg out of Clarence House, into those lush, fragrant gardens, feeling exultant.

Well, that's that then, I thought. Welcome to the family.

18.

I FLEW TO TORONTO. End of October 2016. Meg was excited to show me **her** life, **her** dogs—**her** little house, which she adored. And I was eager to see it all, to know every last detail about her. (Though I'd snuck into Canada once before, briefly, this would be my first proper visit.) We walked the dogs in big, open ravines and parks. We explored the sparsely populated nooks and crannies of her neighborhood. Toronto wasn't London, but it also wasn't Botswana. So, be ever cautious, we said. Maintain the bubble. Keep wearing disguises.

Speaking of disguises. We invited Euge and Jack to join us for Halloween. And Meg's best friend Markus. Toronto's Soho House was having a big party and the theme was "Apocalypse." Dress accordingly.

I mumbled to Meg that I'd not had great luck with themed fancy-dress parties, but I'd give it another go. For help with my costume, I'd turned to a friend, the actor Tom Hardy, before I left home. I'd phoned him to ask if I could borrow his costume from **Mad Max**.

The whole thing?

Yes, please, mate! The whole kit.

He'd given it all to me before I left Britain, and now I tried it on in Meg's little bathroom. When I came out, she roared with laughter.

It was funny. And a little scary. But the main thing was: I was unrecognizable.

Meg, meanwhile, wore torn black shorts, a camo

top, fishnet stockings. If that's the Apocalypse, I thought, bring on the end of the world.

The party was loud, dark, drunk—ideal. Several people did double-takes as Meg passed through the rooms, but no one looked twice at her dystopian date. I wished I could wear this disguise every day. I wished I could reuse it the next day and visit her on the set of **Suits**.

Then again, maybe not. I'd made the mistake of googling and watching some of her love scenes online. I'd witnessed her and a castmate mauling each other in some sort of office or conference room . . . It would take electric-shock therapy to get those images out of my head. I didn't need to see such things live. Still, the point was moot: the next day was Sunday, so she wasn't working.

And then everything was rendered moot, everything was changed forever, because the next day was when news of our relationship broke wide open.

Well, we said, staring anxiously at our phones, it was going to happen eventually.

In fact, we'd had a heads-up that it was likely to happen that day. We'd been tipped, before heading off to the Halloween Apocalypse, that another apocalypse might be coming. More proof that the universe had a wicked sense of humor.

Meg, you ready for what's headed our way?

Kinda. Are you?

Yes.

We were sitting on her sofa, moments before I left for the airport.

Are you scared?

Yes. No. Maybe.

We're going to be hunted. No two ways about it.

I'll just treat it as if we're in the bush.

She reminded me of what I'd said in Botswana, when the lions were roaring.

Trust me. I'll keep you safe.

She'd believed me then, she said. She believed me now.

By the time I touched down at Heathrow, the story had . . . fizzled?

It was all unconfirmed, and there were no photos, so there was nothing to fuel it.

A moment's reprieve? Maybe, I thought, all will be well.

Nah. Calm before the shit storm.

19.

IN THOSE FIRST HOURS and days of November 2016 there was a new low every few minutes. I was shocked, and scolded myself for being shocked. And for being unprepared. I'd been braced for the usual madness, the standard libels, but I hadn't anticipated this level of unrestrained lying.

Above all, I hadn't been ready for the racism. Both the dog-whistle racism and the glaring, vulgar, in-your-face racism.

The **Daily Mail** took the lead. Its headline: **Harry's girl is (almost) straight outta Compton.** Subhead:

Gang-scarred home of her mother revealed—so will he be dropping in for tea?

Another tabloid jumped into the fray with this jaw-dropper: **Harry to marry into gangster royalty?**

My face froze. My blood stopped. I was angry, but more: ashamed. My Mother Country? Doing this? To her? To us? Really?

As if its headline wasn't disgraceful enough, the **Mail** went on to say that Compton had been the scene of forty-seven crimes in the last week alone. Forty-seven, imagine that. Never mind that Meg had never lived in Compton, never even lived near it. She'd lived half an hour away, as far from Compton as Buckingham Palace was from Windsor Castle. But forget that: Even if she **had** lived in Compton, years ago or currently, so what? Who cared how many crimes were committed in Compton, or anywhere else, so long as Meg wasn't the one committing them?

A day or two later the **Mail** weighed in again, this time with an essay by the sister of London's former mayor Boris Johnson, predicting that Meg would . . . do something . . . genetically . . . to the Royal Family. "If there is issue from her alleged union with Prince Harry, the Windsors will thicken their watery, thin blue blood and Spencer pale skin and ginger hair with some rich and exotic DNA."

Sister Johnson further opined that Meg's mother, Doria, was from "the wrong side of the tracks," and as stone-cold proof she cited Doria's dreadlocks. This filth was being blasted out to three million Britons, about Doria, lovely Doria, born in Cleveland, Ohio, graduate of Fairfax High School, in a quintessentially middle-class part of Los Angeles.

The Telegraph entered the fray with a piece slightly less disgusting, but equally insane, in which the writer examined from all angles the burning question of whether or not I was legally able to marry a (gasp) divorcée.

God, they were already into her past and looking at her first marriage.

Never mind that my father, a divorcé, was currently married to a divorcée, or my aunt, Princess Anne, was a remarried divorcée—the list went on. Divorce in 2016 was deemed by the British press to be a scarlet letter.

Next **The Sun** combed through Meg's social media, discovered an old photo of her with a friend and a professional hockey player, and created an elaborate yarn about Meg and the hockey player having a torrid affair. I asked Meg about it.

No, he was hooking up with my friend. I introduced them.

So I asked the Palace lawyer to contact this paper and tell them the story was categorically false, and defamatory, and to remove it immediately.

The paper's response was a shrug and a raised middle finger.

You're being reckless, the lawyer told the newspaper's editors.

Yawn, said the editors.

We already knew for a fact that the papers had put private investigators onto Meg, and onto everyone in her circle, in her life, even many not in her life, so we knew that they were experts on her background and boyfriends. They were Meg-ologists; they knew more about Meg than anyone in the world apart from Meg, and thus they knew that every word they'd written about her and the hockey player was hot garbage. But they continued to answer the Palace lawyer's repeated warnings with the same non-answers, which amounted to a mocking taunt:

We. Don't. Care.

I huddled with the lawyer, trying to work out how to protect Meg from this attack and all the others. I spent most of every day, from the moment I opened my eyes until long past midnight, trying to make it stop.

Sue them, I kept telling the lawyer, over and over. He explained over and over that suing was what the papers wanted. They were hungry for me to sue, because if I sued that would confirm the relationship, and then they could really go to town.

I felt wild with rage. And guilt. I'd infected Meg, and her mother, with my contagion, otherwise known as my life. I'd promised her that I'd keep her safe, and I'd already dropped her into the middle of this danger.

When I wasn't with the lawyer, I was with Kensington Palace's comms person, Jason. He was very smart, but a tad too cool about this unfolding crisis for my liking. He urged me to do nothing. **You're just going to feed the beast. Silence is the best option.**

But silence wasn't an option. Of all the options, silence was the least desirable, the least defensible. We couldn't just let the press continue to do this to Meg.

Even after I'd convinced him that we needed to do something, say something, anything, the Palace said no. Courtiers blocked us hard. Nothing can be done, they said. And therefore nothing **will** be done.

I accepted this as final. Until I read an essay in the **Huffington Post.** The essayist said the mild reaction of Britons to this explosion of racism was to be expected, since they were the heirs of racist colonialists. But what was truly "unforgivable," she added, was my silence.

Mine.

I showed the essay to Jason, said we needed a course correction immediately. No more debate, no more discussion. We needed a statement out there.

Within a day we had a draft. Strong, precise, angry, honest. I didn't think it would be the end, but maybe the beginning of the end.

I read it one last time and asked Jason to let it fly.

20.

JUST HOURS BEFORE THAT statement went out, Meg was on her way to see me. She drove to Toronto's Pearson International Airport, paps chasing her, and made her way carefully through the crowds of travelers, feeling jittery, exposed. The lounge was full, so an Air Canada representative took pity on her and hid her in a side room. Even brought her a plate of food.

By the time she landed at Heathrow my statement was everywhere. And changing nothing. The onslaught continued.

In fact, my statement generated a whole new onslaught—from my family. Pa and Willy were furious. They gave me an earful. My statement made them look bad, they both said.

Why in hell?

Because they'd never put out a statement for **their** girlfriends or wives when **they** were being harassed.

So this visit wasn't like previous ones. It was the complete opposite. Instead of walking around Frogmore gardens, or sitting in my kitchen talking dreamily about the future, or just getting to know each other, we were stressed out, meeting lawyers, searching for ways to combat this madness.

As a rule, Meg wasn't looking at the internet. She wanted to protect herself, keep that poison out of her brain. Smart. But not sustainable if we were going to wage a battle for her reputation and physical safety. I needed to know exactly what was fact, what was false, and that meant asking her every few hours about something else that had appeared online.

Is this true? Is that true? Is there a grain of truth in this?

She'd often begin to cry. **Why would they say that, Haz? I don't understand. Can they just make stuff up?**

Yes they can. And yes they do.

Still, despite the mounting stress, the terrible pressure, we managed to protect our essential bond, never snapping at each other during those few days. As we came to the final hours of her visit, we were solid, happy, and Meg announced she wanted to make me a special goodbye lunch.

There was nothing in my fridge, as usual. But there was a Whole Foods down the street. I gave her directions, the safest route, past the Palace guards, turn right, towards Kensington Palace Gardens, down to Kensington High Street, there's a police barrier, take a right and you'll see Whole Foods. **It's massive, you can't miss it.**

I had an engagement but I'd be home soon.

Baseball cap, jacket, head down, side gate. You'll be fine, I promise.

Two hours later, when I got home, I found her inconsolable. Sobbing. Shaking.

What is it? What's happened?

She could barely get the story out.

She'd dressed just as I'd advised, and she'd run happily, anonymously, up and down the supermarket aisles. But as she rode the escalator a man approached. **Excuse me, do you know where the exit is?**

Oh, yes, I think it's just up here to the left.

Hey! You're on that program—Suits, am I right? My wife loves you.

Oh. That's so nice! Thanks. What's your name?

Jeff.

Nice to meet you, Jeff. Please tell her I said thanks for watching.

I will. Can I get a picture . . . you know, for my mum?

Thought you said it was your wife.

Oh. Yeah. Heh.

Sorry, I'm just grocery shopping today.

His face changed. **Well, even if I can't take a picture WITH you . . . that doesn't stop me taking pictures OF you!**

He whipped out his phone and followed her to the deli counter, snapping away while she looked at the turkey. F the turkey, she thought, hurrying to the checkouts. He followed her there too.

She got into the queue. Before her were rows and rows of magazines and newspapers, and on all of them, under the most shocking and disgusting headlines . . . was her. The other customers noticed as well. They looked at the magazines, looked at her, and now they too pulled out their phones, like zombies.

Meg caught two cashiers sharing a horrible smile. After paying for her groceries, she walked outside, straight into a group of four men with their iPhones aimed at her. She kept her head down, rushed up Kensington High Street. She was nearly home when a horse-drawn carriage came rolling out of Kensington Palace Gardens. Some sort of parade: the Palace gate was blocked. She was forced back along the main road, where the four men picked up the scent again, and chased her all the way to the main gate, screaming her name.

When she finally got inside Nott Cott, she'd

phoned her best girlfriends, each of whom asked: **Is he worth this, Meg? Is anyone worth this?**

I put my arms around her, said I was sorry. So sorry.

We just held each other, until I slowly became aware of the most delicious smells.

I looked around. **Hang on. You mean . . . after all that . . . you still made lunch?**

I wanted to feed you before I left.

21.

THREE WEEKS LATER I was getting an HIV test at a drop-in clinic in Barbados.

With Rihanna.

Royal life.

The occasion was the upcoming World AIDS Day, and I'd asked Rihanna, at the last minute, to join me, help raise awareness across the Caribbean. To my shock she'd said yes.

November 2016.

Important day, vital cause, but my head wasn't in the game. I was worried about Meg. She couldn't go home because her house was surrounded by paps. She couldn't go to her mother's house, in Los Angeles, because it too was surrounded by paps. Alone, adrift, she was on break from filming, and it was Thanksgiving time. So I'd reached out to friends who had a house sitting empty in Los Angeles, and they'd generously offered it to her. Problem solved, for the moment. Still, I was feeling worried, and intensely hostile towards the press, and I was now surrounded by . . . press.

The same royal reporters . . .

Gazing at them all, I thought: **Complicit**.

Then the needle went into my finger. I watched the blood spurt and remembered all the people, friends and strangers, fellow soldiers, journalists, novelists, schoolmates, who'd ever called me and my family blue bloods. That old shorthand for aristocracy, for royalty, I wondered where it had come from. Someone said our blood was blue because it was colder than other people's, but that couldn't be right, could it? My family always said it was blue because we were special, but that couldn't be right either. Watching the nurse channel my blood into a test tube, I thought: Red, just like everyone else's.

I turned to Rihanna and we chatted while I awaited the result. Negative.

Now I just wanted to run, find somewhere with Wi-Fi, check on Meg. But it wasn't possible. I had a full slate of meetings and visits—a royal schedule that didn't leave much wiggle room. And then I had to hurry back to the rusty Merchant Navy ship taking me around the Caribbean.

By the time I reached the ship, late that night, the onboard Wi-Fi signal was barely a pulse. I was only able to text Meg, and only if I stood on the bench in my cabin, phone pressed against the porthole. We were connected just long enough for me to learn that she was safe at my friend's house. Better yet, her mother and father had been able to sneak in and spend Thanksgiving with her. Her father had brought an armful of tabloids, however, which he inexplicably wanted to talk about. That didn't go well, and he'd ended up leaving early.

While she was telling me the story the Wi-Fi went out.

The merchant ship chugged on to its next destination.

I put down the phone and stared out of the porthole at the dark sea.

22.

MEG, DRIVING HOME FROM set, noticed five cars following her.

Then they started chasing her.

Each car was driven by a man—shady-looking. Wolfish.

It was winter, Canada, so the roads were ice. Plus, the way the cars were spinning around her, cutting her off, running red lights, tailgating her, while also trying to photograph her, she felt sure she was going to be in a crash.

She told herself not to panic, not to drive erratically, not to give them what they wanted. Then she phoned me.

I was in London, in my own car, my bodyguard driving, and her tearful voice brought me right back to my childhood. Back to Balmoral. **She didn't make it, darling boy.** I pleaded with Meg to stay calm, keep her eyes on the road. My air-controller training took over. I talked her to the nearest police station. As she got out of the car, I could hear, in the background, paps following her to the door.

C'mon, Meghan, give us a smile!

Click click click.

She told the police what was happening, begged them for help. They had sympathy, or said they did, but she was a public figure, so they insisted there was nothing to be done. She went back to her car, paps swarming her again, and I guided her to her house, through the front door, where she collapsed.

I did too, a little. I felt helpless, and this, I realized, was my Achilles heel. I could deal with most things so long as there was some action to be taken. But when I had nothing to do . . . I wanted to die.

There was no real respite for Meg once she was inside her house. Like every previous night, paps and so-called journalists knocked at her door, rang the bell, constantly. Her dogs were losing their minds. They couldn't understand what was happening, why she wasn't answering the door, why the house was under assault. As they howled and paced in circles she cowered in the corner of her kitchen, on the floor. After midnight, when things quietened down, she dared to peep through the blinds and saw men sleeping in cars outside, engines running.

Neighbors told Meg they'd been harassed too. Men had gone up and down the street, asking questions, offering sums of money for any tidbit about Meg—or else a nice juicy lie. One neighbor reported being offered a fortune to mount, on their roof, live streaming cameras aimed at Meg's windows. Another neighbor actually accepted the offer, hitched a camera to his roof and pointed it straight at Meg's backyard. Again she contacted the police, who again did nothing. Ontario laws don't prohibit that, she was told. If the neighbor wasn't **physically** trespassing, he could hook the Hubble telescope up to his house and point it into her backyard, no problem.

Meanwhile, in Los Angeles, her mother was being chased every day, to and from her house, to and from the launderette, to and from work. She was also being libeled. One story called her "trailer trash." Another called her a "stoner." In fact, she worked in palliative care. She traveled all over Los Angeles to help people at the end of their lives.

Paps scaled the walls and fences of many patients she visited. In other words, every day there was yet another person, like Mummy, whose last sound on earth . . . would be a click.

23.

REUNITED. A quiet night at Nott Cott, preparing dinner together.

December 2016.

Meg and I had discovered that we shared the same favorite food: roast chicken.

I didn't know how to cook it, so that night she was teaching me.

I remember the warmth of the kitchen, the wonderful smells. Lemon wedges on the cutting board, garlic and rosemary, gravy bubbling in a saucepan.

I remember rubbing salt on the skin of the bird, then opening a bottle of wine.

Meg put on music. She was expanding my horizons, teaching me about folk music and soul, James Taylor and Nina Simone.

It's a new dawn. It's a new day.

Maybe the wine went to my head. Maybe the weeks of battling the press had worn me down. For some reason, when the conversation took an unexpected turn, I became touchy.

Then angry. Disproportionately, sloppily angry.

Meg said something I took the wrong way. It was partly a cultural difference, partly a language barrier, but I was also just over-sensitive that night. I thought: Why's she having a go at me?

I snapped at her, spoke to her harshly—cruelly. As the words left my mouth, I could feel everything in the room come to a stop. The gravy stopped bubbling, the molecules of air stopped orbiting. Even Nina Simone seemed to pause. Meg walked out of the room, disappearing for a full fifteen minutes.

I went and found her upstairs. She was sitting in the bedroom. She was calm, but said in a quiet, level tone that she would never stand for being spoken to like that.

I nodded.

She wanted to know where it came from.

I don't know.

Where did you ever hear a man speak like that to a woman? Did you overhear adults speak that way when you were growing up?

I cleared my throat, looked away. **Yes.**

She wasn't going to tolerate that kind of partner. Or co-parent. That kind of life. She wasn't going to raise children in an atmosphere of anger or disrespect. She laid it all out, super-clear. We both knew my anger hadn't been **caused** by anything to do with our conversation. It came from somewhere deep inside, somewhere that needed to be excavated, and it was obvious that I could use some help with the job.

I've tried therapy, I told her. Willy told me to go. Never found the right person. Didn't work.

No, she said softly. Try again.

24.

WE LEFT KENSINGTON PALACE in a dark car, a completely different and unmarked car, both of us hiding in the back. We went through the rear gate, around 6:30 P.M. My bodyguards said we weren't being followed, so when we got stuck in traffic on Regent Street, we hopped out. We were going to the theater and didn't want to draw attention by arriving after the show had started. We were so intent on not being late, on watching the clock, that we didn't see "them" trailing us—in brazen violation of stalking laws.

They shot us close to the theater. From a moving vehicle, through a bus stop window.

The shooters, of course, were Tweedle Dumb and Tweedle Dumber.

We didn't love being papped, especially by those two. But we'd managed to elude them for five months. Good run, we said.

The next time we got papped was a few weeks later, leaving dinner with Doria, who'd flown in with Meg. The paps got us, but missed Doria, happily. She'd turned to go to her hotel, we'd turned with my bodyguards to go to our car. The paps never saw her.

I'd been quite nervous about that dinner. It's always nerve-racking to meet a girlfriend's mother, but especially when you're currently making her daughter's life hell. The Sun had just recently run a front-page headline: **Harry's girl on Pornhub.** The story showed images of Meg, from **Suits,** which some perverts had posted on some porn site. **The Sun** didn't say, of course, that the images were used illegally, that Meg knew nothing about them, that Meg had had as much to do with porn as Granny had. It was just a trick, a way to bait readers into buying the paper or clicking on the story. Once the reader discovered there was nothing there, too late! Ad money was in the purse of **The Sun.**

We'd fought it, filed a formal complaint, but thankfully the subject didn't come up that night over dinner. We had happier things to discuss. Meg had just done a trip to India with World Vision, working on menstrual health management and education access for young girls, after which she'd taken Doria on a yoga retreat in Goa—a belated celebration of Doria's sixtieth birthday. We were celebrating Doria, celebrating being together, and doing it all at our favorite place, Soho House at 76 Dean Street. On the subject of India: we laughed about the advice I'd given Meg before she'd left: Do **not** take a photo in front of the Taj Mahal. She'd asked why and I'd said: **My mum.**

I'd explained that my mother had posed for a photo there, and it had become iconic, and I didn't want anyone thinking Meg was trying to mimic my mother. Meg had never heard of this photo, and found the whole thing baffling, and I loved her for being baffled.

That dinner with Doria was wonderful, but I look back on it now as the end of the beginning. The next day, the pap photos appeared, and there was a new flood of stories, a new surge along the many channels of social media. Racism, misogyny, criminal stupidity—it all increased.

Not knowing where else to turn, I phoned Pa.

Don't read it, darling boy.

It's not that simple, I said angrily. I might lose this woman. She might either decide I'm not worth the bother, or the press might so poison the public that some idiot might do something bad, harm her in some way.

It was already happening in slow motion. Death

threats. Her workplace on lockdown because someone, reacting to what they'd read, had made a credible threat. She's isolated, I said, and afraid, she hasn't raised the blinds in her house for months—and you're telling me not to read it?

He said I was overreacting. **This is sadly just the way it is.**

I appealed to his self-interest. Doing nothing was a terrible look for the monarchy. **People out there have strong feelings about what's happening to her, Pa. They take it personally, you need to understand that.**

He was unmoved.

25.

THE ADDRESS WAS HALF an hour from Nott Cott. Just a quick drive across the Thames, past the park . . . but it felt like one of my polar journeys.

Heart pounding, I took a deep breath, knocked at the door.

The woman opened it, welcomed me. She led me down a short corridor to her office.

First door on the left.

Small room. Windows with venetian blinds. Right on the busy street. You could hear cars, shoes clicking on the pavement. People talking, laughing.

She was fifteen years older than me, but youthful. She reminded me of Tiggy. It was shocking, really. Such a similar vibe.

She pointed me to a dark green sofa and took a

chair across the room. The day was autumnal, yet I was sweating profusely. I apologized. **I overheat easily. Also, I'm a bit nervous.**

Say no more.

She jumped up, ran out. Moments later she returned with a little fan, which she aimed at me.

Ah, lovely. Thank you.

She waited for me to begin. But I didn't know where to begin. So I began with my mum. I said I was afraid of losing her.

She gave me a long, searching look.

She knew, of course, that I'd already lost my mum. How surreal, to meet a therapist who already knows part of your life story, who's possibly spent beach holidays reading whole books about you.

Yes, I've already lost my mum, of course, but I'm afraid that by talking about her, now, here, to a perfect stranger, and perhaps alleviating some of the pain of that loss, I'll be losing her again. I'll be losing that feeling, that presence of her—or what I've always felt as her presence.

The therapist squinted. I tried again.

You see . . . the pain . . . if that's what it is . . . that's all I have left of her. And the pain is also what drives me. Some days the pain is the only thing holding me together. And also, I suppose, without the pain, well, she might think . . . I've forgotten her.

That sounded silly. But, well, there it was.

Most memories of my mother, I explained, with sudden and overwhelming sorrow, were gone. On the

other side of the Wall. I told her about the Wall. I told
her I'd spoken to Willy about my lack of memories of
our mother. He'd advised me to look through photo
albums, which I'd promptly done. Nothing.

So, my mother wasn't images, or impressions, she
was mainly just a hole in my heart, and if I healed
that hole, patched it up—what then?

I asked if all this sounded crazy.

No.

We were silent.

A long time.

She asked me what I needed. **Why are you here?**

Look, I said. **What I need . . . is to be rid of
this heaviness in my chest. I need . . . I need . . .**

Yes?

To cry. Please. Help me cry.

26.

THE NEXT SESSION I asked if it would be all right
for me to lie down.

She smiled. **I was wondering when you'd ask.**

I stretched out on the green sofa, tucked a pillow
under my neck.

I spoke about the physical and emotional suffering.
The panic, the anxiety. The sweats.

How long has this been going on?

Two or three years now. It used to be much worse.

I told her about the talk with Cress. During the

skiing holiday. The top coming off the bottle, emotions fizzing all over the place. I'd cried a bit then . . . but it wasn't enough. I needed to cry more. And I couldn't.

I got around to talking about the deep rage, the ostensible trigger for seeking her out in the first place. I described the scene with Meg, in the kitchen.

I shook my head.

I vented about my family. Pa and Willy. Camilla. I frequently stopped myself, mid-sentence, at the sound of passersby outside the window. If they ever knew. Prince Harry in there yapping about his family. His problems. Oh, the papers would have a field day.

Which led us on to the subject of the press. Firmer ground. I let fly. My own countrymen and countrywomen, I said, showing such contempt, such vile disrespect, to the woman I loved. Sure, the press had been cruel to me through the years, but that was different. I was born into it. And sometimes I'd asked for it, brought it on myself.

But this woman has done nothing to deserve such cruelty.

And whenever I complained about it, privately or publicly, people just rolled their eyes. They said I was whingeing, said I only pretended to want privacy, said Meg was pretending as well. **Oh, she's getting chased, is she? Wah-wah, give us a break! She'll be fine, she's an actress, she's used to paps, in fact, wants them.**

But no one wanted this. No one could ever get used to it. All those eye-rollers couldn't take ten minutes of it. Meg was having panic attacks for the first time in her life. She'd recently received a text from a perfect stranger who knew her address in Toronto and promised to put a bullet into her head.

The therapist said I sounded angry.

Shit, yes, I was angry!

She said that, no matter how valid my complaints, I also sounded stuck. Granted, Meg and I were living through an ordeal, but the Harry who'd snapped at Meg with such anger wasn't this Harry, the reasonable Harry, lying on this sofa and laying out his case. That was twelve-year-old Harry, traumatized Harry.

What you're going through right now is reminiscent of 1997, Harry, but I also fear that part of you is trapped in 1997.

I didn't like the sound of that. I felt a bit insulted. **Calling me a child? Seems a bit rude.**

You say you want truth, you value truth above all—well, there's the truth.

The session went over the allotted time. It lasted nearly two hours. When our time was up, we made a date to get together again soon. I asked if it would be all right if I gave her a hug.

Yes, of course.

I embraced her lightly, thanked her.

Outside, on the street, my head was swimming. In each direction there was an amazing collection of restaurants and shops, and I'd have given anything to walk up and down, look in the windows, give myself time to process all I'd said and learned.

But, of course, impossible.

Didn't want to cause a scene.

27.

THE THERAPIST, it so happened, had met Tiggy. Astounding coincidence. Smallest of all possible worlds. So in another session we talked about Tiggy, how she'd been a surrogate mum to me and Willy, how Willy and I had often turned women into surrogate mums. How often they'd eagerly cast themselves in that role.

Surrogate mums made me feel better, I admitted, and worse, because I felt guilty. **What would Mummy think?**

We talked about guilt.

I mentioned Mummy's experience with therapy, as I understood it. Didn't help her. Might've made things worse, actually. So many people preyed on her, exploited her—including therapists.

We talked about Mummy's parenting, how she could sometimes over-mother, then disappear for stretches. It seemed an important discussion, but also disloyal.

More guilt.

We talked about life inside the British bubble, inside the royal bubble. A bubble inside a bubble— impossible to describe to anyone who hasn't actually experienced it. People simply didn't realize: they heard the word "royal," or "prince," and lost all rationality. **Ah, a prince—you have no problems.**

They assumed . . . no, they'd been taught . . . it was all a fairytale. We weren't human.

A writer many Britons admired, a writer of thick historical novels that racked up literary prizes, had penned an essay about my family, in which she said we were simply . . . pandas.

Our current royal family doesn't have the difficulties in breeding that pandas do, but pandas and royal persons alike are expensive to conserve and ill-adapted to any modern environment. But aren't they interesting? Aren't they nice to look at?

I'll never forget the highly respected essayist who wrote in Britain's most highly respected literary publication that my mother's "early death spared us all a lot of tedium." (He referred in the same essay to "Diana's tryst with the underpass.") But this panda crack always struck me as both acutely perceptive and uniquely barbarous. We did live in a zoo, but by the same token I knew, as a soldier, that turning people into animals, into non-people, is the first step in mistreating them, in destroying them. If even a celebrated intellectual could dismiss us as animals, what hope for the man or woman on the street?

I gave the therapist an overview of how this dehumanization had played out in the first half of my life. But now, with the dehumanizing of Meg, there was so much more hate, more vitriol—plus racism. I told her what I'd seen, heard, witnessed, over the last few months. At one point I sat up on the couch, crooked my neck to see if she was listening. Her mouth was hanging open. A lifelong resident of Britain, she'd thought she knew.

She didn't know.

At the end of the session I asked her professional opinion:

Is what I'm feeling . . . normal?

She laughed. What's normal anyway?

But she conceded that one thing was abundantly clear: I found myself in highly unusual circumstances.

Do you think I have an addictive personality?

More accurately, what I wanted to know was, if I did have an addictive personality, where would I be right now?

Hard to say. Hypotheticals, you know.

She asked if I'd used drugs.

Yes.

I told her some wild stories.

Well, I am rather surprised you're not a drug addict.

If there was one thing to which I did seem undeniably addicted, however, it was the press. Reading it, raging at it, she said, these were obvious compulsions.

I laughed. **True. But they're such shit.**

She laughed. They are.

28.

I ALWAYS THOUGHT CRESSIDA had performed a miracle, opening me up, releasing suppressed emotions. But she'd only started the miracle, and now the therapist brought it to completion.

All my life I'd told people I couldn't remember the past, couldn't remember my mum, but I never gave anyone the full picture. My memory was dead. Now, through months of therapy, my memory twitched, kicked, sputtered.

It came to life.

Some days I'd open my eyes to find Mummy . . . standing before me.

A thousand images returned, some so bright and vivid that they were like holograms.

I remembered mornings in Mummy's apartment at Kensington Palace, the nanny waking Willy and me, helping us down to Mummy's bedroom. I remembered that she had a waterbed, and Willy and I would jump up and down on the mattress, screaming, laughing, our hair standing straight up. I remembered the breakfasts together, Mummy loving grapefruit and lychees, seldom drinking coffee or tea. I remembered that after breakfast we'd embark on the working day with her, sitting by her side during her first phone calls, auditing her business meetings.

I remembered Willy and me joining her for a chat with Christy Turlington, Claudia Schiffer, and Cindy Crawford. Very confusing. Especially for two shy boys, at or about the age of puberty.

I remembered bedtimes in Kensington Palace, saying goodnight at the foot of the stairs, kissing her soft neck, inhaling her perfume, then lying in bed, in the dark, feeling so far away, so alone, and longing to hear her voice just one more time. I remembered my bedroom being the farthest from hers, and in the dark, in the terrible silence, being unable to relax, unable to let go.

The therapist urged me to press on. **We're breaking through**, she said. **Let's not stop.** I brought to her office a bottle of Mummy's favorite perfume. (I'd reached out to Mummy's sister, asked for the name.) First, by Van Cleef & Arpels. At the start of our session I lifted the lid, took a deep sniff.

Like a tab of LSD.

I read somewhere that smell is our oldest sense, and that fitted with what I experienced in that moment, images rising from what felt like the most primal part of my brain.

I remembered one day at Ludgrove, Mummy stuffing sweets into my sock. Outside sweets were forbidden, so Mummy was flouting school rules, giggling as she did so, which made me love her even more. I remembered both of us laughing as we buried the sweets deep in the sock, and me squealing: **Oh, Mummy, you're so naughty!** I remembered the brand of those sweets. Opal Fruits!

Hard squares of bright colors . . . not unlike these resurrected memories.

No wonder I was so keen on Grub Days.

And Opal Fruits.

I remembered going to tennis lessons in the car, Mummy driving, Willy and me in the back. Without warning she trod on the accelerator and we went rocketing ahead, up narrow streets, blasting through red lights, whipping around corners. Willy and

I were strapped into our seats, so we couldn't look out of the back window, but we had a sense of what was chasing us. Paps on motorbikes and mopeds. **Are they going to kill us, Mummy? Are we going to die?** Mummy, wearing big sunglasses, peering into the mirrors. After fifteen minutes and several near smashes Mummy slammed on the brakes, pulled over, jumped out and walked towards the paps: **Leave us alone! For God's sake, I'm with my children, can't you leave us alone?** Trembling, pink-cheeked, she got back into the car, slammed the door, rolled up the windows, leaned her head on the steering wheel and wept while the paps kept clicking and clicking. I remembered the tears falling from her big sunglasses and I remembered Willy looking frozen, like a statue, and I remembered the paps just firing and firing and firing, and I remembered feeling such hatred for them and such deep and eternal love for everyone in that car.

I remembered being on holiday, Necker Island, all three of us sitting in a cliffside hut, and here came a boat with a gang of photographers, looking for us. We'd been playing with water balloons that day and we had a bunch of them lying about. Mummy quickly rigged up a catapult and divided the balloons among us. On the count of three we began raining them down on the heads of the photographers. The sound of her laughter that day, lost to me all these years, was back—it was back. Loud and clear as the traffic outside the therapist's windows.

I cried with joy to hear it.

29.

THE SUN RAN A CORRECTION for their porn story. In a tiny box, on page two, where no one would see it.

What did it matter? The damage had been done.

Plus it cost Meg tens of thousands of dollars in legal fees.

I rang Pa yet again.

Don't read it, darling—

I cut him off. I wasn't about to hear that nonsense again.

Also, I wasn't a boy anymore.

I tried a new argument. I reminded Pa that these were the same shoddy bastards who'd been portraying him as a clown all his life, ridiculing him for sounding the alarm about climate change. These were **his** tormentors, **his** bullies, and now they were tormenting and bullying his son and his son's girlfriend—did that not inspire his outrage? **Why have I got to beg you, Pa? Why is this not already a priority for you? Why is this not causing you anguish, keeping you up at night, that the press are treating Meg like this? You adore her, you told me so yourself. You bonded over your shared love of music, you think she's funny and witty, and impeccably mannered, you told me— so why, Pa? Why?**

I couldn't get a straight answer. The conversation went in circles and when we hung up I felt—abandoned.

Meg, meanwhile, reached out to Camilla, who tried to counsel her by saying this was just what the press always did to newcomers, that it would all pass in due time, that Camilla had been the bad guy once.

The implication being what? Now it was Meg's turn? As if it were apples to apples.

Camilla also suggested to Meg that I become Governor General of Bermuda, which would solve all our problems by removing us from the red-hot center of the maelstrom. Right, right, I thought, and one added bonus of that plan would be to get us out of the picture.

In desperation I went to Willy. I took advantage of the first quiet moment I'd had with him in years: The end of August 2017, at Althorp. Twentieth anniversary of Mummy's death.

We rowed the little boat out to the island. (The bridge had been removed, to give my mother privacy, to keep intruders away.) We each had a bouquet of flowers, which we set on the grave. We stood there awhile, having our own thoughts, and then we talked about life. I gave him a quick summary of what Meg and I had been dealing with.

Don't worry, Harold. No one believes that shit.

Not true. They do. It's drip-fed to them, day by day, and they come to believe it without even being aware.

He didn't have a satisfying answer for that, so we were silent.

Then he said something extraordinary. He said he thought Mummy was here. Meaning . . . among us.

Yes, me too, Willy.

I think she's been in my life, Harold. Guiding me. Setting things up for me. I think she's helped me start a family. And I feel as though she's helping you now too.

I nodded. Totally agree. I feel as though she helped me find Meg.

Willy took a step back. He looked concerned. That seemed to be taking things a bit far.

Well, now, Harold, I'm not sure about that. I wouldn't say THAT!

30.

MEG CAME TO LONDON. September 2017. We were in Nott Cott. In the kitchen. Preparing dinner.

The whole cottage was filled with . . . love. Filled to overflowing. It even seemed to spill out the open door, into the garden outside, a scrubby little patch of ground that no one had wanted, for a very long time, but which Meg and I had slowly reclaimed. We'd raked and mown, planted and watered, and many evenings we sat out there on a blanket, listening to classical music concerts wafting over from the park. I told Meg about the garden just on the other side of our wall: Mummy's garden. Where Willy and I played as kids. It was now sealed off from us forever.

As my memories had once been.

Whose garden is it now? she asked.

It belongs to Princess Michael of Kent. And her Siamese cats. Mummy despised those cats.

As I smelt the garden, and considered this new life, cherished this new life, Meg was sitting on the other side of the kitchen, scooping Wagamama from cartons into bowls. Without thinking I blurted out: **I don't know, I just . . .**

I had my back to her. I froze, mid-sentence, hesitant to go on, hesitant to turn around.

You don't know what, Haz?

I just . . .

Yes?

I love you.

I listened for a response. There was none.

Now I could hear her, or feel her, walking towards me.

I turned and there she was, right before me.

I love you too, Haz.

The words had been on the tip of my tongue almost from the start, so in one sense they didn't feel particularly revelatory, or even necessary. Of course I loved her. Meg knew that, Meg could see it, the whole world could. I loved her with all my heart as I'd never loved anyone before. And yet saying it made everything real. Saying it set things in motion, automatically. Saying it was a step.

It meant we now had a few more very big steps ahead.

Like . . . moving in together?

I asked if she'd consider moving to Britain, moving into Nott Cott with me.

We talked about all that would mean, and how it would work, and what she'd be giving up. We talked about the logistics of winding down her life in Toronto. When, and how, and above all . . . for what? Exactly?

I can't just leave my show and quit my job to give it a shot. Would moving to Britain mean a forever commitment?

Yes, I said. It would.

In that case, she said with a smile, yes.

We kissed, hugged, sat down to our supper.

I sighed. On the road, I thought.

But later, after she'd fallen asleep, I analyzed myself. A holdover from therapy, perhaps. I realized that, mixed in with all my roiling emotions, there was a big streak of relief. She'd said it back, the actual words, **I love you,** and it hadn't been inevitable, it hadn't been a formality. Part of me, I couldn't deny, had been braced for the worst case. **Haz, I'm sorry but I just don't know if I can do this . . .** Part of me feared she'd bolt. Go back to Toronto, change her number. Heed the advice of her girlfriends.

Is anyone worth this?

Part of me thought she'd be smart to do so.

31.

BY PURE CHANCE THE 2017 Invictus Games were going to be in Toronto. Meg's backyard. Perfect occasion, the Palace decided, for our first official public outing.

Meg was a bit nervous. Me too. But we had no choice. Has to be done, we said. We've hidden from the world long enough. Also, this would be the most controlled, predictable environment we could ever hope for.

Above all, once we did a public date, it might reduce the bounty on our heads among the paps, which at that point was running at around a hundred thousand pounds.

We tried to make the whole thing as normal as possible. We watched wheelchair tennis from the front row, focused on the game and the good cause, ignored the whir of cameras. We managed to have fun, to crack a few jokes with some Kiwis sitting beside us, and the photos that appeared the following day were sweet, though several in the British press slammed Meg for wearing ripped jeans. No one mentioned that everything she wore, down to the flats and button-down shirt, had been pre-approved by the Palace.

And by "no one," I mean not anyone at the Palace.

One statement, that week, in defense of Meg . . . it might've made a world of difference.

32.

I TOLD ELF AND JASON that I wanted to propose. Congratulations, both men said.

But then Elf said he'd need to do some fast digging, find out the protocols. There were strict rules governing such things.

Rules? Really?

He came back days later and said before doing anything I'd need to ask Granny's permission.

I asked him if that was a real rule, or the kind we could work around.

Oh, no, it's very real.

It didn't make sense. A grown man asking his grandmother for permission to marry? I couldn't recall Willy asking before he proposed to Kate. Or my cousin Peter asking before he proposed to his wife, Autumn. But come to think of it I did remember Pa asking permission when he wanted to marry Camilla. The absurdity of a fifty-six-year-old man asking his mother's permission had been lost on me at the time.

Elf said there was no point in examining the whys and hows, this was the inalterable rule. The first six in line to the throne had to ask permission. The Royal Marriages Act of 1772, or the Succession to the Crown Act of 2013—he was going on and on and I could barely believe my ears. The point was, love took a decided back seat to law. Indeed, law had trumped love on more than one occasion. A fairly recent relative had been . . . strongly dissuaded . . . from marrying the love of their life.

Who?

Your aunt Margaret.

Really?

Yes. She'd wanted to marry a divorcé and . . . well.

Divorcé?

Elf nodded.

Oh, shit, I thought. This might not be a slam dunk.

But Pa and Camilla were divorcés, I said, and they'd got permission. Didn't that mean the rule no longer applied?

That's them, Elf said. This is you.

To say nothing about the furor over a certain king who'd wanted to marry an American divorcée, which Elf reminded me had ended with the King's abdication and exile. **Duke of Windsor? Ever heard of him?**

And so, heart full of fear, mouth full of dust, I turned to the calendar. With Elf's help I circled a weekend in late October. A family shooting trip at Sandringham. Shooting trips always put Granny in a good mood.

Perhaps she'd be more open to thoughts of love?

33.

CLOUDY, BLUSTERY DAY. I jumped into the venerable old Land Rover, the ancient Army ambulance that Grandpa had repurposed. Pa was behind the wheel, Willy was in the back. I got into the passenger seat and wondered if I should tell them both what I was intending.

I decided against it. Pa already knew, I assumed, and Willy had already warned me not to do it.

It's too fast, he'd told me. Too soon.

In fact, he'd actually been pretty discouraging about

my even dating Meg. One day, sitting together in his garden, he'd predicted a host of difficulties I could expect if I hooked up with an "American actress," a phrase he always managed to make sound like "convicted felon."

Are you sure about her, Harold?

I am, Willy.

But do you know how difficult it's going to be?

What do you want me to do? Fall out of love with her?

The three of us were wearing flat caps, green jackets, plus fours, as if we played for the same sports team. (In a way, I suppose, we did.) Pa, driving us out into the fields, asked about Meg. Not with great interest, just casually. Still, he didn't always ask, so I was pleased.

She's good, thanks.

Does she want to carry on working?

Say again?

Does she want to keep on acting?

Oh. I mean, I don't know, I wouldn't think so. I expect she'll want to be with me, doing the job, you know, which would rule out Suits . . . since they film in . . . Toronto.

Hmm. I see. Well, darling boy, you know there's not enough money to go around.

I stared. What was he banging on about?

He explained. Or tried to. I can't pay for anyone else. I'm already having to pay for your brother and Catherine.

I flinched. Something about his use of the name Catherine. I remembered the time he and Camilla wanted Kate to change the spelling of her name, because there were already two royal cyphers with a C and a crown above: Charles and Camilla. It would be too confusing to have another. Make it **Katherine** with a **K**, they suggested.

I wondered now what came of that suggestion.

I turned to Willy, gave him a look that said: **You listening to this?**

His face was blank.

Pa didn't financially support Willy and me, and our families, out of any largesse. That was his job. That was the whole deal. We agreed to serve the monarch, go wherever we were sent, do whatever we were told, surrender our autonomy, keep our hands and feet inside the gilded cage at all times, and in exchange the keepers of the cage agreed to feed and clothe us. Was Pa, with all his millions from the hugely lucrative Duchy of Cornwall, trying to say that our captivity was starting to cost him a bit too much?

Besides which—how much could it possibly cost to house and feed Meg? I wanted to say, She doesn't eat much, you know! And I'll ask her to make her own clothes, if you like.

It was suddenly clear to me that this wasn't about money. Pa might have dreaded the rising cost of maintaining us, but what he really couldn't stomach was someone new dominating the monarchy, grabbing the limelight, someone shiny and new coming in and overshadowing him. And Camilla. He'd lived through that before, and had no interest in living through it again.

I couldn't deal with any of that right now. I had no time for petty jealousies and Palace intrigue. I was still trying to work out exactly what to say to Granny, and the time had come.

The Land Rover stopped. We piled out and lined up along the hedge being placed by Pa. We waited for the birds to appear. The wind was blowing, and my mind was all over the place, but as the first drive began I found that I was shooting well. I got into the zone. Maybe it was a relief to think about something else. Maybe I preferred focusing on the next shot, rather than the Big Shot I was planning to take. I just kept swinging that barrel, squeezing that trigger, hitting every target.

We broke for lunch. I tried, repeatedly, but wasn't able to get Granny by herself. Everyone was surrounding her, talking her ear off. So I tucked into the meal, biding my time.

A classic royal shooting luncheon. Cold feet warming by the fires, toasty potatoes, juicy meat, creamy soups, staff overseeing every detail. Then perfect puds. Then a little tea, a drink or two. Then back to the birds.

During the day's final two drives I was constantly sneaking peeks in Granny's direction, to see how she was doing. She seemed good. And very locked in.

Did she really have no idea what was coming?

After the final drive the party scattered. Everyone finished picking up their birds and returned to the Land Rovers. I saw Granny jump into her smaller Range Rover and drive out to the middle of the stubble field. She began looking for dead birds, while her dogs hunted.

There was no security around her, so this looked to be my chance.

I walked out to the middle of the stubble field, fell in alongside her, began helping. While we scanned the ground for dead birds, I tried to engage her in some light chat, to loosen her up, and to loosen up my vocal cords. The wind was stronger, and Granny's cheeks looked cold, despite the scarf wrapped tightly around her head.

Not helping matters: my subconscious. It was popping. The full seriousness of all this was finally starting to sink in. If Granny said no . . . would I have to say goodbye to Meg? I couldn't imagine being without her . . . but I also couldn't imagine being openly disobedient to Granny. My Queen, my Commander in Chief. If she withheld her permission, my heart would break, and of course I'd look for another occasion to ask again, but the odds would be against me. Granny wasn't exactly known for changing her mind. So this moment was either the start of my life, or the end. It would all come down to the words I chose, how I delivered them, and how Granny heard them.

If all that wasn't enough to make me tongue-tied, I'd seen plenty of press reports, sourced to "the Palace," that some in my family didn't quite, shall we say, **approve** of Meg. Didn't fancy her directness. Didn't feel altogether comfortable with her strong work ethic. Didn't even enjoy her occasional questions. What was healthy and natural inquisitiveness they deemed to be impertinence.

There were also whispers about a vague and pervasive unease regarding her race. "Concern" had been expressed in certain corners about whether or not Britain was "ready." Whatever that meant. Was any of that rubbish reaching Granny's ears? If so, was this request for permission merely a hopeless exercise?

Was I doomed to be the next Margaret?

Oh. A biro. Wow.

I thought back over the many hinge moments in my life when permission was required. Requesting permission from Control to fire on the enemy. Requesting permission from the Royal Foundation to create the Invictus Games. I thought of pilots requesting permission from me to cross my airspace. My life all at once felt like an endless series of permission requests, all of them a prelude to this one.

Granny started walking back to her Range Rover. I quick-stepped after her, the dogs circling my feet. Looking at them, my mind began to race. My mother used to say that being around Granny and the corgis was like standing on a moving carpet, and I used to know most of them, living and dead, as if they were my cousins, Dookie, Emma, Susan, Linnet, Pickles, Chipper, they were all said to descend from the corgis that belonged to Queen Victoria, the more things change the more they stay the same, but these weren't corgis, these were hunting dogs, and they had a different purpose, and I had a different purpose, and I realized that I needed to get to it, without one second more of hesitation, so as Granny lowered the tailgate, as the dogs leaped up, as I thought of petting them but then remembered I had a dead bird in each hand, their limp necks nestled between my fingers, their glazed eyes rolled all the way back (I feel you, birds), their bodies still warm through my gloves, I turned instead to Granny and saw her turn to me and frown (Did she recognize that I was afraid? Of both the request for permission and of Her Majesty? Did she realize that, no matter how much I loved her, I was often nervous in her presence?) and I saw her waiting for me to speak—and not waiting patiently.

Her face radiated: **Out with it.**

I coughed. **Granny, you know I love Meg very much, and I've decided that I would like to ask her to marry me, and I've been told that, er, that I have to ask your permission before I can propose.**

You have to?

Um. Well, yes, that's what your staff tell me, and my staff as well. That I have to ask your permission.

I stood completely still, as motionless as the birds in my hands. I stared at her face but it was unreadable. At last she replied: **Well, then, I suppose I have to say yes.**

I squinted. You feel you **have** to say yes? Does that mean you are saying yes? But that you want to say no?

I didn't get it. Was she being sarcastic? Ironic? Deliberately cryptic? Was she indulging in a bit of wordplay? I'd never known Granny to do any wordplay, and this would be a surpassingly bizarre moment (not to mention wildly inconvenient) for her to start, but maybe she just saw the chance to play off my unfortunate use of the word "have" and couldn't resist?

Or else, perhaps there was some hidden meaning beneath the wordplay, some message I wasn't comprehending?

I stood there squinting, smiling, asking myself over and over: What is the Queen of England saying to me right now?

At long last I realized: She's saying yes, you muppet! She's granting permission. Who cares how she words it, just know when to take yes for an answer.

So I sputtered: **Right. OK, Granny! Well. Fabulous. Thank you! Thank you so much.**

I wanted to hug her.

I longed to hug her.

I didn't hug her.

I saw her into the Range Rover, then marched back to Pa and Willy.

34.

I TOOK A RING from Meg's jewelry box and gave it to a designer, so he'd know her size.

Since he was also the keeper of Mummy's bracelets, earrings and necklaces, I asked him to harvest the diamonds from one particularly beautiful bracelet of Mummy's and use those to create a ring.

I'd cleared all this in advance with Willy. I'd asked my brother if I could have the bracelet, and told him what it was for. I don't recall him hesitating, for one second, in giving it to me. He seemed to **like** Meg, despite his oft-cited concerns. Kate seemed to like her too. We'd had them over for dinner during one of Meg's visits, and Meg cooked, and everything was good. Willy had a cold: he was sneezing and coughing, and Meg ran upstairs to get him some of her homeopathic cure-alls. Oregano oil, turmeric. He seemed charmed, moved, though Kate announced to the table that he'd never take such unconventional remedies.

We talked about Wimbledon that night, and **Suits**, and Willy and Kate weren't brave enough to admit to being superfans. Which was sweet.

The only possibly discordant note I could think of was the marked difference in how the two women dressed, which both of them seemed to notice.

Meg: ripped jeans, barefoot.

Kate: done up to the nines.

No big deal, I thought.

Along with the diamonds from the bracelet I'd asked the designer to add a third—a blood-free diamond from Botswana.

He asked if there was a rush.

Well . . . now that you mention it . . .

35.

MEG PACKED UP her house, gave up her role in **Suits**. After seven seasons. A difficult moment

for her, because she loved that show, loved the character she was playing, loved her cast and crew—
loved Canada. On the other hand life there had
become untenable. Especially on set. The show writers were frustrated, because they were often advised
by the Palace comms team to change lines of dialogue, what her character would do, how she
would act.

She'd also shut down her website and abandoned all
social media, again at the behest of the Palace comms
team. She'd said goodbye to her friends, goodbye to
her car, goodbye to one of her dogs—Bogart. He'd
been so traumatized by the siege of her house, by the
constant ringing of the doorbell, that his demeanor
changed when Meg was around. He'd become an
aggressive guard dog. Meg's neighbors had graciously
agreed to adopt him.

But Guy came. Not my friend, Meg's other dog,
her beat-up little beagle, who was even more beat-up
of late. He missed Bogart, of course, but more, he was
badly injured. Days before Meg left Canada, Guy had
run away from his minder. (Meg was at work.) He'd
been found miles from Meg's house, unable to walk.
His legs were now in casts.

I often had to hold him upright so he could pee.

I didn't mind in the least. I loved that dog. I couldn't
stop kissing him, petting him. Yes, my intense feelings for Meg spilled over onto anyone or anything
she loved, but also I'd wanted a dog for so long, and
I'd never been able to have one because I'd been such
a nomad. One night, not long after Meg's arrival in

Britain, we were at home, making dinner, playing with Guy, and the kitchen of Nott Cott was as full of love as any room I'd ever been in.

I opened a bottle of champagne—an old, old gift I'd been saving for a special occasion.

Meg smiled. **What's the occasion?**

No occasion.

I scooped up Guy, carried him outside, into the walled garden, put him down on a blanket I'd spread on the grass. Then I ran back inside and asked Meg to grab her champagne flute and come with me.

What's up?

Nothing.

I led her out to the garden. Cold night. We were both wrapped in big coats, and hers had a hood lined with fake fur that framed her face like a cameo. I set electric candles around the blanket. I wanted it to look like Botswana, the bush, where I'd first thought of proposing.

Now I knelt on the blanket, Guy at my side. Both of us looked up searchingly at Meg.

My eyes already full of tears, I brought the ring out of my pocket and said my piece. I was shivering, and my heart was audibly thumping, and my voice was unsteady, but she got the idea.

Spend your life with me? Make me the happiest guy on this planet?

Yes.

Yes?

Yes!

I laughed. She laughed. What other reaction could

there be? In this mixed-up world, this pain-filled life, we'd done it. We'd managed to find each other.

Then we were crying **and** laughing, and petting Guy, who looked frozen solid.

We started for the house.

Oh, wait. Don't you want to see the ring, my love?

She hadn't even thought about it.

We hurried inside, finished our celebration in the warmth of the kitchen.

It was November 4.

We managed to keep it secret for about two weeks.

36.

ORDINARILY, I'D HAVE GONE to Meg's father first, asked for his blessing. But Thomas Markle was a complicated man.

He and Meg's mother split when she was two, and thereafter she divided her time between them. Monday to Friday with Mum, weekends with Dad. Then, for part of high school, she'd moved in with her father full-time. They were that close.

After college she'd traveled the world, but always stayed in constant contact with Daddy. She still, even in her thirties, called him Daddy. She loved him, worried about him—his health, his habits—and often relied upon him. Throughout her run on **Suits** she'd consulted him every week about the lighting. (He'd been a lighting director in Hollywood, won two Emmys.) In recent years, however, he hadn't been working regularly, and he'd sort of disappeared. He'd rented a small house in a Mexican border town and wasn't doing well overall.

In every way, Meg felt, her father would never be able to withstand the psychological pressures that come with being stalked by the press, and that was now happening to him. It had long been open season on everyone in Meg's circle, every current friend and ex-boyfriend, every cousin, including those she'd never known, every former employer or former co-worker, but after I proposed there was a frenzy around . . . the Father. He was considered the prize catch. When the **Daily Mirror** published his location, paps descended on his house, taunting him, trying to tempt or lure him outside. No fox hunt, no bear baiting was ever more depraved. Strange men and women dangled offers of money, gifts, friendship. When none of that worked, they rented the house next door and shot him day and night through his windows. The press reported that, as a result, Meg's father had nailed plywood over his windows.

But this wasn't true. He'd often had plywood nailed over his windows, even when living in Los Angeles, well before Meg started dating me.

Complicated man.

They'd then begun following him into town, tailing him on his errands, walking behind him as he went up and down the aisles of local shops. They'd run photos of him with the headline: GOT HIM!

Meg would often phone her father, urge him to remain calm. **Don't speak to them, Daddy. Ignore** them, they'll go away eventually, as long as you don't react. That's what the Palace says to do.

37.

I T WAS HARD for both of us, while dealing with all that, to focus on the million and one details of planning a royal wedding.

Strangely, the Palace had trouble focusing too.

We wanted to get married quickly. Why give the papers and paps time to do their worst? But the Palace couldn't seem to pick a date. Or a venue.

While waiting for a decree from on high, from the nebulous upper regions of the royal decision-making apparatus, we went off on a traditional "engagement tour." England, Ireland, Scotland, Wales—we traveled up and down and all over the UK, introducing Meg to the public.

Crowds went wild for her. **Meg, Diana would've loved you!** I heard women scream this again and again. A total departure from the tone and tenor of the tabloids, and also a reminder: the British press wasn't reality.

On our return from that trip I rang Willy, sounded him out, asked his thoughts about where we might get married.

I told him we were thinking of Westminster Abbey.

No good. We did it there.

Right, right. St. Paul's?

Too grand. Plus Pa and Mummy did it there.

Hm. Yes. Good point.

He suggested Tetbury.

I snorted. **Tetbury? The chapel near Highgrove? Seriously, Willy? How many does that place seat?**

Isn't that what you said you wanted—a small, quiet wedding?

In fact we wanted to elope. Barefoot in Botswana, with maybe a friend officiating, that was our dream. But we were expected to share this moment with other people. It wasn't up to us.

38.

I TURNED BACK TO the Palace. Any progress on a date? A venue?

Nope, was the reply.

How about March?

Alas, March was all booked.

How about June?

Sorry. Garter Day.

At last they came to us with a date: May 2018.

And they accepted our request for the location: St. George's Chapel.

That settled, we made our first public outing with Willy and Kate.

The Royal Foundation Forum. February 2018.

All four of us sat on a stage while a woman asked us softball questions before a fairly good-sized audience. The Foundation was nearing ten years of existence, and we spoke about its past while looking to its future.

with us four at the helm. The audience was keen, all four of us were having fun, the whole atmosphere was hugely positive.

Afterwards, one journalist dubbed us the Fab Four.

Here we go, I thought hopefully.

Days later, controversy. Something about Meg showing support for #metoo, and Kate not showing support—via their outfits? I think that was the gist, though who can say? It wasn't real. But I think it had Kate on edge, while putting her and everyone else on notice that she was now going to be **compared** to, and forced to compete with, Meg.

All this came on the heels of an awkward moment backstage. Meg asked to borrow Kate's lip gloss. An American thing. Meg forgot hers, worried she needed some, and turned to Kate for help. Kate, taken aback, went into her handbag and reluctantly pulled out a small tube. Meg squeezed some onto her finger and applied it to her lips. Kate grimaced. Small clash of styles, maybe? Something we should've been able to laugh about soon after. But it left a little mark. And then the press sensed something was up and tried to turn it into something bigger.

Here we go, I thought sorrowfully.

39.

GRANNY FORMALLY APPROVED the marriage in March 2018.

By royal decree.

Meanwhile, Meg and I were already a growing family. We brought home a new puppy—a sibling for little Guy. He'd been needing one, poor thing. So when a friend in Norfolk told me his black Labrador had a litter, and offered me a gorgeous amber-eyed female, I couldn't say no.

Meg and I named her Pula. The Setswana word for rain.

And good fortune.

Many mornings I'd wake to find myself surrounded by beings I loved, who loved me, and depended on me, and I thought I simply had no right to this much good fortune. Work challenges aside, this was happiness. Life was good.

And following along a predestined track, seemingly. The decree about the wedding coincided uncannily with the airing of Meg's farewell season of **Suits**, in which her character, Rachel, was also preparing to get married. Art and life, imitating each other.

Decent of **Suits**, I thought, marrying Meg off the show, instead of pushing her down a lift shaft. There were enough people in real life trying to do that.

That spring, however, the press was quieter. Keener about breaking news of wedding details than inventing new libels. Each day there was another "world exclusive" about the flowers, the music, the food, the cake. No detail too small, not even the Portaloos. It was reported that we'd be providing the poshest Portaloos on earth—porcelain basins, gold-plated seats—after being inspired by the ones at Pippa Middleton's wedding. In reality, we didn't notice anything different about how or where people went pee or poo at Pippa's, and we had nothing to do with choosing the Portaloos for ours. But we sincerely hoped that everyone would be able to do their thing in comfort and peace.

Above all, we hoped the royal correspondents would continue to write about poo instead of trying to stir it up.

So when the Palace encouraged us to feed more wedding details to those correspondents, known as the Royal Rota, we obeyed. At the same time, I told the Palace that on the Big Day, the happiest day of our lives, I didn't want to see one single royal correspondent inside that chapel, unless Murdoch himself apologized for phone hacking.

The Palace scoffed. It would be all-out war, the courtiers warned, to bar the Royal Rota from the wedding.

Then let's go to war.

I'd had it with the Royal Rota, both the individuals and the system, which was more outdated than the horse and cart. It had been devised some forty years earlier, to give British print and broadcast reporters first crack at the Royal Family, and it stank to high heaven. It discouraged fair competition, engendered cronyism, encouraged a small mob of hacks to feel entitled.

After weeks of wrangling, it was agreed: The Royal Rota wouldn't be allowed in the chapel, but they could gather outside.

A small win, which I hugely celebrated.

40.

Pa WANTED TO HELP choose the music for the ceremony so he invited us one night to Clarence House, for dinner and . . . a concert.

He brought out his wireless and we began sampling music, wonderful music, all kinds of music. He wholly endorsed our desire to have an orchestra rather than an organist, and he played an assortment of orchestras to get us in the mood.

After a time, we segued into classical, and he talked about his love of Beethoven.

Meg spoke about her own deep feeling for Chopin.

She'd always loved Chopin, she said, but in Canada she grew dependent on him, because Chopin was the only thing that could soothe Guy and Bogart.

She played them Chopin day and night.

Pa smiled sympathetically.

As one piece ended, he'd quickly reload his wireless, begin humming or tapping his foot to the next. He was airy, witty, charming, and I kept shaking my head in amazement. I knew Pa loved music, but I never knew he loved it this much.

Meg evoked so much in him, qualities I'd rarely seen. In her presence Pa became boyish. I saw it, saw the bond between them growing stronger, and I felt strengthened in my own bond with him. So many people were treating her shabbily, it filled my heart to see my father treating her like the princess she was about to—maybe **born** to—become.

41.

AFTER ALL THE STRESS OF ASKING Granny for permission to marry Meg, I thought I'd never have the courage to ask her for anything else.

And yet I now dared to make another ask: **Granny, please, may I, for my wedding, keep my beard?**

Not a small ask either. A beard was thought by some to be a clear violation of protocol and long-standing norms, especially since I was getting married in my Army uniform. Beards were forbidden in the British Army.

But I was no longer in the Army and I desperately wanted to hang on to something that had become an effective check on my anxiety.

Illogical, but true. I'd grown the beard during my voyage to the South Pole, and I'd kept it after returning home, and it helped, along with therapy, and meditation, and a few other things, to quell my nerves. I couldn't explain it, though I did find articles describing the phenomenon. Maybe it was Freudian—beard as security blanket. Maybe it was Jungian—beard as mask. Whatever, it made me calmer, and I wanted to feel as calm as possible on the day of my wedding.

Also, my wife-to-be had never seen me without it. She loved my beard, she loved to grab it and pull me in for a kiss. I didn't want her coming down the aisle and seeing a total stranger.

I explained all this to Granny, and she said she

understood. Plus, her own husband liked to rock a bit of scruff now and then. Yes, she said, you may keep your beard. But then I explained it to my brother and he . . . bristled?

Not the done thing, he said. Military, rules, so forth.

I gave him a quick history lesson. I mentioned the many royals who'd been bearded and uniformed. King Edward VII. King George V. Prince Albert. More recently, Prince Michael of Kent.

Helpfully I referred him to Google Images.

Not the same, he said.

When I informed him that his opinion didn't really matter, since I'd already gone to Granny and got the green light, he became livid. He raised his voice.

You went to ask her!

Yes.

And what did Granny say?

She said keep the beard.

You put her in an uncomfortable position, Harold! She had no choice but to say yes.

No choice? She's the Queen! If she didn't want me to have a beard I think she can speak for herself.

But Willy always thought Granny had a soft spot for me, that she indulged me while holding him to an impossibly high standard. Because . . . Heir, Spare, etc. It irked him.

The argument went on, in person, on the phone, for more than a week. He wouldn't let it go.

At one point he actually ordered me, as the Heir speaking to the Spare, to shave.

Are you serious?

I'm telling you, shave it off.

For the love of God, Willy, why does this matter so much to you?

Because I wasn't allowed to keep my beard.

Ah—there it was. After he'd come back from an assignment with Special Forces, Willy was sporting a full beard, and someone told him to be a good boy, run along and shave it. He hated the idea of me enjoying a perk he'd been denied.

It also, I suspected, brought back bad memories of being told he couldn't marry in the uniform of his choice.

Then he confirmed my suspicion. He said it outright: In one of our beard debates he complained bitterly about my being allowed to marry in my Household Cavalry frock coat, which he'd wanted to wear for **his** wedding.

He was being ridiculous, and I told him so. But he kept getting angrier and angrier.

Finally I told him flatly and defiantly that his bearded brother was getting married soon, and he could either get on board or not. The choice was up to him.

42.

I SHOWED UP TO my stag ready to party. To laugh, to have a good time, to get clear of all this stress. And yet I also feared that if I got too clear, got too drunk and passed out, Willy and his mates would hold me down and shave me.

In fact Willy told me, explicitly, in all seriousness, **that this was his plan.**

So, while having fun, I was also at all times keeping my older brother in my sight.

The stag was at a friend's house in the Hampshire countryside. Not on the south coast, or in Canada, or in Africa, all of which were reported as its location.

Aside from my older brother, fifteen mates were in attendance.

The host kitted out his indoor tennis court with various boy toys:

Giant boxing gloves.

Bows and arrows, à la **Lord of the Rings**.

A mechanical bull.

We painted our faces and rough-housed like idiots. Great fun.

After an hour or two I was tired, and relieved when someone shouted that lunch was ready.

We had a big picnic in a large, airy barn, then trooped off to a makeshift shooting range.

Arming that drunken lot to the teeth—dangerous idea. But somehow no one was hurt.

When everyone was bored of firing rifles, they dressed me as a giant yellow feathered chicken and sent me downrange to shoot fireworks at me. All right, I **offered** to do it. **Whoever comes closest wins!** I flashed back to those long-ago weekends in Norfolk, dodging fireworks with Hugh and Emilie's boys.

I wondered if Willy did too.

How had we drifted so far from the closeness of those days?

Or had we?

Maybe, I thought, we can **still** recapture it.

Now that I'm to be married.

43.

THERE HAD BEEN SPIRITED ARGUMENTS in the back corridors of the Palace about whether or not Meg could—or should—wear a veil. Not possible, some said.

For a divorcée, a veil was thought to be out of the question.

But the powers that be, unexpectedly, showed some flexibility on the subject.

Next came the question of a tiara. My aunts asked if Meg would like to wear my mother's. We were both touched. Meg then spent hours and hours with her dress designer, getting the veil to match the tiara, giving it a similar scalloped edge.

Shortly before the wedding, however, Granny reached out. She offered us access to **her** collection of tiaras. She even invited us to Buckingham Palace to try them on. **Do come over**, I remember her saying.

Extraordinary morning. We walked into Granny's private dressing room, right next to her bedroom, a space I'd never been in. Along with Granny was a jewelry expert, an eminent historian who knew the lineage of each stone in the royal collection. Also present was Granny's dresser and confidante, Angela. Five tiaras were arrayed on a table, and Granny directed Meg to try on each one before a full-length mirror. I stood behind, watching.

One was all emeralds. One was aquamarines. Each was more dazzlingly stunning than the last. Each took my breath.

I wasn't the only one. Granny said to Meg quite tenderly: **Tiaras suit you.**

Meg melted. **Thank you, Ma'am.**

One of the five, however, stood out. Everyone agreed. It was beautiful, seemingly made for Meg. Granny said it would be placed in a safe directly and she looked forward to seeing it on Meg's head come the Big Day.

Make sure, she added, **that you practice putting it on. With your hairdresser. It's tricky and you don't want to be doing it for the first time on the wedding day.**

We left the Palace feeling awed and loved and grateful.

A week later we contacted Angela and asked her to please send us the chosen tiara so we could practice putting it on. We'd done research, and we'd spoken to Kate about her own experience, and we'd learned that Granny's warning was spot on. The placing of the tiara was an intricate, elaborate process. It had to be first sewn to the veil, then Meg's hairdresser would need to fix it to a small plait in her hair. Complicated, time-consuming—we'd need at least one dress rehearsal.

For some reason, however, Angela didn't respond to any of our messages.

We kept trying.

No response.

When we finally reached her, she said the tiara would require an orderly and a police escort to leave the Palace.

That sounded . . . a bit much. But all right, I said, if that's protocol, let's find an orderly and a police officer and get the ball rolling. Time was running out.

Inexplicably, she replied: **Can't be done.**

Why can't it?

Her schedule was too busy.

She was being obstructive, obviously, but for what reason? We couldn't even hazard a guess. I considered going to Granny, but that would probably mean sparking an all-out confrontation, and I wasn't quite sure with whom Granny would side.

Also, to my mind, Angela was a troublemaker, and I didn't need her as an enemy.

Above all, **she was still in possession of that tiara.**

She held all the cards.

44.

THOUGH THE PRESS WAS mostly laying off Meg, mostly staying focused on the approaching wedding, the harm was already done. After eighteen months of trashing her, they'd riled up all the trolls, who were now crawling out of their cellars and lairs. Ever since we'd acknowledged that we were a couple, we'd been flooded with racist taunts and death threats on social media. (**See ya later, race traitor!**) But now the official threat level, used by Palace security to allocate personnel and guns, had reached vertiginous heights. In pre-wedding conversations with police we learned that we'd become **the** prized target for terrorists and extremists. I remembered General Dannatt saying I was a bullet magnet, that anyone standing next to me would be unsafe. Well, I was a bullet magnet again, but standing next to me would be the person I loved most in the world.

There's been some reporting about the Palace deciding to instruct Meg in guerrilla warfare, and survival tactics, in the event of a kidnapping attempt. A bestselling book describes the day Special Forces came to our house, grabbed Meg, put her through several intense days of drills, pushing her into back seats and car boots, speeding away to safe houses—all of which is utter nonsense. Meg wasn't given one minute of training. On the contrary, the Palace floated the idea of not giving her any security at all, because I was now sixth in line to the throne. How I wished reports about Special Forces were even partly true! How I longed to phone my mates in Special Forces, have them come and train Meg and re-train me. Or, better yet, pitch in, protect us. For that matter, how

I wished I could send Special Forces to go and grab that tiara.

Angela still hadn't delivered it.

Meg's hairdresser had come in from France for the rehearsal, and the tiara still wasn't there. So he'd gone back.

Again, we phoned Angela. Again, nothing.

Finally, Angela appeared out of thin air at Kensington Palace. I met her in the Audience Room.

She put before me a release, which I signed, and then she handed me the tiara.

I thanked her, though I added that it would've made our lives so much easier to have had it sooner.

Her eyes were fire. She started having a go at me.

Angela, you really want to do this now? Really? Now?

She fixed me with a look that made me shiver. I could read in her face a clear warning.

This isn't over.

45.

MEG HAD SPENT MONTHS trying to soothe her father. There was always something new that he'd read about himself, something derogatory he'd taken to heart. His pride was constantly wounded. Every day there was another humiliating photo in the papers. Thomas Markle buying a new loo. Thomas Markle buying a six-pack. Thomas Markle with his belly hanging over his belt.

We understood. Meg told him we knew how he felt. The press, the paps, they were awful. Impossible to totally ignore what's written, she acknowledged. But please do try to ignore them **in person**. Ignore anyone who approaches, Daddy. Be on guard against anyone who pretends to be your best friend. He seemed to be listening. He started to sound as if he was in a better place, mentally.

Then, the Saturday before the wedding, Jason phoned us. **We've got a problem.**

What?

The Mail on Sunday **is going to run a story saying that Meg's father has been working with the paps and, for money, has staged some candid photos.**

We immediately phoned Meg's dad, told him what was coming. We asked if it was true. Had he staged a bunch of candid photos for money?

No.

Meg said: **We might be able to kill this story, Daddy, but if it turns out you're lying, we'll never be able to kill a false story about ourselves, or our children, again. So this is serious. You must tell us the truth.**

He swore that he'd never staged any photos, that he hadn't taken part in any such charade, that he didn't know the pap in question.

Meg whispered to me: **I believe him.**

In that case, we told him, leave Mexico right now: A whole new level of harassment is about to rain down on you, so come to Britain. Now. We'll arrange for an apartment where you can hole up safely until your flight.

Air New Zealand, first class, booked and paid for by Meg.

We would immediately send a car with private security to pick him up.

He said he had things to do.

Now Meg's face changed. Something was up.

She turned to me again and sighed: **He's lying.**

The story broke the next morning and it was worse than we feared. There was video of Meg's father meeting the pap at an internet café. There was a series of farcically staged shots, including one of him reading a book about Britain as if studying for the wedding. The photos, reportedly worth a hundred thousand pounds, seemed to prove beyond all doubt that Meg's father had indeed been lying. He'd taken part in this fakery, maybe to make some money, or maybe they had some leverage on him. We didn't know.

Headlines read: **Meg Markle's father a con artist! Staged candid photos for money!**

A week before the wedding, this now became **the** story.

Though the photos had been taken weeks before, they'd been held in reserve until the most devastating possible moment.

Soon after the story broke, Thomas Markle sent us a text:

I'm so ashamed.

We phoned him.

And texted him.

And phoned again.

We're not angry, please pick up.

He didn't answer.

Then we heard, along with the rest of the world, that he'd apparently had a heart attack and wasn't coming to the wedding.

46.

THE NEXT DAY Meg had a text from Kate. There was a problem with the dresses for the bridesmaids, apparently. They needed altering. The dresses were French couture, hand-sewn from measurements only. So it wasn't a big shock that they might need altering.

Meg didn't reply to Kate straightaway. Yes, she had endless wedding-related texts, but mostly she was dealing with the chaos surrounding her father. So the next morning she texted Kate that our tailor was standing by. At the Palace. His name was Ajay.

This wasn't sufficient.

They set up a time to speak that afternoon

Charlotte's dress is too big, too long, too baggy. She cried when she tried it on at home, Kate said.

Right, and I told you the tailor has been standing by since eight a.m. Here. At KP. Can you take

Charlotte to have it altered, as the other moms are doing?

No, all the dresses need to be remade.

Her own wedding dress designer agreed, Kate added.

Meg asked if Kate was aware of what was going on right now. With her father.

Kate said she was well aware, but the dresses. **And the wedding is in four days!**

Yes, Kate, I know . . .

And Kate had other problems with the way Meg was planning her wedding. Something about a party for the page boys?

The page boys? Half the kids in the wedding are from North America. They haven't even arrived yet.

It went back and forth.

I'm not sure what else to say. If the dress doesn't fit then please take Charlotte to see Ajay. He's been waiting all day.

Fine.

A short time later I arrived home and found Meg on the floor. Sobbing.

I was horrified to see her so upset, but I didn't think it a catastrophe. Emotions were running high, of course, after the stress of the last week, the last month, the last day. It was intolerable—but temporary. Kate hadn't meant any harm, I told her.

Indeed the next morning Kate came by with flowers and a card that said she was sorry. Meg's best friend, Lindsay, was in the kitchen when she turned up.

Simple misunderstanding, I told myself.

47.

ON THE EVE OF the wedding I stayed at Coworth Park Hotel. A private cottage. Several mates sat with me and had drinks. One commented that I seemed a bit distracted.

Yes, well. There's been a lot going on.

I didn't want to say too much. The business with Meg's father, Kate and the dress, the constant worry about someone in the crowd doing something crazy—better not to talk about it.

Someone asked about my brother. Where's Willy?

I gave another non-answer. Another sore subject.

He'd been scheduled to join us for the evening. But, like Meg's father, he'd canceled last minute.

He'd told me, just before he attended tea with Granny: Can't do it, Harold. Kate and the kids.

I'd reminded him that this was our tradition, that we'd had dinner before his wedding, that we'd gone together and visited the crowds.

He held fast. **Can't do it.**

I pushed. **Why you being like this, Willy? I was with you the whole night before you married Kate. Why you doing this?**

I asked myself what was really going on. Was he feeling bad about not being my best man? Was he upset that I'd asked my old mate Charlie? (The Palace put out the story that Willy was the best man, as they'd done with me when he and Kate married.) Could that be part of it?

Or was it a hangover from Beardgate?

Or was he feeling guilty about the business between Kate and Meg?

He wasn't giving any indication. He just kept saying no. While asking me why it even mattered so much.

Why are you even saying hello to the crowds, Harold?

Because the press office told me to. As we did at your wedding.

You don't need to listen to them.

Since bloody when?

I felt sick about it. I'd always believed, despite our problems, that our underlying bond was strong. I'd thought brotherhood would always trump a brides-maid's dress or a beard. Suppose not.

Then, just after leaving Granny, around six P.M., Willy texted. He'd changed his mind. He'd come.

Maybe Granny intervened?

Whatever. I thanked him happily, heartily.

Moments later, we met outside and got into a car, which drove us down to King Edward Gate. We hopped out, walked up and down the crowd, thanking people for coming.

People wished us well, blew us kisses.

We waved goodbye, got back into the car.

As we drove off, I asked him to come have dinner with me. I mentioned maybe staying the night, as I'd done before his wedding.

He'd come for dinner, he said, but wouldn't be able to stay.

Come on, please, Willy.
Sorry, Harold. Can't. Kids.

48.

I STOOD AT THE ALTAR, smoothed the front of my Household Cavalry uniform, watched Meg floating towards me. I'd worked hard to choose the right music for her procession, and ultimately I'd landed on Handel's **Eternal Source of Light Divine.**

Now, as the soloist's voice rang out above our heads, I thought I'd chosen well.

Indeed, as Meg came nearer and nearer, I was giving thanks for all my choices.

Amazing that I could even hear the music over the sound of my own heartbeat as Meg stepped up, took my hand. The present dissolved, the past came rushing back. Our first tentative messages on Instagram. Our first meeting at Soho House. Our first trip to Botswana. Our first excited exchanges after my phone went into the river. Our first roast chicken. Our first flights back and forth across the Atlantic. The first time I told her: I love you. Hearing her say it back. Guy in splints. Steve the grumpy swan. The brutal fight to keep her safe from the press. And now here we were, the finishing line. The starting line.

For the last few months, not much had gone according to plan. But I reminded myself that none of **that** was the plan. This was the plan. This. Love.

I shot a glance at Pa, who'd walked Meg down the

last part of the aisle. Not her father, but special just the same, and she was moved. It didn't make up for her father's behavior, for how the press had used him, but it very much helped.

Aunt Jane stood and gave a reading in honor of Mummy. **Song of Solomon.**

Meg and I chose it.

Arise, my love, my fair one, and come away . . .
Set me as a seal upon your heart, as a seal upon
your arm;
For love is strong as death, passion fierce as the
grave . . .

Strong as death. Fierce as the grave. Yes, I thought. Yes.

I saw the archbishop extend the rings, his hands shaking. I'd forgotten, but he clearly hadn't: twelve cameras pointed at us, two billion people watching on TV, photographers in the rafters, massive crowds outside roistering and cheering.

We exchanged the rings, Meg's made from the same hunk of Welsh gold that had provided Kate's.

Granny had told me that this was nearly the last of it.

Last of the gold. That was how I felt about Meg.

The archbishop reached the official part, spoke the few words that made us The Duke and Duchess of Sussex, titles bestowed by Granny, and he joined us until death parted us, though he'd already done similar days earlier, in our garden, a small ceremony,

just the two of us, Guy and Pula the only wit-
nesses. Unofficial, non-binding, except in our souls.
We were grateful for every person in and around
St. George's, and watching on TV, but our love
began in private, and being public had been mostly
pain, so we wanted the first consecration of our love,
the first vows, to be private as well. Magical as the
formal ceremony was, we'd both come to feel slightly
frightened of . . . crowds.

Underscoring this feeling: The first thing we saw
upon walking back up the aisle and out of the church,
other than a stream of smiling faces, were snipers. On
the rooftops, amid the bunting, behind the water-
falls of streamers. Police told me it was unusual, but
necessary.

Due to the unprecedented number of threats they
were picking up.

49.

OUR HONEYMOON WAS a closely guarded secret.
We left London in a car disguised as a removals
van, the windows covered with cardboard, and went
to the Mediterranean for ten days. Glorious to be
away, on the sea, in the sun. But we were also sick.
The build-up to the wedding had worn us down.

We returned just in time for the official June celebration of Granny's birthday. Trooping the Color: one of
our first public appearances as newlyweds. Everyone
present was in a good mood, upbeat. But then:

Kate asked Meg what she thought of her first Trooping the Color.

And Meg joked: Colorful.

And a yawning silence threatened to swallow us all whole.

Days later Meg went off on her first royal trip with Granny. She was nervous, but they got on famously. They also bonded over their love of dogs.

She returned from the trip glowing. **We bonded**, she told me. **The Queen and I really bonded! We talked about how much I wanted to be a mom and she told me the best way to induce labor was a good bumpy car ride! I told her I'd remember that when the time came.**

Things are going to turn around now, we both said.

The papers, however, pronounced the trip an unmitigated disaster. They portrayed Meg as pushy, uppity, ignorant of royal protocol, because she'd made the unthinkable mistake of getting into a car before Granny.

In truth she'd done exactly what Granny had told her to do. Granny said get in; she got in.

No matter. There were stories for days about Meg's breach, about her overall lack of class—about her daring not to wear a hat in Granny's presence. The Palace had specifically directed Meg not to wear a hat. Granny also wore green to honor the victims of Grenfell Tower, and no one told Meg to wear green—so they said she didn't give a fig about the victims.

I said: The Palace will make a phone call. They'll correct the record.

They didn't.

50.

WILLY AND KATE INVITED US for tea. To clear the air.

June 2018.

We walked over one late afternoon. I saw Meg's eyes widen as we entered their front door, walked past their front sitting room, down their hallway, into their study.

Wow, Meg said several times.

The wallpaper, the crown molding, the walnut bookshelves lined with color-coordinated volumes, the priceless art. Gorgeous. Like a museum. And we both told them so. We complimented them lavishly on their renovation, though we also thought sheepishly of our IKEA lamps, our discount sofa recently bought on sale, with Meg's credit card, from sofa.com.

In the study, Meg and I sat on a love seat at one end of the room, Kate opposite us on a leather-clad fender before the fireplace. Willy was to her left, in an armchair. There was a tray of tea and biscuits. For ten minutes we did the classic small talk. **How are the kids? How was your honeymoon?**

Meg then acknowledged the tension among the

four of us and ventured that it might go back to those early days when she'd first joined the family—a misunderstanding that had almost passed without notice. Kate thought Meg had wanted her fashion contacts. But Meg had her own. They'd got off on the wrong foot perhaps? And then, Meg added, everything got magnified by the wedding, and those infernal bridesmaids' dresses.

But it turned out there were other things . . . about which we'd been unaware.

Willy and Kate were apparently upset that we hadn't given them Easter presents.

Easter presents? Was that a thing? Willy and I had never exchanged Easter presents. Pa always made a big deal about Easter, sure, but that was Pa.

Still, if Willy and Kate were upset, we apologized.

For our part, we chipped in that we weren't too pleased when Willy and Kate switched place cards and changed seats at our wedding. We'd followed the American tradition, placing couples next to each other, but Willy and Kate didn't like that tradition, so their table was the only one where spouses were apart.

They insisted it wasn't them, it was someone else.

And they said we'd done the same thing at Pippa's wedding.

We hadn't. Much as we'd wanted to. We'd been separated by a huge flower arrangement between us, and though we'd desperately wanted to sit together, we hadn't done a thing about it.

None of this airing of grievances was doing us any good, I felt. We weren't getting anywhere.

Kate looked out into the garden, gripping the edges of the leather so tightly that her fingers were white, and said she was owed an apology.

Meg asked: **For what?**

You hurt my feelings, Meghan.

When? Please tell me.

I told you I couldn't remember something and you said it was my hormones.

What are you talking about?

Kate mentioned a phone call in which they'd discussed the timing of wedding rehearsals.

Meg said: **Oh, yes! I remember: You couldn't remember something, and I said it's not a big deal, it's baby brain. Because you'd just had a baby. It's hormones.**

Kate's eyes widened: **Yes. You talked about my hormones. We're not close enough for you to talk about my hormones!**

Meg's eyes got wide too. She looked genuinely confused. **I'm sorry I talked about your hormones. That's just how I talk with my girlfriends.**

Willy pointed at Meg. **It's rude, Meghan. It's not what's done here in Britain.**

Kindly take your finger out of my face.

Was this really happening? Had it actually come to this? Shouting at each other about place cards and hormones?

Meg said she'd never intentionally do anything to

hurt Kate, and if she ever did, she asked Kate to please just let her know so it wouldn't happen again.

We all hugged. Kind of.

And then I said we'd better be going.

51.

OUR STAFF SENSED THE friction, read the press, and thus there was frequent bickering around the office. Sides were taken. Team Cambridge versus Team Sussex. Rivalry, jealousy, competing agendas—it all poisoned the atmosphere.

It didn't help that everyone was working around the clock. There were so many demands from the press, such a constant stream of errors that needed clearing up, and we didn't have nearly enough people or resources. At best we were able to address 10 percent of what was out there. Nerves were shattering, people were sniping. In such a climate there was no such thing as constructive criticism. All feedback was seen as an affront, an insult.

More than once a staff member slumped across their desk and wept.

For all this, every bit of it, Willy blamed one person. Meg. He told me so several times, and he got cross when I told him he was out of line. He was just repeating the press narrative, spouting fake stories he'd read or been told. The great irony, I told him, was that the real villains were the people he'd imported into the office, people from government, who didn't seem impervious to this kind of strife—but addicted to it. They had a knack for backstabbing, a talent for intrigue, and they were constantly setting our two groups of staff against each other.

Meanwhile, in the midst of all this, Meg managed to remain calm. Despite what certain people were saying about her, I never heard her speak a bad word about anybody, or to anybody. On the contrary, I watched her redouble her efforts to reach out, to spread kindness. She sent out handwritten thank-you notes, checked on staff who were ill, sent baskets of food or flowers or goodies to anyone struggling, depressed, off sick. The office was often dark and cold, so she warmed it up with new lamps and space heaters, all bought with her personal credit card. She brought pizza and biscuits, hosted tea parties and ice-cream socials. She shared all the freebies she received, clothes and perfumes and makeup, with all the women in the office.

I stood back in awe at her ability, or determination, to always see the good in people. The size of her heart was really brought home for me one day. I learned that Mr. R, my former upstairs neighbor when I was in the badger sett, had suffered a tragedy. His adult son had died.

Meg didn't know Mr. R. Neither did she know the son. But she knew the family had been my neighbors, and she'd often seen them walking their dogs. So she felt tremendous sorrow for them, and wrote the father a letter, expressing condolences, telling him she wanted to give him a hug but didn't know if it would be appropriate. With the letter she included a gardenia, to plant in the son's memory.

A week later Mr. R appeared at our front door at Nott Cott. He handed Meg a thank-you note and gave her a tight hug.

I felt so proud of her, so regretful about my feud with Mr. R.

More, I felt regretful about my family feuding with my wife.

52.

WE DIDN'T WANT TO wait. We both wanted to start a family straightaway. We were working crazy hours, our jobs were demanding, the timing wasn't ideal, but too bad. This had always been our main priority.

We worried about the stress of our daily lives, that it might prevent us getting pregnant. The toll was starting to be visible on Meg; she'd lost a great deal of weight in the last year, despite all the shepherd's pie. I'm eating more than ever, she reported—yet her weight kept dropping.

Friends recommended an ayurvedic doctor who'd helped them conceive. As I understood it, ayurvedic medicine sorted people into categories. I don't recall which category this doctor sorted Meg into, but she did confirm our suspicion that Meg's weight loss might be a barrier to conceiving.

Gain five pounds, the doctor promised, and you'll get pregnant.

So Meg ate, and ate, and soon put on the recommended five pounds, and we looked hopefully at the calendar.

Towards the end of summer 2018 we went to Scotland, the Castle of Mey, to spend a few days with Pa. The bond between Meg and Pa, always strong, grew even stronger during that weekend. One night, over pre-dinner cocktails, Fred Astaire playing in the background, it emerged that Meg shared a birthdate with Pa's favorite person: Gan-Gan.

August 4.

Amazing, Pa said with a smile.

At the memory of Gan-Gan, and the link between her and my bride, he suddenly became buoyant, telling stories I'd never heard, essentially performing, showing off for Meg.

One story in particular delighted us both, captured our imagination. It was about the selkies.

The what, Pa?

Scottish mermaids, he said. They took the form of seals and cruised along the shore outside the castle, within a stone's throw of where we were sitting. **So, when you see a seal**, he advised, **you never can tell . . . Sing to it. They often sing back.**

Oh, come on. You're telling fairytales, Pa!

No, it's absolutely true!

Did I imagine—did Pa promise—that the selkies might also grant a wish?

We talked a bit during that dinner about the stress we'd been under. If we could just convince the papers to back off, we said . . . for a little while.

Pa nodded. But he felt it very important to remind us—

Yes, yes, Pa. We know. Don't read it.

At tea the next day the good vibes continued. We were all laughing, talking about one thing and another, when Pa's butler burst into the room, pulling a land line behind him.

Your Royal Highness, Her Majesty.

Pa sat bolt upright. **Oh, yes.** He reached for the phone.

I'm sorry, sir, but she's calling for the Duchess.
Oh.

We all looked stunned. Meg tentatively reached for the phone.

It seemed Granny was calling to talk about Meg's father. She was responding to a letter Meg had written her, asking for advice and help. Meg said she didn't know how to make the press stop interviewing him, enticing him to say horrid things. Granny now suggested that Meg forget the press, go and see her father, try to talk some sense into him.

Meg explained that he lived in a Mexican border town and she didn't know how she'd ever get through the airport, through the press surrounding his house, then through that part of town, and back again, quietly, safely.

Granny acknowledged the many problems with this plan.

In that case, perhaps write him a letter?

Pa agreed. Splendid idea.

53.

MEG AND I WENT DOWN to the beach in front of the castle. Chilly day, but the sun was bright.

We stood on the rocks, looking out at the sea. Amid all the silky islands of seaweed we saw . . . something.

A head.

A pair of soulful eyes.

Look! Seal!

The head bobbed up and down. The eyes very clearly watched us.

Look! Another!

Just as Pa instructed, I ran to the water's edge, sang to them. Serenaded them.

Arooo.

No answer.

Meg joined me, and sang to them, and now of course they sang back.

She really is magic, I thought. Even the seals know it.

Suddenly, all over the water, heads were bobbing up, singing to her.

Arooo.

A seal opera.

Silly superstition, maybe, but I didn't care. I counted it a good omen. I took off my clothes, jumped into the water, swam to them.

Later, Pa's Aussie chef was horrified. He told us that this had been a supremely bad idea, more ill-advised than diving heedless into the darkest water of the Okavango. This part of the Scottish coast was teeming with killer whales, the chef said, and singing to seals was like calling them to their blood-soaked deaths.

I shook my head.

It had been such a lovely fairytale, I thought.

How did it get so dark so fast?

54.

MEG WAS LATE. We bought two home pregnancy tests, one for a backup, and she took them both into the bathroom at Nott Cott.

I was lying on our bed, and while waiting for her to come out . . . I fell asleep.

When I woke, she was beside me.

What's happened? Is it . . . ?

She said she hadn't looked. She'd waited for me.

The wands were on the nightstand. I only kept a few things there, among them the blue box with my mother's hair. Right, I thought, good. Let's see what Mummy can do with this situation.

I reached for the wands, peered into their little windows.

Blue.

Bright, bright blue. Both of them.

Blue meant . . . baby.

Oh wow.
Well.
Well then.
We hugged, kissed.
I put the wands back on the nightstand.
I thought: Thank you, selkies.
I thought: Thank you, Mummy.

55.

EUGE WAS GETTING married, to Jack, and we were deliriously happy for her, and for ourselves, selfishly, since Jack was one of our favorite people. Meg and I were supposed to head off on our first official foreign tour as a married couple, but we delayed the departure several days, so we could be at the wedding.

Also, the various gatherings connected to the wedding would give us a chance to pull aside family members one by one and tell them our good news.

At Windsor, just before a drinks reception for the bride and groom, we cornered Pa in his study. He was sitting behind his big desk, which afforded his favorite view, straight down the Long Walk. Every window was open, to cool the room, and a breeze was fluttering his papers, which were all stacked in squat little towers, each crowned with a paperweight. He was delighted to learn that he was going to be a grandfather for a fourth time; his wide smile warmed me.

After the drinks reception, in St. George's Hall, Meg and I pulled Willy aside. We were in a big room, suits of armor on the walls. Strange room, strange moment. We whispered the news, and Willy smiled and said we must tell Kate. She was across the room, talking to Pippa. I said we could do it later, but he insisted. So we went and told Kate and she also gave a big smile and hearty congratulations.

They both reacted exactly as I'd hoped—as I'd wished.

56.

DAYS LATER THE pregnancy was announced publicly. The papers reported that Meg was battling fatigue and dizzy spells and couldn't hold any food down, especially in the mornings, all of which was untrue. She was tired, but otherwise a dynamo. Indeed, she felt lucky not to be suffering severe morning sickness, since we were embarking on a hugely demanding tour.

Everywhere we went, enormous crowds turned out, and she didn't disappoint them. All across Australia, Tonga, Fiji, New Zealand, she dazzled. After one especially rousing speech, she got a standing ovation.

She was so brilliant that midway through the tour I felt compelled . . . to warn her.

You're doing too well, my love. Too damn well. You're making it look too easy. This is how everything started . . . with my mother.

Maybe I sounded mad, paranoid. But everyone

knew that Mummy's situation went from bad to worse when she showed the world, showed the family, that she was better at touring, better at connecting with people, better at being "royal," than she had any right to be.

That was when things really took a turn.

We returned home to jubilant welcomes and exultant headlines. Meg, the expectant mother, the flawless representative of the Crown, was hailed.

Not a negative word was written.

It's changed, we said. It's changed at last.

But then it changed again. Oh, how it changed.

Stories rolled in, like breakers on a beach. First a rubbish hit piece by a hack biographer of Pa, who said I'd thrown a tantrum before the wedding. Then a work of fiction about Meg making her staff miserable, driving them too hard, committing the unpardonable sin of emailing people early in the morning. (She just happened to be up at that hour, trying to stay in touch with night-owl friends back in America—she didn't expect an instant reply.) She was also said to have driven our assistant to quit; in fact that assistant was asked to resign by Palace HR after we showed them evidence she'd traded on her position with Meg to get freebies. But because we couldn't speak publicly about the reasons for the assistant's departure, rumors filled the void. In many ways that was the true start of all the troubles. Shortly thereafter, the "Duchess Difficult" narrative began appearing in all the papers.

Next came a novella in one of the tabloids about

the tiara. The article said Meg had demanded a certain tiara that had belonged to Mummy, and when the Queen refused, I'd thrown a fit: **What Meghan wants, Meghan gets!**

Days later came the coup de grâce: from a royal correspondent, a sci-fi fantasy describing the "growing froideur" (good Lord) between Kate and Meg, claiming that, according to "two sources," Meg had reduced Kate to tears about the bridesmaids' dresses.

This particular royal correspondent had always made me ill. She'd always, always got stuff wrong. But this felt more than wrong.

I read the story in disbelief. Meg didn't. She still wasn't reading anything. She heard about it, however, since it was the only thing being discussed in Britain for the next twenty-four hours, and as long as I live I'll never forget the tone of her voice as she looked me in the eye and said:

Haz, I made her cry? I made HER cry?

57.

WE ARRANGED A SECOND summit with Willy and Kate.

This time on our turf.

December 10, 2018. Early evening.

We all gathered in our little front annex, and this time there was no small talk: Kate got things rolling straightaway by acknowledging that these stories in the papers about Meg making her cry were totally false. **I know, Meghan, that I was the one who made you cry.**

I sighed. Excellent start, I thought.

Meg appreciated the apology, but wanted to know why the papers had said this, and what was being done to correct them? In other words: **Why isn't your office standing up for me? Why haven't they phoned this execrable woman who wrote this story, and demanded a retraction?**

Kate, flustered, didn't answer, and Willy chimed in with some very supportive-sounding evasions, but I already knew the truth. No one at the Palace could phone the correspondent, because that would invite the inevitable retort: Well, if the story's wrong, what's the real story? What **did** happen between the two duchesses? And that door must never be opened, because it would embarrass the future queen.

The monarchy, always, at all costs, had to be protected.

We shifted from what to do about the story to where it came from. Who could've planted such a thing? Who could've leaked it to the press in the first place? Who?

We went around and around. The list of suspects became vanishingly small.

Finally, **finally**, Willy leaned back and conceded that, ahem, while we'd been on tour in Australia, he and Kate had gone to dinner with Pa and Camilla . . . and, alas, he said sheepishly, he **might've** let it slip that there'd been strife between the two couples . . .

I put a hand over my face. Meg froze. A heavy silence fell.

So now we knew.

I told Willy: **You . . . of all people . . . should've known . . .**

He nodded. He knew.

More silence.

It was time for them to go.

58.

IT KEPT ON AND ON. One story after another. I thought at times of Mr. Marston ceaselessly ringing his insane bell.

Who can ever forget the spate of front-page stories making Meg out to be singlehandedly responsible for the End Times? Specifically, she'd been "caught" eating avocado toast, and many stories explained breathlessly that the harvesting of avocados was hastening the destruction of the rainforests, destabilizing developing countries, and helping to fund state terrorism. Of course the same media had recently swooned over Kate's love of avocados. (**Oh, how they make Kate's skin glow!**)

Notably, it was around this time that the super-narrative embedded within each story began to shift. It was no longer about two women fighting, two duchesses at odds, or even two households. It was now about one person being a witch and causing everyone to run from her, and that one person was my wife.

And in building this super-narrative the press was clearly being assisted by someone or multiple some-ones inside the Palace.

Someone who had it in for Meg.

One day it was: Yuck—Meg's bra strap was show-ing. (Classless Meghan.)

The next day: Yikes—she's wearing that dress? (Trashy Meghan.)

The next day: God save us, her fingernails are painted black! (Goth Meghan.)

The next day: Goodness—she still doesn't know how to curtsy properly. (American Meghan.)

The next day: Crikey, she shut her own car door again! (Uppity Meghan.)

59.

WE'D RENTED A HOUSE in Oxfordshire. Just a place to get away now and then from the mael-strom, but also from Nott Cott, which was charming but too small. And falling down around our heads.

It got so bad that one day I had to phone Granny. I told her we needed a new place to live. I explained that Willy and Kate hadn't simply outgrown Nott Cott, they'd fled it, because of all the required repairs, and the lack of room, and we were now in the same boat. With two rambunctious dogs . . . and a baby on the way . . .

I told her we'd discussed our housing situation with the Palace, and we'd been offered several properties, but each was too grand, we thought. Too lavish. And too expensive to renovate.

Granny gave it a think and we chatted again days later.

Frogmore, she said.

Frogmore, Granny?

Yes. Frogmore.

Frogmore House?

I knew it well. That was where we'd taken our engagement photos.

No, no—Frogmore Cottage. Near Frogmore House.

Sort of hidden, she said. Tucked away. Originally home to Queen Charlotte and her daughters, then to one of Queen Victoria's aides, and later it was chopped into smaller units. But it could be reassembled. Lovely place, Granny said. Plus, historic. Part of the Crown Estate. Very sweet.

I told her that Meg and I loved the gardens at Frogmore, we went walking there often, and if it was near those, well, what could be better?

She warned: **It's a bit of a building site. Bit of a shell. But go and have a look and do tell me if it works.**

We went that day, and Granny was right. The house spoke to us both. Charming, full of potential. Hard by the Royal Burial Ground, but so what? Didn't bother me or Meg. We wouldn't disturb the dead if they'd promise not to disturb us.

I rang Granny and said Frogmore Cottage would

be a dream come true. I thanked her profusely. With her permission we began sitting down with builders, planning the minimum renovations, to make the place habitable—piping, heating, water.

While the work was being done, we thought we could move into Oxfordshire full time. We loved it out there. The air fresh, the verdant grounds—plus, no paps. Best of all, we'd be able to call upon the talents of my father's longtime butler, Kevin. He knew the Oxfordshire house, and he'd know how to turn it quickly into a home. Better yet, he knew me, held me as a baby, and befriended my mother when she was wandering Windsor Castle in search of a sympathetic face. He told me that Mummy was the only person in the family who ever dared venture "below stairs," to chat with staff. In fact she'd often sneak down and sit with Kevin in the kitchen, over a drink or snack, watching telly. It had fallen to Kevin, on the day of Mummy's funeral, to greet me and Willy on our return to Highgrove. He stood on the front steps, he recalled, waiting for our car, rehearsing what he'd say. But when we pulled up and he opened the car door I said:

How are you holding up, Kevin?

So polite, he said.

So repressed, I thought.

Meg adored Kevin, and vice versa, so I thought this could be the start of something good. A much-needed change of scenery, a much-needed ally in our corner. Then one day I looked down at my phone: a text from our team alerting me to huge splashy stories in **The Sun** and the **Daily Mail**, featuring detailed overhead photos of Oxfordshire.

A helicopter was hovering above the property, a pap hanging out of the door, aiming telephoto lenses at every window, including our bedroom.

Thus ended the dream of Oxfordshire.

60.

I WALKED home from the office and found Meg sitting on the stairs.

She was sobbing. Uncontrollably.

My love, what's happened?

I thought for sure we'd lost the baby.

I went to her on my knees. She choked out that she didn't want to do this anymore.

Do what?

Live.

I didn't catch her meaning at first. I didn't understand, maybe didn't want to understand. My mind just didn't want to process the words.

It's all so painful, she was saying.

What is?

To be hated like this—for what?

What had she **done**? she asked. She really wanted to know. What sin had she committed to deserve this kind of treatment?

She just wanted to make the pain stop, she said.

Not only for her, for everyone. For me, for her mother. But she **couldn't** make it stop, so she'd decided to disappear.

Disappear?

Without her, she said, all the press would go away, and then I wouldn't have to live like this. Our unborn child would never have to live like this.

It's so clear, she kept saying, **it's so clear. Just stop breathing. Stop being. This exists because I exist.**

I begged her not to talk like that. I promised her we'd get through it, we'd find a way. In the meantime, we'd find her the help she needed.

I asked her to be strong, hang on.

Incredibly, while reassuring her, and hugging her, I couldn't entirely stop thinking like a **fucking royal**. We had a Sentebale engagement that night, at the Royal Albert Hall, and I kept telling myself: We can't be late. We **cannot** be late. They'll skin us alive! And they'll blame her.

Slowly—too slowly—I realized that tardiness was the least of our problems.

I said she should skip the engagement, of course. I needed to go, make a quick appearance, but I'd be home fast.

No, she insisted, she didn't trust herself to be at home alone for even an hour with such dark feelings.

So we put on our best kit, and she applied dark, dark lipstick to draw attention away from her bloodshot eyes, and out of the door we went.

The car pulled up outside the Royal Albert Hall,

and as we stepped into the blue flashing lights of the police escort and the whiteout lights of the press's flashbulbs, Meg reached for my hand. She gripped it tightly. As we went inside, she gripped it even tighter. I was buoyed by the tightness of that grip. She's hanging on, I thought. Better than letting go.

But when we settled into the royal box, and the lights dimmed, she let go of her emotions. She couldn't hold back the tears. She wept silently.

The music struck up, we turned and faced the front. We spent the entire length of the performance (Cirque du Soleil) squeezing each other's hands, me promising her in a whisper:

Trust me. I'll keep you safe.

61.

I WOKE TO a text from Jason.
Bad news.
What is it now?
The **Mail on Sunday** had printed the private letter Meg had written to her father. The letter that Granny and Pa urged her to write.
February 2019.
I was in bed, Meg was lying next to me, still asleep.
I waited a bit, then broke the news to her softly.
Your father's given your letter to the Mail.
No.
Meg, I don't know what to say, he's given them your letter.

That moment, for me, was decisive. About Mr. Markle, but also about the press. There had been so many moments, but that for me was The One. I didn't want to hear any more talk of protocols, tradition, strategy. Enough, I thought.

Enough.

The paper knew it was illegal to publish that letter, they knew full well, and did it anyway. Why? Because they also knew Meg was defenseless. They knew she didn't have the **staunch** support of my family, and how else could they have known this, except from people close to the family? Or inside the family? The papers knew that the only recourse Meg had was to sue, and she couldn't do that because there was only one lawyer working with the family, and that lawyer was under the control of the Palace, and the Palace would never authorize him to act on Meg's behalf.

There was nothing in that letter to be ashamed about. A daughter pleading with her father to behave decently? Meg stood by every word. She'd always known it might be intercepted, that one of her father's neighbors, or one of the paps staking out his house, might steal his post. Anything was possible. But she never stopped to think her father would actually offer it, or that a paper would actually take it—and print it.

And edit it. Indeed, that might have been the most galling thing, the way the editors cut and pasted Meg's words to make them sound less loving.

Seeing something so deeply personal smeared

across the front pages, gobbled up by Britons over their morning toast and marmalade, was invasive enough. But the pain was compounded tenfold by the simultaneous interviews with alleged handwriting experts, who analyzed Meg's letter and inferred from the way she crossed her Ts or curved her Rs that she was a terrible person.

Rightward slant? Over-emotional.

Highly stylized? Consummate performer.

Uneven baseline? No impulse control.

The look on Meg's face as I told her about these libels rolling out . . . I knew my way around grief, and there was no mistaking it—this was pure grief. She was mourning the loss of her father, and she was also mourning the loss of her own innocence. She reminded me in a whisper, as if someone might be listening, that she'd taken a handwriting class in high school, and as a result she'd always had excellent penmanship. People complimented her. She'd even used this skill at university to earn spare money. Nights, weekends, she'd inscribed wedding and birthday-party invitations, to pay the rent. Now people were trying to say that this was some kind of window into her soul? And the window was dirty?

Tormenting Meghan Markle has become a national sport that shames us, said a headline in **The Guardian.**

So true. But no one was shamed, that was the problem. No one was feeling the slightest pang of conscience. Would they finally feel some if they caused a divorce? Or would it take another death?

What had become of all the shame they'd felt in the late 1990s?

Meg wanted to sue. Me too. Rather, we both felt we had no choice. If we didn't sue over **this**, we said, what kind of signal would that be sending? To the press? To the world? So we conferred again with the Palace lawyer.

We were given a runaround.

I reached out to Pa and Willy. They'd both sued the press in the past over invasions and lies. Pa sued over so-called Black Spider Letters, his memos to government officials. Willy sued over topless photos of Kate.

But both vehemently opposed the idea of Meg and me taking any legal action.

Why? I asked.

They hummed and hahed. The only answer I could get out of them was that it simply wasn't advisable. The done thing, etc.

I told Meg: **You'd think we were suing a dear friend of theirs.**

62.

WILLY ASKED FOR a meeting. He wanted to talk about everything, the whole rolling catastrophe.

Just him and me, he said.

As it happened, Meg was out of town, visiting girlfriends, so his timing was perfect. I invited him over.

An hour later he walked into Nott Cott, where

he hadn't been since Meg first moved in. He looked piping hot.

It was early evening. I offered him a drink, asked about his family.

Everyone good.

He didn't ask about mine. He just went all in. Chips to the center of the table.

Meg's difficult, he said.

Oh, really?

She's rude. She's abrasive. She's alienated half the staff.

Not the first time he'd parroted the press narrative. Duchess Difficult, all that bullshit. Rumors, lies from his team, tabloid rubbish, and I told him so—again. Told him I expected better from my older brother. I was shocked to see that this actually pissed him off. Had he come here expecting something different? Did he think I'd agree that my bride was a monster?

I told him to step back, take a breath, really ask himself: Wasn't Meg his sister-in-law? Wouldn't this institution be toxic for any newcomer? Worst-case scenario, if his sister-in-law was having trouble adjusting to a new office, a new family, a new country, a new culture, couldn't he see his way clear to cutting her some slack? **Couldn't you just be there for her? Help her?**

He had no interest in a debate. He'd come to lay down the law. He wanted me to agree that Meg was wrong and then agree to do something about it.

Like what? Scold her? Fire her? Divorce her? I

didn't know. But Willy didn't know either, he wasn't rational. Every time I tried to slow him down, point out the illogic of what he was saying, he got louder. We were soon talking over each other, both of us shouting.

Among all the different, riotous emotions coursing through my brother that afternoon, one really jumped out at me. He seemed **aggrieved**. He seemed put upon that I wasn't meekly obeying him, that I was being so impertinent as to deny him, or defy him, to refute his knowledge, which came from his trusted aides. There was a script here and I had the audacity not to be following it. He was in full Heir mode, and couldn't fathom why I wasn't dutifully playing the role of the Spare.

I was sitting on the sofa, he was standing over me. I remember saying: **You need to hear me out, Willy.**

He wouldn't. He simply would not listen.

To be fair, he felt the same about me.

He called me names. All kinds of names. He said I refused to take responsibility for what was happening. He said I didn't care about my office and the people who worked for me.

Willy, give me one example of—

He cut me off, said he was trying to help me.

Are you serious? Help me? Sorry—is that what you call this? Helping me?

For some reason, that really set him off. He stepped towards me, swearing.

To that point I'd been feeling uncomfortable, but

now I felt a bit scared. I stood, brushed past him, went out to the kitchen, to the sink. He was right on my heels, berating me, shouting.

I poured a glass of water for myself, and one for him as well. I handed it to him. I don't think he took a sip.

Willy, I can't speak to you when you're like this.

He set down the water, called me another name, then came at me. It all happened so fast. So very fast. He grabbed me by the collar, ripping my necklace, and he knocked me to the floor. I landed on the dogs' bowl, which cracked under my back, the pieces cutting into me. I lay there for a moment, dazed, then got to my feet and told him to get out.

Come on, hit me! You'll feel better if you hit me!

Do what?

Come on, we always used to fight. You'll feel better if you hit me.

No, only you'll feel better if I hit you. Please . . . just leave.

He left the kitchen, but he didn't leave Nott Cott. He was in the sitting room, I could tell. I stayed in the kitchen. Two minutes passed, two long minutes. He came back looking regretful and apologized.

He walked to the front door. This time I followed. Before leaving he turned and called back: **You don't need to tell Meg about this.**

You mean that you attacked me?

I didn't attack you, Harold.

Fine. I won't tell her.

Good, thank you.

He left.

I looked at the phone. A promise is a promise, I told myself, so I couldn't call my wife, much as I wanted to.

But I needed to talk to someone. So I rang my therapist.

Thank God she answered.

I apologized for the intrusion, told her I didn't know who else to call. I told her I'd had a fight with Willy, he'd knocked me to the floor. I looked down and told her that my shirt was ripped, my necklace was broken.

We'd had a million physical fights in our lives, I told her. As boys we'd done nothing **but** fight. But this felt different.

The therapist told me to take deep breaths. She asked me to describe the scene several times. Each time I did it seemed more like a bad dream.

And made me a bit calmer.

I told her: **I'm proud of myself.**

Proud, Harry? Why's that?

I didn't hit him back.

I stayed true to my word, didn't tell Meg.

But not long after she returned from her trip, she saw me coming out of the shower and gasped.

Haz, what are those scrapes and bruises on your back?

I couldn't lie to her.

She wasn't that surprised, and she wasn't at all angry.

She was terribly sad.

63.

SOON AFTER THAT DAY it was announced that the two royal households, Cambridge and Sussex, would no longer share an office. We'd no longer be working together in any capacity. The Fab Four . . . **finis.**

Reaction was about as expected. The public groaned, journalists brayed. The more disheartening response was from my family. Silence. They never commented publicly, never said anything privately to me. I never heard from Pa, never heard from Granny. It made me think, really think, about the silence that surrounded everything else that happened to me and Meg. I'd always told myself that, just because everyone in my family didn't explicitly condemn press attacks, it didn't mean they **condoned** them. But now I asked: Is that true? How do I know? If they never say anything, why do I so often assume that I know how they feel?

And that they're unequivocally on our side?

Everything I'd been taught, everything I'd grown up believing about the family, and about the monarchy, about its essential fairness, its job of uniting rather than dividing, was being undermined, called into question. Was it all fake? Was it all just a show? Because if we couldn't stand up for one another, rally around our newest member, our first biracial member, then what were we really? Was that a true constitutional monarchy? Was that a real family?

Isn't "defending each other" the first rule of every family?

64.

MEG AND I MOVED our office into Buckingham Palace.

We also moved into a new home.

Frogmore was ready.

We loved that place. From the first minute. It felt as if we were destined to live there. We couldn't wait to wake up in the morning, go for a long walk in the gardens, check in with the swans. Especially grumpy Steve.

We met the Queen's gardeners, got to know their names and the names of all the flowers. They thrilled at how much we appreciated, and praised, their artistry.

Amid all this change we huddled with our new head of comms, Sara. We plotted a new strategy with her, the centerpiece of which was having nothing whatsoever to do with the Royal Rota, and hoped we might soon be able to make a fresh start.

Towards the end of April 2019, days before Meg was due to give birth, Willy rang.

I took the call in our new garden.

Something had happened between him and Pa and Camilla. I couldn't get the whole story, he was talking too fast, and was way too upset. He was seething actually. I gathered that Pa and Camilla's people had planted a story or stories about him and Kate, and the kids, and he wasn't going to take it anymore. Give Pa and Camilla an inch, he said, they take a mile.

They've done this to me for the last time.

I got it. They'd done the same to me and Meg as well.

But it wasn't them, technically, it was the most gung-ho member of Pa's comms team, a true believer who'd devised and launched a new campaign of getting good press for Pa and Camilla at the expense of bad press for us. For some time this person had been peddling unflattering stories, fake stories, about the Heir and Spare, to all the papers. I suspected that this person had been the lone source for stories about a hunting trip I'd made to Germany in 2017, stories that made me out to be some fat-bottomed seventeenth-century baron who craved blood and trophies, when in reality I was working with German farmers to cull wild boar and save their crops. I believed the story had been offered as a straight swap, in exchange for greater access to Pa, and also as a reward for the suppression of stories about Camilla's son, who'd been gadding around London, generating tawdry rumors. I was displeased about being used like this, and livid about it being done to Meg, but I had to admit it was happening much more often lately to Willy. And he was justifiably incandescent.

He'd already confronted Pa once about this woman, face-to-face. I'd gone along for moral support. The scene took place at Clarence House, in Pa's study. I remember the windows being wide open, the white curtains blowing in and out, so it must've been a warm night. Willy put it to Pa: **How can you be letting a stranger do this to your sons?**

Pa instantly got upset. He began shouting that Willy was paranoid. We both were. Just because **we** were getting bad press, and he was getting good, that didn't mean his staff was behind it.

But we had proof. Reporters, inside actual newsrooms, assuring us that this woman was selling us out.

Pa refused to listen. His response was churlish, pathetic. **Granny has her person, why can't I have mine?**

By Granny's person he meant Angela. Among the many services she performed for Granny, she was said to be skilled at planting stories.

What a rubbish comparison, Willy said. Why would anyone in their right mind, let alone a grown man, want their own Angela?

But Pa just kept saying it. Granny had her person, Granny had her person. High time he had a person too.

I was glad that Willy felt he could still come to me about Pa and Camilla, even after all we'd been through recently. Seeing an opportunity to address our recent tensions, I tried to connect what Pa and Camilla had done to him with what the press had done to Meg.

Willy snapped: **I've got different issues with you two!**

In a blink he shifted all his rage onto me. I can't recall his exact words, because I was beyond tired from all our fighting, to say nothing of the recent move into Frogmore, and into new offices—and I was focused on the imminent birth of our first child. But I recall every physical detail of the scene. The daffodils out, the new grass sprouting, a jet taking off from Heathrow, heading west, unusually low, its engines making my chest vibrate. I remember thinking how remarkable that I could still hear Willy above that jet. I couldn't imagine how he had that much anger left after the confrontation in Nott Cott.

He was going on and on and I lost the thread. I couldn't understand and I stopped trying. I fell silent, waiting for him to subside.

Then I looked back. Meg was coming from the house, directly towards me. I quickly took the phone off speaker, but she'd already heard. And Willy was being so loud, even with the speaker off, she could still hear.

The tears in her eyes glistened in the spring sunshine. I started to say something, but she stopped, shook her head.

Holding her stomach, she turned and walked back to the house.

65.

DORIA WAS STAYING with us, waiting for the baby to come. Neither she nor Meg ever strayed far. None of us did. We all just sat around waiting, going for the occasional walk, looking at the cows.

When Meg was a week past her due date, the

comms team and the Palace began pressuring me. When's the baby coming? The press can't wait forever, you know.

Oh. The press is getting frustrated? Heaven forbid!

Meg's doctor had tried several homeopathic ways to get things moving, but our little visitor was just intent on staying put. (I don't remember if we ever tried Granny's suggestion of a bumpy car ride.) Finally we said: Let's just go and make sure nothing's wrong. And let's be prepared in case the doctor says it's time.

We got into a nondescript people-carrier and crept away from Frogmore without alerting any of the journalists stationed at the gates. It was the last sort of vehicle they suspected we'd be riding in. A short time later we arrived at the Portland Hospital and were spirited into a secret lift, then into a private room. Our doctor walked in, talked it through with us, and said it was time to induce.

Meg was so calm. I was calm too. But I saw two ways of **enhancing** my calm. One: Nando's chicken. (Brought by our bodyguards.) Two: A canister of laughing gas beside Meg's bed. I took several slow, penetrating hits. Meg, bouncing on a giant purple ball, a proven way of giving Nature a push, laughed and rolled her eyes.

I took several more hits and now I was bouncing too.

When her contractions began to quicken, and deepen, a nurse came and tried to give some laughing gas to Meg. There was none left. The nurse looked at the tank, looked at me, and I could see the thought slowly dawning: Gracious, the husband's had it all.

Sorry, I said meekly.

Meg laughed, the nurse had to laugh, and quickly changed the canister.

Meg climbed into a bath, I turned on soothing music. Deva Premal: she remixed Sanskrit mantras into soulful hymns. (Premal claimed she heard her first mantra in the womb, chanted by her father, and when he was dying she chanted the same mantra to him.) Powerful stuff.

In our overnight bag we had the same electric candles I'd arranged in the garden the night I proposed. Now I placed them around the hospital room. I also set a framed photo of my mother on a little table. Meg's idea.

Time passed. Hour melted into hour. Minimal dilation.

Meg was doing a lot of deep breathing for pain. Then the deep breathing stopped working. She was in so much pain that she needed an epidural.

The anesthetist hurried in. Off went the music, on went the lights.

Whoa. Vibe change.

He gave her an injection at the base of her spine.

Still the pain didn't let up. The medicine apparently wasn't getting where it needed to go.

He came back, did it again.

Now things both quietened and accelerated.

Her doctor came back two hours later, slipped both hands into a pair of rubber gloves. **This is it, everybody.** I stationed myself at the head of the bed, holding Meg's hand, encouraging her. **Push, my love.**

Breathe. The doctor gave Meg a small hand mirror. I tried not to look, but I had to. I glanced, saw a reflection of the baby's head emerging. Stuck. Tangled. **Oh, no, please, no.** The doctor looked up, her mouth set in a particular way. Things were getting serious.

I said to Meg: **My love, I need you to push.**

I didn't tell her why. I didn't tell her about the cord, didn't tell her about the likelihood of an emergency C-section. I just said: **Give me everything you've got.**

And she did.

I saw the little face, the tiny neck and chest and arms, wriggling, writhing. Life, life—amazing! I thought, Wow, it really all begins with a struggle for freedom.

A nurse swept the baby into a towel and placed him on Meg's chest and we both cried to see him, meet him. A healthy little boy, and he was **here.**

Our ayurvedic doctor had advised us that, in the first minute of life, a baby absorbs everything said to them. **So whisper to the baby, tell the baby your wish for him, your love. Tell.**

We told.

I don't remember phoning anyone, texting them. I remember watching the nurses run tests on my hour-old son, and then we were out of there. Into the lift, into the underground car park, into the people-carrier, and gone. Within two hours of our son being born we were back at Frogmore. The sun had risen and we were behind closed doors before the official announcement was released . . .

Saying Meg had gone into labor?

I had a tiff with Sara about that. You know she's not in labor anymore, I said.

She explained that the press must be given the dramatic, suspenseful story they demanded.

But it's not true, I said.

Ah, truth didn't matter. Keeping people tuned to the show, that was the thing.

After a few hours I was standing outside the stables at Windsor, telling the world: It's a boy. Days later we announced the name to the world. Archie.

The papers were incensed. They said we'd pulled a fast one on them.

Indeed we had.

They felt that, in doing so, we'd been . . . bad partners?

Astonishing. Did they still think of us as partners? Did they really expect special consideration, preferential treatment—given how they'd treated us these last three years?

And then they showed the world what kind of "partners" they really were. A BBC radio presenter posted a photo on his social media—a man and a woman holding hands with a chimpanzee.

The caption read: **Royal baby leaves hospital.**

66.

I HAD A LONG TEA WITH GRANNY, just before she left for Balmoral. I gave her a recap, all the latest. She knew a bit, but I was filling in important gaps.

She looked shocked.

Appalling, she said.

She vowed to send the Bee to talk to us.

I'd spent my life dealing with courtiers, scores of them, but now I dealt mostly with just three, all middle-aged white men who'd managed to consolidate power through a series of bold Machiavellian maneuvers. They had normal names, exceedingly British names, but they sort more easily into zoological categories. The Bee. The Fly. And the Wasp.

The Bee was oval-faced and fuzzy and tended to glide around with great equanimity and poise, as if he was a boon to all living things. He was so poised that people didn't fear him. Big mistake. Sometimes their last mistake.

The Fly had spent much of his career adjacent to, and indeed drawn to, shit. The offal of government, and media, the wormy entrails, he loved it, grew fat on it, rubbed his hands in glee over it, though he pretended otherwise. He strove to give off an air of casualness, of being above the fray, coolly efficient and ever helpful.

The Wasp was lanky, charming, arrogant, a ball of jazzy energy. He was great at pretending to be polite, even servile. You'd assert a fact, something seemingly incontrovertible—**I believe the sun rises in the mornings**—and he'd stammer that perchance you might consider for a moment the possibility that you'd been misinformed: **Well, heh-heh, I don't know about that, Your Royal Highness, you see, it all depends what you mean by mornings, sir.**

Because he seemed so weedy, so self-effacing, you might be tempted to push back, insist on your point, and that was when he'd put you on his list. A short time later, without warning, he'd give you such a stab with his outsized stinger that you'd cry out in confusion. **Where the fuck did that come from?**

I disliked these men, and they didn't have any use for me. They considered me irrelevant at best, stupid at worst. Above all, they knew how I saw them: as usurpers. Deep down, I feared that each man felt **himself** to be the One True Monarch, that each was taking advantage of a Queen in her nineties, enjoying his influential position while merely appearing to serve.

I'd come to this conclusion through cold hard experience. For instance, Meg and I had consulted with the Wasp about the press, and he'd agreed that the situation was abominable, that it needed to be stopped before someone got hurt. **Yes! You'll get no argument from us on that!** He suggested the Palace convene a summit of all the major editors, make our case to them.

Finally, I said to Meg, someone gets it.

We never heard from him again.

So I was skeptical when Granny offered to send us the Bee. But I told myself to keep an open mind. Maybe this time would be different, because this time Granny was dispatching him personally.

Days later, Meg and I welcomed the Bee into Frogmore, made him comfortable in our new sitting room, offered him a glass of rosé, gave a detailed presentation. He took meticulous notes, frequently putting a hand over his mouth and shaking his head. He'd seen the headlines, he said, but he'd not appreciated the full impact this might have on a young couple.

This deluge of hate and lies was unprecedented in British history, he said. **Disproportionate to anything I've ever seen.**

Thank you, we said. Thank you for seeing it.

He promised to discuss the matter with all the necessary parties and get back to us soon with an action plan, a set of concrete solutions.

We never heard from him again.

67.

MEG AND I WERE ON THE phone with Elton John and his husband, David, and we confessed: We need help.

We're sort of losing it here, guys.

Come to us, Elton said.

By which he meant their home in France.

Summer 2019.

So we did. For a few days we sat on their terrace and soaked up their sunshine. We spent long healing moments gazing out at the azure sea, and it felt decadent, not just because of the luxurious setting. Freedom of any kind, in any measure, had come to feel like scandalous luxury. To be out of the fishbowl for even an afternoon felt like day release from prison.

One afternoon we took a scooter ride with David, around the local bay, down the coastal road. I was driving, Meg was on the back, and she threw out her arms and shouted for joy as we zoomed through little towns, smelt people's dinners from open windows, waved to children playing in their gardens. They all waved back and smiled. They didn't know us.

The best part of the visit was watching Elton and David and their two boys fall in love with Archie. Often I'd catch Elton studying Archie's face and I knew what he was thinking: Mummy. I knew because it happened so often to me as well. Time and again I'd see an expression cross Archie's face and it would bring me up short. I nearly said so to Elton, how much I wished my mother could hold her grandson, how often it happened that, while hugging Archie, I felt her—or wanted to. Every hug tinged with nostalgia; every tuck-in touched with grief.

Does anything bring you face-to-face with the past like parenthood?

On the last night we were all experiencing that familiar end-of-holiday malaise: **Why can't it be like this forever?** We were drifting from the terrace to the pool, and back again, Elton offering cocktails, David and I chatting about the news. And the sorry state of the press. And what it meant for the state of Britain.

We got onto books. David mentioned Elton's memoir, at which he'd been toiling for years. It was finally done, and Elton was mighty proud of it, and the publication date was drawing near.

Bravo, Elton!

Elton mentioned that it was going to be serialized.

Is that so?

Yes. Daily Mail.

He saw my face. He quickly looked away.

Elton, how in the absolute—?

I want people to read it!

But, Elton—? The very people who've made your life miserable?

Exactly. Who better to excerpt it? Where better than the very newspaper that's been so poisonous to me my whole life?

Who better? I just . . . I don't understand.

It was a warm night, so I'd already been sweating. But now beads were dripping off my forehead. I reminded him of the specific lies the **Mail** had famously printed about him. Hell—he'd sued them, just over a decade earlier, after they claimed he forbade people at a charity event from speaking to him. They'd ultimately written him a check for a hundred thousand pounds.

I reminded him that he'd stirringly said in one interview: "They can say I'm a fat old c—. They can say I'm an untalented bastard. They can call me a poof. But they mustn't lie about me."

He didn't have an answer.

But I didn't push it.

I loved him. I'll always love him.

And I also didn't want to spoil the holiday.

68.

IT FELT GLORIOUS TO watch an entire country fall in love with my wife.

South Africa, that is.

September 2019.

Another foreign tour, representing the Queen, and another triumph. From Cape Town to Johannesburg, people couldn't get enough of Meg.

We both felt a bit more confident, therefore, a bit more courageous, just days before our return home, when we strapped on the battle armor and announced that we were suing three of the four British tabloids (including the one that printed Meg's letter to her father) over their disgraceful conduct, and over their longstanding practice of hacking into people's phones.

It was partially down to Elton and David. At the end of our recent visit they'd introduced us to a barrister, an acquaintance of theirs, a lovely fellow who knew more about the phone-hacking scandal than anyone I'd ever met. He'd shared with me his expertise, plus loads of open-court evidence, and when I told him I wished there was something I could do with it, when I complained that we'd been blocked at every turn by the Palace, he offered a breathtakingly elegant work-around.

Why not hire your own lawyer?

I stammered: **You mean . . . are you telling me we could just . . . ?**

What a thought. It had never occurred to me.

I'd been so conditioned to do as I was told.

69.

I RANG GRANNY TO TELL her beforehand. Pa too. And I sent Willy a text.

I also told the Bee, giving him advance notice of the lawsuit, letting him know we had a statement ready to go, asking him to please redirect to our office all the press inquiries it would inevitably trigger. He wished us luck! It was amusing, therefore, when I heard that he and the Wasp were claiming to have had no advance warning.

In announcing the lawsuit I laid out my case to the world:

My wife has become one of the latest victims of a British tabloid press that wages campaigns against individuals with no thought to the consequences—a ruthless campaign that has escalated over the past year, throughout her pregnancy and while raising our newborn son . . . I cannot begin to describe how painful it has been . . . Though this action may not be the safe one, it is the right one. Because my deepest fear is history repeating itself . . . I lost my mother and now I watch my wife falling victim to the same powerful forces.

The lawsuit wasn't covered as widely as, say, Meg's daring to shut her own car door. In fact, it was barely covered at all. Nonetheless, friends took note. Many texted: **Why now?**

Simple. In a few days the privacy laws in Britain were going to change in the tabloids' favor. We wanted our case to be heard before a crooked bat was introduced into the game.

Friends also asked: **Why sue at all when you're riding so high in the press? The South Africa tour was a triumph, coverage was wildly positive.**

That's the whole point, I explained. **This isn't about wanting or needing good press. It's about not letting people get away with abuse. And lies. Especially the kind of lies that can destroy innocents.**

Maybe I sounded a bit self-righteous. Maybe I sounded as if I was on my high horse. But shortly after announcing our lawsuit I felt energized by a ghastly story in the **Express.**

How Meghan Markle's flowers may have put Princess Charlotte's life at risk.

This latest "scandal" concerned the flower crowns worn by our bridesmaids, more than a year earlier. Included in the crowns were a few lilies of the valley, which can be poisonous to children. Provided the children **eat** the lilies.

Even then, the reaction would be discomfort, concerning to parents, but only in the rarest cases would such a thing be fatal.

Never mind that an official florist put together these crowns. Never mind that it wasn't Meg who made this "dangerous decision." Never mind that previous royal brides, including Kate and my mother, had also used lilies of the valley.

Never mind all that. The story of Meghan the Murderess was just too good.

An accompanying photo showed my poor little niece wearing her crown, face contorted in a paroxysm of agony, or a sneeze. Alongside this photo was a shot of Meg looking sublimely unconcerned about the imminent death of this angelic child.

70.

I WAS SUMMONED TO Buckingham Palace. A lunch with Granny and Pa. The invitation was contained in a terse email from the Bee, and the tone wasn't: Would you mind popping around?

It was more: Get your arse over here.

I threw on a suit, jumped into the car.

The Bee and the Wasp were the first faces I saw when I walked into the room. An ambush. I thought this was to be a family lunch. Apparently not.

Alone, without my staff, without Meg, I was confronted directly about my legal action. My father said it was massively damaging to the reputation of the family.

How so?

It makes our relationship with the media complicated.

Complicated. There's a word.

Anything you do affects the whole family.

One could say the same about all your actions and decisions. They affect us as well. Like, for instance, wining and dining the same editors and journalists who've been attacking me and my wife . . .

The Bee or the Wasp jumped in to remind me: One has to have a relationship with the press . . . Sir, we've talked about this before!

A relationship yes. But not a sordid affair.

I tried a new tack. Everyone in this family has sued the press, including Granny. Why's this any different?

Chirping crickets. Silence.

There was some more wrangling, and then I said:

We had no other option. And we wouldn't have had to do it if you'd all protected us. And protected the monarchy in the process. You're doing a disservice to yourselves by not protecting my wife.

I looked around the table. Stony faces. Was it incomprehension? Cognitive dissonance? A long-term mission at play? Or . . . did they really not know? Were they so deep inside a bubble inside a bubble that they really hadn't fully appreciated how bad things were?

For instance, **Tatler** magazine quoting an old Etonian saying I'd married Meg because "foreigners" like her are "easier" than girls "with the right background."

Or the **Daily Mail** saying Meg was "upwardly

mobile," because she'd gone from "slaves to royalty" in just 150 years.

Or the social media posts about her being a "yacht girl" and an "escort," or calling her a "gold-digger," and "a whore," and "a bitch," and "a slut," and the N-word—repeatedly. Some of those posts were in the comments section on the pages of all three Palaces' social media accounts—and still hadn't been expunged.

Or the tweet that said: "Dear Duchess, I'm not saying that I hate you but I hope your next period happens in a shark tank."

Or the revelation of racist texts from Jo Marney, girlfriend of UKIP leader Henry Bolton, including one saying that my "black American" fiancée would "taint" the Royal Family, setting the stage for "a black king," and another averring that Ms. Marney would never have sex with "a Negro."

"This is Britain, not Africa."

Or the **Mail** complaining that Meg couldn't keep her hands off her baby bump, that she was rubbing it and rubbing it as if she were a succubus.

Things had got so out of hand, seventy-two women in Parliament, from both main parties, had condemned the "colonial undertones" of all newspaper coverage of The Duchess of Sussex.

None of these things had merited one comment, public or private, from my family.

I knew how they rationalized it all, saying it was no different from what Camilla got. Or Kate. But it **was** different. One study looked closely at four hundred vile tweets about Meg. Employing a team of data specialists and computer analysts the study found that this avalanche of hate was wildly atypical, light-years from anything directed at Camilla or Kate. A tweet calling Meg "the queen of monkey island" had no historical precedent or equivalent.

And this wasn't about hurt feelings or bruised egos. Hate had physical effects. There was a ton of science showing how unhealthy it is to be publicly hated and mocked. Meanwhile, the wider societal effects were even scarier. Certain kinds of people are more susceptible to such hate, and incited by it. Hence the package of suspicious white powder that had been sent to our office, with a disgusting racist note attached.

I looked at Granny, looked around the room, reminded them that Meg and I had been coping with a wholly unique situation, and doing it all by ourselves. Our dedicated staff was too small, too young, grossly underfunded.

The Bee and the Wasp harrumphed and said we should've let it be known that we were under-resourced.

Let it be known? I said I'd begged them repeatedly, all of them, and one of our top aides had sent in pleas as well—multiple times.

Granny looked directly at the Bee and the Wasp: **Is this true?**

The Bee looked her right in the eye, and, with the Wasp nodding vigorously in assent, said: **Your Majesty, we never received any of these requests for support.**

71.

MEG AND I ATTENDED the WellChild Awards, an annual event that honored children suffering from serious illnesses. October 2019.

I'd attended many times through the years, having been a royal patron of the organization since 2007, and it was always gutting. The children were so brave, their parents so proud—and tortured. Various awards were given that night for inspiration, fortitude, and I was presenting one to an especially resilient preschooler.

I walked onstage, began my brief remarks, and caught sight of Meg's face. I thought back to a year ago, when she and I attended this event just weeks after taking that home pregnancy test. We'd been filled with hope, and worry, like all expectant parents, and now we had a healthy little boy at home. But these parents and children hadn't been so lucky. Gratitude and sympathy converged in my heart, and I choked up. Unable to get the words out, I held the lectern tight and leaned forward. The presenter, who'd been a friend of my mother, stepped over and gave my shoulder a rub. It helped, as did the burst of applause, which gave me a moment to restart my vocal cords. Soon after, I got a text from Willy. He was in Pakistan on tour. He said I was clearly struggling, and he was worried about me.

I thanked him for his concern, assured him I was fine. I'd become emotional in front of a roomful of sick kids and their folks just after becoming a father myself—nothing abnormal in that.

He said I wasn't well. He said again that I needed help.

I reminded him that I was doing therapy. In fact, he'd recently told me he wanted to accompany me to a session because he suspected I was being "brainwashed."

Then come, I said. **It will be good for you. Good for us.**

He never came.

His strategy was patently obvious: I was unwell, which meant I was unwise. As if all my behavior needed to be called into question.

I worked hard at keeping my texts to him civil. Nonetheless, the exchange turned into an argument, which stretched over seventy-two hours. Back and forth we went, all day, late into the night—we'd never had a fight like that over text before. Angry, but also miles apart, as if we were speaking different languages. Now and then I realized that my worst fear was coming true: after months of therapy, after working hard to become more aware, more independent, I was a stranger to my older brother. He could no longer relate to me—tolerate me.

Or maybe it was just the stress of the last few years, the last few decades, finally pouring out.

I saved the texts. I have them still. I read them sometimes, with sadness, with confusion, thinking: How did we ever get there?

In his final texts, Willy wrote that he loved me. That he cared for me deeply. That he would do whatever is needed to help me.

He told me to never feel any other way.

72.

Meg and I discussed getting away, but this time we weren't talking about a day at Wimbledon or a weekend with Elton.

We were talking about escape.

A friend knew someone who had a house we could borrow on Vancouver Island. Quiet, green— seemingly remote. Only reachable by ferry or plane, the friend said.

November 2019.

We arrived with Archie, Guy, Pula, and our nanny, under cover of darkness, on a stormy night, and spent the next few days trying to unwind. It wasn't hard. From morning to night we didn't have to give a thought to being ambushed. The house was right on the edge of a sparkling green forest, with big gardens where Archie and the dogs could play, and it was nearly surrounded by the clean, cold sea. I could take a bracing swim in the morning. Best of all, no one knew we were there. We hiked, we kayaked, we played—in peace.

After a few days we needed supplies. We ventured out timidly, drove down the road into the nearest village, walked along the pavement like people in a horror movie. Where will the attack come from? Which direction?

But it didn't happen. People didn't freak. They didn't stare. They didn't reach for their iPhones. Everyone knew, or sensed, that we were going through something. They gave us space, while also managing to make us feel welcome, with a kind smile, a wave. They made us feel like part of a community. They made us feel normal.

For six weeks.

Then the **Daily Mail** printed our address.

Within hours the boats arrived. An invasion by sea. Each boat bristled with telephoto lenses, arrayed like guns along the decks, and every lens was aimed at our windows. At our boy.

So much for playing in the gardens.

We grabbed Archie, pulled him into the house.

They shot through the kitchen windows during his feeds.

We pulled down the blinds.

The next time we drove into town, there were forty paps along the route. Forty. We counted. Some gave chase. At our favorite little general store, a plaintive sign now hung in the window: No Media.

We hurried back to the house, pulled the blinds even tighter, returned to a kind of permanent twilight.

Meg said she'd officially come full circle. Back in Canada, afraid to raise the blinds.

But blinds weren't enough. Security cameras along the back fence of the property soon picked up a skeletal man pacing, peering, looking for a way in. And taking photos over the fence. He wore a filthy puffer vest, dirty trousers bunched around his raggedy shoes, and he looked as if nothing was beneath him. Nothing. His name was Steve Dennett. He was a freelance pap who'd spied on us before, in the employ of **Splash!**

He was a pest. But maybe the next guy would be more than a pest.

Can't stay here, we said.

And, yet . . . ?

Brief as it was, that taste of freedom had got us thinking. What if life could be like that . . . all the time? What if we could spend at least part of each year somewhere far away, still doing work for the Queen, but beyond the reach of the press?

Free. Free from the British press, free from the drama, free from the lies. But also free from the supposed "public interest" that was used to justify the frenzied coverage of us.

The question was . . . where?

We talked about New Zealand. We talked about South Africa. Half the year in Cape Town maybe? That could work. Away from the drama, but closer to my conservation work—and to eighteen other Commonwealth countries.

I'd run the idea by Granny once before. She'd even signed off on it. And I'd run it by Pa, at Clarence House, the Wasp present. He told me to put it in writing, which I'd done immediately. Within a few days it was in all the papers and caused a huge stink.

So now, at the end of December 2019, when I was chatting with Pa on the phone, saying we were more serious than ever about spending part of the year away from Britain, I wasn't having it when he said that I must write it down.

Yeah, um, did that once before, Pa. And our plan immediately got leaked and scuppered.

I can't help you if you don't put it in writing, darling boy. These things have to go through government.

For the love of . . .

So. In the first days of January 2020, I sent him a watermarked letter broadly outlining the idea, with bullet points, and many details. Throughout the exchanges that followed, all marked PRIVATE AND CONFIDENTIAL, I hammered the essential theme: we were prepared to make any sacrifice necessary to find some peace and safety, including relinquishing our Sussex titles.

I rang to get his thoughts.

He wouldn't come to the phone.

I soon received a long email from him saying we'd have to sit down and discuss the whole thing in person. He'd like us to come back as soon as possible.

You're in luck, Pa! We're coming back to Britain in the next few days—to see Granny. So . . . when can we meet?

Not before the end of January.

What? That's more than a month away.

I'm in Scotland. I can't get there before then.

I really hope and trust that we will be able to have

further conversations without this getting into the public domain and it becoming a circus, I wrote.

He responded with what felt like an ominous threat: **You'll be disobeying orders from the monarch and myself if you persist in this course of action before we have a chance to sit down.**

73.

I RANG GRANNY on January 3.

We're coming back to Britain, I said. We'd love to see you.

I told her explicitly that we hoped to discuss with her our plan to create a different working arrangement.

She wasn't pleased. Neither was she shocked. She knew how unhappy we were, she'd seen this day on the horizon.

One good chat with my grandmother, I felt, would bring this ordeal to an end.

I said: **Granny, are you free?**

Yes, of course! I'm free all week. The diary is clear.

That's great. Meg and I can come up for tea and then drive back to London. We have an engagement at Canada House the next day.

You'll be exhausted from the travel. Do you want to stay here?

By "here" she meant Sandringham. Yes, that would be easier, and I told her so.

That would be lovely, thank you.

Are you planning to see your father too?

I asked, but he said it's impossible. He's in Scotland and can't leave until the end of the month.

She made a little sound. A sigh or a knowing grunt. I had to laugh.

She said: **I have only one thing to say about that. Yes?**

Your father always does what he wants to do.

Days later, January 5, as Meg and I boarded a flight in Vancouver, I got a frantic note from our staff, who'd received a frantic note from the Bee. Granny wouldn't be able to see me. **Initially Her Majesty thought this would be possible, it will not . . . The Duke of Sussex cannot come to Norfolk tomorrow. Her Majesty will be able to arrange another mtg this month. No announcements about anything shall be issued until such a meeting takes place.**

I said to Meg: They're blocking me from seeing my own grandmother.

When we landed I considered driving straight to Sandringham anyway. To hell with the Bee. Who was he to try to block me? I imagined our car being stopped at the gate by Palace police. I imagined smashing past security, the gate snapping across the bonnet. Diverting fantasy, and a fun way to spend the trip from the airport, but no. I'd have to bide my time.

When we reached Frogmore I rang Granny again. I imagined the phone ringing on her desk. I could actually hear it in my mind, **brrrang**, like the red phone in the VHR tent.

Troops in Contact!

Then I heard her voice.

Hello?

Hi, Granny, it's Harry. Sorry, I must have misunderstood you the other day when you said you didn't have anything going on today.

Something came up that I wasn't aware of.

Her voice was strange.

Can I pop in tomorrow then, Granny?

Um. Well. I'm busy all week.

At least, she added, that was what the Bee told her . . .

Is he in the room with you, Granny?

No answer.

74.

WE GOT WORD from Sara that **The Sun** was about to run a story saying The Duke and Duchess of Sussex were stepping away from their royal duties to spend more time in Canada. A sad little man, the newspaper's showbiz editor, was said to be the lead reporter on the story.

Why him? Why, of all people, the showbiz guy?

Because lately he'd refashioned himself into some sort of quasi royal correspondent, largely on the strength of his secret relationship with one particularly close friend of Willy's comms secretary—who fed him trivial (and mostly fake) gossip.

He was sure to get everything wrong, as he'd got everything wrong on his last big "exclusive," Tiaragate.

He was equally sure to cram his story into the paper as fast as possible, because he was likely working in concert with the Palace, whose courtiers were determined to get ahead of us and spin the story. We didn't want that. We didn't want anyone else breaking our news, **twisting** our news.

We'd have to rush out a statement.

I phoned Granny again, told her about **The Sun**, told her we might need to hurry out a statement. She understood. She'd allow it, so long as it didn't "add to speculation."

I didn't tell her exactly what our statement would say. She didn't ask. But also I didn't fully know yet. I gave her the gist, however, and mentioned some of the basic details I'd outlined in the memo Pa had demanded and which she'd seen.

The wording needed to be precise. And it needed to be bland—calm. We didn't want to assign any blame, didn't want to stoke the fires. Mustn't add to speculation.

Formidable writing challenge.

We soon realized it wasn't possible; we didn't have time to get our statement out there first.

We opened a bottle of wine. Proceed, sad little man, proceed.

He did. **The Sun** posted his story late that night, and again on the morning's front page.

Headline: WE'RE ORF!

As expected, the story depicted our departure as a rollicking, carefree, hedonistic **tapping out**, rather than a careful retreat and attempt at self-preservation.

It also included the telling detail that we'd offered to relinquish our Sussex titles. There was only one document on earth in which that detail was mentioned—my private and confidential letter to my father.

To which a shockingly, damningly small number of people had access. We hadn't mentioned it to even our closest friends.

January 7, we worked some more on the draft, did a brief public appearance, met with our staff. Finally, knowing more details were about to be leaked, on January 8 we hunkered down deep inside Buckingham Palace, in one of the main state rooms, with the two most senior members of our staff.

I'd always liked that state room. Its pale walls, its sparkly crystal chandelier. But now it struck me as especially lovely and I thought: Has it always been so? Has it always looked so . . . **royal**?

In a corner of the state room was a grand wooden desk. We used this as our workspace. We took turns sitting there, typing on a laptop. We tried out different phrases. We wanted to say that we were taking a reduced role, stepping back but not down. Hard to get the exact wording, the right tone. Serious, but respectful.

Occasionally one of us would stretch out in a nearby armchair, or give the eyes a rest by gazing out of the two huge windows onto the gardens. When I needed a longer break I set off on a trek across the oceanic carpet. On the far side of the room, in the left corner, a small door led to the Belgian Suite, where

Meg and I had once spent the night. In the near corner stood two tall wooden doors, the kind people think of when they hear the word "palace." These led to a room in which I'd attended countless cocktail parties. I thought back on those gatherings, on all the good times I'd had in this place.

I remembered: The room right next door was where the family always gathered for drinks before Christmas lunch.

I went out into the hall. There was a tall, beautiful Christmas tree, still brightly lit. I stood before it, reminiscing. I removed two ornaments, soft little corgis, and brought them back to the staffers. One each. Souvenir of this strange mission, I said.

They were touched. But a bit guilty.

I assured them: **No one will miss 'em.**

Words that seemed double-edged.

Late in the day, as we crawled closer to a final draft, the staffers began to feel anxious. They worried aloud if their involvement would be discovered. If so, what would it mean for their jobs? But mostly they were excited. They felt that they were on the side of right; both had read every word of abuse in the press and on social media, going back months and months.

At six P.M. it was done. We gathered around the laptop, read the draft one last time. One staffer messaged the private secretaries of Granny, Pa and Willy, told them what was coming. Willy's guy replied immediately: **This is going to go nuclear.**

I knew, of course, that many Britons would be shocked, and saddened, which made my stomach churn. But in due course, once they knew the truth, I felt confident they'd understand.

One of the staffers said: **Are we doing this?**

Meg and I both said:

Yes. There's no other choice.

We sent the statement to our social media person. Within a minute there it was, live, on our Instagram page, the only platform available to us. We all hugged, wiped our eyes, and quickly gathered our things.

Meg and I walked out of the Palace and jumped into our car. As we sped towards Frogmore the news was already on the radio. Every channel. We picked one. Magic FM. Meg's favorite. We listened to the presenter work himself into a very British lather. We held hands and shared a smile with our bodyguards in the front seat. Then we all gazed silently out of the windows.

75.

DAYS LATER THERE was a meeting at Sandringham. I don't remember who called it the Sandringham Summit. Someone in the press, I suspect.

On my way there I got a text from Marko about a story in **The Times**.

Willy was declaring that he and I were now "separate entities."

"I've put my arm around my brother all our lives and I can't do that anymore," he said.

Meg had gone back to Canada to be with Archie,

so I was on my own for this summit. I got there early, hoping to have a quick chat with Granny. She was sitting on a bench before the fireplace and I sat down beside her. I saw the Wasp react with alarm. He went buzzing off and moments later returned with Pa, who sat beside me. Immediately after him came Willy, who looked at me as if he planned to murder me. **Hello, Harold.** He sat across from me. Separate entities indeed.

When all participants had arrived, we shifted to a long conference table, with Granny at the head. Before each chair was a royal notepad and pencil.

The Bee and the Wasp conducted a quick summary of where we were. The subject of the press came up pretty quickly. I referenced their cruel and criminal behavior, but said they'd had a ton of help. This family had enabled the papers by looking the other way, or by actively courting them, and some of the staff had worked directly with the press, briefing them, planting stories, occasionally rewarding and fêting them. The press was a big part of why we'd come to this crisis—their business model demanded that we be in constant conflict—but they weren't the only culprits.

I looked at Willy. This was his moment to jump in, echo what I was saying, talk about his maddening experiences with Pa and Camilla. Instead he complained about a story in the morning papers suggesting that he was the reason we were leaving.

I'm now being accused of bullying you and Meg out of the family!

I wanted to say: We had nothing to do with that story . . . but imagine how you might feel if we **had** leaked it. Then you'll know how Meg and I have felt the last three years.

The private secretaries began to address Granny about the Five Options.

Your Majesty, you've seen the Five Options.

Yes, she said.

We all had. They'd been emailed to us, five different ways of proceeding. Option 1 was continuance of the status quo: Meg and I don't leave, everyone tries to go back to normal. Option 5 was full severance, no royal role, no working for Granny, and total loss of security.

Option 3 was somewhere in between. A compromise. Closest to what we'd originally proposed.

I told everyone assembled that, above all, I was desperate to keep security. That was what worried me most, my family's physical safety. I wanted to prevent a repeat of history, another untimely death like the one that had rocked this family to its core twenty-three years earlier, and from which we were still trying to recover.

I'd consulted with several Palace veterans, people who knew the inner workings of the monarchy and its history and they all said Option 3 was best for all parties. Meg and I living elsewhere part of the year, continuing our work, retaining security, returning to Britain for charities, ceremonies, events. Sensible solution, these Palace veterans said. And eminently doable.

But the family, of course, pushed me to take

Option 1. Barring that, they would only accept Option 5.

We discussed the Five Options for nearly an hour. At last the Bee got up and went around the table, handing out a draft of a statement the Palace would soon be releasing. Announcing implementation of Option 5.

Wait. I'm confused. You've already drafted a statement? Before any discussion? Announcing Option 5? In other words, the fix was in, this whole time? This summit was just for show?

No answer.

I asked if there were drafts of other statements. Announcing the other options.

Oh yes, of course, the Bee assured me.

Can I see them?

Alas—his printer had gone on the blink, he said. The odds! At the very moment he was about to print out those other drafts!

I started laughing. **Is this some kind of joke?**

Everyone was staring away or down at their shoes.

I turned to Granny: **Do you mind if I take a moment, get some air?**

Of course!

I left the room. I walked into a big hall and ran into Lady Susan, who'd worked for Granny for years, and Mr. R, my former upstairs neighbor in the badger sett. They could see I was upset and they asked if there was anything they could do for me. I smiled and said, No, thank you, then went back into the room.

There was some discussion at this point of

Option 3. Or was it Option 2? It was all starting to give me a headache. They were wearing me down. I didn't bloody care which option we adopted, so long as security remained in place. I pleaded for continuation of the same armed police protection I'd had, and needed, since birth. I'd never been allowed to go anywhere without three armed bodyguards, even when I was supposedly the most popular member of the family, and now I was the target, along with my wife and son, of unprecedented hate—and the leading proposal under discussion called for total abandonment?

Madness.

I offered to defray the cost of security out of my own pocket. I wasn't sure how I'd do that, but I'd find a way.

I made one last pitch: **Look. Please. Meg and I don't care about perks, we care about working, serving—and staying alive.**

This seemed simple and persuasive. All the heads around the table went up and down.

As the meeting came to a close there was a basic, general agreement. The many fine, granular details of this hybrid arrangement would be sorted out over a twelve-month transitional period, during which we'd continue to have security.

Granny rose. We all rose. She walked out.

For me there was one more piece of unfinished business. I went off to find the office of the Bee. Luckily, I ran into the Queen's friendliest page, who'd always liked me. I asked for directions; he said he'd take me himself. He led me through the kitchen, up some back stairs, down a narrow corridor.

Just that way, he said, pointing.

A few steps later I came upon a huge printer, churning out documents. The Bee's assistant swung into view.

Hello!

I pointed at the printer and said: **This seems to be working fine?**

Yes, Your Royal Highness!

Not broken?

That thing? It's indestructible, sir!

I asked about the printer in the Bee's office. **That one work too?**

Oh, yes, sir! Did you need to print something out?

No, thank you.

I went farther down the corridor, through a door. Everything suddenly looked familiar. Then I remembered. This was the corridor where I'd slept that Christmas after returning from the South Pole. And now along came the Bee. Head on. He saw me and looked extremely sheepish . . . for a bee. He could tell what I was up to. He heard the printer whirring away. He knew he was busted. **Oh, sir, please, sir, don't worry about that, it's really not important.**

Isn't it?

I walked away from him, went downstairs. Someone suggested that before I left I should step outside with Willy. Cool our heads.

All right.

We went up and down the yew hedges. The day

was freezing. I was wearing only a light jacket, and Willy was in a jumper, so both of us were shivering.

I was struck again by the beauty of it all. As in the state room, I felt as if I'd never seen a palace before. These gardens, I thought, they're paradise. Why can't we just enjoy them?

I was braced for a lecture. It didn't come. Willy was subdued. He wanted to listen. For the first time in a long time my brother heard me out, and I was so grateful.

I told him about one past staff member sabotaging Meg. Plotting against her. I told him about one current staff member, whose close friend was taking payments for leaking private stuff to the press about Meg and me. My sources on this were above reproach, including several journalists and barristers. Plus, I'd made a visit to New Scotland Yard.

Willy frowned. He and Kate had their own suspicions. He'd look into it.

We agreed to keep talking.

76.

I JUMPED INTO THE car and was immediately told that a strongly worded denial had been put out by the Palace, squashing that morning's bullying story. The denial was signed by none other than . . . me. And Willy. My name attached by faceless others to words I'd never even seen—let alone approved? I was stunned.

I went back to Frogmore. From there, remotely, over the next few days, I took part in the drafting of a final statement, which went out January 18, 2020.

The Palace announced that The Duke and Duchess of Sussex had agreed to "step back," that we'd no longer "formally" represent the Queen, that our HRH titles would be in "abeyance" during this transitional year—and that we'd offered to reimburse the Sovereign Grant for refurbishments to Frogmore Cottage.

A firm "no comment" on the status of our security.

I flew back to Vancouver. Delicious reunion with Meg, Archie and the dogs. And yet, for a few days, I didn't feel fully back. Part of me was still in Britain. Still at Sandringham. I spent hours glued to my phone, and the internet, monitoring the fallout. The ire directed at us by the papers and the trolls was alarming.

"Make no mistake, it's an insult," cried the **Daily Mail**, which convened a "Fleet Street jury" to consider our "crimes." Among them was the Queen's ex–press secretary, who concluded, with his fellow jurors, that we should hereafter "expect no mercy."

I shook my head. No mercy. The language of war?

Clearly this was more than simple anger. These men and women saw me as an existential threat. If our leaving posed a threat to the monarchy, as some were saying, then it posed a threat to all those covering the monarchy for a living.

Hence, we had to be destroyed.

One of this lot, who'd written a book about me and thus provably depended on me to pay her rent, went on live TV to explain confidently that Meg and I had departed from Britain without so much as a by-your-leave to Granny. We'd discussed it with no one, she said, not even Pa. She announced these false-hoods with such unfaltering certainty that even I was tempted to believe her, and thus her version of events quickly became "the truth" in many circles. **Harry blindsided the Queen!** That was the narrative that took hold. I could feel it oozing into history books, and I could imagine boys and girls at Ludgrove, decades hence, having that hogwash rammed down their throats.

I sat up late, brooding on it all, going over the progression of events and asking myself: What's the matter with these people? What makes them like this?

Is it all just about the money?

Isn't it always? All my life I've heard people saying the monarchy was expensive, anachronistic, and Meg and I were now served up as proof. Our wedding was cited as Exhibit A. It cost millions, and thereafter we'd up and left. Ingrates.

But the family paid for the actual wedding, and a huge portion of the remaining cost was for security, much of which was made necessary by the press stirring up racism and class resentment. And the security experts themselves told us the snipers and sniffer dogs weren't just for us: they were to prevent a shooter from strafing the crowds on the Long Walk, or a suicide bomber blowing up the parade route.

Maybe money sits at the heart of every controversy

about monarchy. Britain has long had trouble making up its mind. Many support the Crown, but many also feel anxious about the cost. That anxiety is increased by the fact that the cost is unknowable. Depends on who's crunching the numbers. Does the Crown cost taxpayers? Yes. Does it also pay a fortune into government coffers? Also yes. Does the Crown generate tourism income that benefits all? Of course. Does it also rest upon lands obtained and secured when the system was unjust and wealth was generated by exploited workers and thuggery, annexation and enslaved people?

Can anyone deny it?

According to the last study I saw, the monarchy costs the average taxpayer the price of a pint each year. In light of its many good works that seems a pretty sound investment. But no one wants to hear a prince argue for the existence of a monarchy, any more than they want to hear a prince argue against it. I leave cost-benefit analyses to others.

My emotions are complicated on this subject, naturally, but my bottom-line position isn't. I'll forever support my Queen, my Commander in Chief, my Granny. Even after she's gone. My problem has never been with the monarchy, nor the concept of monarchy. It's been with the press and the sick relationship that's evolved between it and the Palace. I love my Mother Country, and I love my family, and I always will. I just wish, at the second-darkest moment of my life, they'd both been there for me.

And I believe they'll look back one day and wish they had too.

77.

THE QUESTION WAS: Where to live?

We considered Canada. By and large it had been good to us. It had already come to feel like home. We could imagine spending the rest of our lives there. If we could just find a place the press didn't know about, we said, Canada might be the answer.

Meg got in touch with a Vancouver friend, who connected us with an estate agent, and we started looking at houses. We were taking first steps, trying to be positive. Doesn't really matter where we live, we said, so long as the Palace fulfills its obligation—and what I felt was its implicit promise—to keep us safe.

Meg asked me one night: **You don't think they'd ever pull our security, do you?**

Never. Not in this climate of hate. And not after what happened to my mother.

Also, not in the wake of my Uncle Andrew. He was embroiled in a shameful scandal, accused of the sexual assault of a young woman, and no one had so much as suggested that he lose his security. Whatever grievances people had against us, sex crimes weren't on the list.

February 2020.

I scooped Archie from his nap and took him out to the lawn. It was sunny, cold, and we gazed at the water, touched the dry leaves, collected rocks and twigs. I kissed his chubby little cheeks, tickled him, then glanced down at my phone to see a text from the head of our security team, Lloyde.

He needed to see me.

I carried Archie across the garden and handed him to Meg, then went across the soggy grass to the cottage where Lloyde and the other bodyguards were staying. We sat on a bench, both of us wearing puffer jackets. Waves rolling gently in the background, Lloyde told me that our security was being pulled. He and the whole team had been ordered to evacuate.

Surely they can't.

I would tend to agree. But they are.

So much for the year of transition.

The threat level for us, Lloyde said, was still higher than for that of nearly every other royal, equal to that assigned the Queen. And yet the word had come down and there was to be no arguing.

So here we are, I said. The ultimate nightmare. The worst of all worst-case scenarios. Any bad actor in the world would now be able to find us, and it would just be me with a pistol to stop them.

Oh wait. No pistol. I'm in Canada.

I rang Pa. He wouldn't take my calls.

Just then I got a text from Willy. **Can you speak?**

Great. I was sure my older brother, after our recent walk in the Sandringham gardens, would be sympathetic. That he'd step up.

He said it was a government decision. Nothing to be done.

78.

LLOYDE WAS PLEADING with his superiors at home, trying to get them at least to postpone the date when he and his team pulled out. He showed me the emails. He wrote: **We can't just . . . leave them here!**

The person at the other end wrote: **The decision has been made. As of March 31 they're by themselves.**

I scrambled to find new security. I spoke to consultants, gathered estimates. I filled a notebook with research. The Palace directed me to a firm, which quoted me a price. Six million a year.

I slowly hung up.

In the midst of all this darkness came the horrible news that my old friend Caroline Flack had taken her life. She couldn't stand it anymore, apparently. The relentless abuse at the hands of the press, year after year, had finally broken her. I felt so awful for her family. I remembered how they'd all suffered for her mortal sin of going out with me.

She'd been so light and funny that night we met. The definition of carefree.

It would've been impossible then to imagine this outcome.

I told myself it was an important reminder. I wasn't being overdramatic, I wasn't warning about things that would never happen. What Meg and I were dealing with was indeed a question of life and death.

And time was running out.

In March 2020 the World Health Organization declared a global pandemic, and Canada began to discuss the possibility of closing its borders.

But Meg had zero doubt. **They're definitely going to close those borders, so we need to figure out somewhere else to go . . . and get there.**

79.

WE WERE HAVING a chat with Tyler Perry, the actor-writer-director. He'd sent a note to Meg before the wedding, out of the blue, telling her that she wasn't alone, that he saw what was happening. Now, FaceTiming with him, Meg and I were trying to put on a brave face, but we were both a mess.

Tyler saw. He asked what was up.

We gave him the highlights, the loss of security, the borders closing. Nowhere to turn.

Whoa. OK, that's a lot. But . . . just breathe. Breathe.

That was the problem. We couldn't breathe.

Look . . . take my house.

What?

My house in Los Angeles. It's gated, it's secure—you'll be safe there. I'll keep you safe.

He was traveling, he explained, working on a project, so the house was empty, waiting for us.

It was too much. Too generous.

But we accepted. Eagerly.

I asked why he was doing this.

My mother.

Your . . . ?

My mother loved your mother.

I was caught completely by surprise. He said: **After your mother visited Harlem, that was it. She could do no wrong in Maxine Perry's book.**

He went on to say that his mother had died ten years earlier, and he was still grieving.

I wanted to tell him it gets easier.

I didn't.

80.

THE HOUSE WAS XANADU. High ceilings, priceless art, beautiful swimming pool. Palatial, but above all, ultra-safe. Better yet, it came with security, paid for by Tyler.

We spent those last days of March 2020 exploring, unpacking. Trying to get our bearings. Halls, wardrobes, bedrooms, there seemed no end of spaces to discover, and niches for Archie to hide.

Meg introduced him to everything. Look at this statue! Look at this fountain! Look at these hummingbirds in the garden!

In the front hall was a painting he found especially interesting. He started every day locked on to it. A scene from ancient Rome. We asked each other why.

No clue.

Within a week Tyler's house felt like home. Archie took his first steps in the garden a couple of months later, at the height of the global pandemic lockdown. We clapped, hugged him, cheered. I thought, for a moment, how nice it would be to share the news with Grandpa or Uncle Willy.

Not long after those first steps Archie went marching up to his favorite painting in the front hall. He stared at it, made a gurgle of recognition.

Meg leaned in for a closer look.

She noticed, for the first time, a nameplate on the frame.

Goddess of the hunt. **Diana.**

When we told Tyler, he said he hadn't known. He'd forgotten the painting was even there.

He said: **Gives me chills.**

Us too.

81.

LATE AT NIGHT, WITH everyone asleep, I'd walk the house, checking the doors and windows. Then I'd sit on the balcony or the edge of the garden and roll a joint.

The house looked down onto a valley, across a hillside thick with frogs. I'd listen to their late-night song, smell the flower-scented air. The frogs, the smells, the trees, the big starry sky, it all brought me back to Botswana.

But maybe it's not just the flora and fauna, I thought.

Maybe it's more the feeling of safety. Of life.

We were able to get a lot of work done. And we had a lot of work to do. We launched a foundation, I reconnected with my contacts in world conservation. Things were getting under control . . . and then the press somehow learned we were at Tyler's. It had taken six weeks exactly, same as Canada. Suddenly there were drones overhead, paps across the street. Paps across the valley.

They cut the fence.

We patched the fence.

We stopped venturing outside. The garden was in full view of the paps.

Next came the helicopters.

Sadly, we were going to have to flee. We'd need to find somewhere new, and soon, and that would mean paying for our own security. I went back to my notebooks, started contacting security firms again. Mcg and I sat down to work out exactly how much security we could afford, and how much house. Exactly then, while we were revising our budget, word came down: Pa was cutting me off.

I recognized the absurdity, a man in his mid-thirties being financially cut off by his father. But Pa wasn't merely my father, he was my boss, my banker, my comptroller, keeper of the purse strings throughout my adult life. Cutting me off therefore meant firing me, without redundancy pay, and casting me into the void after a lifetime of service. More, after a lifetime of rendering me otherwise unemployable.

I felt fatted for the slaughter. Suckled like a veal calf. I'd never asked to be financially dependent on Pa. I'd been forced into this surreal state, this unending **Truman Show** in which I almost never carried money, never owned a car, never carried a house key, never once ordered anything online, never received a single box from Amazon, **almost** never traveled on the Underground. (Once, at Eton, on a theater trip.) Sponge, the papers called me. But there's a big difference between being a sponge and being **prohibited** from learning independence. After decades of being rigorously and systematically infantilized, I was now abruptly abandoned, and mocked for being immature? For not standing on my own two feet?

The question of how to pay for a home and security kept Meg and me awake at nights. We could always spend some of my inheritance from Mummy, we said, but that felt like a last resort. We saw that money as belonging to Archie. And his sibling.

It was then that we learned Meg was pregnant.

82.

WE FOUND A PLACE. Priced at a steep discount. Just up the coast, outside Santa Barbara. Lots of room, large gardens, a climbing frame—even a pond with koi carp.

The koi were stressed, the estate agent warned.

So are we. We'll all get along famously.

No, the agent explained, the koi need very particular care. You'll have to hire a koi guy.

Uh-huh. And where does one find a koi guy?

The agent wasn't sure.

We laughed. First-world problems.

We took a tour. The place was a dream. We asked Tyler to look at it too, and he said: Buy it. So we pulled together a down-payment, took out a mortgage, and in July 2020 we moved in.

The move itself required only a couple of hours. Everything we owned fitted into thirteen suitcases. That first night we had a quiet drink in celebration, roasted a chicken, went to bed early.

All was well, we said.

And yet Meg was still under loads of stress.

There was a pressing issue with her legal case against the tabloids. The **Mail** was up to its usual tricks. Their first crack at offering a defense had been patently ridiculous, so now they were trying a new defense, which was even more ridiculous. They were arguing that they'd printed Meg's letter to her father because of a story in **People** magazine, which quoted a handful of Meg's friends—anonymously. The tabloids argued that Meg had orchestrated these quotes, used her friends as **de facto** spokespeople, and thus the **Mail** had every right to publish her letter to her father.

More, they now wanted the names of Meg's previously anonymous friends read into the official court record—to destroy them. Meg was determined to do everything in her power to prevent that. She'd been staying up late, night after night, trying to work out how to save these people, and now, on our first morning in the new house, she reported abdominal pains.

And bleeding.

Then she collapsed to the floor.

We raced to the local hospital. When the doctor walked into the room, I didn't hear one word she said, I just watched her face, her body language. I already knew. We both did. There had been so much blood.

Still, hearing the words was a blow.

Meg grabbed me, I held her, we both wept.

In my life I've felt **totally** helpless only four times.

In the back of the car while Mummy and Willy and I were being chased by paps.

In the Apache above Afghanistan, unable to get clearance to do my duty.

At Nott Cott when my pregnant wife was planning to take her life.

And now.

We left the hospital with our unborn child. A tiny package. We went to a place, a secret place only we knew.

Under a spreading banyan tree, while Meg wept, I dug a hole with my hands and set the tiny package softly in the ground.

83.

FIVE MONTHS LATER. Christmas 2020.

We took Archie to find a Christmas tree. A pop-up lot in Santa Barbara.

We bought one of the biggest spruces they had.

We brought it home, set it up in the living room. Magnificent. We stood back, admiring, counting our blessings. New home. Healthy boy. Plus, we'd signed several corporate partnerships, which would give us the chance to resume our work, to spotlight the causes we cared about, to tell the stories we felt were vital. And to pay for our security.

It was Christmas Eve. We FaceTimed with several friends, including a few in Britain. We watched Archie running around the tree.

And we opened presents. Keeping to the Windsor family tradition.

One present was a little Christmas ornament of . . . the Queen!

I roared. **What the—?**

Meg had spotted it in a local store and thought I might like it.

I held it to the light. It was Granny's face to a T. I hung it on an eye-level branch. It made me happy to see her there. It made Meg and me smile. But then Archie, playing around the tree, jostled the stand, shook the tree, and Granny fell.

I heard a smash and turned.

Pieces lay all over the floor.

Archie ran and grabbed a spray bottle. For some reason he thought spraying water on the broken pieces would fix it.

Meg said: **No, Archie, no—do not spray Gan-Gan!** I grabbed a dustpan and swept up the pieces, all the while thinking: This is weird.

84.

THE PALACE ANNOUNCED THAT a review had been conducted of our roles, and of the agreement reached in Sandringham.

Henceforth, we were stripped of everything but a few patronages.

February 2021.

They took it all away, I thought, even my military associations. I'd no longer be captain general of the Royal Marines, a title handed down by my grandfather. I'd no longer be permitted to wear my ceremonial military uniform.

I told myself they could never take away my real uniform, or my real military status. But still.

Furthermore, the statement continued, we'd no longer be doing any service whatsoever for the Queen.

They made it sound as if there'd been an agreement between us. There was nothing of the sort.

We pushed back in our own statement, released the same day, saying we'd never cease living a life of service.

This new slap-down from the Palace was like petrol on a bonfire. We'd been under media attack non-stop since leaving, but this official severing of ties set off a new wave, which felt different. We were vilified every day, every hour, on social media, and found ourselves the subjects of scurrilous, wholly fictional stories in the newspapers, stories always attributed to "royal aides" or "royal insiders" or "palace sources," stories clearly spoon-fed by Palace staff—and presumably sanctioned by my family.

I didn't read any of it, seldom even heard about it. I was now avoiding the internet as I once avoided downtown Garmsir. I kept my phone on silent. Not even vibrate. Sometimes a well-meaning friend would text: **Gosh, sorry about such and such.** We had to ask such friends, all friends, to stop informing us what they'd read.

In all honesty, I hadn't been totally surprised when the Palace cut ties. I'd had a sneak preview months earlier. Just before Remembrance Day I'd asked the Palace if someone could lay a wreath for me at the Cenotaph, since, of course, I couldn't be there.

Request denied.

In that case, I said, could a wreath be laid somewhere else in Britain on my behalf?

Request denied.

In that case, I said, perhaps a wreath could be laid somewhere in the Commonwealth, anywhere at all, on my behalf?

Request denied.

Nowhere in the world would any proxy be permitted to lay any sort of wreath at any military grave on behalf of Prince Harry, I was told.

I pleaded that this would be the first time I'd let a Remembrance Day pass without paying tribute to the fallen, some of whom had been dear friends.

Request denied.

In the end I rang one of my old instructors at Sandhurst and asked him to lay my wreath for me. He suggested the Iraq and Afghanistan Memorial, in London, which had just been unveiled a few years earlier.

By Granny.

Yes. That's perfect. Thank you.

He said it would be his honor.

Then added: **And by the by, Captain Wales. Fuck this. It's proper wrong.**

85.

I WASN'T SURE WHAT TO call her, or what exactly she did. All I knew was that she claimed to have "powers."

I recognized the high-percentage chance of humbuggery. But the woman came with strong recommendations from trusted friends, so I asked myself: What's the harm?

Then, the minute we sat down together, I felt an energy around her.

Oh, I thought. Wow. There's something here.

She felt an energy around me too, she said. **Your mother is with you.**

I know. I've felt that of late.

She said: **No. She's with you. Right now.**

I felt my neck grow warm. My eyes watered.

Your mother knows you're looking for clarity. Your mother feels your confusion. She knows that you have so many questions.

I do.

The answers will come in time. One day in the future. Have patience.

Patience? The word caught in my throat.

In the meantime, the woman said, my mother was very proud of me. And fully supportive. She knew it wasn't easy.

What wasn't?

Your mother says: You're living the life she couldn't. You're living the life she wanted for you.

I swallowed. I wanted to believe. I wanted every word this woman was saying to be true. But I needed proof. A sign. Anything.

Your mother says . . . the ornament?

Ornament?

She was there.

Where?

Your mother says . . . something about a Christmas ornament? Of a mother? Or a grand-mother? It fell? Broke?

Archie tried to fix it.

Your mother says she had a bit of a giggle about that.

86.

FROGMORE GARDENS.
Hours after Grandpa's funeral.

I'd been walking with Willy and Pa for about half an hour, but it felt like one of those days-long marches the Army put me through when I was a new soldier. I was beat.

We'd reached an impasse. And we'd reached the Gothic ruin. After a circuitous route we'd arrived back where we'd begun.

Pa and Willy were still claiming not to know why I'd fled Britain, still claiming not to know anything, and I was getting ready to walk away.

Then one of them brought up the press. They asked about my hacking lawsuit.

They still hadn't asked about Meg, but they were keen to know how my lawsuit was going, because that directly affected them.

Still ongoing.

Suicide mission, Pa mumbled.

Maybe. But it's worth it.

I'd soon prove that the press were more than liars, I said. That they were lawbreakers. I was going to see some of them thrown into jail. That was why they were attacking me so viciously: they knew I had hard evidence.

It wasn't about me, it was a matter of public interest.

Shaking his head, Pa allowed that journalists were the **scum of the earth**. His phrase. **But** . . .

I snorted. There was always a **but** with him when it came to the press, because he hated their hate, but oh how he loved their love. One could make the argument that therein lay the seeds of the whole problem, indeed all problems, going back decades. Deprived of love as a boy, bullied by schoolmates, he was dangerously, compulsively drawn to the elixir they offered him.

He cited Grandpa as a sterling example of why the press wasn't anything to get too vexed about. Poor Grandpa had been abused by the papers for most of his life, but now look. He was a national treasure! The papers couldn't say enough good things about the man.

So that's it, then? Just wait till we're dead and all will be sorted?

If you could just endure it, darling boy, for a little while, in a funny way they'd respect you for it.

I laughed.

All I'm saying is, don't take it personally.

Speaking of taking things personally, I told them I might learn to endure the press, and even forgive their abuse, **I might**, but my own family's complicity— that was going to take longer to get over. Pa's office, Willy's office, enabling these fiends, if not outright collaborating?

Meg was apparently a bully—that was the latest vicious campaign they'd helped orchestrate. It was so shocking, so egregious, that even after Meg and I demolished their lie with a twenty-five-page, evidence-filled report to Human Resources, I was going to have trouble simply shrugging that one off.

Pa stepped back. Willy shook his head. They began talking over each other. We've been down this road a hundred times, they said. You're delusional, Harry.

But they were the delusional ones.

Even if, for the sake of argument, I accepted that Pa and Willy and their staff had never done one overt thing against me or my wife—their silence was an undeniable fact. And that silence was damning. And continuing. And heartrending.

Pa said: **You must understand, darling boy, the Institution can't just tell the media what to do!**

Again, I yelped with laughter. It was like Pa saying he couldn't just tell his valet what to do.

Willy said I was a fine one to talk about cooperating with the press. What about my chat with Oprah?

A month earlier Meg and I had done an interview with Oprah Winfrey. (Days before it aired, those Meg-is-a-bully stories started popping up in the papers—what a coincidence!) Since leaving Britain, the attacks on us had been increasing exponentially. We had to try something to make it stop. Being silent wasn't working. It was only making it worse. We felt we had no choice.

Several close mates and beloved figures in my life, including one of Hugh and Emilie's sons, Emilie herself, and even Tiggy, had chastised me for **Oprah.**

How could you reveal such things? About your family? I told them that I failed to see how speaking to Oprah was any different from what my family and their staffs, had done for decades—briefing the press on the sly, planting stories. And what about the endless books on which they'd cooperated, starting with Pa's 1994 crypto-autobiography with Jonathan Dimbleby? Or Camilla's collaborations with the editor Geordie Greig? The only difference was that Meg and I were upfront about it. We chose an interviewer who was above reproach, and we didn't once hide behind phrases like "Palace sources," we let people see the words coming out of our mouths.

I looked at the Gothic ruin. What's the point? I thought. Pa and Willy weren't hearing me and I wasn't hearing them. They'd never had a satisfactory explanation for their actions and inactions, and never would, because there was no explanation. I started to say goodbye, good luck, take care, but Willy was really steaming, shouting that if things were as bad as I made out, then it was my fault for never asking for help.

You never came to us! You never came to me!

Since boyhood that had been Willy's position on everything. I must come to him. Pointedly, directly, formally—bend the knee. Otherwise, no aid from the Heir. I wondered why I should have to ask my brother to help when my wife and I were in peril.

If we were being mauled by a bear, and he saw, would he wait for us to ask for help?

I mentioned the Sandringham Agreement. I'd

asked for his help about that, when the agreement was violated, shredded, when we were stripped of everything, and he hadn't lifted a finger.

That was Granny! Take it up with Granny!

I waved a hand, disgusted, but he lunged, grabbed my shirt. **Listen to me, Harold.**

I pulled away, refused to meet his gaze. He forced me to look into his eyes.

Listen to me, Harold, listen! I love you, Harold! I want you to be happy.

The words flew out of my mouth: **I love you too . . . but your stubbornness . . . is extraordinary!**

And yours isn't?

I pulled away again.

He grabbed me again, twisting me to maintain eye contact.

Harold, you must listen to me! I just want you to be happy, Harold. I swear. . . . I swear on Mummy's life.

He stopped. I stopped. Pa stopped.

He'd gone there.

He'd used the secret code, the universal password. Ever since we were boys those three words were to be used only in times of extreme crisis. **On Mummy's life.** For nearly twenty-five years we'd reserved that soul-crushing vow for times when one of us needed to be heard, to be believed, quickly. For times when nothing else would do.

It stopped me cold, as it was meant to. Not because he'd used it, but because it didn't work. I simply didn't believe him, didn't fully trust him. And vice versa. He saw it too. He saw that we were in a place of such hurt and doubt that even those sacred words couldn't set us free.

How lost we are, I thought. How far we've strayed. How much damage has been done to our love, our bond, and why? All because a dreadful mob of dweebs and crones and cut-rate criminals and clinically diagnosable sadists along Fleet Street feel the need to get their jollies and plump their profits—and work out their personal issues—by tormenting one very large, very ancient, very dysfunctional family.

Willy wasn't quite ready to accept defeat. **I've felt properly sick and ill after everything that's happened and—and . . . I swear to you now on Mummy's life that I just want you to be happy.**

My voice broke as I told him softly: **I really don't think you do.**

My mind suddenly flooded with memories of our relationship. But one in particular was crystalline. Willy and I, years before in Spain. A beautiful valley, the air glittery with that uncommonly clear Mediterranean light, the two of us kneeling behind a green canvas wall as the first hunting horns sounded. Lowering our flat caps as the first partridges burst towards us, **bang bang,** a few falling, handing our guns to the loaders, who handed us new ones, **bang bang,** more falling, passing our guns back, our shirts darkening with sweat, the ground filling with birds that would feed nearby villages for weeks, **bang,** one last shot, neither of us able to miss, then standing at last, drenched, starved, happy, because we were young and together and this was our place, our one true space, away from Them and close to Nature. It was such a transcendent moment that we turned and did that rarest of things—we hugged. Really hugged.

But now I saw that even our finest moments, and my best memories, somehow involved death. Our lives were built on death, our brightest days shadowed by it. Looking back, I didn't see spots of time, but dances with death. I saw how we **steeped** ourselves in it. We christened and crowned, graduated and married, passed out and passed over our beloveds' bones. Windsor Castle itself was a tomb, the walls filled with ancestors. The Tower of London was held together with the blood of animals, used by the original builders a thousand years ago to temper the mortar between the bricks. Outsiders called us a cult, but maybe we were a **death** cult, and wasn't that a little bit more depraved? Even after laying Grandpa to rest, had we not had our fill? Why were we here, lurking along the edge of that "undiscover'd country, from whose bourn no traveller returns"?

Though maybe that's a more apt description of America.

Willy was still talking, Pa was talking over him, and I could no longer hear a word they said. I was already gone, already on my way to California, a voice in my head saying: **Enough death—enough.**

When is someone in this family going to break free and live?

87.

IT WAS SLIGHTLY EASIER this time. Maybe because we were an ocean away from the old chaos and stress.

When the big day came we were both surer, calmer—steadier. What bliss, we said, not having to worry about timing, protocols, journalists at the front gate.

We drove calmly, sanely to the hospital, where our bodyguards once again fed us. This time they brought burgers and fries from In-N-Out. And fajitas from a local Mexican restaurant for Meg. We ate and ate and then did the Baby Mama dance around the hospital room.

Nothing but joy and love in that room.

Still, after many hours Meg asked the doctor: **When?**

Soon. We're close.

This time I didn't touch the laughing gas. (Because there was none.) I was fully present. I was with Meg through every push.

When the doctor said it was a matter of minutes, I told Meg that I wanted mine to be the first face our little girl saw.

We knew we were having a daughter.

Meg nodded, squeezed my hand.

I went and stood beside the doctor. We both crouched. As if about to pray.

The doctor called out: **The head is crowning.**

Crowning, I thought. Incredible.

The skin was blue. I worried the baby wasn't getting enough air. Is she choking? I looked at Meg. **One more push, my love! We're so close.**

Here, here, here, the doctor said, guiding my hands, **right here.**

A scream, then a moment of pure liquid silence. It wasn't, as sometimes happens, that past and future were suddenly one. It was that the past didn't matter, and the future didn't exist. There was only this intense present, and then the doctor turned to me and shouted: **Now!**

I slid my hands under the tiny back and neck. Gently, but firmly, as I'd seen in films, I pulled our precious daughter from that world into this, and cradled her just a moment, trying to smile at her, to see her, but honestly, I couldn't see anything. I wanted to say: Hello. I wanted to say: Where have you come from? I wanted to say: Is it better there? Is it peaceful? Are you frightened?

Don't be, don't be, all will be well.

I'll keep you safe.

I surrendered her to Meg. Skin to skin, the nurse said.

Later, after we'd brought her home, after we'd settled into all the new rhythms of a family of four, Meg and I were skin to skin and she said: **I've never been more in love with you than in that moment.**

Really?

Really.

She jotted some thoughts in a kind of journal. Which she shared.

I read them as a love poem.

I read them as a testament, a renewal of our vows.

I read them as a citation, a remembrance, a proclamation.

I read them as a decree.

She said: **That was everything.**

She said: **That is a man.**

My love. She said: **That is not a Spare.**

Epilogue

I HELPED MEG INTO THE BOAT. It wobbled, but I quick-stepped to the middle, got it righted in time.

As she found a seat in the stern, I took up the oars. They didn't work.

We're stuck.

The thick mud of the shallows had us in its grip.

Uncle Charles came down to the water's edge, gave us a little shove. We waved to him, and to my two aunts. **Bye. See you in a bit.**

Gliding across the pond, I gazed around at Althorp's rolling fields and ancient trees, the thousands of green acres where my mother grew up, and where, though things weren't perfect, she'd known some peace.

Minutes later we reached the island and gingerly stepped onto the shore. I led Meg up the path, around a hedge, through the labyrinth. There it was, looming: the grayish white oval stone.

No visit to this place was ever easy, but this one . . .

Twenty-fifth anniversary.

And Meg's first time.

At long last I was bringing the girl of my dreams home to meet mum.

We hesitated, hugging, and then I went first. I placed flowers on the grave. Meg gave me a moment, and I spoke to my mother in my head, told her I missed her, asked her for guidance and clarity.

Feeling that Meg might also want a moment, I went around the hedge, scanned the pond. When I came back, Meg was kneeling, eyes shut, palms against the stone.

I asked, as we walked back to the boat, what she'd prayed for.

Clarity, she said. And guidance.

The next few days were given over to a whirlwind work trip. Manchester, Dusseldorf, then back to London for the WellChild Awards. But that day—September 8, 2022—a call came in around lunchtime.

Unknown number.

Hello?

It was Pa. Granny's health had taken a turn.

She was up at Balmoral, of course. Those beautiful, melancholy late-summer days. He hung up—he had many other calls to make—and I immediately texted Willy to ask whether he and Kate were flying up. If so, when? And how?

No response. Meg and I looked at flight options.

The press started phoning; we couldn't delay a decision any longer. We told our team to confirm: We'd be missing the WellChild Awards and hurrying up to Scotland.

Then came another call from Pa.

He said I was welcome at Balmoral, but he didn't

want . . . her. He started to lay out his reason, which was nonsensical, and disrespectful, and I wasn't having it. **Don't ever speak about my wife that way.**

He stammered, apologetic, saying he simply didn't want a lot of people around. No other wives were coming, Kate wasn't coming, he said, therefore Meg shouldn't.

Then that's all you needed to say.

By now it was midafternoon; no more commercial flights that day to Aberdeen. And I still had no response from Willy. My only option, therefore, was a charter out of Luton.

I was on board two hours later.

I spent much of the flight staring at the clouds, replaying the last time I'd spoken with Granny. Four days earlier, long chat on the phone. We'd touched on many topics. Her health, of course. The turmoil at Number 10. The Braemar Games—she was sorry about not being well enough to attend. We talked also about the biblical drought. The lawn at Frogmore, where Meg and I were staying, was in terrible shape. **Looks like the top of my head, Granny! Balding and brown in patches.**

She laughed.

I told her to take care, I looked forward to seeing her soon.

As the plane began its descent, my phone lit up. A text from Meg. **Call me the moment you get this.**

I checked the BBC website.

Granny was gone.

Pa was King.

I put on my black tie, walked off the plane into a thick mist, sped in a borrowed car to Balmoral. As I pulled through the front gates it was wetter, and pitch-dark, which made the white flashes from the dozens of cameras that much more blinding.

Hunched against the cold, I hurried into the foyer. Aunt Anne was there to greet me.

I hugged her. **Where's Pa and Willy? And Camilla?**

Gone to Birkhall, she said.

She asked if I wanted to see Granny.

Yes . . . I do.

She led me upstairs, to Granny's bedroom. I braced myself, went in. The room was dimly lit, unfamiliar— I'd been inside it only once in my life. I moved ahead uncertainly, and there she was. I stood, frozen, staring. I stared and stared. It was difficult, but I kept on, thinking how I'd regretted not seeing my mother at the end. Years of lamenting that lack of proof, postponing my grief for want of proof. Now I thought: Proof. Careful what you wish for.

I whispered to her that I hoped she was happy, that I hoped she was with Grandpa. I said that I was in awe of her carrying out her duties to the last. The Jubilee, the welcoming of a new prime minister. On her ninetieth birthday my father had given a touching tribute, quoting Shakespeare on Elizabeth I:

. . . no day without a deed to crown it.

Ever true.

I left the room, went back along the corridor, across

the tartan carpet, past the statue of Queen Victoria. **Your Majesty**. I rang Meg, told her I'd made it, that I was OK, then walked into the sitting room and ate dinner with most of my family, though still no Pa, Willy, or Camilla.

Towards the end of the meal, I braced myself for the bagpipes. But out of respect for Granny there was nothing. An eerie silence.

The hour getting late, everyone drifted off to their rooms, except me. I went on a wander, up and down the stairs, the halls, ending up at the nursery. The old-fashioned basins, the tub, everything the same as it had been twenty-five years ago. I passed most of the night time-traveling in my thoughts while trying to make actual travel arrangements on my phone.

The quickest way back would've been a lift with Pa or Willy . . . Barring that, it was British Airways, departing Balmoral at daybreak. I bought a seat and was among the first to board.

Soon after settling into a front row, I sensed a presence on my right. Deepest sympathies, said a fellow passenger before heading down the aisle.

Thank you.

Moments later, another presence.

Condolences, Harry.

Thanks . . . very much.

Most passengers stopped to offer a kind word, and I felt a deep kinship with them all.

Our country, I thought.

Our Queen.

Meg greeted me at the front door of Frogmore with a long embrace, which I desperately needed. We sat down with a glass of water and a calendar. Our quick trip would now be an odyssey. Another ten days, at least. Difficult days at that. More, we'd have to be away from the children for longer than we'd planned, longer than we'd ever been.

When the funeral finally took place, Willy and I, barely exchanging a word, took our familiar places, set off on our familiar journey, behind yet another coffin draped in the Royal Standard, sitting atop another horse-pulled gun carriage. Same route, same sights—though this time, unlike at previous funerals, we were shoulder to shoulder. Also, music was playing.

When we got to St. George's Chapel, amid the roar of dozens of bagpipes, I thought of all the big occasions I'd experienced under that roof. Grandpa's farewell, my wedding. Even the ordinary times, simple Easter Sundays, felt especially poignant, the whole family alive and together. Suddenly I was wiping my eyes.

Why now? I wondered. Why?

The following afternoon Meg and I left for America.

For days and days we couldn't stop hugging the children, couldn't let them out of our sight—though I also couldn't stop picturing them with Granny. The final visit. Archie making deep, chivalrous bows, his baby sister Lilibet cuddling the monarch's shins.

Sweetest children, Granny said, sounding bemused. She'd expected them to be a bit more . . . American, I think? Meaning, in her mind, more rambunctious.

Now, while overjoyed to be home again, doing drop-offs again, reading **Giraffes Can't Dance** again, I couldn't stop . . . remembering. Day and night, images flitted through my mind.

Standing before her during my passing-out parade, shoulders thrown back, catching her half smile. Stationed beside her on the balcony, saying something that caught her off guard and made her, despite the solemnity of the occasion, laugh out loud. Leaning into her ear, so many times, smelling her perfume as I whispered a joke. Kissing both cheeks at one public event, just recently, placing a hand lightly on her shoulder, feeling how frail she was becoming. Making a silly video for the first Invictus Games, discovering that she was a natural comedienne. People around the world howled, and said they'd never suspected she possessed such a wicked sense of humor—but she did, she always did! That was one of our little secrets. In fact, in every photo of us, whenever we're exchanging a glance, making solid eye contact, it's clear: We had secrets.

Special relationship, that's what they said about us, and now I couldn't stop thinking about the specialness that would no longer be. The visits that wouldn't take place.

Ah well, I told myself, that's just the deal, isn't it? That's life.

Still, as with so many partings, I just wished there'd been . . . one more goodbye.

Soon after our return, a hummingbird got into the house. I had a devil of a time guiding it out, and the thought occurred that maybe we should start shutting the doors, despite those heavenly ocean breezes.

Then a mate said: Could be a sign, you know?

Some cultures see hummingbirds as spirits, he said. Visitors, as it were. Aztecs thought them reincarnated warriors. Spanish explorers called them "resurrection birds."

You don't say?

I did some reading and learned that not only are hummingbirds visitors, they're voyagers. The lightest birds on the planet, and the fastest, they travel vast distances—from Mexican winter homes to Alaskan nesting grounds. Whenever you see a hummingbird, what you're actually seeing is a tiny, glittering Odysseus.

So, naturally, when this hummingbird arrived, and swooped around our kitchen, and flitted through the sacred airspace we call Lili Land, where we've set the baby's playpen with all her toys and stuffed animals, I thought hopefully, greedily, foolishly:

Is our house a detour—or a destination?

For half a second I was tempted to let the hummingbird be. Let it stay.

But no.

Gently I used Archie's fishing net to scoop it from the ceiling, carry it outside.

Its legs felt like eyelashes, its wings like flower petals.

With cupped palms I set the hummingbird gently on a wall in the sun.

Goodbye, my friend.

But it just lay there.

Motionless.

No, I thought. No, not that.

Come on, come on.

You're free.

Fly away.

And then, against all odds, and all expectations, that wonderful, magical little creature bestirred itself, and did just that.

Acknowledgments

The length of this list alone leaves me deeply humbled.

On the publishing side, thank you to everyone at Penguin Random House, U.S. and U.K., beginning of course with the sage and forbearing Gina Centrello, plus super-genius-editor (and all-around top bloke) Ben Greenberg. Thanks to Markus Dohle and Madeline McIntosh for the understanding as timelines changed, not once, but twice. Thanks to Bill Scott-Kerr, Tom Weldon, Andy Ward, David Drake, Madison Jacobs, Larry Finlay, Theresa Zoro, Bill Takes, Lisa Feuer, Katrina Whone, Benjamin Dreyer, Sally Franklin, Catriona Hillerton, Linnea Knollmueller, Mark Birkey, Kelly Chian, Derek Bracken, Kate Samano, Simon Sullivan, Chris Brand, Jenny Pouech, Susan Corcoran, Maria Braeckel, Leigh Marchant, Windy Dorresteyn, Leslie Prives, Aparna Rishi, Ty Nowicki, Matthew Martin, Anke Steinecke, Sinead Martin, Vanessa Milton, Martin Soames, Kaeli Subberwal, Denise Cronin, Sarah Lehman, Jaci Updike, Cynthia Lasky, Allyson Pearl, Skip Dye, Stephen Shodin, Sue Malone-Barber, Sue Driskill,

Michael DeFazio, Annette Danek, Valerie VanDelft, Stacey Witcraft, Nihar Malaviya, Kirk Bleemer, Matthew Schwartz, Lisa Gonzalez, Susan Seeman, Eric Tessen, Gina Wachtel, Daniel Christensen, Jess Wells, Thea James, Holly Smith, Patsy Irwin, Nicola Bevin, Robert Waddington, Thomas Chicken, Chris Turner, Stuart Anderson, Ian Sheppard, Vicky Palmer, and Laura Ricchetti.

On the audio side, thanks goes to Kelly Gildea, Dan Zitt, Scott Sherratt, Noah Bruskin, Alan Parsons, Ok Hee Kolwitz, Tim Bader, Amanda D'Acierno, Lance Fitzgerald, Donna Passannante, Katie Punia, Ellen Folan, and Nicole McArdle.

Special thanks to Ramona Rosales for her sensitivity, humor, and artistry, Hazel Orme for her careful copyedits, Hilary McClellen for her superb fact-checking, Tricia Wygal for her eagle-eyed readings—likewise Elizabeth Carbonell, Tory Klose, Janet Renard, and Megha Jain. Thank you for the huge team effort.

To my mates in the U.K., who have stuck by me, who may not have seen it all clearly as it was happening, but who always saw me, knew me, stood by me—in amongst the fog—thank you for everything. And thank you for the laughs. Next round's on me.

Love and thanks to friends and colleagues who helped jog my memory or else restored important details lost in the haze of youth, including Tania Jenkins and Mike Holding, Mark Dyer, Thomas, Charlie, Bill, and Kevin. To my entire military family, for challenging me, prodding me, encouraging me, and for always having my back. I'll always have yours. Special gratitude goes to Glenn Haughton and Spencer Wright, my two color sergeants from Sandhurst. Thanks and hugs to Jennifer Rudolph Walsh for her always positive energy and soulful counsel, and to Oprah Winfrey, Tyler Perry, Chris Martin, Nacho Figueras and Delphi Blaquier, and James Corden for their unwavering friendship and support.

Thank you to all the professionals, medical experts, and coaches for keeping me physically and mentally strong over the years. Dr. Lesley Parkinson, Dr. Ben Carraway and Kevin Lidlow, and also Ross Barr, Jessie Blum, Dr. Kevin English, Winston Squire, Esther Lee, John Amaral, and Peter Charles. Also Kasey, Eric Goodman, and the two Petes. Special thanks to my U.K. therapist for helping unravel years of unresolved trauma.

Thanks from the bottom of my heart to the A Team on the home front, plus the whole wonderful gang at Archewell for the endless support. To Rick, Andrew, the two Tims, Matt, Jenny and team, David, my deepest thanks for your wisdom and guidance. You're always there—whenever, however.

Thanks to my collaborator and friend, confessor and sometime sparring partner, J. R. Moehringer, who spoke to me so often and with such deep conviction about the beauty (and sacred obligation) of Memoir, and to all the faculty and students at the Moehringer-Welch Memoir Academy, including Shannon Welch,

Gracie Moehringer, Augie Moehringer, John Stillman, Kit Rachlis, Amy Albert. Special thanks to Shannon for her countless reads and brilliant, incisive notes.

Stand out thanks to my mother's siblings for their love, support, time, and perspective.

Above all my deepest and adoringest thanks to Archie and Lili, for letting Papa go off to read and think and reflect, to my mother-in-law (a.k.a. Grandma), and to my incredible wife, for too many millions of gifts and sacrifices, great and small, to ever enumerate. Love of my life, thank you, thank you, thank you. This book would've been impossible (logistically, physically, emotionally, spiritually) without you. Most things would be impossible without you.

And to you, the reader: Thank you for wanting to know my story in my words. I am so grateful to be able to share it thus far.